Avizandum Statutes on

Scots Family Law
2005–2006

3rd edition

Avizandum Statutes on

Scots Family Law
2005–2006

Third edition

Editor

Jane Mair LLM, PhD
Senior lecturer in law, University of Glasgow

Avizandum Publishing Ltd
Edinburgh
2005

Published by
Avizandum Publishing Ltd
58 Candlemaker Row
Edinburgh EH1 2QE

First published   2002
Reprinted   2003
2nd Edition   2004
3rd Edition   2005

ISBN 1-904968-04-X

British Library Cataloguing in Publication Data
A catalogue record for this book is available from the British Library

Typeset by AFS Image Setters Ltd, Glasgow
Printed and bound by Bell & Bain Ltd, Glasgow

EDITOR'S PREFACE

The last few years have seen significant amendments to Scots family law and in particular the introduction of the new legal concept of civil partnership. Those parts of the Civil Partnership Act 2004 which are relevant to Scots law have been included in this third edition of *Statutes on Scots Family Law*, together with considerable consequential amendments. Part 2 of the Vulnerable Witnesses (Scotland) Act 2004 has also been included as it relates in particular to the evidence of children and is therefore of relevance to those studying child law.

This volume is intended primarily as a resource for undergraduate students of child and family law and the provisions which have been included reflect the content of undergraduate courses. As with previous editions, statutory instruments have not been included. Students are unlikely to refer to these on a regular basis, and when they need to do so, statutory instruments are reasonably accessible on the internet. To ensure that this collection continues to reflect the needs of its users, we would welcome their further comment.

I have endeavoured to update the materials to the end of June 2005. Material which was not included in the statute as originally enacted has been identified by the use of square brackets.

Jane Mair
Glasgow University
August 2005

CONTENTS

PART I

STATUTES

REGISTRATION OF BIRTHS, DEATHS AND MARRIAGES (SCOTLAND)
ACT 1965
(1965, c 49)

PART II
REGISTRATION OF BIRTHS

13 Particulars of births to be registered

(1) For every registration district there shall be kept by the district registrar—

(a) a register of births, and

(b) a register of still-births,

containing such particulars as may be prescribed for them respectively; and the prescribed particulars of the birth of every child born in Scotland shall, subject to the following provisions of this Part of this Act, be registered by the registrar in the relevant register kept for the appropriate district, or, if there are two appropriate districts, in the relevant register kept for either of them.

(2) In the foregoing subsection, and in the following provisions of this Part of this Act, 'the registrar' in relation to the birth of any child means the district registrar for the appropriate district, or, if there are two appropriate districts, the district registrar for either of them; and any reference in the following provisions of this Part of this Act to the register of births or stillbirths in relation to the birth of any child shall be construed as a reference to the register in which the particulars of the birth are, or may be, registered in pursuance of the said subsection.

(3) For the purposes of the foregoing subsections the appropriate districts in relation to the birth of any child shall be—

(a) the registration district in which the birth took place, and

(b) any other registration district in which the mother of the child was ordinarily resident at the time of the birth, and

(c) in a case where a living infant child is found exposed, or the body of a dead infant child is found, and the place in which the birth took place is not known, the registration district in which the child, or, as the case may be, the body of the dead child, was found.

(4) Where a child is born (whether within or out of Scotland) in a ship, aircraft or land vehicle in the course of a journey, and that child is brought by such ship, aircraft or land vehicle to any place in Scotland, the birth shall, unless the Registrar General [of Births, Deaths and Marriages for Scotland] otherwise directs, be deemed for the purposes of this section to have occurred at that place.

14 Duty to give information of particulars of birth

(1) Subject to the subsequent provisions of this Part of this Act, in the case of every birth it shall be the duty of—

(a) the [child's father or mother (whether or not they have attained the age of sixteen years)], or

(b) in the case of the death or inability of the father and mother, each other person who under the next following subsection is qualified to give information concerning the birth,

within twenty-one days from the date of the birth, to attend personally at the registration office and give to the registrar information of the particulars required to be registered concerning the birth and sign the register in the presence of the registrar:

Provided that the giving of that information and the signing of the register by the father or the mother or by any one of those persons shall constitute a discharge of any duty imposed by this subsection on any other person.

(2)   The following persons, in addition to the father and mother, shall be qualified to give information concerning the birth of a child, that is to say—

(a)   any relative of either parent of the child, being a relative who has knowledge of the birth;

(b)   the occupier of the premises in which the child was, to the knowledge of that occupier, born;

(c)   any person present at the birth;

(d)   any person having charge of the child.

(3)   Nothing in this or the last foregoing section shall authorise the registration of the particulars of any birth in two or more registers, or more than once in any one register.

(4)   If it appears to the Registrar General that the particulars of the birth of any child have been registered in two or more registers, or more than once in any one register, he may give directions for the cancellation of all those registrations except such one of them as may be specified in the directions.

[(5)   In this section, any reference to the father or parent of the child shall not include a reference to a father who is not married to the mother and has not been married to her since the child's conception.]

18   Births of children born out of wedlock

[(1)   Subject to section 182A of this Act no person who is not married to the mother of a child and has not been married to her since the child's conception shall be required, as father of the child, to give information concerning the birth of the child and, save as provided in section 20 of this Act, the registrar shall not enter in the register the name and surname of any such person as father of the child except—

(a)   at the joint request of the mother and the person acknowledging himself to be the father of the child (in which case that person shall sign the register together with the mother); or

(b)   at the request of the mother—

(i)   on the production of—

(aa)   a declaration in the prescribed form made by the mother stating that that person is the father of the child; and

(bb)   a statutory declaration made by that person acknowledging himself to be the father of the child; or

(ii)   on production of a decree by a competent court finding or declaring that person to be the father of the child; or

(c)   at the request of that person on production of—

(i)   a declaration in the prescribed form by that person acknowledging himself to be the father of the child; and

(ii)   a statutory declaration made by the mother stating that that person is the father of the child.

(1A)   Where a person acknowledging himself to be the father of a child makes a request to the registrar in accordance with paragraph (c) of subsection (1) of this section, he shall be treated as a qualified informant concerning the birth of the child for the purposes of this Act; and the giving of information concerning the birth of the child by that person and the signing of the register by him in the presence of the registrar shall act as a discharge of any duty of any other qualified informant under section 14 of this Act.]

(2)   In any case where the name and surname of the father of a [. . .] child has not been entered in the register, the Registrar General may record that name and

surname by causing an appropriate entry to be made in the Register of Corrections Etc.—

(a)   if a decree of paternity has been granted by a competent court; or

(b)   if there is produced to him [a declaration and a statutory declaration such as are mentioned in paragraph (b) or (c) of subsection 1 of this section]; or

(c)   if, where the mother is dead [or cannot be found or is incapable of making a request under subsection (1)(b) of this section, or a declaration under subsection (1)(b)(i)(aa) of this section, or a statutory declaration under subsection (1)(c)(ii) of this section] he is ordered so to do by the sheriff upon application made to the sheriff [. . .] by the person acknowledging himself to be the father of the child.

Where a decree of paternity has been granted by any court the clerk of court shall, where no appeal has been made against such decree, on the expiration of the time within which such an appeal may be made, or where an appeal has been made against such a decree, on the conclusion of any appellate proceedings, notify the import of such decree in the prescribed form to the Registrar General.

[(3)   A person under the age of sixteen years has legal capacity—

(a)   to make a request, declaration or statutory declaration under subsection (1) or (2)(b) above if, in the opinion of the registrar; or

(b)   to make an application under subsection (2)(c) above if, in the opinion of the sheriff,

that person understands the nature of the request or, as the case may be, of the declaration, statutory declaration or application; and without prejudice to the generality of this subsection a person twelve years of age or more shall be presumed to be of sufficient age and maturity to have such understanding.]

[18ZA   Registration of father by virtue of certain provisions of the Human Fertilisation and Embryology Act 1990

(1)   The registrar shall not enter in the register as the father of a child the name of a man who is to be treated for that purpose as the father of the child by virtue of section 28(5A), (5B), (5C) or (5D) of the Human Fertilisation and Embryology Act 1990 (circumstances in which man to be treated as father of child for purposes of registration of birth where fertility treatment undertaken after his death) unless the condition in subsection (2) below is satisfied.

(2)   The condition in this subsection is satisfied if—

(a)   the mother requests the registrar to make such an entry in the register and produces the relevant documents; or

(b)   in the case of the death or inability of the mother, the relevant documents are produced by some other person who is a qualified informant.

(3)   In this section 'the relevant documents' means—

(a)   the consent in writing and election mentioned in section 28(5A), (5B), (5C) or (as the case may be) (5D) of the Act of 1990;

(b)   a certificate of a registered medical practitioner as to the medical facts concerned; and

(c)   such other documentary evidence (if any) as the registrar considers appropriate.]

[18A   Decrees of parentage and non-parentage

(1)   Where a decree of parentage or non-parentage has been granted by any court the clerk of court shall—

(a)   where no appeal has been made against such decree, on the expiration of the time within which such an appeal may be made, or

(b)   where an appeal has been made against such a decree, on the conclusion of any appellate proceedings,

notify the import of such decree in the prescribed form to the Registrar General.

(2)   Where it appears to the Registrar General that the import of a decree noti-

fied to him under subsection (1) above does not correspond with the entry in the register of births in respect of any person to whom the decree relates he shall cause an appropriate entry to be made in the Register of Corrections Etc.]

19   Free abbreviated certificate of birth
(1)   At the time of registering the birth of any child, the registrar shall without charge give to the informant, or transmit by post to him within two working days after the date of registration, an abbreviated certificate of birth.

(2)   Any such certificate shall be in the prescribed form and shall contain such particulars as may be prescribed including particulars of the name, surname, sex, date and place of birth of the child, but shall not include any particulars relating to parentage.

(3)   This section shall not apply to re-registration of a birth under section 20 of this Act or to the registration of a still-birth under section 21 of this Act.

20   Re-registration in certain cases
(1)   In the case of any person, if—

(a)   the entry relating to him in the register of births is affected by any matter contained in the Register of Corrections Etc. respecting his status [parentage or non-parentage], or

(b)   the entry relating to him in the register of births has been so made as to imply that he was found exposed, or

(c)   the entry relating to him in the register of births [has been so made as to imply that his parents were not then married to one another and his parents have subsequently married one another],

the Registrar General may at any time authorise the re-registration of the birth, and any such re-registration shall be effected in such manner as may be prescribed:

Provided that the Registrar General shall not authorise the re-registration of a birth in pursuance of paragraph (c) of this subsection, in a case where the paternity of the person has not been entered in the register of births or in the Register of Corrections Etc. in accordance with section 18 of this Act, or any corresponding enactment in force before the commencement of this Act, save with the sanction of the sheriff granted upon the application—

(i)   of both parents of the person jointly, or

(ii)   where one of the parents is dead, of the surviving parent, or

(iii)   where both parents are dead, of or on behalf of the person,

after such intimation as the sheriff may direct, and after due inquiry, and a hearing of any party having interest who may appear to oppose such application.

(2)   In this section any reference to the register of births includes a reference to any register of births kept under any enactment in force at any time before the commencement of this Act.

[(3)   Subject to the proviso in subsection (1) of this section, an application for re-registration of a person's birth under this section may be made—

(a)   if the person is under 16 years of age [by any person (whether or not he has himself attained the age of 16 years) having parental responsibilities in relation to that person];

[(b)]   if the person is of or over [16] years of age, by the person himself, or

[(c)]   in any case, by any person who may be prescribed by regulations made under the Act.]

43   Recording of baptismal name or change of name or surname
(1)   The following provisions of this section, except subsection 6(b), shall apply only to persons whose births are registered in Scotland, and, without prejudice to the provisions of section 24 of the Adoption Act 1958 relating to the giving or taking of a new name, to persons in respect of whom there is an entry in the Adopted

Children Register maintained by the Registrar General under section 22 of that Act.

(2)   In this section 'change' in relation to a name or surname includes any change by way of substitution, addition, omission, spelling or hyphenation.

(3)   Where, within twelve months from the date of the birth of any child, the name by which it was registered is changed or, if it was registered without a name, a name is given to the child, the Registrar General upon delivery to him, within two years from the date of the birth of the child, of a certificate in the pre-scribed form signed—

(a)   if the name was changed or given in baptism, by the person who per-formed the ceremony of baptism or his successor in office, or

(b)   if the name was changed or given otherwise than in baptism, by the qualified applicant,

shall cause an entry containing the name mentioned in the certificate to be made in the Register of Corrections Etc., and only one such entry may be made under this subsection in respect of any one child. [. . .]

(4)   Where an application in the prescribed form is made to the Registrar General by the qualified applicant in respect of the change of name or surname of a child under sixteen years of age the Registrar General may record that change of name or surname by causing an appropriate entry to be made in the Register of Corrections Etc.—

(a)   if evidence to the satisfaction of the Registrar General is produced that the name or surname which the qualified applicant wishes to have recorded has been in use by or in respect of the child to whom the application relates for a period of not less than two years prior to the date of application, and

(b)   if the Registrar General is not satisfied with the evidence so produced, there is also produced to him a copy of a notice inserted in a newspaper circu-lating in the area of the child's usual residence specifying the qualified appli-cant's intention to apply to the Registrar General for the recording of the name or surname proposed and specifying also that such name or surname has been in use by the child for a period of not less than two years prior to the date of the insertion of the notice in the newspaper.

Only one change of name and one change of surname in respect of any one child may be recorded under this subsection, but no change of name shall be recorded under this subsection in the case of a child in respect of whom a change of name has been recorded by virtue of the last foregoing subsection.

(5)   Where an application in the prescribed form is made to the Registrar General in respect of a change of name or surname, in the case of a person over sixteen years of age [. . .] by that person, the Registrar General may record that change of name or surname by causing an appropriate entry to be made in the Register of Corrections Etc.—

(a)   if evidence to the satisfaction of the Registrar General is produced that the name or surname which the applicant wishes to have recorded has been in use by him for a period of not less than two years prior to the date of applica-tion, and

(b)   if the Registrar General is not satisfied with the evidence so produced, there is also produced to him a copy of a notice inserted in a newspaper circu-lating in the area of the applicant's usual residence specifying the applicant's intention to apply to the Registrar General for the recording of the name or sur-name proposed and specifying also that such name or surname has been in use by him for a period of not less than two years prior to the date of the insertion of the notice in the newspaper.

Only one change of name and three changes of surname in respect of any one person may be recorded under this subsection, and a period of five years must elapse after one change of surname is recorded before another such change may be recorded.

(6)   Notwithstanding the foregoing provisions of this section, where an application is made to the Registrar General in respect of a change of name or surname—
(a)   in the case of a child under sixteen years of age, by the [qualified applicant] of that child, in the case of a person over sixteen years of age [. . .] by that person, and there is produced to the Registrar General—
(i)   a decree or certificate of change of name or surname pronounced or, as the case may be, granted by or on behalf of the Lyon King of Arms, or
(ii)   a certified copy of a will, settlement, or deed of trust containing a condition that the person concerned shall take a name or surname different from that in which his birth was registered, together with evidence to the satisfaction of the Registrar General that the name or surname has thereafter been so changed, or
(b)   in the case of a male person who has married in Scotland and who has changed his name or surname following his marriage, by that person, and there is produced to the Registrar General a decree or certificate as described in the foregoing paragraph,
the Registrar General may record that change of name or surname by causing an appropriate entry to be made in the Register of Corrections Etc.
(7)   Where an application is made to the Registrar General in respect of the recording of an alternative name, being the English equivalent of a non-English name, in the case of a child under sixteen years of age, by the [qualified applicant] of that child, in the case of a person over sixteen years of age [. . .] by that person the Registrar General may record that name as an alternative name by causing an appropriate entry to be made in the Register of Corrections Etc.
(8)   On making an application under any of the provisions of this section the applicant shall pay such fees as may be prescribed.
(9)   Nothing in this section shall affect any rule of law as respects change of name or surname, and in particular, without prejudice to that generality, the validity as evidence of change of name or surname of a decree or certificate pronounced or, as the case may be, granted by or on behalf of the Lyon King of Arms.
[(9A)   In this section 'qualified applicant' means—
(a)   where only one parent has parental responsibilities in relation to the child, that parent;
(b)   where both parents have such responsibilities in relation to the child, both parents; and
(c)   where neither parent has such responsibilities, any other person who has such responsibilities.
(9B)   A person may be a qualified applicant for the purposes of this section whether or not he has attained the age of sixteen years].

ABORTION ACT 1967
(1967, c 87)

1   Medical termination of pregnancy
(1)   Subject to the provisions of this section, a person shall not be guilty of an offence under the law relating to abortion when a pregnancy is terminated by a registered medical practitioner if two registered medical practitioners are of the opinion, formed in good faith—
[(a)   that the pregnancy has not exceeded its twenty-fourth week and that the continuance of the pregnancy would involve risk, greater than if the pregnancy were terminated, of injury to the physical or mental health of the pregnant woman or any existing children of her family; or
(b)   that the termination is necessary to prevent grave permanent injury to the physical or mental health of the pregnant woman; or
(c)   that the continuance of the pregnancy would involve risk to the life of the pregnant woman, greater than if the pregnancy were terminated; or

(d)   that there is a substantial risk that if the child were born it would suffer from such physical or mental abnormalities as to be seriously handicapped.]

(2)   In determining whether the continuance of a pregnancy would involve such risk of injury to health as is mentioned in paragraph (a) [or (b)] of subsection (1) of this section, account may be taken of the pregnant woman's actual or reasonably foreseeable environment.

(3)   Except as provided by subsection (4) of this section, any treatment for the termination of pregnancy must be carried out in a hospital vested in [. . .] the Secretary of State [. . .] for the purposes of [his functions under the National Health Service Act 1977 or the National Health Service (Scotland) Act 1978 or in a hospital vested in a Primary Care Trust or in a National Health Service Trust [or an NHS foundation trust] or in a place approved for the purposes of this section by the Secretary of State.]

[(3A)   The power under subsection (3) of this section to approve a place includes power, in relation to treatment consisting primarily in the use of such medicines as may be specified in the approval and carried out in such manner as may be so specified, to approve a class of places.]

(4)   Subsection (3) of this section, and so much of subsection (1) as relates to the opinion of two registered medical practitioners, shall not apply to the termination of a pregnancy by a registered medical practitioner in a case where he is of the opinion, formed in good faith, that the termination is immediately necessary to save the life or to prevent grave permanent injury to the physical or mental health of the pregnant woman.

SOCIAL WORK (SCOTLAND ACT 1968
(1968, s 49)

Central authority

5   Powers of the Secretary of State
(1)   Local authorities shall perform their functions under this Act [and Part II of the Children (Scotland) Act 1995] under the general guidance of the Secretary of State.

[(1A)   Without prejudice to subsection (1) above, the Secretary of State may issue directions to local authorities, either individually or collectively, as to the manner in which they are to exercise any of their functions under this Act or any of the enactments mentioned in [subsection (1B) below] and a local authority shall comply with any direction made under this subsection.

(1B)   The enactments referred to in subsection (1A) above are—
(a)   this Act as read with sections 1 and 2(1) of the Chronically Sick and Disabled Persons Act 1970 and the Disabled Persons (Services, Consultation and Representation) Act 1986;
(b)   Part IV of the Children and Young Persons (Scotland) Act 1937;
(c)   section 22(2) to (5A), (7) and (8), section 26(2) to (4) and sections 43, 45, 47 and 48 of the National Assistance Act 1948;
(d)   the Disabled Persons (Employment) Act 1958;
(e)   sections 10 to 12 of the Matrimonial Proceedings (Children) Act 1958, and sections 11 and 12 of the Guardianship Act 1973;
(f)   [section 51 of the Criminal Procedure (Scotland) Act 1995;]
(g)   the Children Act 1975;
(h)   the Adoption Act 1976;
(i)   the Adoption (Scotland) Act 1978;
(j)   sections 21 to 23 of the Health and Social Services and Social Security Adjudications Act 1983;
(k)   the Mental Health (Scotland) Act 1984;
(l)   the Foster Children (Scotland) Act 1984;

(m)   sections 38(6) and 235 of the Housing (Scotland) Act 1987;
(n)   the Access to Personal Files Act 1987; [. . .] and
[. . .]
(p)   Part II of the Children (Scotland) Act 1995.
(2)   The Secretary of State may make regulations in relation to—
(a)   the performance of the functions assigned to local authorities by this Act;
(b)   the activities of voluntary organisations in so far as those activities are concerned with the like purposes;
[(c)   the performance of the functions of local authorities under any of the enactments mentioned in paragraphs (b), (d), (e), (g), (h), (i), (1), (o) and (p) of subsection (1B) above.
[. . .]
(3)   Without prejudice to the generality of subsection (2) above, regulations under this section may make such provision as is mentioned in subsection (4) of this section as regards—
(a)   the boarding out of persons other than children by local authorities and voluntary organisations, whether under any enactment or otherwise; and
(b)   the placing of children under paragraph (a), or the making of arrangements in respect of children under paragraph (c), of section 26(1) of the Children (Scotland) Act 1995, by local authorities.
(4)   The provision referred to in subsection (3) of this section is—
(a)   for the recording—
(i)   by local authorities and voluntary organisations, of information relating to those with whom persons are so boarded out, or who are willing to have persons so boarded out with them; and
(ii)   by local authorities, of information relating to those with whom children are so placed or with whom such arrangements are made or who are willing to have children so placed with them or to enter into such arrangements,
(b)   for securing that—
(i)   persons are not so boarded out in any household unless it is for the time being approved by such local authority or voluntary organisation as may be prescribed by the regulations; and
(ii)   children are not so placed or, in accordance with such arrangements, provided with accommodation, in any household unless it is for the time being approved by the local authority placing the child or as the case may be making the arrangements;
(c)   for securing that, where possible, the person with whom a child is so placed or with whom such arrangements are made is either of the same religious persuasion as the child or gives an undertaking that the child shall be brought up in that persuasion;
(d)   for securing—
(i)   that a person who is, and the place in which he is, so boarded out by a local authority or voluntary organisation is supervised and inspected by that authority or organisation; and
(ii)   that a child who is, and the place in which he is, so placed or, in accordance with such arrangements, provided with accommodation, by a local authority is supervised and inspected by that authority,
and that he shall be removed from the place in question if his welfare appears to require it.
(5)   In subsections (3) and (4) of this section, 'child' has the same meaning as in Chapters 2 and 3 of Part II of the Children (Scotland) Act 1995.]

[5A   Local authority plans for community care services
(1)   Within such period after the day appointed for the coming into force of this section as the Secretary of State may direct, and in accordance with the provisions

of this section, each local authority shall prepare and publish a plan for the provision of community care services in their area.

(2)   Each local authority shall from time to time review any plan prepared by
them under subsection (1) above, and shall, in the light of any such review, prepare and publish—
      (a)   any modifications to the plan under review; or
      (b)   if the case requires, a new plan.

(3)   In preparing any plan or carrying out any review under subsection (1) or,
as the case may be, subsection (2) above the authority shall consult—
      (a)   any Health Board providing services under the National Health Service
(Scotland) Act 1978 in the area of the authority;
      [. . .]
      (c)   such voluntary organisations as appear to the authority to represent the
interests of persons who use or are likely to use any community care services
within the area of the authority or the interests of private carers who, within that
area, provide care to persons for whom, in the exercise of their functions under
this Act or any of the enactments mentioned in [section 5(1B)] of this Act, the
local authority have a power or a duty to provide, or to secure the provision of,
a service;
      (d)   such voluntary housing agencies and other bodies as appear to the
authority to provide housing or community care services in their area; and
      (e)   such other persons as the Secretary of State may direct.

(4)   In this section—
'community care services' means services, other than services for children,
which a local authority are under a duty or have a power to provide, or to secure
the provision of, under Part II of this Act or section 7 (functions of local authorities), 8 (provision of after-care services) or 11 (training and occupation of the
mentally handicapped) of the Mental Health (Scotland) Act 1984; and
'private carer' means a person who is not employed to provide the care in question by any body in the exercise of its functions under any enactment.

5B   Complaints procedure

(1)   Subject to the provisions of this section, the Secretary of State may by order
require local authorities to establish a procedure whereby a person, or anyone acting on his behalf, may make representations (including complaints) in relation to
the authority's discharge of, or failure to discharge, any of their functions under
this Act, or any of the enactments [mentioned in section 5(1B)] of this Act, in
respect of that person.

(2)   For the purposes of subsection (1) of this section, 'person' means any person for whom the local authority have a power or a duty to provide, or to secure
the provision of, a service, and whose need or possible need for such a service has
(by whatever means) come to the attention of the authority.

(3)   An order under subsection (1) of this section may be commenced at
different times in respect of such different classes of person as may be specified in
the order.

(4)   In relation to a child, representations may be made by virtue of subsection
(1) above by the child, or on his behalf by—
      (a)   his parent;
      (b)   any person having parental [responsibilities and parental rights (within
the meaning of section 1(3) and section 2(4) respectively of the Children (Scotland) Act 1995 in relation to him];
      (c)   any local authority foster parent; or
      (d)   any other person appearing to the authority to have a sufficient interest in
the child's wellbeing to warrant his making representations on the child's behalf.

(5)   In this section—
'child' means a child under the age of 18 years; [. . .]

(6)   A local authority shall comply with any directions given by the Secretary of State as to the procedure to be adopted in considering representations made as mentioned in subsection (1) of this section and as to the taking of such action as may be necessary in consequence of such representations.

(7)   Every local authority shall give such publicity to the procedure established under this section as they consider appropriate.]

6   Supervision of establishments providing accommodation for persons and inspection of records etc

(1)   Any person duly authorised by the Secretary of State may enter any of the following places for the purpose of making such examinations into the state and management of the place, the facilities and services provided therein and the condition and treatment of the persons in it, as he thinks necessary and for the purpose of inspecting any records or registers (in whatever form they are held) relating to the place or to any person for whom services have been or are provided there by virtue of this Act or section 7 (functions of local authorities) or 8 (provision of after-care services) of the Mental Health (Scotland) Act 1984, that is to say—

(a)   any residential or other establishment provided by a local authority or a voluntary organisation or other person for the purposes of this Act or section 7 or 8 of the said Act of 1984 or Part II of the Children (Scotland) Act 1995;

(b)   any place where there is being maintained—

(i)   a foster child within the meaning of the Foster Children (Scotland) Act 1984,

[. . .]

(iii)   a child who has been placed for adoption by an adoption agency (within the meaning of section 1 of the Adoption (Scotland) Act 1978);

(c)   any place where any person, other than a child, is for the time being boarded out by a local authority or a voluntary organisation;

[(cc)   any place where a child is for the time being accommodated under paragraph (a) of, or by virtue of paragraph (c) of, section 26(1) of the Children (Scotland) Act 1995.

[. . .]

(2)   Any such person as aforesaid may at all reasonable times enter the offices of a local authority or of a voluntary organisation for the purpose of inspecting any records or registers relating to any establishment or place mentioned in the foregoing subsection or relating to any persons to whom the authority or organisation has made available advice, guidance or assistance in pursuance of this Act or section 7 or 8 of the said Act of 1984 or Part II of the Children (Scotland) Act 1995, or who may require such advice, guidance or assistance, and may carry out that inspection.

[(2A)   Any such person may require the owner of, or any person employed in, the establishment or place in question to furnish him with such information as he may request.

(2B)   In exercising the power to inspect records and registers under this section a person—

(a)   shall be entitled at any reasonable time to have access to, and inspect and check the operation of, any computer and any associated apparatus or material which is or has been in use in connection with the records or register in question; and

(b)   may require—

(i)   the person by whom or on whose behalf the computer is or has been so used; or

(ii)   any person having charge of or otherwise concerned with the operation of the computer, apparatus or material,

to give him such reasonable assistance as he may require.

(2C)   In exercising the power to inspect places under this section a person—

(a)   may interview any person residing there in private—

(i)   for the purpose of investigating any complaint as to that place or the services provided there; or

(ii)   if he has reason to believe that the services being provided there for that person are not satisfactory; and

(b)   may examine any such person in private.

(2D)   No person may—

(a)   exercise the power to inspect records or registers under subsection (1) or (2) above so as to inspect medical records; or

(b)   exercise the power conferred by subsection (2C)(b) above, unless he is a registered medical practitioner and, in the case of the power conferred by subsection (1) or (2) above, the records or register relate to medical treatment given at the place in question.]

(3)   The power conferred by subsection (1) of this section may be exercised in respect of any place which an authorised person has reasonable cause to believe to be used as an establishment in respect of which the person carrying on the establishment is registrable under Part IV of this Act.

(4)   A person who proposes to exercise any power of entry or inspection conferred by this section shall if so required, produce a duly authenticated document showing his authority to exercise the power.

(5)   Any person who obstructs the exercise of any such power as aforesaid shall be guilty of an offence and liable on summary conviction to a fine not exceeding [level 4 on the standard scale].

[6A   Inquiries

(1)   Without prejudice to section 6B(1) of this Act, the Secretary of State may cause an inquiry to be held into—

(a)   the functions of a local authority under this Act or any of the enactments mentioned in section 5(1B) of this Act;

(b)   the functions of an adoption society, within the meaning of section 65 of the Adoption (Scotland) Act 1978;

[. . .]

(d)   the detention of a child under—

(i)   section 57 of the Children and Young Persons (Scotland) Act 1937; or

(ii)   section 44 or 208 of the Criminal Procedure (Scotland) Act 1995;

(e)   the functions of the Principal Reporter under Part III of the Local Government (Scotland) Act 1994, the Children (Scotland) Act 1995 or any other enactment.

(2)   The Secretary of State may, before an inquiry is commenced, direct that it shall be held in private, but where no such direction has been given the person holding the inquiry may if he thinks fit hold it or any part of it in private.

(3)   Subsections (2) to (8) of section 210 of the Local Government (Scotland) Act 1973 (powers in relation to local inquiries) shall apply in relation to an inquiry under this section as they apply in relation to a local inquiry under that section.]

[6B   Local authority inquiries into matters affecting children

(1)   Without prejudice to section 6A(1) of this Act, a local authority may cause an inquiry to be held into their functions under this Act, or any of the enactments mentioned in section 5(1B) of this Act, in so far as those functions relate to children.

(2)   The local authority may, before an inquiry under this section is commenced, direct that it be held in private; but where no such direction is given, the person holding the inquiry may if he thinks fit hold it, or any part of it, in private.

(3)   Subsections (2) to (6) of section 210 of the Local Government (Scotland) Act 1973 (powers in relation to local inquiries) shall apply in relation to an inquiry under this section as they apply in relation to a local inquiry under that section, so

however that, for the purposes of the application, any reference in those subsections to a Minister shall be construed as a reference to the local authority and any reference to an officer of his Department as a reference to an officer of that authority.

(4)   The expenses incurred by a local authority in relation to an inquiry under this section (including such reasonable sum as the authority may determine for the services of any of their officers engaged in the inquiry) shall, unless the authority are of the opinion that those expenses should be defrayed in whole or in part by them, be paid by such party to the inquiry as they may direct; and the authority may certify the amount of the expenses so incurred.

(5)   Any sum certified under subsection (4) above and to be defrayed in accordance with a direction under that subsection shall be a debt due by the party directed and shall be recoverable accordingly.

(6)   The local authority may make an award as to the expenses of the parties at the inquiry and as to the parties by whom such expenses shall be paid.]

PART II
PROMOTION OF SOCIAL WELFARE BY LOCAL AUTHORITIES

General

12   General social welfare services of local authorities

(1)   It shall be the duty of every local authority to promote social welfare by making available advice, guidance and assistance on such a scale as may be appropriate for their area, and in that behalf to make arrangements and to provide or secure the provision of such facilities (including the provision or arranging for the provision of residential and other establishments) as they may consider suitable and adequate, and such assistance may, [subject to subsections (3) to (5) of this section, be given in kind or in cash on, or in respect of, any relevant person.

(2)   A person is a relevant person for the purposes of this section if, not being less than eighteen years of age, he is] in need requiring assistance in kind or, in exceptional circumstances constituting an emergency, in cash, where the giving of assistance in either form would avoid the local authority being caused greater expense in the giving of assistance in another form, or where probable aggravation of the person's need would cause greater expense to the local authority on a later occasion.

[(2A)   A person to whom section 115 of the Immigration and Asylum Act 1999 (exclusion from benefits) applies is not to receive assistance under subsection (1) of this section (whether by way of residential accommodation or otherwise) if his need for assistance has arisen solely—

(a)   because he is destitute; or
(b)   because of the physical effects, or anticipated physical effects, of his being destitute.

(2B)   Subsections (3) and (5) to (8) of section 95 of the Immigration and Asylum Act 1999, and paragraph 2 of Schedule 8 to that Act, apply for the purposes of subsection (2A) as they apply for the purposes of that section, but for the references in subsections (5) and (7) of that section and in that paragraph to the Secretary of State substitute references to a local authority.]

(3)   Before giving assistance to, or in respect of, a person in cash under subsection (1) of this section a local authority shall have regard to his eligibility for receiving assistance from any other statutory body and, if he is so eligible, to the availability to him of that assistance in his time of need.

[(3A)   In determining, for the purposes of this section, whether to make available assistance by providing, or securing the provision of, residential accommodation to a person, a local authority shall disregard so much of the person's resources—

(a)   as may be prescribed; or

(b)   as is determined by them in such a way as may be prescribed,

and any order made by virtue of this subsection may make different provision for different cases and for different persons.

(3B)   An order made by virtue of paragraph (a) of subsection (3A) of this section may prescribe circumstances in which assistance such as is mentioned in that subsection is to be made available disregarding entirely a person's resources.

(3C)   In subsections (3A) and (3B) of this section, references to a person's resources are to resources within the meaning of the order prescribing the amount, or as the case may be the way, in question.

(3D)   A statutory instrument made in exercise of the power conferred by paragraph (a) or (b) of subsection (3A) of this section shall be subject to annulment in pursuance of a resolution of the Scottish Parliament.]

(4)   Assistance given in kind or in cash to, or in respect of, persons under this section may be given unconditionally or subject to such conditions as to the repayment of the assistance, or of its value, whether in whole or in part, as the local authority may consider reasonable having regard to the means of the person receiving the assistance and to the eligibility of the person for assistance from any other statutory body.

(5)   Nothing in the provisions of this section shall affect the performance by a local authority of their functions under any other enactment.

[(6)   For the purposes of subsection (2) of this section 'person in need' includes a person who is in need of care and attention arising out of drug or alcohol dependency or release from prison or other form of detention.]

[12A   Duty of local authority to assess needs

(1)   Subject to the provisions of this section, where it appears to a local authority that any person for whom they are under a duty or have a power to provide, or to secure the provision of, community care services may be in need of any such services, the authority—

(a)   shall make an assessment of the needs of that person for those services; and

[(b)   shall then decide, having regard to the results of that assessment, and taking account—

(i)   where it appears to them that a person ('the carer') provides a substantial amount of care on a regular basis for that person, of such care as is being so provided; and

(ii)   in so far as it is reasonable and practicable to do so, both of the views of the person whose needs are being assessed and of the views of the carer (provided that, in either case, there is a wish, or as the case may be a capacity, to express a view),

whether the needs of the person being assessed call for the provision of any such services.]

(2)   Before deciding, under subsection (1)(b) of this section, that the needs of any person call for the provision of nursing care, a local authority shall consult a medical practitioner.

(3)   If, while they are carrying out their duty under subsection (1) of this section, it appears to a local authority that there may be a need for the provision to any person to whom that subsection applies—

(a)   of any services under the National Health Service (Scotland) Act 1978 by the Health Board— (i) in whose area he is ordinarily resident; or (ii) in whose area the services to be supplied by the local authority are, or are likely, to be provided; or

(b)   of any services which fall within the functions of a housing authority (within the meaning of section 130 (housing) of the Local Government (Scotland) Act 1973) which is not the local authority carrying out the assessment, the local authority shall so notify that Health Board or housing authority, and shall request information from them as to what services are likely to be made available to that person by that Health Board or housing authority; and, thereafter, in carrying out their said duty, the local authority shall take into account any information received by them in response to that request.

(4)   Where a local authority are making an assessment under this section and it appears to them that the person concerned is a disabled person, they shall—

(a)   proceed to make such a decision as to the services he requires as is mentioned in section 4 of the Disabled Persons (Services, Consultation and Representation) Act 1986 without his requesting them to do so under that section; and

(b)   inform him that they will be doing so and of his rights under that Act.

(5)   Nothing in this section shall prevent a local authority from providing or arranging for the provision of community care services for any person without carrying out a prior assessment of his needs in accordance with the preceding provisions of this section if, in the opinion of the authority, the condition of that person is such that he requires those services as a matter of urgency.

(6)   If, by virtue of subsection (5) of this section, community care services have been provided for any person as a matter of urgency, then, as soon as practicable thereafter, an assessment of his needs shall be made in accordance with the preceding provisions of this section.

(7)   This section is without prejudice to section 3 of the said Act of 1986.

(8)   In this section—

'community care services' has the same meaning as in section 5A of this Act;

'disabled person' has the same meaning as in the said Act of 1986; and

'medical practitioner' means a fully registered person within the meaning of section 55 (interpretation) of the Medical Act 1983.]

[12AA   Assessment of ability to provide care

(1)   A person ('the carer') who provides, or intends to provide, a substantial amount of care on a regular basis for another person aged eighteen or over ('the person cared for') may, whether or not the carer is a child, request a local authority to make an assessment ('the carer's assessment') of the carer's ability to provide or to continue to provide such care for that person.

(2)   The local authority to whom the request is made shall—

(a)   comply with the request where it appears to them that the person cared for is a person for whom they must or may provide, or secure the provision of, community care services; and

(b)   if they then or subsequently make an assessment under subsection (1)(a) of section 12A of this Act of the needs of the person cared for, have regard to the results of the carer's assessment—

(i)   in the assessment of the person cared for; and

(ii)   in making their decision under subsection (1)(b) of that section as respects that person.

(3)   Subsection (1) above does not apply as respects a carer who provides, or will provide, the care in question—

(a)   by virtue of a contract of employment or other contract; or

(b)   as a volunteer for a voluntary organisation.

(4)   Section 8 of the Disabled Persons (Services, Consultation and Representation) Act 1986 (c 33) (duty of local authority to take into account abilities of carer in deciding whether to provide certain services to disabled person) shall not apply in a case where a local authority make an assessment, by virtue of subsection (2)(a) above, in respect of a carer of a disabled person.

(5)   Subsections (4) to (7) of section 12A of this Act apply to a local authority making an assessment by virtue of subsection (2)(a) of this section as they apply to a local authority making an assessment under subsection (1)(a) of that section.

(6)   In this section, 'community care services', 'disabled person' and 'person' have the same meanings as in section 12A of this Act.]

[12AB   Duty of local authority to provide information to carer
(1)   Where it appears to a local authority both that—
(a)   a person aged eighteen or over ('the person cared for') is a person for whom the authority are under a duty or have a power to provide community care services; and
(b)   another person ('the carer') provides, or intends to provide, a substantial amount of care on a regular basis for the person cared for the local authority shall notify the carer that he may be entitled under section 12AA of this Act to request an assessment of his ability to provide, or continue to provide, care for the person cared for.
(2)   In this section, 'community care services' and 'person' have the same meanings as in section 12A of this Act.]

[12B   Direct payments in respect of community care services
(1)   Where, as respects [any person] in need—
(a)   a local authority
[(i)   have decided under section 12A of this Act that his needs call for the provision of any service which is a community care service; or
(ii)   have a duty to provide a service to him under section 22(1) of the Children (Scotland) Act 1995 (c 36) (promotion of welfare of children in need) other than a service which comprises giving assistance in cash;]
(b)   the person is [not] of a description which is specified for the purposes of this subsection by regulations, the authority [shall, if and while (the payment having been offered by the authority) either the person consents or consent is duly given on his behalf,], make to him, in respect of his securing the provision of the service, a payment of such amount as, subject to subsection (2) below, they [determine to be appropriate].
[(1A)   The amount of any payment made, under subsection (1) above, with or without first assessing the person's ability to contribute to securing the provision of the service in question, may be determined on the supposition that he has no such ability; but this subsection is subject to subsection (5A) below.
(1B)   Consent is duly given as mentioned in subsection (1) above if—
(a)   the authority are satisfied that the person on whose behalf it is given is himself incapable of giving it; and
(b)   the person who gives it is of a category specified for the purposes of that subsection by regulations,
and such regulations may authorise the person so consenting to intromit with the payment and to do anything requisite to secure the provision of the service.
(1C)   The reference in subsections (1) to (1B) above to securing the provision of the service is to securing its provision by any person, including the authority themselves (provided that both they and the consenting person so wish) or any other local authority.]
(2)   If—
(a)   an authority pay under subsection (1) above at a rate below their estimate of the reasonable cost of securing the provision of the service concerned, and
(b)   the person to whom the payment is made satisfies the authority that his means are insufficient for it to be reasonably practicable for him to make up the difference,
the authority shall so adjust the payment to him under that subsection as to avoid there being a greater difference than that which appears to them to be reasonably practicable for him to make up.
(3)   A payment under subsection (1) above shall be subject to the condition that the person to whom it is made shall not secure the provision of the service to

which it relates by a person who is of a description specified for the purposes of this subsection by regulations.

(4)   Regulations may

[(a)   provide that the [duty imposed by subsection (1) above shall not apply] in relation to the provision of residential accommodation for any person for a period in excess of such period as may be specified in the regulations;

[(b)   impose preconditions which must be fulfilled if the service concerned is, by virtue of that subsection, to be provided by the authority by whom the payment under that subsection is made and special conditions which shall apply as respects a service so provided by them;

(c)   specify circumstances in which the authority are not required to make payments under that subsection (whether circumstances relating to the person in question or to the service in question or to both);

(d)   specify circumstances in which the authority may or must terminate the making of such payments; and

(e)   authorise such payments to be made, on behalf of the payee, to some other person of a category specified, for the purposes of this subsection, by regulations.]

(5)   If the authority by whom a payment under subsection (1) above is made are not satisfied, in relation to the whole or any part of the payment—

(a)   that it has been used to secure the provision of the service to which it relates, or

(b)   that the condition imposed by subsection (3) above, or any condition properly imposed by them, has been met in relation to its use,

they may require the payment or, as the case may be, the part of the payment to be repaid.

[(5A)   An authority who have made a determination by virtue of subsection (1A) above in respect of a payment—

(a)   having first assessed the recipient's ability to contribute to securing the provision of the service in question, may; or

(b)   other than is mentioned in paragraph (a) above, shall thereafter make such an assessment and may,

having regard to the assessment, require from him such repayment as appears to them appropriate.

(5B)   If the person from whom a repayment is required under subsection (5A) above satisfies the authority that, notwithstanding the assessment to which regard was had in making the requirement, his means are insufficient for it to be reasonably practicable for him to make that repayment, the authority shall adjust the requirement so that the amount to be repaid becomes an amount which appears to them to be reasonably practical for him to repay.]

(6)   Regulations under this section shall be made by the Secretary of State and may—

(a)   make different provision for different cases; and

(b)   include such supplementary, incidental, consequential and transitional provisions and savings as the Secretary of State thinks fit.

[(7)   The definition of 'community care services' in section 5A of this act shall, with the modification mentioned in subsection (8) below, apply for the purposes of this section as that definition applies for the purposes of that section.

(8)   The modification is that the words ', other than services for children,' in the definition shall be disregarded.]

[12C   Further provisions relating to direct payments

(1)   Except as provided by subsection (2) below, the fact that a local authority make a payment under [subsection (1) of section 12B] of this Act shall not affect their functions with respect to the provision of the service to which the payment relates.

(2) Subject to subsection (3) below, where an authority make a payment under [subsection (i) of section 12B(1)] of this Act they shall not be under any obligation to the person to whom it is made with respect to the provision of the service to which it relates [(except in so far as it is provided by them by virtue of that sub-section)] as long as they are satisfied that the need which calls for the provision of that service will be met by virtue of [that subsection].

(3) The fact that an authority make a payment under section 12B(1) of this Act shall not affect their functions under section 12 of this Act in relation to the pro-vision, to the person to whom the payment is made, of assistance, in exceptional circumstances constituting an emergency, in cash in respect of the service to which the payment under section 12B(1) relates.]

13 Power of local authorities to assist persons in need in disposal of produce of their work

Where, by virtue of [section 12 of this Act], a local authority make arrangements or provide or secure the provision of facilities for the engagement of persons in need (whether under a contract of service or otherwise) in suitable work, that local auth-ority may assist such persons in disposing of the produce of their work.

Residential accommodation with nursing

[13A Residential accommodation with nursing

(1) Without prejudice to section 12 of this Act, a local authority shall—
    [(a) provide and maintain, or
    (b)] make such arrangements as they consider appropriate and adequate for the provision of
suitable residential accommodation where nursing is provided for persons who appear to them to be in need of such accommodation by reason of infirmity, age, illness or mental disorder, dependency on drugs or alcohol or being substantially handicapped by any deformity or disability.

[(2) [A]rrangements made by virtue of subsection (1) above shall be made with a voluntary or other organisation or other person, being an organisation or person providing—
    (a) an independent health care service which is a private psychiatric hos-pital; or
    (b) a care home service.

(2A) Expressions used in subsection (2) above have the same meanings as in the Regulation of Care (Scotland) Act 2001 (asp 8).]

(3) The provisions of section 6 of this Act apply in relation to premises where accommodation is provided for the purposes of this section as they apply in re-lation to establishments provided for the purposes of this Act.

[(4) No arrangements under subsection (1) above may be given effect to in re-lation to a person to whom section 115 of the Immigration and Asylum Act 1999 (exclusion from benefits) applies solely—
    (a) because he is destitute; or
    (b) because of the physical effects, or anticipated physical effects, of his being destitute.

(5) Subsections (3) and (5) to (8) of section 95 of the Immigration and Asylum Act 1999, and paragraph 2 of Schedule 8 to that Act, apply for the purposes of subsection (4) above as they apply for the purposes of that section, but for the references in subsections (5) and (7) of that section and in that paragraph to the Secretary of State substitute references to a local authority.]

Provision of care and after-care

[13B Provision of care and after-care

(1) Subject to subsection (2) below, a local authority may, with the approval of

the Secretary of State, and shall, if and to the extent that the Secretary of State so directs, make arrangements for the purpose of the prevention of illness, the care of persons suffering from illness, and the after-care of such persons.

(2)   The arrangements which may be made under subsection (1) above do not include arrangements in respect of medical, dental or nursing care, or health visiting.

[(3)   No arrangements under subsection (1) above may be given effect to in relation to a person to whom section 115 of the Immigration and Asylum Act 1999 (exclusion from benefits) applies solely—

(a)   because he is destitute; or

(b)   because of the physical effects, or anticipated physical effects, of his being destitute.

(4)   Subsections (3) and (5) to (8) of section 95 of the Immigration and Asylum Act 1999, and paragraph 2 of Schedule 8 to that Act, apply for the purposes of subsection (3) above as they apply for the purposes of that section, but for the references in subsections (5) and (7) of that section and in that paragraph to the Secretary of State substitute references to a local authority.]]

PART IV
RESIDENTIAL AND OTHER ESTABLISHMENTS

Provision of residential and other establishments

59   Provision of residential and other establishments by local authorities, and maximum period for repayment of sums borrowed for such provision

(1)   [Without prejudice to their duties under section 13A of this Act it] shall be the duty of a local authority to provide and maintain such residential and other establishments as may be required for their functions under this Act [or under Part II of the Children (Scotland) Act 1995] or arrange for the provision of such establishments.

(2)   For the purpose of discharging their duty under the foregoing subsection a local authority may—

(a)   themselves provide such establishments as aforesaid; or

(b)   join with another local authority in providing those establishments; or

(c)   secure the provision of such establishments by voluntary organisations or other persons including other local authorities.

(3)   The maximum period for the repayment of sums borrowed by a local authority for the purposes of this section shall be such period not exceeding sixty years as may be sanctioned by the Secretary of State; and accordingly in Schedule 6 to the Local Government (Scotland) Act 1947, at the end, there shall be added the following entry, that is to say—

Section 59 of the Social Work   Such period not exceeding sixty years as
(Scotland) Act 1968.   may be sanctioned by the Secretary of
                                         State.

[59A   Grants in respect of secure accommodation for children

(1)   The Secretary of State may make to a local authority grants of such amount and subject to such conditions as he may with the consent of the Treasury determine in respect of expenditure incurred by the authority in—

(a)   providing;

(b)   joining with another local authority in providing; or

(c)   contributing by way of grant under section 10(3) of this Act to the provision by a voluntary organisation of,

secure accommodation [. . .]

(2)   The conditions subject to which grants are made under subsection (1) of this section may include conditions for securing the repayment in whole or in part of such grants.]

PART VI
CONTRIBUTIONS IN RESPECT OF CHILDREN IN CARE ETC

78 Duty to make contributions in respect of children in care etc

(1) Where a child [is being looked after by a local authority] or a supervision requirement to which this Part of this Act applies has been made in respect of him, contributions in respect of the child (hereinafter in this Part of this Act referred to as the 'maintainable child') shall be payable—

(a) while the maintainable child is under sixteen years of age, by [any natural person who has parental responsibilities (within the meaning of section 1(3) of the Children (Scotland) Act 1995)] in relation to him;

(b) if he is over sixteen years of age [. . .] by the maintainable child himself.

[(2) This Part of this Act applies to any supervision requirement which, under paragraph (a) of section 70(3) of the Children (Scotland) Act 1995, requires the child concerned to reside in a place or places other than his own home.

(2A) No contributions shall be payable under subsection 1(a) of this section by a contributor during a period when he is in receipt of income support, an income-based jobseeker's allowance (payable under the Jobseekers Act 1995) or family credit.]

(3) In this Part of this Act 'contributor' means a person liable to make contributions by virtue of subsection (1) of this section in respect of a maintainable child.

[78A Recovery of contributions

(1) Section 87 of this Act (charges for services and accommodation) shall not apply to the provision of services (including accommodation) under this Act in respect of maintainable children, and the provisions of this section shall apply thereto.

(2) A local authority providing such services may recover from a contributor a contribution (if any) of such amount as is reasonable and, subject to that, may recover—

(a) a standard contribution determined by them in respect of maintainable children who are [looked after by them]; or

(b) such other contribution as they consider reasonable in the circumstances.]

79 Recipients of contributions

(1) Subject to the provisions of the following subsection, contributions payable under the last foregoing section shall be payable to the local authority within whose area the contributor is residing, and shall, in the case of contributions paid in respect of a maintainable child [looked after by] a local authority, other than the authority to whom the contributions are payable as aforesaid, be paid over by the last-mentioned authority to that other authority, but subject to such deductions in respect of services rendered by the local authority to whom the contributions were payable as may be agreed between the authorities concerned or as, in default of agreement, may be determined by the Secretary of State.

(2) Where a contributor is for the time being residing in England or Wales or Northern Ireland contributions payable by him under the last foregoing section shall be payable to the local authority [looking after the child].

80 Enforcement of duty to make contributions

(1) Where a child becomes a maintainable child by virtue of being [looked after by a local authority] any court of summary jurisdiction, having jurisdiction in the place where the contributor is for the time being residing, may, on the application of the local authority, at any time make an order on any contributor, hereinafter in this Act referred to as a contribution order, for weekly contributions in respect of the child of such amount as the court thinks proper.

[. . .]

(4) Subject to the following provisions of this section, a contribution order in

respect of a maintainable child shall remain in force [throughout the period during which he is looked after by a local authority].

(5) No contribution shall be payable, by virtue of a contribution order by a contributor who, [being a natural person, has parental responsibilities (within the meaning of section 1(3) of the Children (Scotland) Act 1995) in relation to the maintainable child], in respect of any period after the maintainable child becomes sixteen.

(6) A contribution order may be revoked or varied by any court of summary jurisdiction having jurisdiction in the place where the contributor is for the time being residing and shall be enforceable in like manner as a decree for aliment.

(7) Where a contributor resides in England or Wales or Northern Ireland this section shall have effect as if for any reference to a court of summary jurisdiction having jurisdiction in a place where the contributor is for the time being residing there were substituted a reference to a court of summary jurisdiction having jurisdiction in any place within the area of the local authority [looking after] the child.

81   Provisions as to decrees for ailment

(1)   [. . .]

(2)   Where [. . .] a decree for aliment [of a maintainable child] is in force, on the application of the local authority concerned, any court of summary jurisdiction having jurisdiction in the place where the [person liable under the decree] is for the time being residing may, at any time, or order the payments under the decree [. . .] to be paid to the local authority who are from time to time entitled under either of the last two foregoing sections to receive contributions in respect of the child.

(3)   Where [. . .] an order made under this section in respect to a decree for aliment is in force any sums received under the decree for aliment shall be applied in like manner as if they were contributions received under a contribution order.

(4)(a)   In this section the local authority concerned means the local authority which may make application for a contribution order in respect of a child under the last foregoing section;

(b)   where the [person liable to pay aliment for a child under a decree] is resident in England or Wales or Northern Ireland, subsection (2) of this section shall have effect as if for the reference to a court of summary jurisdiction having jurisdiction in the place where [that person] is for the time being residing, there were substituted a reference to a court of summary jurisdiction having jurisdiction in any place within the area of the local authority concerned.

82   Recovery of arrears of contributions

(1)   Where, by virtue of an order or decree made under either of the last two foregoing sections, any sum is payable to a local authority, the local authority in whose area the person liable under the order or decree is for the time being residing, or, as the case may be, the local authority [looking after] the child to whom the order or decree relates, shall be entitled to receive and give a discharge for, and, if necessary, enforce payment of, any arrears accrued due under the order or decree, notwithstanding that those arrears may have accrued at a time when he was not resident in that area or, as the case may be, when the authority were not entitled to sums payable under the order or decree.

(2)   In any proceedings under either of the last two foregoing sections, a certificate purporting to be signed by the clerk to a local authority for the time being entitled to receive contributions, or by some other officer of the authority duly authorised in that behalf, and stating that any sum due to the authority under an order or decree is overdue and unpaid, shall be sufficient evidence of the facts stated therein.

83   Variation of trusts

(1)   Where a child is by virtue of a supervision requirement removed from the

care of any person and that person is entitled under any trust to receive any sum of money in respect of the maintenance of the child, on the application of the local authority concerned any court of summary jurisdiction, having jurisdiction in the place where that person is for the time being residing, may at any time order the whole or any part of the sums so payable under the trust to be paid to the local authority, to be applied by the authority for the benefit of the child in such manner as, having regard to the terms of the trust, the court may direct.

(2) Where the person in whose care a child has been residing is for the time being residing in England or Wales or Northern Ireland the foregoing subsection shall have effect as if for the reference to a court having jurisdiction in the place where that person is residing there were substituted a reference to a court of summary jurisdiction having jurisdiction in any place within the area of the local authority [looking after] the child.

[83A   References in this Part of this Act to child being looked after
In this Part of this Act, references to a child being looked after by a local authority shall be construed in accordance with section 17(6) of the Children (Scotland) Act 1995.]

PART VII
MISCELLANEOUS AND GENERAL

General

84   Transfer of assets and liabilities
Where any functions are transferred to a local authority by virtue of this Act all property, rights, liabilities and obligations relating to the performance of those functions which immediately before the date of transfer were the property, rights, liabilities and obligations of the body or person from which the functions are transferred shall on that date be transferred to and vest in the local authority or, as the case may be, the local authorities to which the functions have been transferred, and the provisions of Schedule 6 to this Act shall have effect for the purposes of this section.

86   Adjustments between authority providing accommodation etc, and authority of area of residence
(1)   Any expenditure which apart from this section would fall to be borne by a local authority—

(a)   in the provision under this Act [or under section 25 of the Children (Scotland) Act 1995] of accommodation for a person ordinarily resident in the area of another local authority, or

(b)   in the provision under Part II of this Act [, or under or by virtue of Part II of the said Act of 1995, of services and facilities for a person ordinarily so resident (including, in the case of a child, any expenses incurred after he has ceased to be a child, and, in the event of another local authority taking over, under section 24(4) of that Act, the provision of accommodation for him,] including also any travelling or other expenses incurred in connection with the taking over), or

(c)   for the conveyance of a person ordinarily resident as aforesaid, or

(d)   in administering a supervision requirement in respect of a person ordinarily resident as aforesaid, [or

(e)   in the provision of accommodation, services or facilities for persons ordinarily so resident under section 7 (functions of local authorities) or 8 (provision of after-care services) of the Mental Health (Scotland) Act 1984,]

shall be recoverable from the other local authority, and in this subsection any reference to another local authority includes a reference to a local authority in England and Wales.

(2)   Any question arising under this section as to the ordinary residence of a

person shall be determined by the Secretary of State, and the Secretary of State may determine that a person has no ordinary residence.

(3)   In determining for the purposes of subsection (1) of this section the ordinary residence of any person or child, any period during which he was a patient in a hospital [. . .] provided under [sections 2 and 3 of the National Health Service Act 1977] or Part II of the National Health Service (Scotland) Act [1978 or in a hospital managed by a National Health Service Trust established under Part I of the National Health Service and Community Care Act 1990 or section 12A of the National Health Service (Scotland) Act 1978] or, in the case of a child, any period during which he resided in any place as an inmate of a school or other institution, or in accordance with the requirements of a supervision requirement, supervision order or probation order or the conditions of a recognizance, or while boarded out under this Act or under [. . .] the Children and Young Persons (Scotland) Act 1937 by a local authority or education authority [or placed with local authority foster parents under the Children Act 1989, or provided with accommodation under paragraph (4) of, or by virtue of paragraph (c) of section 26(1) of the Children (Scotland) Act 1995] shall be disregarded.

[. . .]

87   Charges that may be made for services and accommodation

(1)   [Subject to sections 78 and 78A of this Act (contributions in respect of maintainable children) and to the following provisions of this section, a local authority providing a service under this Act [or section 7 (functions of local authorities) or 8 (provision of after-care services) of the Mental Health (Scotland) Act 1984 or under or by virtue of Part II of the Children (Scotland) Act 1995] may recover such charge (if any) for it as they consider reasonable.]

[(1A)   If a person—

(a)   avails himself of a service provided under this Act [or section 7 or 8 of the said Act of 1984 or under or by virtue of Part II of the Children (Scotland) Act 1995]; and

(b)   satisfies the authority providing the service that his means are insufficient for it to be reasonably practicable for him to pay for the service the amount which he would otherwise be obliged to pay for it,

the authority shall not require him to pay more for it than it appears to them that it is reasonably practicable for him to pay.]

[(1B)   Subsections (1) and (1A) above do not apply as respects any amount required not to be charged by subsection (1) of section 1 of the Community Care and Health (Scotland) Act 2002 (asp 5) (charging and not charging for social care) or required to be charged or not to be charged by virtue of subsection (4) of that section.]

(2)   Persons, other than maintainable children, for whom accommodation is provided under this Act or section 7 of the said Act of 1984; shall be required to pay for that accommodation in accordance with the subsequent provisions of this section.

(3)   Subject to the following provisions of this section, accommodation provided under this Act shall be regarded as accommodation provided under Part III of the National Assistance Act 1948, and sections 22(2) to [(8)] and 26(2) to (4) [as amended by the Schedule to the Housing (Homeless Persons) Act 1977, paragraph 2(1) of Schedule 4 to the Social Security Act 1980, section 20 of the Health and Social Services and Social Security Adjudications Act 1983 and paragraph 32 of Schedule 10 to the Social Security Act 1986] (charges for accommodation and provision of accommodation in premises maintained by voluntary organisations) and sections 42 [(as amended by paragraph 5 of Schedule 1 to the Law Reform (Parent and Child) (Scotland) Act 1986) and 43].

(4)   In the application of the said section 22, for any reference to the Minister there shall be substituted a reference to the Secretary of State, and in the applica-

tion of the said section 26, any references to arrangements under a scheme for the provision of accommodation shall be construed as references to arrangements made by a local authority with a voluntary organisation [or any other person or body] for the provision of accommodation under this Act [or section 7 of the said Act of 1984].

(5) The Secretary of State may, with the consent of the Treasury, make regulations for modifying or adjusting the rates at which payments under this section are made, where such a course appears to him to be justified, and any such regulations may provide for the waiving of any such payment in whole or in part in such circumstances as may be specified in the regulations.

[. . .]

[. . .]

90 Orders, regulations etc

(1) Any power to make regulations or orders [. . .] or to make rules conferred on the Secretary of State by this Act shall be exercisable by statutory instrument.

(2) Any statutory instrument made in the exercise of any power to make regulations conferred by this Act shall be subject to annulment in pursuance of a resolution of either House of Parliament.

(3) Any power conferred by this Act to make orders shall include a power, exercisable in the like manner and subject to the same conditions, to vary or revoke any such order.

91 Expenses

There shall be defrayed out of moneys provided by Parliament—

(a) any sums required for the payment of grants under this Act or any other expenses of the Secretary of State under this Act, and

(b) any increase attributable to the provisions of this Act in the sums payable out of such money under any other Act.

92 Effect of Act on rate support grant

(1) The Secretary of State shall have power, by an order made in the like manner and subject to the like provisions as a rate support grant order, to vary the provisions of any rate support grant order made before the commencement of this Act for a grant period ending after the commencement of this Act.

(2) Any order made by virtue of this section may be made for all or any of the years comprised in the said rate support grant period, as may be specified in the order, and in respect of the year or years so specified shall increase the annual aggregate amount of the rate support grants to such extent as may appear to the Secretary of State to be appropriate having regard to any additional expenditure incurred or likely to be incurred by councils of counties or of large burghs in consequence of the passing of this Act.

(3) The provisions of this section shall have effect without prejudice to the exercise of any power conferred by section 4 of the Local Government (Scotland) Act 1966 (which confers power to vary rate support grant orders in consequence of unforeseen increases in the level of prices, costs or remuneration).

(4) In this section the expressions 'rate support grant order' and 'grant period' have the meanings respectively assigned to them by subsection (1) and subsection (3) of section 3 of the Local Government (Scotland) Act 1966.

[92A Power of the Secretary of State to make grants

The Secretary of State may, with the approval of the Treasury, make grants out of money provided by Parliament towards any expenses of local authorities in respect to their functions under—

(a) Part II of this Act; and

(b) sections 7 and 8 of the Mental Health (Scotland) Act 1984,

in relation to persons suffering from mental illness.]

Supplementary

93 Transitional provisions

The transitional provisions set out in Schedule 7 to this Act shall have effect for the purposes of the transition to the provisions of this Act from the law in force before the commencement of this Act.

94 Interpretation

(1)   In this Act, except where otherwise expressly provided or the context otherwise requires, the following expressions have the meanings hereby respectively assigned to them—

'approved school' means a school approved by the Secretary of State under section 79 of the Children and Young Persons Act 1933,

'approved school order' has the meaning assigned to it by section 107(1) of the Children and Young Persons Act 1933,

[. . .]

'community rehabilitation order' has the meaning given by section 43 of the Criminal Justice and Court Services Act 2000],

'constable' means a constable of a police force within the meaning of the Police (Scotland) Act 1967,

'contribution' and 'contribution order' have the meanings respectively assigned to them by sections 78 and 80 of this Act,

'domiciliary services' means any services, being services provided in the home, which appear to a local authority to be necessary for the purpose of enabling a person to maintain as independent an existence as is practicable in his home,]

'establishment' means an establishment managed by a local authority, voluntary organisation or any other person, which provides non-residential accommodation for the purposes of this Act, [or of Part II of the Children (Scotland) Act 1995] whether for reward or not,

'functions' shall include powers and duties,

'hospital' means—

(a)   any hospital vested in the Secretary of State under the National Health Service (Scotland) Act [1978],

[(aa) any hospital managed by a National Health Service trust established under section 12A of the National Health Service (Scotland) Act 1978,]

(b)   any private hospital registered under the Mental Health (Scotland) Act 1984, and

(c)   any State hospital, within the meaning of [Part VIII of the said Act of 1984],

'local authority', in relation to Scotland, has the meaning assigned to it by section 1(2) of this Act,

'maintainable child' has the meaning assigned to it by section 78 of this Act,

'mental disorder' has the meaning assigned to it by [section 1(2) of the Mental Health (Scotland) Act 1984],

'mental health officer' means an officer of a local authority appointed to act as a mental health officer for the purposes of the said Act of [1984],

'parent' means either parent or both parents, except that where the child was born out of wedlock and the parents have not subsequently married each other it means the natural mother but not the natural father,]

'performance', in relation to functions, includes the exercise of powers as well as the performance of duties, and 'perform' shall be construed accordingly,

'persons in need' means persons who,

(a)   are in need of care and attention arising out of infirmity, youth or age; or

(b)   suffer from illness or mental disorder or are substantially handicapped by any deformity or disability; or

(c)   being persons prescribed by the Secretary of State who have asked for assistance, are, in the opinion of a local authority, persons to whom the authority may appropriately make available the services and facilities provided by them under this Act,

'prescribed' means

(a)   in section 3 prescribed by regulations; and

(b)   [. . .]

[(c)   in sections 12(3A), 27A, 27B, 62(2), 64A(3), 66(1) and (2), 94, paragraphs 2(2) and (3), 4(3) and (4) of Schedule 7, prescribed by order, and 'prescribe' shall be construed accordingly.]

['probation order'—

(a)   in relation to an order imposed by a court in England or Wales, means a community rehabilitation order,

(b)   in relation to an order imposed by a court in Northern Ireland, has the same meaning as in the Criminal Justice (Northern Ireland) Order 1996;]

'residential establishment' means an establishment managed by a local authority, voluntary organisation or any other person, which provides residential accommodation for the purposes of this Act [or of Part II of the Children (Scotland) Act 1995], whether for reward or not,

'supervision order', in relation to an order imposed by a court in England or Wales, has the meaning assigned to it by section 5 of the Children and Young Persons Act 1963 [and includes a supervision order within the meaning of the Powers of Criminal Courts (Sentencing) Act 2000], and in relation to an order imposed by a court in Northern Ireland [means a supervision order under the Children and Young Persons Act (Northern Ireland) 1968 or the Children (Northern Ireland) Order 1995],

'supervision requirement' has the meaning assigned to it by [section 70(1) of the Children (Scotland) Act 1995],

'training school' has the meaning assigned to it by section 180(1) of the Children and Young Persons Act (Northern Ireland) 1968,]

'training school order' means an order made by a court in Northern Ireland sending a child or young person to a training school,

'voluntary organisation' means a body the activities of which are carried on otherwise than for profit, but does not include any public or local authority,

'welfare authority' means a welfare authority constituted under the Public Health and Local Government (Administrative Provisions) Act (Northern Ireland) 1946.

(2)   Unless the context otherwise requires, any reference in this Act to any other enactment is a reference thereto as amended, and includes a reference thereto as extended or applied by or under any other enactment including this Act.

(3)   Without prejudice to the last foregoing subsection, any reference in this Act to an enactment of the Parliament of Northern Ireland, or to an enactment which that Parliament has power to amend, shall be construed, in relation to Northern Ireland, as a reference to that enactment as amended by any Act of that Parliament, whether passed before or after this Act, and to any enactment of that Parliament passed after this Act and re-enacting the said enactment with or without modifications.

95   Minor and consequential amendments, repeals and savings

(1)   The enactments described in Schedule 8 to this Act shall have effect subject to the amendments therein specified, being minor amendments and amendments consequential on the foregoing provisions of this Act.

(2)   The enactments described in Schedule 9 to this Act are hereby repealed to the extent specified in the third column of that Schedule.

(3)   Subject to any expression in this Act to the contrary, in so far as any appointment, agreement or any provision in a regulation or order made or any notice, direction, consent, approval, warrant or certificate given under any enactment repealed by this Act or registration effected, or deemed to have been effected, proceedings instituted or other thing done under any such enactment

could have been made, passed, given, granted, effected, instituted or done under a corresponding provision of this Act, it shall not be invalidated by this repeal, but shall have effect as if it had been made, passed, given, granted, effected, instituted or done to that corresponding provision and may be amended, varied, revoked or enforced accordingly, and, in the case of any legal proceedings, may be continued and appealed against as if this Act had not been passed.

97 Extension of certain provisions of Act to England and Wales, Northern Ireland and the Channel Islands

(1) The following provisions of this Act shall extend to England and Wales, that is to say—

[. . .]

sections 86 and 87

section 98(3)

Schedule 2, paragraphs 7 and 13

Schedule 8

Part II of Schedule 9.

[. . .]

(4) Save as aforesaid, and except in so far as it relates to the interpretation or commencement of the provisions, this Act shall extend only to Scotland.

98 Commencement

(1) This Act (except this section) shall come into operation on such date as the Secretary of State may by order appoint.

(2) Different dates may be appointed by order under this section for different purposes of this Act; and any reference in any provision of this Act to the commencement of this Act shall, unless otherwise provided by any such order, be construed as a reference to the date on which that provision comes into operation.

(3) An order under this section may make such transitional provisions as appear to the Secretary of State to be necessary or expedient in connection with the provisions thereby brought into force, including such adaptations of those provisions or of any provision of this Act then in force as appear to the Secretary of State necessary or expedient for the purposes or in consequence of the operation of any provision of this Act before the coming into force of any other provision of this Act or of the Children and Young Persons Act 1969.

99 Short title

This Act may be cited as the Social Work (Scotland) Act 1968.

DOMICILE AND MATRIMONIAL PROCEEDINGS ACT 1973
(1973, c 45)

PART I
DOMICILE

Husband and wife

1 Abolition of wife's dependent domicile

(1) Subject to subsection (2) below, the domicile of a married woman as at any time after the coming into force of this section shall, instead of being the same as her husband's by virtue only of marriage, be ascertained by reference to the same factors as in the case of any other individual capable of having an independent domicile.

(2) Where immediately before this section came into force a woman was married and then had her husband's domicile by dependence, she is to be treated as retaining that domicile (as a domicile of choice, if it is not also her domicile of origin) unless and until it is changed by acquisition or revival of another domicile either on or after the coming into force of this section.

(3)   This section extends to England and Wales, Scotland and Northern Ireland.

4   Dependent domicile of child not living with his father

(1)   Subsection (2) of this section shall have effect with respect to the dependent domicile of a child as at any time after the coming into force of this section when his father and mother are alive but living apart.

(2)   The child's domicile as at that time shall be that of his mother if—

(a)   he then has his home with her and has no home with his father; or

(b)   he has at any time had her domicile by virtue of paragraph (a) above and has not since had a home with his father.

(3)   As at any time after the coming into force of this section, the domicile of a child whose mother is dead shall be that which she last had before she died if at her death he had her domicile by virtue of subsection (2) above and he has not since had a home with his father.

(4)   Nothing in this section prejudices any existing rule of law as to the cases in which a child's domicile is regarded as being, by dependence, that of his mother.

(5)   In this section, 'child' means a person incapable of having an independent domicile. [. . .]

(6)   This section extends to England and Wales, Scotland and Northern Ireland.

PART III

JURISDICTION IN CONSISTORIAL CAUSES (SCOTLAND)

7   Jurisdiction of Court of Session

(1)   Subsections (2) to (8) below shall have effect, subject to section 12(6) of this Act, with respect to the jurisdiction of the Court of Session to entertain—

(a)   an action for divorce, separation, declarator of nullity of marriage, declarator of marriage, declarator of freedom and putting to silence.

(2)   The Court shall have jurisdiction to entertain an action for [. . .] declarator of freedom and putting to silence if (and only if) either of the parties to the marriage in question—

(a)   is domiciled in Scotland on the date when the action is begun; or

(b)   was habitually resident in Scotland throughout the period of one year ending with that date.

[(2A)   The Court shall have jurisdiction to entertain an action for divorce or separation if (and only if)—

(a)   the Scottish courts have jurisdiction under the Council Regulation; or

(b)   the action is an excluded action and either of the parties to the marriage in question is domiciled in Scotland on the date when the action is begun.]

(3)   The Court shall have jurisdiction to entertain an action for declarator of marriage . . . if (and only if) either of the parties to the marriage—

(a)   is domiciled in Scotland on the date when the action is begun; or

(b)   was habitually resident in Scotland throughout the period of one year ending with that date; or

(c)   died before that date and either—

(i)   was at death domiciled in Scotland, or

(ii)   had been habitually resident in Scotland throughout the period of one year ending with the date of death.

[(3A)   The Court shall have jurisdiction to entertain an action for declarator of nullity of marriage if (and only if)—

(a)   the Scottish courts have jurisdiction under the Council Regulation; or

(b)   the action is one to which subsection (3B) below applies and either of the parties to the marriage—

(a)   is domiciled in Scotland on the date when the action is begun, or

(b)   died before that date and either—

(i)   was at death domiciled in Scotland; or

(ii)   had been habitually resident in Scotland throughout the period of one year ending with the date of death.

(3B)   This subsection applies to an action—

(a)   which is an excluded action; or

(b)   where one of the parties to the marriage died before the date when the action is begun.]

[. . .]

(5)   The Court shall, at any time when proceedings are pending in respect of which it has jurisdiction by virtue of subsection (2) [(2A), (3) or (3A)] above (or of this subsection), also have jurisdiction to entertain other proceedings, in respect of the same marriage, for divorce, separation or declarator of marriage, declarator of nullity of marriage or declarator of freedom and putting to silence, notwithstanding that jurisdiction would not be exercisable [under any of those subsections].

[(5A)   Subsection (5) does not give the Court jurisdiction to entertain proceedings in contravention of Article 6 of the Council Regulation.]

(6)   Nothing in this section affects the rules governing the jurisdiction of the Court of Session to entertain, in an action for divorce, an application for payment by a co-defender of damages or expenses.

(7)   The foregoing provisions of this section are without prejudice to any rule of law whereby the Court of Session has jurisdiction in certain circumstances to entertain actions for separation as a matter of necessity and urgency.

(8)   No action for divorce in respect of a marriage shall be entertained by the Court of Session by virtue of [this section] while proceedings for divorce or nullity of marriage, begun before the commencement of this Act, are pending (in respect of the same marriage) in England and Wales, Northern Ireland, the Channel Islands or the Isle of Man; and provision may be made by rules of court as to when, for the purposes of this subsection, proceedings are to be treated as begun or pending in any of those places.

8   Jurisdiction of sheriff court in respect of actions for separation

(1)   Subsections (2) to (4) below shall have effect, subject to section 12(6) of this Act, with respect to the jurisdiction of the sheriff court to entertain an action for separation [or divorce.]

(2)   The court shall have jurisdiction to entertain an action for separation [or divorce] if (and only if)—

[(a)   either—

(i)   the Scottish courts have jurisdiction under the Council Regulation; or

(ii)   the action is an excluded action where either party to the marriage in question is domiciled in Scotland at the date when the action is begun;]

(b)   either party to the marriage—

(i)   was resident in the sheriffdom for a period of forty days ending with that date, or

(ii)   had been resident in the sheriffdom for a period of not less than forty days ending not more than forty days before the said date, and has no known residence in Scotland at that date.

(3)   In respect of any marriage, the court shall have jurisdiction to entertain an action for separation [or divorce] (notwithstanding that jurisdiction would not be exercisable under subsection (2) above) if it is begun at a time when an original action is pending in respect of the marriage; and for this purpose 'original action' means an action in respect of which the court has jurisdiction by virtue of subsection (2), or of this subsection.

[(3A)   Subsection (3) does not give the Court jurisdiction to entertain an action in contravention of Article 6 of the Council Regulation.]

(4)   The foregoing provisions of this section are without prejudice to any jurisdiction of a sheriff court to entertain an action of separation [or divorce] remitted

to it in pursuance of any enactment or rule of court, [provided that entertaining the action would not contravene Article 6 of the Council Regulation].

10   Ancillary and collateral orders

(1)   [Where after the commencement of this Act, an application is competently made to the Court of Session or to a sheriff court for the making, or the variation or recall, of an order which is ancillary or collateral to] an action for any of the following remedies, namely, divorce, separation, declarator of marriage and declarator of nullity of marriage (whether the application is made in the same proceedings or in other proceedings and whether it is made before or after the pronouncement of a final decree in the action), then, if the court has or, as the case may be, had by virtue of this Act or of any enactment or rule of law in force before the commencement of this Act jurisdiction to entertain the action, it shall have jurisdiction to entertain the application [. . .] whether or not it would have jurisdiction to do so apart from this subsection.

[(1A)   For the purposes of subsection (1) above, references to an application for the making, or the variation or recall, of an order are references to the making, or the variation or recall, of an order relating to children, aliment, financial provision on divorce, judicial separation, nullity of marriage or expenses.]

[(1B)   Subsection (1) above does not give the Court of Session or a sheriff court jurisdiction to entertain an application in proceedings where—

(a)   the court is exercising jurisdiction in the proceedings by virtue of Article 2 of the Council Regulation; and

(b)   the making or variation of an order in consequence of the application would contravene Article 6 of the Council Regulation.]

(2)   It is hereby declared that where—

(a)   the Court of Session has jurisdiction by virtue of this section to entertain an application for the variation or recall as respects any person of an order made by it, and

(b)   the order is one to which section 8 (variation and recall by the sheriff of certain orders made by the Court of Session) of the Law Reform (Miscellaneous Provisions) (Scotland) Act 1966 applies,

then, for the purposes of any application under the said section 8 for the variation or recall of the order in so far as it relates to that person, the sheriff, as defined in that section, has jurisdiction as respects that person to exercise the power conferred on him by that section.

11   Sisting of certain actions

[(1)]   The provisions of Schedule 3 to this Act shall have effect with respect to the sisting of actions for any of the following remedies, namely, divorce, separation, declarator of marriage or declarator of nullity of marriage, and with respect to the other matters mentioned in that Schedule; but nothing in that Schedule—

(a)   requires or authorises a sist of an action which is pending when this Act comes into force; or

(b)   prejudices any power to sist an action which is exercisable by any court apart from the Schedule.

[(2)   Subsection (1) above and Schedule 3 to this Act and any power mentioned in subsection (1)(b) are subject to Article 19 of the Council Regulation.]

12   Supplementary

(1)   In relation to any action for any of the following three remedies, namely, declarator of marriage, declarator of nullity of marriage, and declarator of freedom and putting to silence, references in this Part of this Act to the marriage shall be construed as including references to the alleged, or, as the case may be, the purported, marriage.

(2)   References in this Part of this Act to an action for a particular remedy shall be construed, in relation to a case where the remedy is sought along with other

remedies in one action, as references to so much of the proceedings in the action as relates to the particular remedy.

(3)   References in this Part of this Act to the remedy of separation shall be construed, in relation to an action in a sheriff court, as references to the remedy of separation and aliment.

(4)   For the purposes of this Act the period during which an action in the Court of Session or a sheriff court is pending shall be regarded as including any period while the taking of an appeal is competent and the period while any proceedings on appeal are pending; and in this subsection references to an appeal include references to a reclaiming motion.

(5)   In this Part of this Act—

(a)   any reference to an enactment shall, unless the contrary intention appears, be construed as a reference to that enactment as amended or extended, and as including a reference thereto as applied, by or under any other enactment (including this Act);

[(b)   'Contracting State' means Belgium, Germany, Greece, Spain, France Ireland, Italy, Luxembourg, the Netherlands, Austria, Portugal, Finland, Sweden, and the United Kingdom;

(c)   'the Council Regulation' means Council Regulation (EC) No 2201/2003 of 27th November 2003 concerning] jurisdiction and the recognition and enforcement of judgments in matrimonial matters and in matters of parental responsibility [. . .]; and

(d)   'excluded action' means an action in respect of which no court of a Contracting State has jurisdiction under the Council Regulation and the defender is not a person who is—

(i)   a national of a Contracting State (other than the United Kingdom or Ireland); or

(ii)   domiciled in Ireland.]

(6)   Nothing in this Part of this Act affects any court's jurisdiction to entertain any proceedings begun before the commencement of this Act.

(7)   Subject to subsection (6) above, the enactments described in Schedule 4 to this Act shall have effect subject to the amendments therein specified, being amendments consequential on the provisions of this Part of this Act.

DAMAGES (SCOTLAND) ACT 1976
(1976, c 13)

1   Rights of relatives of a deceased person

(1)   Where a person dies in consequence of personal injuries sustained by him as a result of an act or omission of another person, being an act or omission giving rise to liability to pay damages to the injured person or his executor, then, subject to the following provisions of this Act, the person liable to pay those damages (in this section referred to as 'the responsible person') shall also be liable to pay damages in accordance with this section to any relative of the deceased, being a relative within the meaning of Schedule 1 to this Act.

(2)   No liability shall arise under this section if the liability to the deceased or his executor in respect of the act or omission has been excluded or discharged (whether by antecedent agreement or otherwise) by the deceased before his death, or is excluded by virtue of any enactment.

(3)   The damages which the responsible person shall be liable to pay to a relative of a deceased under this section shall (subject to the provisions of this Act) be such as will compensate the relative for any loss of support suffered by him since the date of the deceased's death or likely to be suffered by him as a result of the act or omission in question, together with any reasonable expense incurred by him in connection with the deceased's funeral.

(4)   If the relative is a member of the deceased's immediate family (within the

meaning of section 10(2) of this Act) there shall be awarded, without prejudice to any claim under subsection (3) above, such sum of damages, if any, as the court thinks just by way of compensation for [all or any of the following—

(a) distress and anxiety endured by the relative in contemplation of the suffering of the deceased before his death;

(b) grief and sorrow of the relative caused by the deceased's death;

(c) the loss of such non-patrimonial benefit as the relative might have been expected to derive from the deceased's society and guidance if the deceased had not died,

and the court in making an award under this subsection shall not be required to ascribe specifically any part of the award to any of paragraphs (a), (b) and (c) above.]

(5) [Subject to subsection (5A) below] in assessing for the purposes of this section the amount of any loss of support suffered by a relative of a deceased no account shall be taken of—

(a) any patrimonial gain or advantage which has accrued or will or may accrue to the relative from the deceased or from any other person by way of succession or settlement;

(b) any insurance money, benefit, pension or gratuity which has been, or will be or may be, paid as a result of the deceased's death;

and in this subsection—

'benefit' means benefit under the Social Security Act 1975 or the Social Security (Northern Ireland) Act 1975, and any payment by a friendly society or trade union for the relief or maintenance of a member's dependants;

'insurance money' includes a return of premiums; and

'pension' includes a return of contributions and any payment of a lump sum in respect of a person's employment.

[(5A) Where a deceased has been awarded a provisional award of damages under section 12(2) of the Administration of Justice Act 1982, the making of that award does not prevent liability from arising under this section but in assessing for the purposes of this section the amount of any loss of support suffered by a relative of the deceased the court shall take into account such part of the provisional award relating to future patrimonial loss as was intended to compensate the deceased for a period beyond the date on which he died.]

(6) In order to establish loss of support for the purposes of this section it shall not be essential for a claimant to show that the deceased was, or might have become, subject to a duty in law to provide or contribute to the support of the claimant; but if any such fact is established it may be taken into account in determining whether, and if so to what extent, the deceased, if he had not died, would have been likely to provide or contribute to such support.

(7) Except as provided in this section [or in Part II of the Administration of Justice Act 1982 or under section 1 of the International Transport Conventions Act 1983] no person shall be entitled by reason of relationship to damages (including damages by way of solatium) in respect of the death of another person.

[1A Transmissibility to executor of rights of deceased relative

Any right to damages under any provision of section 1 of this Act which is vested in the relative concerned immediately before his death shall be transmitted to the relative's executor; but, in determining the amount of damages payable to an executor by virtue of this section, the court shall have regard only to the period ending immediately before the relative's death.]

2 Rights transmitted to executor in respect of deceased person's injuries

(1) Subject to the following provisions of this section, there shall be transmitted to the executor of a deceased person the like rights to damages in respect of personal injuries (including a right to damages by way of solatium) sustained by the deceased as were vested in him immediately before his death.

(2)   There shall not be transmitted to the executor under this section a right to damages by way of compensation for patrimonial loss attributable to any period after the deceased's death.

(3)   In determining the amount of damages by way of solatium payable to an executor by virtue of this section, the court shall have regard only to the period ending immediately before the deceased's death.

(4)   In so far as a right to damages vested in the deceased comprised a right to damages (other than for patrimonial loss) in respect of injury resulting from defamation or any other verbal injury or other injury to reputation sustained by the deceased, that right shall be transmitted to the deceased's executor only if an action to enforce that right had been brought by the deceased before his death and had not been concluded by then within the meaning of section 2A(2) of this Act.]

[2A   Enforcement by executor of rights transmitted to him

(1)   For the purpose of enforcing any right transmitted to an executor under section 1A or 2 of this Act the executor shall be entitled—

(a)   to bring an action; or

(b)   if an action for that purpose had been brought by the deceased but had not been concluded before his death, to be sisted as pursuer in that action.

(2)   For the purpose of subsection (1) above, an action shall not be taken to be concluded while any appeal is competent or before any appeal taken has been disposed of.]

[. . .]

4   Executor's claim not to be excluded by relatives' claim: and *vice versa*

A claim by the executor of a deceased person for damages under section 2 of this Act is not excluded by the making of a claim by a relative of the deceased for damages under section 1 of this Act [or by a decreased relative's executor under section 1A of this Act; nor is a claim by a relative of a deceased person or by a deceased relative's executor for damages under the said section 1 or (as the case may be) the said section 1A] excluded by the making of a claim by the deceased's executor or damages under the said section 2.

[. . .]

6   Limitation of total amount of liability

(1)   Where in any action to which [this section] of this Act applies, so far as directed against any defender, it is shown that by antecedent agreement, compromise or otherwise, the liability arising in relation to that defender from the personal injuries in question had, before the deceased's death, been limited to damages of a specified or ascertainable amount, or where that liability is so limited by virtue of any enactment, nothing in this Act shall make the defender liable to pay damages exceeding that amount; and accordingly where in such an action there are two or more pursuers any damages to which they would respectively be entitled under this Act apart from the said limitation shall, if necessary, be reduced *pro rata*.

(2)   Where two or more such actions are conjoined, the conjoined actions shall be treated for the purposes of this section as if they were a single action.

[(3)   This section applies to any action in which, following the death of any person from personal injuries, damages are claimed—

(a)   by the executor of the deceased, in respect of the injuries from which the deceased died;

(b)   in respect of the death of the deceased, by any relative of his or if the relative has died, by the relative's executor.]

7   Amendment of references in other Acts

In any Act passed before this Act, unless the context otherwise requires, any reference to solatium in respect of the death of any person (however expressed) shall be construed as a reference to a loss of society award within the meaning of section 1 of this Act; and any reference to a dependant of a deceased person, in relation to an action claiming damages in respect of the deceased person's death, shall be construed as including a reference to a relative of the deceased person within the meaning of this Act.

8 Abolition of right of assythment

After the commencement of this Act no person shall in any circumstances have a right to assythment, and accordingly any action claiming that remedy shall (to the extent that it does so) be incompetent.

9 Damages due to injured person for patrimonial loss caused by personal injuries whereby expectation of life is diminished

(1) This section applies to any action for damages in respect of personal injuries sustained by the pursuer where his expected date of death is earlier than it would have been if he had not sustained the injuries.

(2) In assessing, in any action to which this section applies, the amount of any patrimonial loss in respect of the period after the date of decree—

(a) it shall be assumed that the pursuer will live until the date when he would have been expected to die if he had not sustained the injuries (hereinafter referred to as the 'notional date of death');

(b) the court may have regard to any amount, whether or not it is an amount related to earnings by the pursuer's own labour or other gainful activity, which in its opinion the pursuer, if he had not sustained the injuries in question, would have received in the period up to his notional date of death by way of benefits in money or money's worth, being benefits derived from sources other than the pursuer's own estate;

(c) the court shall have regard to any diminution of any such amount as aforesaid by virtue of expenses which in the opinion of the court the pursuer, if he had not sustained the injuries in question, would reasonably have incurred in the said period by way of living expenses.

[9A Solatium for loss of expectation of life

(1) In assessing, in an action for damages in respect of personal injuries, the amount of damages by way of solatium, the court shall, if—

(a) the injured person's expectation of life has been reduced by the injuries; and

(b) the injured person is, was at any time or is likely to become, aware of that reduction,

have regard to the extent that, in consequence of that awareness, he has suffered or is likely to suffer.

(2) Subject to subsection (1) above, no damages by way of solatium shall be recoverable in respect of loss of expectation of life.

(3) The court in making an award of damages by way of solatium shall not be required to ascribe specifically any part of the award to loss of expectation of life.]

10 Interpretation

(1) In this Act, unless the context otherwise requires—

[. . .]

'personal injuries' includes any disease or an impairment of a person's physical or mental condition [and injury resulting from defamation or any other verbal injury or other injury to reputation, or injury resulting from harassment actionable under section 8 of the Protection from Harassment Act 1997];

'relative', in relation to a deceased person, has the meaning assigned to it by Schedule 1 to this Act.

(2) References in this Act to a member of a deceased person's immediate family are references to any relative of his who falls within sub-paragraph (a), [(aa)], (b) or (c) of paragraph 1 of Schedule 1 to this Act.

(3)   References in this Act to any other Act are references to that Act as amended, extended or applied by any other enactment, including this Act.

12   Citation, application to Crown, commencement and extent

(1)   This Act may be cited as the Damages (Scotland) Act 1976.

(2)   This Act binds the Crown.

(5)   This Act extends to Scotland only.

SCHEDULES

SCHEDULE 1
DEFINITION OF 'RELATIVE'

(1)   In this Act 'relative' in relation to a deceased person includes—

(a)   any person who immediately before the deceased's death was the spouse [or civil partner] of the deceased;

[(aa)   any person, not being the spouse [or civil partner] of the deceased, who was, immediately before the deceased's death, living with the deceased as husband or wife or in a relationship which had the characteristics of the relationship between civil partners;]

(b)   any person who was a parent or child of the deceased;

(c)   any person not falling within paragraph (b) above who was accepted by the deceased as a child of his family;

(d)   any person who was an ascendant or descendant (other than a parent or child) of the deceased;

(e)   any person who was, or was the issue of, a brother, sister, uncle or aunt of the deceased;

(f)   any person who, having been a spouse of the deceased, had ceased to be so by virtue of a divorce; [and

(g)   any person who, having been a civil partner of the deceased, had ceased to be so by virtue of the dissolution of the civil partnership,]

but does not include any other person.

(2)   In deducing any relationship for the purposes of the foregoing paragraph—

(a)   any relationship by affinity shall be treated as a relationship by consanguinity; any relationship of the half blood shall be treated as a relationship of the whole blood; and the stepchild of any person shall be treated as his child; and

(b)   section 1(1) of the Law Reform (Parent and Child) (Scotland) Act 1986 shall apply; and any reference (however expressed) in this Act to a relative shall be construed accordingly.

CONGENITAL DISABILITIES (CIVIL LIABILITY) ACT 1976
(1976, c 28)

1   Civil liability to child born disabled

(1)   If a child is born disabled as the result of such an occurrence before its birth as is mentioned in subsection (2) below, and a person (other than the child's own mother) is under this section answerable to the child in respect of the occurrence, the child's disabilities are to be regarded as damage resulting from the wrongful act of that person and actionable accordingly at the suit of the child.

(2)   An occurrence to which this section applies is one which—

(a)   affected either parent of the child in his or her ability to have a normal, healthy child; or

(b)   affected the mother during her pregnancy, or affected her or the child in the course of its birth, so that the child is born with disabilities which would not otherwise have been present.

(3) Subject to the following subsections, a person (here referred to as 'the defendant') is answerable to the child if he was liable in tort to the parent or would, if sued in due time, have been so; and it is no answer that there could not have been such liability because the parent suffered no actionable injury, if there was a breach of legal duty which, accompanied by injury, would have given rise to the liability.

(4) In the case of an occurrence preceding the time of conception, the defendant is not answerable to the child if at that time either or both of the parents knew the risk of their child being born disabled (that is to say, the particular risk created by the occurrence); but should it be the child's father who is the defendant, this subsection does not apply if he knew of the risk and the mother did not.

(5) The defendant is not answerable to the child, for anything he did or omitted to do when responsible in a professional capacity for treating or advising the parent, if he took reasonable care having due regard to then received professional opinion applicable to the particular class of case; but this does not mean that he is answerable only because he departed from received opinion.

(6) Liability to the child under this section may be treated as having been excluded or limited by contract made with the parent affected, to the same extent and subject to the same restrictions as liability in the parent's own case; and a contract term which could have been set up by the defendant in an action by the parent, so as to exclude or limit his liability to him or her, operates in the defendant's favour to the same, but no greater, extent in an action under this section by the child.

(7) If in the child's action under this section it is shown that the parent affected shared the responsibility for the child being born disabled, the damages are to be reduced to such extent as the court thinks just and equitable having regard to the extent of the parent's responsibility.

[1A Extension of section 1 to cover infertility treatments

(1) In any case where—

(a) a child carried by a woman as the result of the placing in her of an embryo or of sperm and eggs or her artificial insemination is born disabled,

(b) the disability results from an act or omission in the course of the selection, or the keeping or use outside the body, of the embryo carried by her or of the gametes used to bring about the creation of the embryo, and

(c) a person is under this section answerable to the child in respect of the act or omission,

the child's disabilities are to be regarded as damage resulting from the wrongful act of that person and actionable accordingly at the suit of the child.

(2) Subject to subsection (3) below and the applied provisions of section 1 of this Act, a person (here referred to as 'the defendant') is answerable to the child if he was liable in tort to one or both of the parents (here referred to as 'the parent or parents concerned') or would, if sued in due time, have been so; and it is no answer that there could not have been such liability because the parent or parents concerned suffered no actionable injury, if there was a breach of legal duty which, accompanied by injury, would have given rise to the liability.

(3) The defendant is not under this section answerable to the child if at the time the embryo, or the sperm and eggs, are placed in the woman or at the time of her insemination (as the case may be) either or both of the parents knew the risk of their child being born disabled (that is to say, the particular risk created by the act or omission).

(4) Subsections (5) to (7) of section 1 of this Act apply for the purposes of this section as they apply for the purposes of that section but as if references to the parent or the parent affected were references to the parent or parents concerned.]

2   Liability of woman driving when pregnant
A woman driving a motor vehicle when she knows (or ought reasonably to know)
herself to be pregnant is to be regarded as being under the same duty to take care
for the safety of her unborn child as the law imposes on her with respect to the
safety of other people; and if in consequence of her breach of that duty her child is
born with disabilities which would not otherwise have been present, those disabilities are to be regarded as damage resulting from her wrongful act and actionable accordingly at the suit of the child.

DIVORCE (SCOTLAND) ACT 1976
(1976, c 39)

Divorce

1   [Grounds of divorce]
   (1)   In an action for divorce the court may grant decree of divorce if, but only if,
it is established in accordance with the following provisions of this Act that—
      [(a)]   the marriage has broken down irretrievably [, or
      (b)   an interim gender recognition certificate under the Gender Recognition
Act 2004 has, after the date of the marriage, been issued to either party to the
marriage.]
   References in this Act (other than in sections 5(1) and 13 of this Act) to an action
for divorce are to be construed as references to such an action brought after the
commencement of this Act.
   (2)   The irretrievable breakdown of a marriage shall, subject to the following
provisions of this Act, be taken to be established in an action for divorce if—
      (a)   since the date of the marriage the defender has committed adultery; or
      (b)   since the date of the marriage the defender has at any time behaved
(whether or not as a result of mental abnormality and whether such behaviour
has been active or passive) in such a way that the pursuer cannot reasonably be
expected to cohabit with the defender; or
      (c)   the defender has wilfully and without reasonable cause deserted the pur-
suer; and during a continuous period of two years immediately succeeding the
defender's desertion—
         (i)   there has been no cohabitation between the parties, and
         (ii)   the pursuer has not refused a genuine and reasonable offer by the
      defender to adhere; or
      (d)   there has been no cohabitation between the parties at any time during a
continuous period of two years after the date of the marriage and immediately
preceding the bringing of the action and the defender consents to the granting of
decree of divorce; or
      (e)   there has been no cohabitation between the parties at any time during a
continuous period of five years after the date of the marriage and immediately
preceding the bringing of the action.
   (3)   The irretrievable breakdown of a marriage shall not be taken to be established in an action for divorce by reason of subsection (2)(a) of this section if the
adultery mentioned in the said subsection (2)(a) has been connived at in such a
way as to raise the defence of *lenocinium* or has been condoned by the pursuer's
cohabitation with the defender in the knowledge or belief that the defender has
committed the adultery.
   (4)   Provision shall be made by act of sederunt—
      (a)   for the purpose of ensuring that, where in an action for divorce to which
subsection (2)(d) of this section relates the defender consents to the granting of
decree, he has been given such information as will enable him to understand—
         (i)   the consequences to him of his consenting as aforesaid; and
         (ii)   the steps which he must take to indicate his consent; and

(b) prescribing the manner in which the defender in such an action shall indicate his consent, and any withdrawal of such consent, to the granting of decree;

and where the defender has indicated (and not withdrawn) his consent in the pre-scribed manner, such indication shall be sufficient evidence of such consent.

(5) Notwithstanding that irretrievable breakdown of a marriage has been estab-lished in an action for divorce by reason of subsection (2)(e) of this section, the court shall not be bound to grant decree in that action if in the opinion of the court the grant of decree would result in grave financial hardship to the defender.

For the purposes of this subsection, hardship shall include the loss of the chance of acquiring any benefit.

(6) In an action for divorce the standard of proof required to establish the ground of the action shall be on balance of probability.

2 Encouragement of reconciliation

(1) At any time before granting decree [under paragraph (a) of section 1(1)], if it appears to the court that there is a reasonable prospect of a reconciliation between the parties, it shall continue, or further continue, the action for such period as it thinks proper to enable attempts to be made to effect such a recon-ciliation; and if during any such continuation the parties cohabit with one another, no account shall be taken of such cohabitation for the purposes of that action.

(2) Adultery shall not be held to have been condoned within the meaning of section 1(3) of this Act by reason only of the fact that after the commission of the adultery the pursuer has continued or resumed cohabitation with the defender, provided that the pursuer has not cohabited with the defender at any time after the end of the period of three months from the date on which such cohabitation as is referred to in the said section 1(3) was continued or resumed as aforesaid.

(3) The irretrievable breakdown of a marriage shall not be taken to be estab-lished in an action for divorce by reason of section 1(2)(c) of this Act if, after the expiry of the period mentioned in the said section 1(2)(c), the pursuer has resumed cohabitation with the defender and has cohabited with the defender at any time after the end of the period of three months from the date on which the cohabi-tation was resumed as aforesaid.

(4) In considering whether any period mentioned in paragraph (c), (d), or (e) of section 1(2) of this Act has been continuous no account shall be taken of any period or periods not exceeding six months in all during which the parties co-habited with one another; but no such period or periods during which the parties cohabited with one another shall count as part of the period of non-cohabitation required by any of those paragraphs.

3 Action for divorce following on decree of separation

(1) The court may grant decree in an action for divorce notwithstanding that decree of separation has previously been granted to the pursuer on the same, or substantially the same, facts as those averred in support of the action for divorce; and in any such action (other than an action for divorce by reason of section 1(2)(a) of this Act) the court may treat an extract decree of separation lodged in process as sufficient proof of the facts upon which such decree was granted.

(2) Nothing in this section shall entitle the court to grant decree of divorce without receiving evidence from the pursuer.

Actions for separation

4 Actions for separation

(1) Sections 1, 2 and 11 of this Act shall apply to an action for separation or separation and aliment brought after the commencement of this Act and decree in such action as those sections apply to an action for divorce and decree therein subject to—

(a) the modification that any reference to irretrievable breakdown of a marriage shall be construed as a reference to grounds justifying decree of separation of the parties to a marriage; and

(b) all other necessary modifications.

(2) In an action for separation or separation and aliment brought after the commencement of this Act, decree of separation shall not be pronounced except in accordance with the provisions of this section.

[. . .]

Supplemental

9 Abolition of oath of calumny

In a consistorial action (whether brought before or after the commencement of this Act) the oath of calumny shall not be administered to the pursuer, and accordingly that oath is hereby abolished, but nothing in this section shall affect any rule of law relating to collusion.

10 Right of husband to cite paramour as a co-defender and to sue for damages abolished

(1) After the commencement of this Act the following rights of a husband shall be abolished, that is to say—

(a) the right to cite a paramour of his wife as a co-defender in an action for divorce, and

(b) the right to claim or to obtain damages (including solatium) from a paramour by way of reparation.

(2) Nothing in the provisions of the foregoing subsection shall preclude the court from awarding the expenses of the action for or against the paramour or alleged paramour in accordance with the practice of the court.

(3) Section 7 of the Conjugal Rights (Scotland) Amendment Act 1861 (citation of a co-defender in an action for divorce and decree for expenses against him) shall cease to have effect.

11 Curator *ad litem* to be appointed in certain cases

Provision shall be made by act of sederunt for the purpose of securing that, where in an action for divorce the defender is suffering from mental illness, the court shall appoint a curator *ad litem* to the defender.

12 Amendments, repeals and transitional provisions

(1) The enactments described in Schedule 1 to this Act shall have effect subject to the amendments specified therein in relation to them respectively.

(2) The enactments specified in columns 1 and 2 of Schedule 2 to this Act are hereby repealed to the extent specified in relation to them respectively in column 3 of that Schedule.

(3) Subject to the following provisions of this section and without prejudice to the operation of section 38 of the Interpretation Act 1889 (effect of repeals), nothing in this section shall affect any proceedings brought, anything done, or the operation of any order made, under any enactment repealed by this section; nor shall anything in this Act be taken to revive any rule of law superseded by any enactment repealed by this section.

(4) Anything which, prior to the commencement of this Act, could have been done under section 2 of the Divorce (Scotland) Act 1938 or section 26 or 27 of the Succession (Scotland) Act 1964 may, after the commencement of this Act, be done under the corresponding provision of section 5 or 6 of this Act.

(5) An order under section 2 of the Divorce (Scotland) Act 1938 for the payment of an annual or periodical allowance to or for the behoof of a child of the marriage may, after the commencement of this Act, be varied or recalled by a subsequent order under subsection (2) of that section as if that section had not been repealed by this Act.

(6)   Subsection (5) of section 5 of this Act shall apply in relation to an order for the payment of an annual or periodical allowance under section 2 of the Divorce (Scotland) Act 1938 or of a periodical allowance under section 26 of the Succession (Scotland) Act 1964 as it applies in relation to an order for the payment of a periodical allowance under the said section 5.

13   Interpretation
(1)   In this Act, unless the context otherwise requires—
'action for divorce' has the meaning assigned to it by section 1(1) of this Act;
'the court' means in relation to an action [. . .] the Court of Session or the sheriff [court] as the case may require.
(2)   For the purposes of this Act, the parties to a marriage shall be held to co-habit with one another only when they are in fact living together as man and wife; and 'cohabitation' shall be construed accordingly.
(3)   References in this Act to any enactment are references to that enactment as amended, and include references thereto as applied, by any other enactment, including, except where the context otherwise requires, this Act.

14   Citation, commencement and extent
(1)   This Act may be cited as the Divorce (Scotland) Act 1976.
(2)   This Act except section 8 shall come into operation on 1st January 1977.
(3)   So much of section 12 of, and Schedule 1 to, this Act as affects the operation of section 16 of the Maintenance Orders Act 1950 shall extend to England and Wales and to Northern Ireland as well as Scotland, but save as aforesaid this Act shall extend to Scotland only.

MARRIAGE (SCOTLAND) ACT 1977
(1977, c 15)

Minimum age for marriage

1   Minimum age for marriage
(1)   No person domiciled in Scotland may marry before he attains the age of 16.
(2)   A marriage solemnised in Scotland between persons either of whom is under the age of 16 shall be void.

Forbidden degrees

2   Marriage of related persons
(1)   [Subject to subsections (1A) and (1B) below,] a marriage between a man and any woman related to him in a degree specified in column 1 of Schedule 1 to this Act, or between a woman and any man related to her in a degree specified in column 2 of that Schedule shall be void if solemnised—
     (a)   in Scotland; or
     (b)   at a time when either party is domiciled in Scotland.
     [(1A)   Subsection (1) above does not apply to a marriage between a man and any woman related to him in a degree specified in column 1 of paragraph 2 of Schedule 1 to this Act, or between a woman and any man related to her in a degree specified in column 2 of that paragraph, if—
     (a)   both parties have attained the age of 21 at the time of the marriage; and
     (b)   the younger party has not at any time before attaining the age of 18 lived in the same household as the other party and been treated by the other party as a child of his family.
     (1B)   Subsection (1) above does not apply to a marriage between a man and any woman related to him in a degree specified in column 1 of paragraph 2A of Schedule 1 to this Act, or between a woman and any man related to her in a

degree specified in column 2 of that paragraph, if both parties to the marriage have attained the age of 21 and the marriage is solemnised—

(a)   in the case of a man marrying the mother of a former wife of his, after the death of both the former wife and the former wife's father;

(b)   in the case of a man marrying a former wife of his son, after the death of both his son and his son's mother;

(c)   in the case of a woman marrying the father of a former husband of hers, after the death of both the former husband and the former husband's mother;

(d)   in the case of a woman marrying a former husband of her daughter, after the death of both her daughter and her daughter's father.]

(2)   For the purposes of this section a degree of relationship exists—

(a)   in the case of a degree specified in paragraph 1 of Schedule 1 to this Act, whether it is of the full blood or the half blood.

[. . .]

(3)   Where a person is related to another person in a degree not specified in Schedule 1 to this Act that degree of relationship shall not, in Scots law, bar a valid marriage between them; but this subsection is without prejudice to—

(a)   the effect which a degree of relationship not so specified may have under the provisions of a system of law other than Scots law in a case where such provisions apply as the law of the place of celebration of a marriage or as the law of a person's domicile; or

(b)   any rule of law that a marriage may not be contracted between persons either of whom is married to a third person.

[(4)   References in this section and in Schedule 1 to this Act to relationships and degrees of relationship shall be construed in accordance with section 1(1) of the Law Reform (Parent and Child) (Scotland) Act 1986.

(5)   Where the parties to an intended marriage are related in a degree specified in paragraph 2 of Schedule 1 to this Act, either party may (whether or not an objection to the marriage has been submitted in accordance with section 5(1) of this Act) apply to the Court of Session for a declarator that the conditions specified in paragraphs (a) and (b) of subsection (1A) above are fulfilled in relation to the intended marriage.]

[(6)   Subsections (1A) and (1B) above and paragraphs 2 and 2A of Schedule 1 to this Act have effect subject to the following modifications in the case of a party to a marriage whose gender has become the acquired gender under the Gender Recognition Act 2004 ('the relevant person').

(7)   Any reference in those provisions to a former wife or former husband of the relevant person includes (respectively) any former husband or former wife of the relevant person.

(8)   And—

(a)   the reference in paragraph (b) of subsection (1B) above to the relevant person's son's mother is to the relevant person's son's father if the relevant person is the son's mother; and

(b)   the reference in paragraph (d) of that subsection to the relevant person's daughter's father is to the relevant person's daughter's mother if the relevant person is the daughter's father.]

Preliminaries to regular marriage

3   Notice of intention to marry

(1)   Subject to subsections (2) to (4) below, each of the parties to a marriage intended to be solemnised in Scotland shall submit to the district registrar a notice, in the prescribed form, of intention to marry (in this Act referred to as a 'marriage notice') accompanied by the prescribed fee, his birth certificate and—

(a)   if he has previously been married and the marriage has been dissolved, a copy of the decree of divorce, dissolution or annulment;

[(aa) if he has previously been in civil partnership and the civil partnership has been dissolved, a copy of the decree of dissolution or annulment;]

(b) in the case of a widow or widower, the death certificate of the former spouse;

(c) in any case where a certificate is required under subsection (5) below, that certificate;

[(d) where he is related to the other party in a degree specified in paragraph 2 of Schedule 1 to this Act, a declaration in the prescribed form stating—

(i) the degree of relationship; and

(ii) that the younger party has not at any time before attaining the age of 18 lived in the same household as the other party and been treated by the other party as a child of his family.]

(2) If a party is unable to submit his birth certificate or any document referred to in paragraph (a) [, (aa)] or (b) of subsection (1) above, he may in lieu thereof make a declaration stating that for reasons specified in that declaration it is impracticable for him to submit that certificate or document; and he shall provide the district registrar with such—

(a) information in respect of the matters to which such certificate or document would have related; and

(b) documentary evidence in support of that information, as the district registrar may require.

(3) If any document submitted under subsection (1) above is written in a language other than English, the party submitting it shall attach to that document a translation of it in English certified by the translator as a correct translation.

(4) Where a party to a marriage intended to be solemnised in Scotland is residing in another part of the United Kingdom, he may submit to the district registrar a valid certificate for marriage (in this Act referred to as an 'approved certificate') issued in that other part: and where that party so submits an approved certificate, he need not, unless the Registrar General so directs, comply with the other provisions of this section.

(5) A party to a marriage intended to be solemnised in Scotland who is not domiciled in any part of the United Kingdom is required, if practicable, to submit under subsection (1)(c) above a certificate, issued by a competent authority in the state in which the party is domiciled, to the effect that he is not known to be subject to any legal incapacity (in terms of the law of that state) which would prevent his marrying:

Provided that such a party—

(i) may, where under the law of the state in which he is domiciled his personal law is that of another foreign state, submit in lieu of the said certificate a like certificate issued by a competent authority in that other state;

(ii) need not submit a certificate under paragraph (c) of subsection (1) above—

(a) if he has been resident in the United Kingdom for a period of 2 or more years immediately before the date on which he submits a marriage notice under that subsection in respect of the said marriage; or

[(b) if no such certificate has been issued only by reason of the fact that the validity of a divorce or annulment granted by a court of civil jurisdiction in Scotland or entitled to recognition in Scotland under section 44 or 45 of the Family Law Act 1986 is not recognised in the state in which the certificate would otherwise have been issued.]

4 Marriage notice book and list of intended marriages

(1) On receipt of a marriage notice or an approved certificate in respect of a party to an intended marriage, the district registrar shall forthwith enter such particulars, extracted from such notice or certificate, as may be prescribed, together with the date of receipt by him of such notice or certificate, in a book (in this Act

referred to as 'the marriage notice book') supplied to him for that purpose by the Registrar General.

(2) The district registrar shall, in relation to each intended marriage in respect of which he has received a marriage notice or an approved certificate, and as soon as practicable after such receipt, make an entry giving the names of the parties to, and the proposed date of, that marriage in a list which he shall display in a conspicuous place at the registration office; and such entry shall remain so displayed until the said date has elapsed.

(3) Any person claiming that he may have reason to submit an objection to an intended marriage, or to the issue of a certificate under section 7 of this Act to a party to such marriage, may, free of charge and at any time when the registration office is open for public business, inspect any entry relating to the marriage in the marriage notice book.

5 Objections to marriage

(1) Any person may at any time before the solemnisation of a marriage in Scotland submit an objection in writing thereto to the district registrar:

Provided that where the objection is on the ground mentioned in subsection (4)(d) below, it shall be accompanied by a supporting certificate signed by a registered medical practitioner.

(2) Where the district registrar receives an objection in accordance with subsection (1) above he shall—

(a) in any case where he is satisfied that the objection relates to no more than a misdescription or inaccuracy in the marriage notice or approved certificate, notify the parties to the marriage of the nature of the objection and make such enquiries into the matter mentioned in it as he thinks fit; and thereafter he shall, subject to the approval of the Registrar General, make any necessary correction to any document relating to the marriage;

(b) in any other case—

(i) forthwith notify the Registrar General of the objection;

(ii) pending consideration of the objection by the Registrar General, suspend the completion or issue of the Marriage Schedule in respect of the marriage;

(iii) where, in the case of a marriage to be solemnised by an approved celebrant, the Marriage Schedule has already been issued to the parties, if possible notify that celebrant of the objection and advise him not to solemnise the marriage pending the said consideration.

(3) [Subject to subsection (3A) below,] if the Registrar General is satisfied, on consideration of an objection of which he has received notification under subsection (2)(b)(i) above, that—

(a) there is a legal impediment to the marriage, he shall direct the district registrar to take all reasonable steps to ensure that the marriage does not take place and shall notify, or direct the district registrar to notify, the parties to the intended marriage accordingly;

(b) there is no legal impediment to the marriage, he shall inform the district registrar to that effect.

[(3A) Where—

(a) an objection of which the Registrar General has received notification under subsection (2)(b)(i) above is on the ground that—

(i) the parties are related in a degree specified in paragraph 2 of Schedule 1 to this Act; and

(ii) the conditions specified in paragraphs (a) and (b) of section 2(1A) of this Act are not satisfied; and

(b) an extract decree of declarator that those conditions are satisfied, granted on an application under section 2(5) of this Act, is produced to the Registrar General, the Registrar General shall inform the district registrar that there is no legal impediment to the marriage on that ground.

(4) For the purposes of [this section] and section 6 of this Act, there is a legal impediment to a marriage where—

(a) that marriage would be void by virtue of section 2(1) of this Act;

(b) one of the parties is, or both are, already married [or in civil partnership];

(c) one or both of the parties will be under the age of 16 on the date of solemnisation of the intended marriage;

(d) one or both of the parties is or are incapable of understanding the nature of a marriage ceremony or of consenting to marriage;

(e) both parties are of the same sex; or

(f) one or both of the parties is, or are, not domiciled in Scotland and, on a ground other than one mentioned in paragraphs (a) to (e) above, a marriage in Scotland between the parties would be void *ab initio* according to the law of the domicile of the party or parties as the case may be.

(5) A person who has submitted an objection in accordance with subsection (1) above may at any time withdraw it:

Provided that the Registrar General shall be entitled to have regard to that objection notwithstanding such withdrawal.

6 The Marriage Schedule

(1) Where the district registrar has received a marriage notice or approved certificate in respect of each of the parties to a marriage intended to be solemnised in Scotland and is satisfied that there is no legal impediment to the marriage or, as the case may be, is informed by the Registrar General under section 5(3)(b) [or (3A)] of this Act that there is no such legal impediment, he shall, subject to subsection (2) below, complete a Marriage Schedule in the prescribed form.

(2) If a period of more than 3 months has elapsed since the date of receipt (as entered by the district registrar in the marriage notice book) of a marriage notice or an approved certificate in respect of a party to the marriage, the Registrar General may direct that the district registrar shall not complete the Marriage Schedule unless that party submits a new marriage notice or approved certificate to the district registrar.

(3) Subject to subsection (4) below, in the case of a marriage to be solemnised by an approved celebrant, the Marriage Schedule completed in accordance with subsection (1) above shall be issued by the district registrar at the registration office to one or both of the parties to the intended marriage.

(4) The district registrar shall not issue a Marriage Schedule under subsection (3) above—

(a) within 14 days of the date of receipt (as entered by him in the marriage notice book) of a marriage notice in respect of the marriage to which the Marriage Schedule relates, except where—

(i) he has received a written request from one or both of the parties for the issue of the Marriage Schedule on a specified date within the said 14 days stating the reason for the request; and

(ii) he has been authorised to issue the Marriage Schedule on that specified date by the Registrar General;

(b) on a date earlier than 7 days before the date of the intended marriage unless he has been authorised to issue the Marriage Schedule on that earlier date by the Registrar General.

(5) Subject to subsections (6) and (7) below and section [23A] of this Act, a religious marriage may be solemnised only on the date and at the place specified in the Marriage Schedule

(6) Subject to subsection (7) below, if, for any reason, the marriage cannot be solemnised on the date or at the place so specified and a new date or place is fixed for the marriage, the district registrar shall—

(a)   issue another Marriage Schedule under subsection (3) above, in lieu of that already issued, specifying that new date or place; or

(b)   substitute, or direct the approved celebrant to substitute, that new date or place in the Marriage Schedule already issued.

(7)   Subsection (6) above shall not apply in a case where the new date fixed for the marriage is more than 3 months after the date for the marriage as specified in the Marriage Schedule already issued or where the new place so fixed is in a different registration district, but in such a case the Registrar General may, according to the circumstances, direct—

(a)   the district registrar for the district in which the marriage is to be solemnised to proceed as in paragraph (a) or (b) (whichever the Registrar General considers the more appropriate) of subsection (6) above; or

(b)   each party to the marriage to submit to the said district registrar a new marriage notice or approved certificate.

7   Marriage outside Scotland where a party resides in Scotland

(1)   Where a person residing in Scotland is a party to a marriage intended to be solemnised in—

(a)   England or Wales with a party residing in England or Wales and desires; or

(b)   any country, territory or place outside Great Britain, and, for the purpose of complying with the law in force in that country, territory or place, is required to obtain from a competent authority in Scotland,

a certificate in respect of his legal capacity to marry, he may submit, in the form and with the fee and documents specified in section 3(1)(a), (b) [and (d)] of this Act, notice of intention to marry to the district registrar for the district in which he resides (the said registrar being in this section referred to as the 'appropriate registrar') as if it were intended that the marriage should be solemnised in that district, and sections 3(2) and (3) and 4 of this Act shall apply accordingly.

(2)   The appropriate registrar shall, if satisfied (after consultation, if the appropriate registrar considers it necessary, with the Registrar General) that a person who has by virtue of subsection (1) above submitted a marriage notice to him is not subject to any legal incapacity (in terms of Scots law) which would prevent his marrying, issue to that person a certificate in the prescribed form that he is not known to be subject to any such incapacity:

Provided that the certificate shall not be issued earlier than 14 days after the date of receipt (as entered by the appropriate registrar in the marriage notice book) of the marriage notice.

(3)   Any person may, at any time before a certificate is issued under subsection (2) above, submit to the appropriate registrar an objection in writing to such issue; and the objection shall be taken into account by the appropriate registrar in deciding whether, in respect of the person to whom the certificate would be issued, he is satisfied as mentioned in the said subsection (2).

Persons who may solemnise marriage

8   Persons who may solemnise marriage

(1)   [Subject to section 23A of this Act,] a marriage may be solemnised by and only by—

(a)   a person who is—

(i)   a minister of the Church of Scotland; or

(ii)   a minister, clergyman, pastor, or priest of a religious body prescribed by regulations made by the Secretary of State, or who, not being one of the foregoing, is recognised by a religious body so prescribed as entitled to solemnise marriages on its behalf; or

(iii)   registered under section 9 of this Act; or

(iv)   temporarily authorised under section 12 of this Act; or

(b)   a person who is a district registrar or assistant registrar appointed under section 17 of this Act.

(2)   In this Act—

(a)   any such person as is mentioned in subsection (1)(a) above is referred to as an 'approved celebrant', and a marriage solemnised by an approved celebrant is referred to as a 'religious marriage';

(b)   any such person as is mentioned in subsection (1)(b) above is referred to as an 'authorised registrar', and a marriage solemnised by an authorised registrar is referred to as a 'civil marriage'.

Religious marriages

9   Registration of nominated persons as celebrants

(1)   A religious body, not being—

(a)   the Church of Scotland; or

(b)   prescribed by virtue of section 8(1)(a)(ii) of this Act,

may nominate to the Registrar General any of its members who it desires should be registered under this section as empowered to solemnise marriages:

Provided that any such nominee must, at the date of his nomination, be 21 years of age or over.

(2)   The Registrar General shall reject a nomination made under subsection (1) above if in his opinion—

(a)   the nominating body is not a religious body; or

(b)   the marriage ceremony used by that body is not of an appropriate form; or

(c)   the nominee is not a fit and proper person to solemnise a marriage; or

(d)   there are already registered under this section sufficient members of the same religious body as the nominee to meet the needs of that body.

(3)   For the purposes of subsection (2)(b) above, a marriage ceremony is of an appropriate form if it includes, and is in no way inconsistent with—

(a)   a declaration by the parties, in the presence of each other, the celebrant and two witnesses, that they accept each other as husband and wife; and

(b)   a declaration by the celebrant, after the declaration mentioned in paragraph (a) of this subsection, that the parties are then husband and wife,

and the Registrar General may, before deciding whether to accept or reject a nomination, require the nominating body to produce to him in writing the form of words used at its marriage ceremonies.

(4)   Where the Registrar General accepts a nomination made to him under subsection (1) above, he—

(a)   shall determine the period during which the nominee shall be empowered to solemnise marriages, being a period of not more than 3 years; and

(b)   may determine that the nominee shall be empowered to solemnise marriages only in such area as the Registrar General may specify,

and may make his acceptance subject to such other conditions as he thinks fit:

Provided that nothing in paragraph (a) above shall preclude the Registrar General from accepting a further nomination of that nominee, in accordance with this section, to take effect at any time after the end of the period determined by the Registrar General under the said paragraph (a).

(5)   The Registrar General shall—

(a)   where he accepts a nomination made to him under subsection (1) above—

(i)   so inform the nominee and the nominating body, specifying the period during which the acceptance shall have effect and any condition to which the acceptance is subject;

(ii)   enter the name of the nominee, the nominating body and such other particulars as he deems appropriate in a register which he shall establish and maintain and which shall be made available for public inspection at all reasonable times without charge;

(b)   where he rejects the nomination, by notice in writing inform the nominating body of the reasons for that rejection.

(6)   The nominating body may, if aggrieved by a rejection under this section, within 28 days of receiving notice of that rejection, appeal to the Secretary of State, and on any such appeal the Secretary of State may direct the Registrar General to accept the nomination or may confirm its rejection and shall inform the nominating body of his direction or confirmation, as the case may be, and the reason for it; and such direction or confirmation shall be final:

Provided that if a reason given for a confirmation of the rejection of a nomination is that the nominating body is not a religious body, that body may, within 42 days of receiving notice of the confirmation, appeal against the confirmation to the Court of Session and seek the determination of that court as to whether the body is a religious body; and if—

(a)   the court determine that the nominating body is a religious body; and

(b)   the said reason was the only reason given for the confirmation,

that determination shall be given effect to by the Registrar General as if it were a direction under this subsection to accept the nomination.

10   Removal of celebrant's name from registers

(1)   Subject to the provisions of this section, the Registrar General may remove the name of a person registered under section 9 of this Act from the register on the ground that—

(a)   that person has requested that his name should be so removed; or

(b)   the body which nominated that person under section 9(1) of this Act no longer desires that he should be so registered; or

(c)   the marriage ceremony used by the said body is no longer of an appropriate form within the meaning of section 9(3) of this Act; or

(d)   that person—

(i)   has, while registered as an approved celebrant, been convicted of an offence under this Act; or

(ii)   has, for the purpose of profit or gain, been carrying on a business of solemnising marriages; or

(iii)   is not a fit and proper person to solemnise marriages; or

(iv)   for any other reason, should not be so registered.

(2)   The Registrar General shall not remove the name of a person from the register on any ground mentioned in subsection (1)(d) above unless he has given to that person at least 21 days notice in writing of his intention to do so.

(3)   The Registrar General shall—

(a)   in the notice given under subsection (2) above, specify the ground of removal and call upon the said person to show cause, within the period specified in the notice, why his name should not be removed from the register; and

(b)   consider any representations made to him within the said period by that person.

(4)   Where a person's name has been removed from the register on any of the grounds mentioned in paragraphs (c) and (d) of subsection (1) above, that person or the body which nominated him under section 9(1) of this Act may, if aggrieved by the removal, within 28 days of receiving notice of the removal appeal to the Secretary of State, and on any such appeal the Secretary of State may give such direction as he thinks proper to the Registrar General as to the removal from, or restoration to, the register of that name; and such direction shall be final.

(5)   Where a person has received a notice in pursuance of subsection (2) above, he shall not solemnise a marriage unless and until his name is restored to the register or, as the case may be, the Registrar General has decided not to remove his name from the register.

11 Alterations to register maintained under s 9

A body registered in pursuance of section 9(5)(a)(ii) of this Act shall notify the Registrar General of any of the following events (if practicable, within 21 days of its occurrence)—

(a) any change in the name or the address of the body or any amalgamation with any other religious body, giving the name and address of any approved celebrant who is a member of the body so registered;

(b) the death of an approved celebrant who is a member of the body so registered;

(c) any change of name, address or designation of an approved celebrant who is a member of the body so registered;

(d) the cessation of an approved celebrant who is a member of the body so registered from exercising the functions of an approved celebrant, giving his name and address;

and the Registrar General shall, on receipt of any such notification, make whatever alteration to the register maintained by him under section 9 of this Act as he considers necessary or desirable.

12 Temporary authorisation of celebrants

The Registrar General may, in accordance with such terms and conditions as may be specified in the authorisation, grant to any person a temporary written authorisation to solemnise—

(a) a marriage or marriages specified in the authorisation, or

(b) marriages during such period as shall be specified in the authorisation:

Provided that the authorised person must at the date of the granting of the authorisation be 21 years of age or over.

13 Preliminaries to solemnisation of religious marriages

(1) A marriage shall not be solemnised by an approved celebrant unless

(a) the parties produce to him before the marriage ceremony a Marriage Schedule, in respect of the marriage, issued in accordance with this Act;

(b) both parties to the marriage are present; and

(c) two persons professing to be 16 years of age or over are present as witnesses.

[. . .]

14 Form of ceremony to be used by approved celebrant

An approved celebrant who is a person specified—

(a) in section 8(1)(a)(i) or (ii) of this Act shall not solemnise a marriage except in accordance with a form of ceremony recognised by the religious body to which he belongs as sufficient for the solemnisation of marriages;

(b) in section 8(1)(a)(iii) or (iv) of this Act shall not solemnise a marriage except in accordance with a form of ceremony which includes and is in no way inconsistent with the declarations specified in section 9(3) of this Act.

15 Registration of religious marriages

(1) Immediately after the solemnisation of the marriage the Marriage Schedule shall be signed by the parties contracting the marriage, by both witnesses present thereat and by the approved celebrant.

(2) The parties to the marriage shall, within 3 days thereafter, deliver the Marriage Schedule, or send it by post or arrange that it is delivered, to the district registrar.

(3) As soon as possible after receipt of the Marriage Schedule, the district registrar shall cause the particulars as set forth in that Schedule to be entered in the register of marriages kept by him; and subject to subsection (4) below, he shall not register a religious marriage unless and until he receives a duly signed Marriage Schedule in respect of that marriage.

(4) Where the Registrar General is satisfied that a marriage has been properly

solemnised and that the Marriage Schedule in respect of the marriage has been duly signed but has been lost or destroyed, he may direct the district registrar to complete an exact copy of the original Marriage Schedule and, so far as practicable, to arrange for its signature by those persons who signed the original Schedule; and as soon as possible thereafter, the district registrar shall cause the particulars as set forth in that copy to be entered in the register of marriages kept by him.

16   Registrar's power to require delivery of Marriage Schedule

(1)   Where after the expiration of 21 days from the date of marriage as entered in the Marriage Schedule that Schedule has not been delivered to the district registrar, he may serve a notice in the prescribed form on either of the parties to the marriage requiring that party within 8 days from the date of service of the notice to deliver the said Schedule, or send it by post, to the district registrar.

(2)   If any party on whom a notice has been served in pursuance of subsection (1) above fails to comply with the notice, the district registrar may serve on that party a second notice in the prescribed form requiring that party to attend personally at the registration office of the district registrar, within 8 days from the date of service of the second notice, for the purpose of delivering the Marriage Schedule to the district registrar to enable him to register the marriage.

Civil marriages

17   Appointment of authorised registrars

For the purpose of affording reasonable facilities for the solemnisation of civil marriages throughout Scotland, the Registrar General—

(a)   shall appoint such number of district registrars as he thinks necessary; and

(b)   may, in respect of any district for which he has appointed a district registrar under paragraph (a) above, appoint one or more assistant registrars,
as persons who may solemnise marriages:

Provided that any person appointed under this section must, at the date of his appointment, be 21 years of age or over.

18   Places at which civil marriages may be solemnised

(1)   Subject to the provisions of this section, an authorised registrar shall solemnise a civil marriage—

[(a)]   in his registration office [; or

(b)   at an approved place in his registration district.]

(2)   An authorised registrar may, with the approval of the Registrar General, solemnise a civil marriage—

[(a)]   in the registration office of another authorised registrar [; or

(b)   at an approved place in the district of another authorised registrar.]

(3)   If either of the parties to an intended civil marriage is unable to attend the registration office of an authorised registrar for the solemnisation of the marriage, an authorised registrar may, subject to the following provisions of this section and on reimbursement of any additional expenditure incurred by him by virtue of this subsection, solemnise the marriage—

(a)   at any place in his registration district other than his registration office; or

(b)   with the approval of the Registrar General, at any place in any registration district in respect of which there is no authorised registrar.

(4)   The authorised registrar shall not solemnise a marriage at any such place as is described in subsection (3)(a) or (b) above unless—

(a)   application has been made to him by either of the parties to the intended marriage requesting him to solemnise the marriage at such a place and stating the reason why one of the parties is unable to attend a registration office; and

(b)   subject to subsection (5) below, he is satisfied on consideration of the application that the party is unable to attend a registration office by reason of serious illness or serious bodily injury and that there is good reason why the marriage cannot be delayed until the party is able to attend a registration office.

(5)   If the authorised registrar is not satisfied as mentioned in subsection (4)(b) above, he shall consult the Registrar General who may direct him to solemnise the marriage in accordance with the application made under subsection (4)(a) above or to refuse so to solemnise it.

[(6)   For the purposes of this section 'approved place' means any place approved by virtue of regulations made under section 18A of this Act.]

[18A   Approved places

(1)   The Scottish Ministers may by regulations make provision for or in connection with the approval by local authorities of places in their areas in which civil marriages may be solemnised.

(2)   Regulations under subsection (1) above may in particular include provision as to—

(a)   the kinds of place in respect of which approvals may be granted;
(b)   the procedure to be followed in relation to applications for approval;
(c)   the considerations to be taken into account by a local authority in determining whether to approve any places;
(d)   the duration and renewal of approvals;
(e)   the conditions that shall or may be imposed by a local authority on granting or renewing an approval;
(f)   the determination and charging by local authorities of fees in respect of—
    (i)   applications for the approval of places;
    (ii)   the renewal of approvals; and
    (iii)   the attendance by authorised registrars at places approved under the regulations;
(g)   the circumstances in which a local authority shall or may revoke or suspend an approval or vary any of the conditions imposed in relation to an approval;
(h)   the notification to the Registrar General of all approvals granted, renewed, revoked, suspended or varied;
(i)   the notification to the district registrar for the district in which a place approved under the regulations is situated of all approvals relating to such a place which are granted, renewed, revoked, suspended or varied;
(j)   the keeping by the Registrar General, district registrars and local authorities of registers of places approved under the regulations; and
(k)   the issue by the Registrar General of guidance supplementing the provision made by the regulations.

(3)   A person who has made an application under regulations made under subsection (1) above may appeal, by summary application, to the sheriff against any decision made by a local authority in relation to the application (including any decision to revoke or suspend, or to vary any of the conditions imposed in relation to, an approval granted in pursuance of that application).

(4)   An appeal under subsection (3) above may be made only on one or more of the following grounds—

(a)   that the local authority's decision was based on an error of law;
(b)   that the local authority's decision was based on an incorrect material fact;
(c)   that the local authority has acted contrary to natural justice; or
(d)   that the local authority has acted unreasonably in the exercise of its discretion.

(5)   An appeal under subsection (3) above shall not, unless on good cause shown, be considered by the sheriff unless lodged with the sheriff clerk within 28

days of the date on which the local authority made the decision being appealed against.

(6)   In upholding an appeal under subsection (3) above, the sheriff may—

(a)   remit the case with the reasons for the sheriff's decision to the local authority for reconsideration by the local authority of its decision; or

(b)   reverse or modify the local authority's decision.

(7)   A party to an appeal under subsection (3) above may appeal, on a point of law only, against the decision of the sheriff to the Court of Session within 28 days of the date of that decision.

(8)   Regulations under subsection (1) above may make different provision for different cases or circumstances.

(9)   The power to make regulations under subsection (1) above shall be exercisable by statutory instrument; and, subject to subsection (10) below, any such statutory instrument shall be subject to annulment in pursuance of a resolution of the Scottish Parliament.

(10)   A statutory instrument containing the first regulations under subsection (1) above shall not be made unless a draft of the instrument has been laid before, and approved by a resolution of, the Scottish Parliament.]

19   Marriage ceremony and registration of marriage

(1)   An authorised registrar shall not solemnise a marriage within 14 days of the date of receipt (as entered in the marriage notice book) of a marriage notice in respect of that marriage, unless—

(a)   he has received a written request from one or both of the parties to solemnise the marriage on a specified earlier date stating the reason for the request, and

(b)   he has been authorised to solemnise the marriage on that earlier date by the Registrar General.

(2)   A marriage shall not be solemnised by an authorised registrar unless—

(a)   he has available to him at the time of the ceremony a Marriage Schedule, in respect of the marriage, completed in accordance with this Act and the prescribed fee for the marriage has been paid;

(b)   both parties to the marriage are present; and

(c)   two persons professing to be 16 years of age or over are present as witnesses.

(3)   Immediately after the solemnisation of the marriage the Marriage Schedule shall be signed by the parties contracting the marriage, by both witnesses present thereat and by the authorised registrar who solemnised it.

(4)   As soon as possible after the Marriage Schedule has been signed in accordance with subsection (3) above—

(a)   in a case where the marriage has been solemnised in the registration office of the authorised registrar who solemnised it or in any such place as is mentioned in section 18(3) of this Act, that authorised registrar;

(b)   in a case where the marriage has been solemnised in the registration office of another authorised registrar, that other authorised registrar,

shall cause the particulars as set forth in that Schedule to be entered in the register of marriages kept by him.

20   Second marriage ceremony

(1)   Where two persons have gone through a marriage ceremony with each other outside the United Kingdom, whether before or after the commencement of this Act, but they are not, or are unable to prove that they are, validly married to each other in Scots law, an authorised registrar, on an application made to him by those persons, may, subject to the approval of the Registrar General and to subsection (2) below, solemnise their marriage as if they had not already gone through a marriage ceremony with each other.

(2)   Sections 3 to 6 and 18 and 19 of this Act shall apply for the purpose of solemnising a marriage under this section except that—

(a)   there shall be submitted to the authorised registrar a statutory declaration by both parties—

(i)   stating that they have previously gone through a marriage ceremony with each other; and

(ii)   specifying the date and place at which, and the circumstances in which, they went through that ceremony;

(b)   section 5(4)(b) of this Act shall not apply in respect of the parties already being married to each other;

(c)   the Marriage Schedule shall contain such modifications as the Registrar General may direct to indicate that the parties have previously gone through a marriage ceremony with each other; and

(d)   after the Marriage Schedule has been signed in accordance with section 19(3) of this Act, the authorised registrar shall make an endorsement on it in the following terms—

'The ceremony of marriage between the parties mentioned in this Schedule was performed in pursuance of section 20 of the Marriage (Scotland) Act 1977, following a statutory declaration by them that they had gone through a ceremony of marriage with each other on the   day of   19   , at

Dated the   day of   19   ,

(Signature of authorised registrar)'.

Irregular marriages

21   Registration of irregular marriages

Where decree of declarator establishing—

(a)   a marriage by cohabitation with habit and repute; or

(b)   a marriage contracted before 1st July 1940 by declaration *de praesenti* or by promise *subsequente copula*,

has been granted in the Court of Session, the principal clerk of Session shall forthwith cause the decree, the names, designations and addresses of the parties, and the date, as determined by the Court, on which the marriage was constituted to be intimated to the Registrar General, and on receipt of such intimation the Registrar General shall cause the marriage to be registered.

General

22   Interpreters at marriage ceremony

(1)   Where the person by whom a marriage is to be solemnised under this Act considers that it is necessary or desirable, he may use the services of an interpreter (not being a party or a witness to the marriage) at the marriage ceremony.

(2)   The interpreter shall—

(a)   before the marriage ceremony, sign a written statement that he understands, and is able to converse in, any language in respect of which he is to act as interpreter at that ceremony; and

(b)   immediately after the marriage ceremony, furnish the person solemnising the marriage with a certificate written in English and signed by the interpreter that he has faithfully acted as interpreter at that ceremony.

(3)   Any fee for the services of the interpreter shall be paid by the parties to the marriage.

23   Cancellation of entry in register of marriages

If a marriage in respect of which an entry has been made in a register of marriages is found or declared to be void, the Registrar General shall direct the cancellation of the entry.

[23A Validity of registered marriage

(1) Subject to sections 1 and 2 of, and without prejudice to section 24(1) of, this Act, where the particulars of any marriage at the ceremony in respect of which both parties were present are entered in a register of marriages by or at the behest of an appropriate registrar, the validity of that marriage shall not be questioned, in any legal proceedings whatsoever, on the ground of failure to comply with a requirement or restriction imposed by, under or by virtue of this Act.

(2) In subsection (1) above, 'appropriate registrar' means

(a) in the case of a civil marriage, an authorised registrar; and

(b) in any other case, a district registrar.]

24 Offences

(1) Any person who—

(a) falsifies or forges any Marriage Schedule, certificate or declaration issued or made, or purporting to be issued, or made, under this Act;

(b) knowingly uses, or gives or sends to any person as genuine, any false or forged Marriage Schedule, certificate, declaration or other document issued or made, or purporting to be issued or made, or required, under this Act;

(c) being an approved celebrant, solemnises a marriage without a Marriage Schedule in respect of the marriage, issued in accordance with this Act, being available to him at the time of the marriage ceremony;

(d) not being an approved celebrant or an authorised registrar, conducts a marriage ceremony in such a way as to lead the parties to the marriage to believe that he is solemnising a valid marriage;

(e) being an approved celebrant or an authorised registrar, solemnises a marriage without both parties to the marriage being present,

shall be guilty of an offence and shall be liable—

(i) on conviction on indictment, to a fine or to imprisonment for a term not exceeding 2 years or to both;

(ii) on summary conviction, to a fine not exceeding £100 or to imprisonment for a term not exceeding 3 months or to both [; or

(f) being an authorised registrar, solemnises a marriage in a place otherwise than in accordance with section 18(1) of this Act.]

(2) Any person who—

(a) solemnises a marriage in an area in which by virtue of section 9(4)(b) of this Act he is not permitted to solemnise a marriage;

(b) solemnises a marriage in contravention of section 10(5) of this Act;

(c) being a person temporarily authorised under section 12(a) of this Act, solemnises a marriage not specified in that authorisation;

(d) solemnises a marriage in contravention of section 14 of this Act; or

(e) being a party to a marriage, fails to comply with a notice served under section 16(2) of this Act,

shall be guilty of an offence and shall be liable on summary conviction to a fine not exceeding £100.

(3) Summary proceedings for an offence under this Act or, in relation to information supplied under or for the purposes of this Act, section 53(1)(a) of the Registration of Births, Deaths and Marriages (Scotland) Act 1965, may be commenced at any time within the period of 3 months from the date on which evidence sufficient in the opinion of the Lord Advocate to justify the proceedings comes to his knowledge or within the period of 12 months from the commission of the offence, whichever period last expires; and subsection (3) of [section 136 of the Criminal Procedure (Scotland) Act 1995] (date of commencement of summary proceedings) shall have effect for the purposes of this section as it has effect for the purposes of that section.

25 Regulations

(1) Any power to make regulations conferred by this Act shall be exercisable

by statutory instrument and no such regulations shall be made by the Registrar General except with the approval of the Secretary of State.

(2)   Any statutory instrument containing regulations which prescribe fees for the purposes of this Act shall be subject to annulment in pursuance of a resolution of either House of Parliament.

(3)   The Statutory Instruments Act 1946 shall apply to a statutory instrument containing regulations made for the purposes of this Act by the Registrar General as if the regulations had been made by a Minister of the Crown.

26   Interpretation

(1)   Except where the context otherwise requires and subject to subsection (2) below, expressions used in this Act and in the Registration of Births, Deaths, and Marriages (Scotland) Act 1965 have the same meanings in this Act as in that Act.

(2)   In this Act, except where the context otherwise requires—

'annulment' includes any decree or declarator of nullity of marriage, however expressed;

'approved celebrant' has the meaning assigned to it by section 8(2)(a) of this Act;

'authorised registrar' has the meaning assigned to it by section 8(2)(b) of this Act;

'district registrar' means the registrar for the registration district in which the marriage is to be or has been solemnised;

'name' includes surname;

'prescribed' means prescribed by regulations made by the Registrar General;

'religious body' means an organised group of people meeting regularly for common religious worship.

(3)   Except where the context otherwise requires, any reference in this Act to any other enactment shall be construed as a reference to that enactment as amended by or under any other enactment, including this Act.

27   Transitional and saving provisions

(1)   Where, before the commencement of this Act—

(a)   proclamation of banns or publication of notice has been applied for by one or both of the parties to; or

(b)   a licence has been granted by a sheriff in respect of,

an intended marriage in accordance with an enactment repealed by this Act, then the marriage shall proceed in accordance with the enactments repealed by this Act as if they had not been so repealed:

Provided that this subsection shall cease to have effect in respect of the marriage if—

(i)   a certificate of proclamation of banns or publication of notice issued in respect of the said application; or

(ii)   the said licence,

ceases to be valid in accordance with any enactment so repealed.

(2)   Any form used, and any requirement as to the particulars to be entered in any form used, for the purposes of any enactment repealed by this Act shall continue in force as though prescribed under this Act until other forms or particulars are so prescribed.

(3)   Nothing in this Act shall affect the validity of any marriage solemnised or contracted before 1st January 1978.

(4)   Nothing in the foregoing provisions of this section shall be taken as prejudicing the operation of section 38 of the Interpretation Act 1889 (which relates to the effect of repeals).

29   Short title, commencement and extent

(1)   This Act may be cited as the Marriage (Scotland) Act 1977.

(2)   This Act, except this section, shall come into force on 1st January 1978.

(3)   This Act, except this section and, in so far as relating to the Marriage with Foreigners Act 1906, the Marriage Act 1939, the Marriage Act 1949 and the Marriage (Scotland) Act 1956, section 28, shall extend to Scotland only.

SCHEDULES

SCHEDULE 1
DEGREES OF RELATIONSHIP

Column 1   *Column 2*

1.—*Relationships by consanguinity*

Mother;	Father;
Daughter;	Son;
Father's mother;	Father's father;
Mother's mother;	Mother's father;
Son's daughter;	Son's son;
Daughter's daughter;	Daughter's son;
Sister;	Brother;
Father's sister;	Father's brother;
Mother's sister;	Mother's brother;
Brother's daughter;	Brother's son;
Sister's daughter;	Sister's son;
Father's father's mother;	Father's father's father;
Father's mother's mother;	Father's mother's father;
Mother's father's mother;	Mother's father's father;
Mother's mother's mother;	Mother's mother's father;
Son's son's daughter;	Son's son's son;
Son's daughter's daughter;	Son's daughter's son;
Daughter's son's daughter;	Daughter's son's son;
Daughter's daughter's daughter;	Daughter's daughter's son.

[2.—*Relationships by affinity referred to in section 2(1A)*

Daughter of former wife;	Son of former husband;
Former wife of father;	Former husband of mother;
Former wife of father's father;	Former husband of father's mother;
Former wife of mother's father;	Former husband of mother's mother;
Daughter of son of former wife;	Son of son of former husband;
Daughter of daughter of former wife;	Son of daughter of former husband.

2A.—*Relationships by affinity referred to in section 2(1B)*

Mother of former wife;	Father of former husband;
Former wife of son;	Former husband of daughter.]

3.—*Relationships by adoption*

Adoptive mother or former adoptive mother;	Adoptive father or former adoptive father;
Adopted daughter or former adopted daughter;	Adopted son or former adopted son.

ADOPTION (SCOTLAND) ACT 1978
(1978, c 28)

PART I
THE ADOPTION SERVICE

The Adoption Service

1 Establishment of Adoption Service
(1) It is the duty of every local authority to establish and maintain within their area a service designed to meet the needs, in relation to adoption, of—
    (a) children who have been or may be adopted;
    (b) parents and guardians of such children; and
    (c) persons who have adopted or may adopt a child;
and for that purpose to provide the requisite facilities, or secure that they are provided by [registered adoption services].
(2) The facilities to be provided as part of the service maintained under subsection (1) include—
    [. . .]
    (b) arrangements for assessing children and prospective adopters, and placing children for adoption;
    [(bb) counselling and assistance (but, without prejudice to sections 51 to 51B, not assistance in cash) to children who have been adopted and to persons who have adopted a child; and
    (c) counselling for other persons if they have problems relating to adoption.]
(3) The facilities of the service maintained under subsection (1) shall be provided in conjunction with the local authority's other social services and with [registered adoption services] in their area, so that help may be given in a co-ordinated manner without duplication, omission or avoidable delay.
[(3A) In this Part, references to adoption are to the adoption of children, wherever they may be habitually resident, effected under the law of any country or territory, whether within or outside the British Islands.]
(4) The services maintained by local authorities under subsection (1) may be collectively referred to as 'the Scottish Adoption Service', and a local authority or [registered adoption service] may be referred to as an adoption agency.
[(5) In this Act 'registered adoption service' means an adoption service provided as mentioned in section 2(11)(b) of the Regulation of Care (Scotland) Act 2001 (asp 8) and registered under Part I of that Act.]

2 Local authorities' social work
The social services referred to in section 1(3) are the functions of a local authority [under any of the enactments mentioned in subsection (18) of section 5 of the Social Work (Scotland) Act 1968 (power of Secretary of State to issue directions to local authorities in respect of their functions under certain enactments)], including, in particular but without prejudice to the generality of the foregoing, a local authority's functions relating to—
    (a) the promotion of the welfare of children by diminishing the need to receive children into care or keep them in care, including (in exceptional circumstances) the giving of assistance in cash;
    (b) the welfare of children in the care of the local authority;
    (c) the welfare of children who are foster children within the meaning of the [Foster Children (Scotland) Act 1984];
    [. . .]
    (e) the provision of residential accommodation for expectant mothers and young children and of day-care facilities;
    [. . .]

(g)   care and other treatment of children through court proceedings and children's hearings.

Adoption societies

[. . .]

[6   Duty to promote welfare of child

(1)   Without prejudice to sections 12(8) and 18(8), in reaching any decision relating to the adoption of a child, a court or adoption agency shall have regard to all the circumstances but—

(a)   shall regard the need to safeguard and promote the welfare of the child concerned throughout his life as the paramount consideration; and

(b)   shall have regard so far as practicable—

(i)   to his views (if he wishes to express them) taking account of his age and maturity; and

(ii)   to his religious persuasion, racial origin and cultural and linguistic background.

(2)   Without prejudice to the generality of paragraph (b) of subsection (1), a child twelve years of age or more shall be presumed to be of sufficient age and maturity to form a view for the purposes of that paragraph.]

[6A   Duty to consider alternatives to adoption

In complying with its duties under section 6 of this Act, an adoption agency shall, before making any arrangements for the adoption of a child, consider whether adoption is likely best to meet the needs of that child or whether for him there is some better, practicable, alternative; and if it concludes that there is such an alternative it shall not proceed to make those arrangements.]

7   Religious upbringing of adopted child

An adoption agency shall in placing a child for adoption have regard (so far as is practicable) to any wishes of the child's parents and guardians as to the religious upbringing of the child.

[. . .]

9   Regulation of adoption agencies

[. . .]

(2)   The Secretary of State may make regulations for any purpose relating to the exercise of its functions by [a registered adoption service].

(3)   The Secretary of State may make regulations with respect to the exercise by local authorities of their functions of making or participating in arrangements for the adoption of children.

[(3A)   Regulations under this section may make provision—

(a)   as to the determination by an adoption agency of whether, as regards a child for whose adoption it proposes to make arrangements, any such agreement as is mentioned in sections 16(1)(b)(i) and 18(1)(a) is likely to be forthcoming and as to a period by the end of which, if they have determined that the agreement is unlikely to be forthcoming and if no application has been made for an adoption order in relation to the child, application for an order under section 18(1) shall require to be made in relation to him; and

(b)   where the case of a child for whose adoption an adoption agency proposes to make arrangements is referred under section 73(4)(c)(ii) or (iii) of the Children (Scotland) Act 1995 to the Principal Reporter (within the meaning of Part II of that Act), as to circumstances in which and, on the occurrence of such circumstances, a period by the end of which, if no application has been made for an adoption order in relation to the child, application for an order under section 18(1) shall require to be made in relation to him.]

(4)   Any person who contravenes or fails to comply with regulations made

under [this section] shall be guilty of an offence and liable on summary conviction to a fine not exceeding [level 5 on the standard scale].

(5) Regulations under this section may make different provisions in relation to different cases or classes of cases and may exclude certain cases or classes of cases.

[. . .]

11 Restriction on arranging adoptions and placing of children

(1) A person other than an adoption agency shall not make arrangements for the adoption of a child, or place a child for adoption, unless the proposed adopter is a relative of the child.

[(2) An adoption society which is—

    (a) a person registered under Part II of the Care Standards Act 2000,

    (b) registered as respects Northern Ireland under Article 4 of the Adoption (Northern Ireland) Order 1987,

but which is not a registered adoption service, shall not act as an adoption society in Scotland except to the extent that the society considers it necessary to do so in the interests of a person mentioned in section 1 of that Act or, as the case may be, Article 3 of that Order.]

(3) A person who—

    (a) takes part in the management or control of a body of persons which exists wholly or partly for the purpose of making arrangements for the adoption of children and which is not [a registered adoption service] or a local authority; or

    (b) contravenes subsection (1); or

    (c) [both receives a child placed with him in contravention of subsection (1) and knows that the placement is with a view to his adopting the child,]

shall be guilty of an offence and liable on summary conviction to imprisonment for a term not exceeding 3 months or to a fine not exceeding [level 5 on the standard scale] or to both.

(4) In any proceedings for an offence under paragraph (a) of subsection (3), proof of things done or of words written, spoken or published (whether or not in the presence of any party to the proceedings) by any person taking part in the management or control of a body of persons, or in making arrangements for the adoption of children on behalf of the body, shall be sufficient evidence of the purpose for which that body exists.

(5) Section 26 shall apply where a person is convicted of a contravention of subsection (1) as it applies where an application for an adoption order is refused.

PART II

ADOPTION ORDERS

The making of adoption orders

12 Adoption orders

(1) An adoption order is an order vesting the parental [responsibilities and parental rights in relation] to a child in the adopters, made on their application by an authorised court; except that an adoption order may be made in relation to a person who has attained the age of 18 years if the application for it was made before such attainment.

(2) The order does not affect the parental [responsibilities and parental rights] so far as they relate to any period before the making of the order.

(3) [Subject to subsection (3A)] the making of an adoption order operates to extinguish—

    (a) any [parental responsibility or parental right] relating to the child which immediately before the making of the order was vested in a person (not being one of the adopters) who was—

    (i) a parent of the child, or

    (ii) a [. . .] guardian of the child appointed by a deed or by the order of a court;

(b) any duty owed to [. . .] the child—

    (i) to pay or provide aliment in respect of any period occurring after the making of the order;

    (ii) to make any payment arising out of parental responsibilities and [parental rights] in respect of such a period.

[(3A) Where the adoption order is made by virtue of section 15(1)(aa), its making shall not operate to extinguish the parental responsibilities and parental rights which immediately before the making of the order were vested in the natural parent to whom the adopter is married.]

(4) Nothing in subsection (3) shall extinguish any duty arising under a deed or agreement which constitutes a trust or which expressly provides that the duty is not to be extinguished by the making of an adoption order. [. . .]

(5) An adoption order may not be made in relation to a child who is or has been married.

(6) An adoption order may contain such terms and conditions as the court thinks fit.

(7) An adoption order may be made notwithstanding that the child is already an adopted child.

[(8) An adoption order shall not be made in relation to a child of or over the age of 12 years unless with the child's consent; except that, where the court is satisfied that the child is incapable of giving his consent to the making of the order, it may dispense with that consent.

(9) Where a court making an adoption order in relation to a child who is subject to a supervision requirement is satisfied that, in consequence of its doing so, compulsory measures of supervision in respect of the child are no longer necessary, it may determine that the child shall forthwith cease to be subject to that requirement.]

13 Child to live with adopters before order made

(1) Where the applicant, or one of the applicants, is a parent, step-parent or relative of the child, or the child was placed with the applicants by an adoption agency, an adoption order shall not be made unless the child is at least 19 weeks old and at all times during the preceding 13 weeks had his home with the applicants or one of them.

(2) Where subsection (1) does not apply, an adoption order shall not be made unless the child is at least 12 months old and at all times during the preceding 12 months had his home with the applicants or one of them.

(3) An adoption order shall not be made unless the court is satisfied that sufficient opportunities to see the child with the applicant, or, in the case of an application by a married couple, both applicants together in the home environment have been afforded—

(a) where the child was placed with the applicant by an adoption agency, to that agency, or

(b) in any other case, to the local authority within whose area the home is.

[(4) In relation to—

(a) an adoption proposed to be effected by a Convention adoption order; or

(b) an adoption of a child habitually resident outside the British Islands which is proposed to be effected by an adoption order other than a Convention adoption order,

subsection (1) shall have effect as if the reference to the preceding 13 weeks were a reference to the preceding six months.]

14 Adoption by married couple

[(1) [. . .] An adoption order shall not be made on the application of more than one person except in the circumstances specified in subsections (1A) and (1B).

(1A) An adoption order may be made on the application of a married couple where both the husband and the wife have attained the age of 21 years.

(1B) An adoption order may be made on the application of a married couple where—
  (a) the husband or the wife—
    (i) is the father or mother of the child; and
    (ii) has attained the age of 18 years; and
  (b) his or her spouse has attained the age of 21 years.]

(2) An adoption order shall not be made on the application of a married couple unless—
  (a) at least one of them is domiciled in a part of the United Kingdom, or in the Channel Islands or the Isle of Man, or
  (b) the application is for a Convention adoption order and [the requirements of regulations under section 17 are] compiled with [, or
  (c) both of them were habitually resident in any of the places mentioned in paragraph (a) above throughout the period of one year which ends with the date of their application.]

15 Adoption by one person

(1) [A]n adoption order may be made on the application of one person where he has attained the age of 21 years and—
  (a) is not married, or
  [(aa) not being a person who may make application by virtue of paragraph (b) below, is married to a person—
    (i) who is the natural parent of the child concerned; and
    (ii) in whom are vested parental responsibilities and parental rights in relation to the child,]
  (b) [not being a person who may make application by virtue of paragraph (aa) above,] is married and the court is satisfied that—
    (i) his spouse cannot be found, or
    (ii) the spouses have separated and are living apart, and the separation is likely to be permanent, or
    (iii) his spouse is by reason of ill-health, whether physical or mental, incapable of making an application for an adoption order.

(2) An adoption order shall not be made on the application of one person unless—
  (a) he is domiciled in a part of the United Kingdom, or in the Channel Islands or the Isle of Man, or
  (b) the application is for a Convention adoption order and [the requirements of regulations under section 17 are] complied with [, or
  (c) he was habitually resident in any of the places mentioned in paragraph (a) above throughout the period of one year which ends with the date of his application].

(3) An adoption order shall not be made on the application of the mother or father of the child alone unless the court is satisfied that—
  (a) the other [. . .] parent is dead or cannot be found [or, by virtue of section 28 of the Human Fertilisation and Embryology Act 1990 (disregarding subsections (5A) to (5I) of that section), there is no other parent,] or
  (b) there is some other reason justifying the exclusion of the other [. . .] parent,
and where such an order is made the reason justifying the exclusion of the other [. . .] parent shall be recorded by the court.

16 Parental agreement

(1) An adoption order shall not be made unless—

(a)   the child is free for adoption by virtue of an order made
[(i)   in Scotland under section 18;
(ii)   in England and Wales under section 18 of the Adoption Act 1976; or
(iii)   in Northern Ireland under Article 17(1) or 18(1) of the Adoption (Northern Ireland) Order 1987,
and not revoked]; or
(b)   in the case of each parent or guardian of the child the court is satisfied that—
(i)   he freely, and with full understanding of what is involved, agrees unconditionally to the making of an adoption order (whether or not he knows the identity of the applicants), or
(ii)   his agreement to the making of the adoption order should be dispensed with on a ground specified in subsection (2).
[(2)   The grounds mentioned in subsection (1)(b)(ii) are, that the parent or guardian—
(a)   is not known, cannot be found or is incapable of giving agreement;
(b)   is withholding agreement unreasonably;
(c)   has persistently failed, without reasonable cause, to fulfil one or other of the following parental responsibilities in relation to the child—
(i)   the responsibility to safeguard and promote the child's health, development and welfare; or
(ii)   if the child is not living with him, the responsibility to maintain personal relations and direct contact with the child on a regular basis;
(d)   has seriously ill-treated the child, whose reintegration into the same household as the parent or guardian is, because of the serious ill-treatment or for other reasons, unlikely.]
[. . .]
(4)   Agreement is ineffective for the purposes of subsection (1)(b)(i) if given by the mother less than six weeks after the child's birth.
[. . .]

[17   Convention adoption orders

An adoption order shall be made as a Convention adoption order if—
(a)   the application is for a Convention adoption order; and
(b)   such requirements as may be prescribed by regulations made by the Secretary of State are complied with.]

Freeing for adoption

18   Freeing child for adoption

(1)   Where, on an application by an adoption agency [which is a local authority], an authorised court is satisfied in the case of each parent or guardian of the child that—
(a)   he freely, and with full understanding of what is involved, agrees generally and unconditionally to the making of an adoption order, or
(b)   his agreement to the making of an adoption order should be dispensed with on a ground specified in section 16(2),
the court shall, subject to subsection (8), make an order declaring the child free for adoption.
(2)   No application shall be made under subsection (1) unless—
(a)   it is made with the consent of a parent or guardian of a child, or
(b)   the adoption agency is applying for dispensation under subsection (1)(b) of the agreement of each parent or guardian of the child, and the child is in the care of the adoption agency.
(3)   No agreement required under subsection (1)(a) shall be dispensed with under subsection (1)(b) unless the child is already placed for adoption or the court is satisfied that it is likely that the child will be placed for adoption.

(4)   An agreement by the mother of the child is ineffective for the purposes of this section if given less than 6 weeks after the child's birth.

[(5)   On the making of an order under this section, the parental responsibilities and parental rights in relation to the child are transferred to the adoption agency.]

(6)   Before making an order under this section, the court shall satisfy itself, in relation to each parent or guardian [. . .] of the child [who can be found,] that he has been given an opportunity of making, if he so wishes, a declaration that he prefers not to be involved in future questions concerning the adoption of the child; and any such declaration shall be recorded by the court.

[(7)   Before making an order under this section in the case of a child whose father is not, and has not been, married to the mother and does not have any parental responsibilities or parental rights in relation to the child, the court shall satisfy itself in relation to any person claiming to be the father that—

(a)   he has no intention of applying for, or, if he did so apply, it is likely that he would be refused, an order under section 11 of the Children (Scotland) Act 1995 (orders in relation to parental responsibilities and parental rights); and

(b)   he has no intention of entering into an agreement with the mother under section 4(1) of that Act (acquisition by natural father by agreement of such responsibilities and rights), or, if he has such an intention, that no agreement under that subsection is likely to be made.]

[(8)   An order under this section shall not be made in relation to a child of or over the age of 12 years unless with the child's consent; except that where the court is satisfied that the child is incapable of giving his consent to the making of the order, it may dispense with that consent.

(9)   Where a court making an order under this section in relation to a child who is subject to a supervision requirement is satisfied that, in consequence of its doing so, compulsory measures of supervision in respect of the child are no longer necessary, it may determine that the child shall forthwith cease to be subject to that requirement.]

19   Progress reports to the former parent

(1)   This section and section 20 apply to any person [(in this section and in section 20 referred to as the 'relevant parent')] who was required to be given an opportunity of making a declaration under section 18(6) but [either—

(a)   did not do so; or

(b)   having done so, subsequently by written notice under this subsection to the adoption agency to which the parental responsibilities and parental rights have been transferred, has withdrawn such declaration].

(2)   Within the 14 days following the date 12 months after the making of the order under section 18; the adoption agency [to which the parental responsibilities and parental rights were transferred] on the making of the order, unless it has previously by notice to the [relevant] parent informed him that an adoption order has been made in respect of the child, shall by notice to the [relevant] parent inform him—

(a)   whether an adoption order has been made in respect of the child, and (if not)

(b)   whether the child has his home with a person with whom he has been placed for adoption.

(3)   If at the time when the [relevant] parent is given notice under subsection (2) an adoption order has not been made in respect of the child, it is thereafter the duty of the adoption agency to give notice to the [relevant] parent of the making of an adoption order (if and when made), and meanwhile to give the [relevant] parent notice whenever the child is placed for adoption or ceases [to be placed with a person to a view to his being adopted by that person].

(4)   If at any time the [relevant] parent by notice makes a declaration to the

adoption agency that he prefers not to be involved in future questions concerning the adoption of the child—
    (a)   the agency shall secure that the declaration is recorded by the court which made the order under section 18, and
    (b)   the agency is released from the duty of complying further with subsection (3) as respects that [relevant] parent [but a declaration under this subsection may be withdrawn in the same way as may a declaration under subsection (6) of section 18, in which event the agency shall no longer be so released].

20   Revocation of s 18 order

(1)   The [relevant] parent, at any time more than 12 months after the making of the order under section 18 when—
    (a)   no adoption order has been made in respect of the child, and
    (b)   the child does not have his home with a person with whom he has been placed for adoption,
may apply to the court which made the order for a further order revoking it on the ground that he wishes to resume the parental [responsibilities and parental rights].

[(1A)   The adoption agency, at any time after the making of the order under section 18 when the conditions mentioned in paragraphs (a) and (b) of subsection (1) above are satisfied, may apply to the court which made the order for a further order revoking it.]

(2)   While [an] application [under subsection (1) or (1A)] is pending the adoption agency having the parental [responsibilities and parental rights] and duties shall not place the child for adoption without the leave of the court.

[(3)   Where an order freeing a child for adoption is revoked under this section, the court shall, by an order under section 11 of the Children (Scotland) Act 1995 determine on whom are to be imposed the parental responsibilities, and to whom are to be given the parental rights in relation to the child.]

(4)   Subject to subsection (5), if [an] application [under subsection (1)] is dismissed on the ground that to allow it would contravene the principle embodied in section 6—
    (a)   the [relevant] parent who made the application shall not be entitled to make any further application under subsection (1) in respect of the child, and
    (b)   the adoption agency is released from the duty of complying further with section 19(3) as respects that parent.

(5)   Subsection (4)(a) shall not apply where the court which dismissed the application gives leave to the [relevant] parent to make a further application under subsection (1), but such leave shall not be given unless it appears to the court that because of a change in circumstances or for any other reason it is proper to allow the application to be made.

[21   Variation of section 18 order so as to substitute one adoption agency for another

(1)   On an application to which this section applies an authorised court may vary an order under section 18 so as to transfer the parental [responsibilities and parental rights] relating to the child from the adoption agency [to which they are transferred by virtue of] the order ('the existing agency') to another adoption agency ('the substitute agency').

(2)   This section applies to any application made jointly by the existing agency and the would-be substitute agency.

(3)   Where an order under section 18 is varied under this section, section 19 shall apply as if the parental [responsibilities and parental rights] relating to the child had [been transferred to] the substitute agency on the making of the order.]

Supplemental

22 Notification to local authority of adoption application

(1)   An adoption order shall not be made in respect of a child who was not placed with the applicant by an adoption agency unless the applicant has, at least 3 months before the date of the order, given notice to the local authority within whose area he has his home of his intention to apply for the adoption order.

(2)   On receipt of such a notice the local authority shall investigate the matter and submit to the court a report of their investigation.

(3)   Under subsection (2), the local authority shall in particular investigate,—

(a)   so far as is practicable, the suitability of the applicant, and any other matters relevant to the operation of section 6 in relation to the application; and

(b)   whether the child was placed with the applicant in contravention of section 11.

(4)   A local authority which receive notice under subsection (1) in respect of a child whom the authority know to be in the care of another local authority shall, not more than 7 days after the receipt of the notice, inform that other local authority in writing that they have received the notice.

[22A Children subject to supervision requirements

(1)   [A registered adoption service] shall refer the case of a child who is subject to a supervision requirement to the Principal Reporter where it is satisfied that the best interests of the child would be served by its placing the child for adoption and it intends so to place him.

(2)   On a case being referred to him under subsection (1), the Principal Reporter shall arrange for a children's hearing to review the supervision requirement in question and shall make any arrangements incidental to that review.

(3)   Subsections (9), (13) and (14) of section 73 of the Children (Scotland) Act 1995 (which provide, respectively, for acting on the review of a supervision requirement, a report by a children's hearing and consideration of that report) shall apply in relation to a children's hearing arranged under this section as those subsections apply in relation to one arranged by virtue of subsection (4)(c)(iii) of that section.

(4)   In this section 'Principal Reporter' has the same meaning as in Part II of the Children (Scotland) Act 1995.]

23 Reports where child placed by agency

Where an application for an adoption order relates to a child placed by an adoption agency, the agency shall submit to the court a report on the suitability of the applicants and any other matters relevant to the operation of section 6, and shall assist the court in any manner the court may direct.

24 Restrictions on making adoption orders

(1)   The court shall not proceed to determine an application for an adoption order in relation to a child where a previous application for a British adoption order made in relation to the child by the same persons was refused by any court unless—

(a)   in refusing the previous application the court directed that this subsection should not apply, or

(b)   it appears to the court that because of a change in circumstances or for any other reason it is proper to proceed with the application.

[(2)   The court may make an adoption order in relation to a child even where it is found that the applicants have, as respects the child, contravened section 51.

(3)   In considering whether to make an adoption order or an order under section 18(1), the court shall regard the welfare of the child concerned as its paramount consideration and shall not make the order in question unless it considers that it would be better for the child that it should do so than that it should not.]

25   Interim orders
(1)   Where on an application for an adoption order the requirements [—
    (a)   of section 16(1); and
    (b)   in a case where the child was not placed with the applicant by an adoption agency, of section 22(1),
are complied with], the court may postpone the determination of the application and make an order giving parental [responsibilities and parental rights] to the applicants for a probationary period not exceeding 2 years upon such terms for the aliment of the child and otherwise as the court thinks fit.
(2)   Where the probationary period specified in an order under subsection (1) is less than 2 years, the court may by a further order extend the period to a duration not exceeding 2 years in all.

[25A   Timetable for resolving question as to whether agreement to adoption order etc should be dispensed with
In proceedings in which the question arises as to whether the court is satisfied as is mentioned in section 16(1)(b)(ii) or 18(1)(b), the court shall, with a view to determining the question without delay—
    (a)   draw up a timetable specifying periods within which certain steps must be taken in relation to those proceedings; and
    (b)   give such directions as it considers appropriate for the purpose of ensuring, so far as is reasonably practicable, that the timetable is adhered to.]

[. . .]

PART III
CARE AND PROTECTION OF CHILDREN AWAITING ADOPTION

Restrictions on removal of children

27   Restrictions on removal where adoption agreed or application made under s 18
[(1)   Where—
    (a)   an adoption agency has placed a child with a person with a view to his being adopted by the person; and
    (b)   the consent of each parent or guardian of the child has been duly obtained to that placement (whether or not in knowledge of the identity of the person),
any such parent or guardian shall not be entitled to remove the child from the care and possession of the person without the leave either of the adoption agency or of the court.
(2)   The reference in subsection (1) to consent having been duly obtained is to its having been obtained in accordance with such regulations as may be made by the Secretary of State for the purposes of this section.]
(3)   Any person who [removes a child in contravention of subsection (1)] shall be guilty of an offence and liable on summary conviction to imprisonment for a term not exceeding 3 months or a fine not exceeding [level 5 on the standard scale] or both.
    [. . .]

28   Restrictions on removal where applicant has provided home for 5 years
(1)   While an application for an adoption order in respect of a child made by the person with whom the child has had his home for the 5 years preceding the application is pending, no person is entitled, against the will of the applicant, to remove the child from the applicant's [care and possession] except with the leave of the court or under authority conferred by any enactment or on the arrest of the child.
(2)   Where a person ('the prospective adopter') gives notice to the local auth-

ority within whose area he has his home that he intends to apply for an adoption order in respect of a child who for the preceding 5 years has had his home with the prospective adopter, no person is entitled, against the will of the prospective adopter, to remove the child from the prospective adopter's [care and possession] except with the leave of a court or under authority conferred by any enactment or on the arrest of the child, before—

(a)   the prospective adopter applies for the adoption order, or

(b)   the period of 3 months from the receipt of the notice by the local authority expires,

whichever occurs first.

(3)   In any case where subsection (1) or (2) applies and—

(a)   the child was in the care of a local authority before he began to have his home with the applicant or, as the case may be, the prospective adopter, and

(b)   the child remains in the care of a local authority,

the authority in whose care the child is shall not remove the child from the care and possession of the applicant or of the prospective adopter except in accordance with section 30 or 31 or with leave of a court.

(4)   Subsection (3) does not apply where the removal of the child is authorised, [under or by virtue of Chapter 2 or 3 or Part II of the Children (Scotland) Act 1995].

(5)   A local authority which receives such notice as is mentioned in subsection (2) in respect of a child whom the authority know to be in the care of another local authority [. . .] shall, not more than 7 days after the receipt of the notice, inform that other authority [. . .] in writing that they have received the notice.

(6)   Subsection (2) does not apply to any further notice served by the prospective adopter on any local authority in respect of the same child during the period referred to in paragraph (b) of that subsection or within 28 days after its expiry.

(7)   Any person who contravenes subsection (1) or (2) shall be guilty of an offence and liable on summary conviction to imprisonment for a term not exceeding 3 months or a fine not exceeding [level 5 on the standard scale] or both.

[. . .]

(10)   The Secretary of State may by order amend subsection (1) or (2) to substitute a different period for the period of 5 years mentioned in that subsection (or the period which, by a previous order under this subsection, was substituted for that period).

(11)   In subsections (2) and (3) 'a court' means a court having jurisdiction to make adoption orders.

29   Return of child taken away in breach of s 27 or 28

(1)   An authorised court may on the application of a person from whose [care and possession] a child has been removed in breach of section 27 or 28 [or section 27 or 28 of the Adoption Act 1976 or article 28 or 29 of the Adoption (Northern Ireland) Order 1987] order the person who has so removed the child to return the child to the applicant.

(2)   An authorised court may on the application of a person who has reasonable grounds for believing that another person is intending to remove a child from the applicant's [care and possession] in breach of section 27 or 28 [or section 27 or 28 of the Adoption Act 1976 or article 28 or 29 of the Adoption (Northern Ireland) Order 1987] by order direct that other person not to remove the child from the applicant's [care and possession] in breach of section 27 or 28 [or section 27 or 28 of the Adoption Act 1976 or article 28 or 29 of the Adoption (Northern Ireland) Order 1987].

30   Return of children placed for adoption by adoption agencies

(1)   Subject to subsection (2), at any time after a child has been delivered into the care and possession of any person in pursuance of arrangements made by [a

registered adoption service, an appropriate voluntary organisation (as defined by
section 1(5) of the Adoption Act 1976 (c 36) or a] local authority for the adoption of
the child by that person, and before an adoption order has been made on the
application of that person in respect of the child—

(a)   that person may give notice in writing to the [service, organisation] or
authority of his intention not to retain the care and possession of the child; or

(b)   the [service, organisation] or authority may cause notice in writing to be
given to that person of their intention not to allow the child to remain in his care
and possession.

(2)   No notice under paragraph (b) of subsection (1) shall be given in respect of
a child in relation to whom an application has been made for an adoption order
except with the leave of the court to which the application has been made.

(3)   Where a notice is given [under subsection (1)(a) or (b)], or where an application for an adoption order made by any person in respect of a child placed in his
care and possession by [a registered adoption service, an appropriate voluntary
organisation such as is mentioned in that subsection or a local authority] is refused
by the court or withdrawn, that person shall, within 7 days after the date on which
notice was given or the application refused or withdrawn, as the case may be,
cause the child to be returned to [that service, organisation] or authority, who shall
receive the child.

(4)   Where the period specified in an interim order made under section 25
(whether as originally made or as extended under subsection (2) of that section)
expires without an adoption order having been made in respect of the child, subsection (3) shall apply as if the application for an adoption order upon which the
interim order was made had been refused at the expiration of that period.

(5)   It shall be sufficient compliance with the requirements of subsection (3) if
the child is delivered to, and is received by a suitable person nominated for the
purpose by the [service, organisation] or local authority.

(6)   Where an application for an adoption order is refused the court may, if it
thinks fit at any time before the expiry of the period of 7 days mentioned in subsection (3), order that period to be extended to a duration, not exceeding 6 weeks,
specified in the order.

(7)   Any person who contravenes the provisions of this section shall be guilty of
an offence and liable on summary conviction to imprisonment for a term not
exceeding 3 months or to a fine not exceeding [level 5 on the standard scale] or to
both; and the court by which the offender is convicted may order the child in
respect of whom the offence is committed to be returned to his parent or guardian
or to the [service organisation] or local authority which made the arrangements
referred to in subsection (1).

31   Application of s 30 where child not placed for adoption

(1)   Where a person gives notice in pursuance of section 22(1) to the local authority within whose area he has his home of his intention to apply for an adoption
order in respect of a child who is for the time being in the care of a local authority,
not being a child who was delivered into the care and possession of that person in
pursuance of such arrangements as are mentioned in section 30(1), that section
shall apply as if the child had been so delivered, except that where the application
is refused by the court or withdrawn the child need not be returned to the local
authority in whose care he is unless that authority so require.

(2)   Where notice of intention is given as aforesaid in respect of any child who
is for the time being in the care of a local authority then, until the application for
an adoption order has been made and disposed of, and right of the local authority
to require the child to be returned to them otherwise than in pursuance of section
30 shall be suspended.

(3)   While the child remains in the care and possession of the person by whom
the notice is given no contribution shall be payable (whether under a contribution

order or otherwise) in respect of the child by any person liable under section 78 of the Social Work (Scotland) Act 1968 to make contributions in respect of him (but without prejudice to the recovery of any sum due at the time the notice is given), unless 12 weeks have elapsed since the giving of the notice without the application being made or the application has been refused by the court or withdrawn.

[. . .]

PART IV
STATUS OF ADOPTED CHILDREN

38   Meaning of 'adoption order' in Part IV

(1)   In this Part 'adoption order' means—

(a)   an adoption order within the meaning of section 65(1);

(b)   an adoption order under the Children Act 1975, the Adoption Act 1958, the Adoption Act 1950 or any enactment repealed by the Adoption Act 1950;

(c)   an order effecting an adoption made in England, Wales, Northern Ireland, the Isle of Man or any of the Channel Islands;

[(cc) a Convention adoption;]

(d)   an 'overseas adoption' within the meaning of section 65(2); or

(e)   any other adoption recognised by the law of Scotland; and cognate expressions shall be construed accordingly.

(2)   The definition of adoption order includes, where the context admits, an adoption order which took effect before the commencement of the Children Act 1975.

39   Status conferred by adoption

[(1)   A child who is the subject of an adoption order shall be treated in law—

(a)   where the adopters are a married couple, as if—

(i)   he had been born as a legitimate child of the marriage (whether or not he was in fact born after the marriage was constituted); and

(ii)   [subject to subsection (2A)] he were not the child of any person other than the adopters;

(b)   where the adoption order is made by virtue of section 15(1)(aa) as if—

(i)   he had been born as a legitimate child of the marriage between the adopter and the natural parent to whom the adopter is married (whether or not he was in fact born after the marriage was constituted); and

(ii)   [subject to subsection (2A)] he were not the child of any person other than the adopter and that natural parent; and

(c)   in any other case, as if—

(i)   he had been born as a legitimate child of the adopter; and

(ii)   [subject to subsection (2A)] he were not the child of any person other than the adopter.]

(2)   Where [a] child has been adopted by one of his natural parents as sole adoptive parent and the adopter thereafter marries the other natural parent, subsection (1) shall not affect any enactment or rule of law whereby, by virtue of the marriage, the child is rendered the legitimate child of both natural parents.

[(2A)   Where, in the case of a child adopted under a Convention adoption, the Court of Session is satisfied, on an application under this subsection—

(a)   that under the law of the country in which the adoption was effected the adoption is not a full adoption;

(b)   that the consents referred to in Article 4(c) and (d) of the Convention have not been given for a full adoption, or that the United Kingdom is not the receiving State (within the meaning of Article 2 of the Convention); and

(c)   that it would be more favourable to the child for a direction to be given under this subsection,

the Court may direct that sub-paragraph (ii) of, as the case may be, paragraph (a),

(b) or (c) of subsection (1) shall not apply, or shall not apply to such extent as may be specified in the direction: and in this subsection 'full adoption' means an adoption by virtue of which the child falls to be treated in law as if he were not the child of any person other than the adopters or adopter.]

(3)   This section has effect—
(a)   in the case of an adoption before 1st January 1976, from that date, and
(b)   in the case of any other adoption, from the date of the adoption.

(4)   Subject to the provisions of this Part, this section—
(a) applies for the construction of enactments or instruments passed or made before or after the commencement of this Act so far as the context admits; and
(b) does not affect things done or events occurring before the adoption or, where the adoption took place before 1st January 1976, before that date.

(5)   This section has effect subject to the provisions of section 44.

[. . .]

41   Miscellaneous enactments

(1)   Section 39 does not apply in determining the forbidden degrees of consanguinity and affinity in respect of the law relating to marriage [, to the eligibility of persons to register as civil partners of each other] or in respect of the crime of incest, except that, on the making of an adoption order, the adopter and the child shall be deemed, for all time coming, to be within the said forbidden degrees in respect of the law relating to marriage [and to such eligibility and to incest].

(2)   [S]ection 39 does not apply for the purposes of any provision of—
(a)   [the British Nationality Act 1981],
(b)   the Immigration Act 1971,
(c)   any instrument having effect under an enactment within paragraph (a) or (b), or
(d)   any other law for the time being in force which determines [British citizenship, British Overseas Territories citizenship, the status of a British National (Overseas) or British Overseas citizenship].

42   Pensions

Section 39(1) does not affect entitlement to a pension which is payable to or for the benefit of a child and is in payment at the time of his adoption.

43   Insurance

Where a child is adopted whose natural parent has effected an insurance with a friendly society or a collecting society or an industrial insurance company for the payment on the death of the child of money for funeral expenses, the rights and liabilities under the policy shall by virtue of the adoption be transferred to the adoptive parents who shall for the purposes of the enactments relating to such societies and companies be treated as the person who took out the policy.

44   Effect of s 39 on succession and *inter vivos* deed

Section 39 (status conferred by adoption) does not affect the existing law relating to adopted persons in respect of—
(a)   the succession to a deceased person (whether testate or intestate), and
(b)   the disposal of property by virtue of any *inter vivos* deed.

PART V
REGISTRATION AND REVOCATION OF ADOPTION ORDERS AND CONVENTION ADOPTIONS

45   Adopted Children Register

(1)   The Registrar General for Scotland shall maintain at the General Register Office a register, to be called the Adopted Children Register, in which [such entries as may be—
(a)   directed to be made in it by adoption orders, or

(b)   required to be made under Schedule 1 to this Act,
and no other entries, shall be made.]

(2)   An extract of any entry in the Adopted Children Register maintained under this section, if purporting to be sealed or stamped with the seal of the General Register Office, shall, without any further or other proof of that entry, be received as evidence of the adoption to which it relates and, where the entry contains a record of the date of the birth or the country of the birth of the adopted person, shall also be received as aforesaid as evidence of that date or country.

(3)   The Registrar General for Scotland shall cause an index of the Adopted Children Register maintained under this section to be made and kept in the General Register Office; and the Registrar General for Scotland shall—
(a)   cause a search to be made of that index on behalf of any person or per-mit that person to search the index himself, and
(b)   issue to any person an extract of any entry in that register which that person may require,
in all respects upon and subject to the same terms, conditions and regulations as to payment of fees and otherwise as are applicable under the Registration of Births, Deaths and Marriages (Scotland) Act 1965 in respect of searches in other indexes kept in the General Register Office and in respect of the supply from that office of extracts of entries in the registers of births, deaths and marriages.

(4)   The Registrar General for Scotland shall, in addition to the Adopted Children Register and the index thereto, keep such other registers and books, and make such entries therein, as may be necessary to record and make traceable the connection between any entry in the register of births which has been marked 'Adopted' pursuant to paragraph 1 of Schedule 1 or any enactment at the time in force and any corresponding entry in the Adopted Children Register maintained under this section.

(5)   The registers and books kept under subsection (4) shall not be, nor shall any index thereof be, open to public inspection or search, nor, except under an order of the Court of Session or a sheriff, shall the Registrar General for Scotland furnish any information contained in or any copy or extract from any such registers or books to any person other than an adopted person who has attained the age of [16] years and to whom that information, copy or extract relates or a local authority [Board or adoption society falling within subsection (6) which is providing counselling for that adopted person.

(6)   Where the Registrar General for Scotland furnishes an adopted person with information under subsection (5), he shall advise that person that counselling ser-vices are available—
(a)   if the person is in Scotland—
(i)   from the local authority in whose area he is living;
(ii)   where the adoption order relating to him was made in Scotland, from the local authority in whose area the court which made the order sat; or
(iii)   from any other local authority in Scotland;
(b)   if the person is in England and Wales—
(i)   from the local authority in whose area he is living;
(ii)   where the adoption order relating to him was made in England and Wales, from the local authority in whose area the court which made the order sat; or
(iii)   from any other local authority in England and Wales;
(c)   if the person is in Northern Ireland—
(i)   from the Board in whose area he is living;
(ii)   where the adoption order relating to him was made in Northern Ireland, from the Board in whose area the court which made the order sat; or
(iii)   from any other Board;
(d)   if the person is in the United Kingdom and his adoption was arranged by
[(i)   a registered adoption service, from that service;

(ii)   an appropriate voluntary organisation (as defined by section 1(5) of the Adoption Act 1976 (c 36)), from that organisation; or
(iii)   an adoption society registered under Article 4 of the Adoption (Northern Ireland) Order 1987, from that society.]
(6A)   Where an adopted person who is in Scotland—
(a)   is furnished with information under subsection (5); or
(b)   applies for information under—
(i)   section 51(1) of the Adoption Act 1976; or
(ii)   Article 54 of the Adoption (Northern Ireland) Order 1987,
any body mentioned in subsection (6B) to which the adopted person applies for counselling shall have a duty to provide counselling for him.
(6B)   The bodies referred to in subsection (6A) are—
(a)   any local authority falling within subsection (6)(a); and
(b)   [any registered adoption service, or any voluntary organisation or adoption society mentioned in subsection (6)(d)(ii) or (iii) insofar as (by virtue of section 11(2) of this Act) that organisation or society is acting as an adoption society in Scotland.]
(7)   where an adopted person has arranged to receive counselling from—
[(a)   a local authority or Board; or
(b)   a service, organisation or society mentioned in subsection (6)(d),]
the Registrar General for Scotland shall, on receipt of a request from the local authority, [Board, service, organisation or society], and on payment of the appropriate fee, send to [them or it] an extract of the entry relating to the adopted person in the register of births.
(8)   The provisions of the Registration of Births, Deaths and Marriages (Scotland) Act 1965 with regard to the correction of errors in entries shall apply to the Adopted Children Register maintained by the Registrar General for Scotland and to registration therein in like manner as they apply to any register of births and to registration therein.
(9)   Schedule 1 to this Act, which, among other things provides for the registration of adoptions and the amendment of adoption orders, shall have effect.
[(10)   In this section—
'Board' means a Health and Social Services Board established under Article 16 of the Health and Personal Social Services (Northern Ireland) Order 1972; and
'local authority', in relation to England and Wales, means the council of a county (other than a metropolitan county), a metropolitan district, a London borough or the Common Council of the City of London.]

46   Revocation of adoptions on legitimation

(1)   Where the natural parents of [a] child, one of whom has adopted him in Scotland, have subsequently married each other, the court by which the adoption order was made may, on the application of any of the parties concerned, revoke that order. [. . .]

47   Annulment etc of overseas adoptions

(1)   The Court of Session may, upon an application under this subsection, by order annul a regulated adoption or an adoption effected by a Convention adoption order—
(a)   on the ground that at the relevant time the adoption was prohibited by a notified provision, if under the internal law then in force in the country of which the adopter was then a national or the adopters were then nationals the adoption could have been impugned on that ground;
(b)   on the ground that at the relevant time the adoption contravened provisions relating to consents of the internal law relating to adoption of the country of which the adopted person was then a national, if under that law the adoption could then have been impugned on that ground;
(c)   on any other ground on which the adoption can be impugned under the

law for the time being in force in the country in which the adoption was effected.

(2) The Court of Session may, upon an application under this subsection—

(a) order that an overseas adoption or a determination shall cease to be valid in Great Britain on the ground that the adoption or determination is contrary to public policy or that the authority which purported to authorise the adoption or make the determination was not competent to entertain the case;

(b) decide the extent, if any, to which a determination has been affected by a subsequent determination.

(3) Any court in Great Britain may, in any proceedings in that court, decide that an overseas adoption or a determination shall, for the purposes of those proceedings, be treated as invalid in Great Britain on either of the grounds mentioned in subsection (2).

(4) An order or decision of the High Court on an application under subsection (2) of section 53 of the Adoption Act 1976 shall be recognised and have effect as if it were an order or decision of the Court of Session on an application under subsection (2) of this section.

(5) Except as provided by this section [. . .] the validity of [a Convention adoption, a Convention adoption order,] an overseas adoption or a determination shall not be impugned in Scotland in proceedings in any court.

48 Provisions supplementary to ss 46(2) and 47

(1) Any application for an order under section 47 or a decision under section 47(2)(b) shall be made in the prescribed manner and within such period, if any, as may be prescribed.

(2) No application shall be made under section [. . .] 47(1) in respect of an adoption unless immediately before the application is made the person adopted or the adopter habitually resides in Scotland or, as the case may be, both adopters habitually reside there.

(3) In deciding in pursuance of section 47 whether such an authority as is mentioned in section 53 was competent to entertain a particular case, a court shall be bound by any finding of fact made by the authority and stated by the authority to be so made for the purpose of determining whether the authority was competent to entertain the case.

(4) In section 47—

'determination' means such a determination as is mentioned in section 53;

[. . .]

PART VI

MISCELLANEOUS AND SUPPLEMENTAL

49 Adoption of children abroad

(1) Where on an application made in relation to a child by a person who is not domiciled in England and Wales or Scotland [or Northern Ireland] an authorised court is satisfied that he intends to adopt the child under the law of or within the country in which the applicant is domiciled, the court may, subject to the following provisions of this section, make an order [transferring to him the parental responsibilities and parental rights in relation] to the child.

(2) The provisions of Part II relating to adoption orders, except sections 12(1), 14(2), 15(2), 17 to 21 and 25, shall apply in relation to orders under this section as they apply in relation to adoption orders subject to the modification that in section 13(1) for '19' and '13' there are substituted '32' and '26' respectively.

(3) Section 45 and paragraphs 1 and 2(1) and (3) of Schedule 1 shall apply in relation to an order under this section as they apply in relation to an adoption order except that any entry in the register of births or the Adopted Children Register which is required to be marked in consequence of the making of an order under this section shall, in lieu of being marked with the word 'Adopted'

or 'Re-adopted' (with or without the addition of the words '(England)' [or '(Northern Ireland)',] be marked with the words 'Proposed foreign adoption' or 'Proposed foreign re-adoption', as the case may require.

[. . .]

50   Restriction on removal of children for adoption outside Great Britain

(1)   Except under the authority of an order under section 49, or under section 55 of the Adoption Act 1976, [or article 57 of the Adoption (Northern Ireland) Order 1987] it shall not be lawful or any person to take or send a child who is a British subject or a citizen of the Republic of Ireland out of Great Britain to any place outside the United Kingdom, the Channel Islands and the Isle of Man with a view to the adoption of the child by any person not being a parent or guardian or relative of the child; and any person who takes or sends a child out of Great Britain to any place in contravention of this subsection, or makes or takes part in any arrangements for transferring the care and possession of a child to any person for that purpose, shall be guilty of an offence and liable on summary conviction to imprisonment for a term not exceeding 3 months or to a fine not exceeding [level 5 on the standard scale] or to both.

(2)   In any proceedings under this section, a report by a British consular officer or a deposition made before a British consular officer and authenticated under the signature of that officer shall, upon proof that the officer or the deponent cannot be found in the United Kingdom, be sufficient evidence of the matters stated therein, and it shall not be necessary to prove the signature or official character of the person who appears to have signed any such report or deposition.

(3)   A person shall be deemed to take part in arrangements for transferring the care and possession of a child to a person for the purpose referred to in subsection (1) if—

(a)   he facilitates the placing of the child in the care and possession of that person; or

(b)   he initiates or takes part in any negotiations of which the purpose or effect is the conclusion of any agreement or the making of any arrangement therefor, or if he causes another person to do so.

[50A   Restriction on bringing children into the United Kingdom for adoption

(1)   A person habitually resident in the British Islands who at any time brings into the United Kingdom for the purpose of adoption a child who is habitually resident outside those Islands shall be guilty of an offence unless such require- ments as may be prescribed by regulations made by the Secretary of State are satisfied either—

(a)   before that time; or

(b)   within such period beginning with that time as may be so prescribed.

(2)   Subsection (1) does not apply where the child is brought into the United Kingdom for the purpose of adoption by a parent, guardian or relative.

(3)   A person guilty of an offence under this section is liable on summary con- viction to imprisonment for a term not exceeding three months, or a fine not exceeding level 5 on the standard scale, or both.

(4)   Proceedings for an offence under this section may be brought within a period of six months from the date on which evidence sufficient in the opinion of the prosecutor to warrant the proceedings came to his knowledge; but no such proceedings shall be brought by virtue of this subsection more than three years after the commission of the offence.]

51   Prohibition on certain payments

(1)   Subject to the provisions of this section [and of section 51A(3)], it shall not be lawful to make or give to any person any payment or reward for or in con- sideration of—

(a)   the adoption by that person of a child;

(b)   the grant by that person of any agreement or consent required in connection with the adoption of a child;
(c)   the transfer by that person of the care and possession of a child with a
view to the adoption of the child; or
(d)   the making by that person of any arrangements for the adoption of a
child.
(2)   Any person who makes or gives, or agrees or offers to make or give, any
payment or reward prohibited by this section, or who receives or agrees to receive
or attempts to obtain any such payment or reward, shall be guilty of an offence
and liable on summary conviction to imprisonment for a term not exceeding 3
months or to a fine not exceeding [level 5 on the standard scale] or to both; and
[without prejudice to any power which the court has to make any order in relation
to the child as respects whom the offence was committed, it may order him] to be
removed to a place of safety until he can be restored to his parents or guardian or
until other arrangements can be made for him.
(3)   This section does not apply to any payment made to an adoption agency by
a parent or guardian of a child or by a person who adopts or proposes to adopt a
child, being a payment in respect of expenses reasonably incurred by the agency in
connection with the adoption of the child, or to any payment or reward authorised
by the court to which an application for an adoption order in respect of a child is
made.
(4)   This section does not apply to—
(a)   any payment made by an adoption agency to a person who has applied
or proposes to apply to a court for an adoption order or an order under section
49, being a payment of or towards any legal or medical expenses incurred or to
be incurred by that person in connection with the application; or
(b)   any payment made by an adoption agency to another adoption agency in
consideration of the placing of a child in the care and possession of any person
with a view to the child's adoption; or
(c)   any payment made by an adoption agency to a voluntary organisation
for the time being approved for the purposes of this paragraph by the Secretary
of State as a fee for the services of that organisation in putting that adoption
agency into contact with another adoption agency with a view to the making of
arrangements between the adoption agencies for the adoption of a child.
(5)   [Subject to section 51B] if an adoption agency submits to the Secretary of
State a scheme for the payment by the agency of allowances to persons who have
adopted or intend to adopt a child where arrangements for the adoption were
made, or are to be made, by that agency, and the Secretary of State approves the
scheme, this section shall not apply to any payment made in accordance with the
scheme [(including any such payment made by virtue of section 51B)].
(6)   The Secretary of State, in the case of a scheme approved by him under subsection (5), may at any time . . . revoke the scheme.
   [. . .]

[51A   Adoption allowances schemes

(1)   Subject to subsection (2), an adoption agency which is—
(a)   a local authority shall, within such period after the coming into force of
this section as the Secretary of State may by order direct;
(b)   [a registered adoption service] may,
prepare a scheme (in this section and in section 51B referred to as an 'adoption
allowances scheme') for the payment by the agency of allowances to any person
who has adopted, or intends to adopt, a child in any case where arrangements for
the adoption were made, or as the case may be are to be made, by the agency.
(2)   The Secretary of State may make regulations as respects adoption allowances schemes; and without prejudice to the generality of this subsection such
regulations may in particular make provision as to—

(a)   the procedure to be followed by an agency in determining whether a person should be paid an allowance;

(b)   the circumstances in which an allowance may be paid;

(c)   the factors to be taken into account in determining the amount of an allowance;

(d)   the procedure for review, variation and termination of allowances;

(e)   the information about allowances which is to be supplied by an agency to a person who intends to adopt a child; and

(f)   the procedure to be followed by an agency in drawing up, in making alterations to, or in revoking and replacing, an adoption allowances scheme.

(3)   Section 51(1) shall not apply to any payment made in accordance with an adoption allowances scheme (including any such payment made by virtue of section 51B).

51B   Transitional provisions as respects adoption allowances

After the coming into force of section 51A—

(a)   no scheme for the payment of allowances shall be submissible under subsection (5) of section 51; and

(b)   a scheme which has been approved under that subsection of that section shall forthwith be revoked under subsection (6)(b) of that section, so however that where a person was before its revocation receiving payments made in accordance with that scheme he may continue to receive payments so made which, had there been no revocation, would have fallen to be made to him or he may agree to receive, instead of the continued payments, payments made in accordance with an adoption allowances scheme.]

52   Restriction on advertisements

(1)   It shall not be lawful for any advertisement to be published indicating—

(a)   that the parent or guardian of a child desires to cause a child to be adopted; or

(b)   that a person desires to adopt a child; or

(c)   that any person (not being an adoption agency) is willing to make arrangements for the adoption of a child.

(2)   Any person who causes to be published or knowingly publishes an advertisement in contravention of the provisions of this section shall be guilty of an offence and liable on summary conviction to a fine not exceeding [level 5 on the standard scale].

53   Effect of determination and orders made in England and Wales and overseas in adoption proceedings

[(1)   Where—

(a)   an authority of a Convention country (other than the United Kingdom) having power under the law of that country—

(i)   to authorise, or review the authorisation of, a Convention adoption; or

(ii)   to give or review a decision revoking or annulling such an adoption or a Convention adoption order; or

(b)   an authority of any of the Channel Islands, the Isle of Man or any colony having power under the law of that territory—

(i)   to authorise, or review the authorisation of, a Convention adoption or an adoption effected in that territory; or

(ii)   to give or review a decision revoking or annulling such an adoption or a Convention adoption order,

makes a determination in the exercise of that power, then, subject to section 47 and any subsequent determination having effect under this subsection, the determination shall have effect in Scotland for the purpose of effecting, confirming or terminating the adoption in question or confirming its termination as the case may be.]

54 Evidence of adoption in England, Wales and Northern Ireland
Any document which is receivable as evidence of any matter—
   (a)   in England and Wales under section 50(2) of the Adoption Act 1976; or
   (b)   in Northern Ireland under [article 63(1) of the Adoption (Northern Ireland) Order 1987];
shall also be so receivable in Scotland.

55 Evidence of agreement and consent
   (1)   Any agreement or consent which is required by this Act to be given to the making of an order or application for an order [. . .] may be given in writing, and, if the document signifying the agreement or consent is witnessed in accordance with rules, it shall be sufficient evidence without further proof of the signature of the person by whom it was executed.
   (2)   A document signifying such agreement or consent which purports to be witnessed in accordance with rules, shall be presumed to be so witnessed, and to have been executed and witnessed on the date and at the place specified in the document, unless the contrary is proved.

56 Courts
   (1)   In this Act, 'authorised court', as respects an application for an order relating to a child, shall be construed as follows.
   (2)   Subject to subsection [. . .] (5), if the child is in Scotland when the application is made, the following are authorised courts—
   (a)   the Court of Session;
   (b)   the sheriff court of the sheriffdom within which the child is.
   (3)   If, in the case of an application for an adoption order or for an order freeing a child for adoption, the child is not in Great Britain when the application is made, the Court of Session is the authorised court.
   [. . .]
   (5)   Subsection (2) does not apply in the case of an application under section 29 but for the purposes of such an application the following are authorised courts—
   (a)   if there is pending in respect of the child an application for an adoption order or an order freeing him for adoption, the court in which that application is pending;
   (b)   in any other case—
      (i)   the Court of Session;
      (ii)   the sheriff court of the sheriffdom within which the applicant resides.

57 Proceedings to be in private
All proceedings before the court under Part II, section 29 or section 49 shall be heard and determined in private unless the court otherwise directs.

58 Curators ad litem and reporting officers
   (1)   For the purpose of any application for an adoption order or an order freeing a child for adoption or an order under section 20 or 49, rules shall provide for the appointment, in such cases as are prescribed—
   (a)   of a person to act as curator ad litem of the child upon the hearing of the application, with the duty of safeguarding the interests of the child in the prescribed manner;
   (b)   of a person to act as reporting officer for the purpose of witnessing agreements to adoption and performing such other duties as the rules may prescribe.
   (2)   A person who is employed—
   (a)   in the case of an application for an adoption order, by the adoption agency by whom the child was placed; or
   (b)   in the case of an application for an order freeing a child for adoption, by the adoption agency by whom the application was made; or

(c)   in the case of an application under section 20, by the adoption agency with the parental [responsibilities and parental rights in relation] to the child,

shall not be appointed to act as curator *ad litem* or reporting officer for the purposes of the application but, subject to that, the same person may if the court thinks fit be both curator *ad litem* and reporting officer.

(3)   Rules may provide for the reporting officer to be appointed before the application is made.

59   Rules of procedure

(1)   Subject to subsection (4), provision shall be made by act of sederunt with regard to any matter to be prescribed under this Act and generally with regard to all matters of procedure and incidental matters arising out of this Act and for carrying this Act into effect.

(2)   In the case of—

(a)   an application for an adoption order in relation to a child who is not free for adoption;

(b)   an application for an order freeing a child for adoption, rules shall require every person who can be found and whose agreement or consent to the making of the order is required to be given or dispensed with under this Act to be notified of a date and place where he may be heard on the application and of the fact that, unless he wishes or the court requires, he need not attend.

(3)   In the case of an application under section 49, rules shall require every person who can be found, and whose agreement to the making of the order would be required if the application were for an adoption order (other than a Convention adoption order), to be notified as aforesaid.

(4)   This section does not apply to sections 9, 10 and 11.

60   Orders, rules and regulations

(1)   Any power to make orders or regulations conferred by this Act on the Secretary of State or the Registrar General for Scotland shall be exercisable by statutory instrument.

(2)   A statutory instrument containing regulations made under any provision of this Act, [. . .] shall be subject to annulment in pursuance of a resolution of either House of Parliament.

(3)   An order under section 28(10) shall not be made unless a draft of the order has been approved by resolution of each House of Parliament.

(4)   An order made under any provision of this Act may be revoked or varied by a subsequent order under that provision.

(5)   Any order, rule or regulation made under this Act may make different provision for different circumstances and may contain such incidental and transitional provisions as the authority making the order or regulation considers expedient.

(6)   The Registrar General for Scotland shall not make regulations under paragraph 1(1) [or 3] of Schedule 1 except with the approval of the Secretary of State.

(7)   The Statutory Instruments Act 1946 shall apply to a statutory instrument containing regulations made for the purposes of this Act by the Registrar General for Scotland as if the regulations had been made by a Minister of the Crown.

61   Offences by bodies corporate

Where an offence under this Act committed by a body corporate is proved to have been committed with the consent or connivance of or to be attributable to any neglect on the part of, any director, manager, member of the committee, secretary or other officer of the body, he as well as the body shall be deemed to be guilty of that offence and shall be liable to be proceeded against and punished accordingly.

62   Service of notices etc

Any notice or information required to be given under this Act may be given by post.

[. . .]

64 Internal law of a country

(1) In this Act 'internal law' in relation to any country means the law applicable in a case where no question arises as to the law in force in any other country.

(2) In any case where the internal law of a country falls to be ascertained for the purposes of this Act by any court and there are in force in that country two or more systems of internal law, the relevant system shall be ascertained in accordance with any rule in force throughout that country indicating which of the systems is relevant in the case in question or, if there is no such rule, shall be the system appearing to that court to be most closely connected with the case.

65 Interpretation

(1) In this Act, unless the context otherwise requires—

'adoption agency' in sections 11, 13, 18 to 23 and 27 includes an adoption agency within the meaning of section 1 of the Adoption Act 1976 (adoption agencies in England and Wales) [and an adoption agency within the meaning of article 3 of the Adoption (Northern Ireland) Order 1987 (adoption agencies in Northern Ireland)];

['adoption order'—

(a)   means an order under section 12(1); and

(b)   in sections 12(3) and (4), 18 to 20, 27, 28, 30 [and 31] and in the definition of 'British adoption order' in this subsection includes an order under section 12 of the Adoption Act 1976 and Article 12 of the Adoption (Northern Ireland) Order 1987 (adoption orders in England and Wales and Northern Ireland respectively); and

(c)   in sections 27, 28, 30 [and 31] includes an order under section 49, section 55 of the Adoption Act 1976 and Article 57 of the Adoption (Northern Ireland) Order 1987 (orders in relation to children being adopted abroad);]

'adoption society' means a body of persons whose functions consist of or include the making of arrangements for [, or in connection with,] the adoption of children;

[. . .]

'authorised court' shall be construed in accordance with section 56;

'body of persons' means any body of persons, whether incorporated or unincorporated;

['British adoption order' means—

(a)   an adoption order as defined in this subsection; and

(b)   an order under any provision for the adoption of a child effected under the law of any British territory outside the United Kingdom;]

'British territory' means, for the purposes of any provision of this Act, any of the following countries, that is to say, Great Britain, Northern Ireland, the Channel Islands, the Isle of Man and a colony, being a country designated for the purposes of that provision by order of the Secretary of State or, if no country is so designated, any of those countries;

'child', except where used to express a relationship, means a person who has not attained the age of 18 years;

['compulsory measures of supervision' has the same meaning as in Part II of the Children (Scotland) Act 1995;]

['the Convention' means the Convention on Protection of Children and Co-operation in respect of Intercountry Adoption, concluded at the Hague on 29th May 1993;

'Convention adoption' means an adoption effected under the law of a Convention country outside the British Islands, and certified in pursuance of Article 23(1) of the Convention;

'Convention adoption order' means an adoption order made in accordance with section 17;

'Convention country' means any country or territory in which the Convention is in force;]

'England' includes Wales;

'guardian' means—

    (a)   a person appointed by deed or will or by a court of competent juris-diction to be the guardian of the child,

[. . .]

'internal law' has the meaning assigned by section 64;

'local authority' means a [council constituted under section 2 of the Local Government etc (Scotland) Act 1994];

'notice' means a notice in writing;

'order freeing a child for adoption' means an order under section 18 [and in sections 27(2) and 53 includes an order under—

    (a)   section 18 of the Adoption Act 1976; and

    (b)   Article 17 or 18 of the Adoption (Northern Ireland) Order 1987];

'overseas adoption' has the meaning assigned by subsection (2);

['parent' means, irrespective of whether or not they are, or have been, married to each other—

    (a)   the mother of the child, where she has parental responsibilities or parental rights in relation to him;

    (b)   the father of the child where he has such responsibilities or rights; and

    (c)   both of his parents, where both have such responsibilities or rights;

'parental responsibilities' and 'parental rights' have the meanings respectively given by sections 1(3) and 2(4) of the Children (Scotland) Act 1995 (analogous expressions being construed accordingly);]

'place of safety' [has the meaning given by section 93(1) of the Children (Scotland) Act 1995;]

'prescribed' means prescribed by act of sederunt;

['registered adoption service' has the meaning given by section 1(5) of this Act;]

'Registrar General for Scotland' means the Registrar General of Births, Deaths and Marriages for Scotland;

[. . .]

'relative' in relation to a child means a grandparent, brother, sister, uncle or aunt, whether of the full blood or half-blood or by affinity and includes, where the child is illegitimate, the father of the child [where he is not a parent within the meaning of this Act, and any person who would be a relative within the meaning of this definition if the father were such a parent];

'rules' means rules made by act of sederunt;

[. . .]

['supervision requirement' has the same meaning as in Part II of the Children (Scotland) Act 1995;]

'United Kingdom national' means, for the purposes of any provision of this Act, a citizen of the United Kingdom and Colonies satisfying such conditions, if any, as the Secretary of State may by order specify for the purposes of that provision;

'voluntary organisation' means a body, other than a public or local authority, the activities of which are not carried on for profit.

(2)   In this Act 'overseas adoption' means an adoption of such a description as the Secretary of State may by order specify, being a description of adoptions of children appearing to him to be effected under the law of any country outside [the British Islands]; and an order under this subsection may contain provision as to the manner in which evidence of an overseas adoption may be given.

(3)   For the purposes of this Act, a person shall be deemed to make arrangements for the adoption of a child if he enters into or makes any agreement or arrangement for, or for facilitating, the adoption of the child by any other person, whether the adoption is effected, or is intended to be effected, in Great Britain or elsewhere, or if he initiates or takes part in any negotiations of which the purpose

or effect is the conclusion of any agreement or the making of any arrangement therefor, or if he causes another person to, do so [but the making, under section 70 of the Children (Scotland) Act 1995, by a children's hearing of a supervision requirement which, in respect that it provides as to where he is to reside, facilitates his being placed for adoption by an adoption agency, shall not constitute the making of such arrangements].

[(3A) In this Act, in relation to the proposed adoption of a child resident outside the British Islands; references to arrangements for the adoption of a child include references to arrangements for an assessment for the purpose of indicating whether a person is suitable to adopt a child or not.

(3B) In this Act, in relation to—

(a) an adoption proposed to be effected by a Convention adoption order; or

(b) an adoption of a child habitually resident outside the British Islands which is proposed to be effected by an adoption order other than a Convention adoption order,

references to a child placed with any persons by an adoption agency include references to a child who, in pursuance of arrangements made by such an agency, has been adopted by or placed with those persons under the law of a country or territory outside the British Islands.]

(4) Except so far as the context otherwise requires, any reference in this Act to an enactment shall be construed as a reference to that enactment as amended by or under any other enactment, including this Act.

(5) In this Act, except where otherwise indicated—

(a) a reference to a numbered Part, section or Schedule is a reference to the Part or section of, or the Schedule to, this Act so numbered, and

(b) a reference in a section to a numbered subsection is a reference to the subsection of that section so numbered, and

(c) a reference in a section, subsection or Schedule to a numbered paragraph is a reference to the paragraph of that section, subsection or Schedule so numbered.

[(6) Any reference in this Act to a child being in, received into or kept in, care (whether or not such care is expressed as being the care of a local authority and except where the context otherwise requires) shall be taken to be a reference to his being looked after by a local authority and shall be construed in accordance with section 17(6) of the Children (Scotland) Act 1995; and any reference to the authority in whose care a child is, shall be construed accordingly.]

66 Transitional provisions, amendments and repeals

(1) The transitional provisions contained in Schedule 2 shall have effect.

(2) The enactments specified in Schedule 3 shall have effect subject to the amendments specified in that Schedule, being amendments consequential upon the provisions of this Act.

(3) The enactments specified in Schedule 4 are hereby repealed to the extent specified in column 3 of that Schedule.

67 Short title, commencement and extent

(1) This Act may be cited as the Adoption (Scotland) Act 1978.

(2) This Act shall come into force on such date as the Secretary of State may by order appoint and different dates may be appointed for different provisions.

(3) Until the date appointed under subsection (2) for sections 3, 4, 5 and 8, in this Act and in the Adoption Act 1958 'adoption agency' means a local authority or a registered adoption society within the meaning of the said Act of 1958.

(4) This Act shall extend to Scotland only.

SCHEDULES

SCHEDULE 1
REGISTRATION OF ADOPTIONS

Section 45

Registration of adoption orders

1.—(1) Every adoption order shall contain a direction to the Registrar General for Scotland to make in the Adopted Children Register maintained by him an entry recording the adoption in such form as the Registrar General for Scotland may by regulations specify.
[. . .]
(3) For the purposes of compliance with the requirements of sub-paragraph (1)—

(a) where the precise date of the child's birth is not proved to the satisfaction of the court, the court shall determine the probable date of his birth and the date so determined shall be specified in the order as the date of his birth;

(b) where the country of birth of the child is not proved to the satisfaction of the court, then, if it appears probable that the child was born within the United Kingdom, the Channel Islands or the Isle of Man, he shall be treated as having been born in Scotland and in any other case the particulars of the country of birth may be omitted from the order and from the entry in the Adopted Children Register;

and the names to be specified in the order as the name and surname of the child shall be the name or names and surname stated in that behalf in the application for the adoption order, or, if no name or surname is so stated, the original name or names of the child and the surname of the applicant.

(4) There shall be produced with every application for an adoption order in respect of a child whose birth has been registered under the Registration of Births, Deaths and Marriages (Scotland) Act 1965 or under any enactment repealed by that Act an extract of the entry of the birth.

(5) Where on an application to a court for an adoption order in respect of a child (not being a child who has previously been the subject of an adoption order made by a court in Scotland under this Act or any enactment at the time in force) there is proved to the satisfaction of the court the identity of the child with a child to whom an entry in the register of births relates, any adoption order made in pursuance of the application shall contain a direction to the Registrar General for Scotland to cause the entry in that register to be marked with the word 'Adopted'.

(6) Where an adoption order is made in respect of a child who has previously been the subject of an adoption order made by a court in Scotland under this Act or any enactment at the time in force, the order shall contain a direction to the Registrar General for Scotland to cause the previous entry in the Adopted Children Register to be marked with the word 'Re-adopted'.

(7) Where an adoption order is made, the clerk of the court which made the order shall cause the order to be communicated to the Registrar General for Scotland and upon receipt of the communication the Registrar General for Scotland shall cause compliance to be made with the directions contained in the order.

Registration of adoptions in England, Northern Ireland, the Isle of Man and the Channel Islands

2.—(1) Where the Registrar General for Scotland is notified by the Registrar General that an adoption order has been made by a court in England in respect of a child to whom an entry in the register of births or the Adopted Children Register relates, the Registrar General for Scotland shall cause the entry to be marked 'Adopted (England)' or, as the case may be, 'Re-adopted (England)'.

(2)   Where the Registrar General for Scotland is notified by the authority main-taining a register of adoptions in Northern Ireland, the Isle of Man or any of the Channel Islands that an order has been made in that country authorising the adop-tion of a child to whom an entry in the register of births or the Adopted Children Register relates, he shall cause the entry to be marked 'Adopted' or 'Re-adopted', as the case may be, followed by the name in brackets of the country in which the order was made.

(3)   Where, after an entry has been marked under the foregoing provisions of this paragraph, the Registrar General for Scotland is notified as aforesaid that the order has been quashed, that an appeal against the order has been allowed or that the order has been revoked, he shall cause the marking to be cancelled; and an extract of an entry in any register, being an entry the marking of which is can-celled under this sub-paragraph, shall be deemed to be accurate if and only if both the marking and the cancellation are omitted therefrom.

(4)   The foregoing provisions of this paragraph shall apply in relation to orders corresponding to orders under section 49 as they apply in relation to orders authorising the adoption of a child; but any marking of an entry required by virtue of this sub-paragraph shall consist of the words 'proposed foreign adoption' or, as the case may require, 'proposed foreign re-adoption' followed by the name in brackets of the country in which the order was made.

Registration of foreign adoptions

[3.—(1)   If the Registrar General [for Scotland] is satisfied, on an application under this paragraph, that he has sufficient particulars relating to a child adopted under a registrable foreign adoption to enable an entry to be made in the Adopted Children Register for the child—

(a)   he must make the entry accordingly, and

(b)   if he is also satisfied that an entry in the register of births relates to the child, he must secure that the entry in that register is marked 'Adopted' or 'Re-adopted', as the case may be, followed by the name in brackets of the country in which the adoption was effected.

(2)   An entry made in the Adopted Children Register by virtue of this para-graph must be made in the specified form.

(3)   An application under this paragraph must be made, in the specified manner, by a specified person and give the specified particulars.

(4)   In this paragraph—

'registrable foreign adoption' means a Convention or overseas adoption which satisfies specified requirements;

'specified' means specified by regulations made by the Registrar General for Scotland.]

Amendment of orders and rectification of registers

4.—(1)   The court by which an adoption order has been made may, on the application of the adopter or of the adopted person, amend the order by the cor-rection of any error in the particulars contained therein. and may—

(a)   if satisfied on the application of the adopter or the adopted person that within one year beginning with the date of the order any new name has been given to the adopted person (whether in baptism or otherwise), or taken by him, either in lieu of or in addition to a name specified in the particulars required to be entered in the Adopted Children Register in pursuance of the order, amend the order by substituting or adding that name in those particulars, as the case may require;

(b)   if satisfied on the application of any person concerned that a direction for the marking of an entry in the register of births or the Adopted Children

Register included in the order in pursuance of sub-paragraph (5) or (6) of paragraph 1 was wrongly so included, revoke that direction.

(2) Where an adoption order is amended or a direction revoked under sub-paragraph (1), the clerk of the court shall cause the amendment to be communicated in the prescribed manner to the Registrar General for Scotland who shall as the case may require—

(a) cause the entry in the Adopted Children Register to be amended accordingly; or

(b) cause the marking of the entry in the register of births or the Adopted Children Register to be cancelled.

(3) Where an adoption order is quashed or an appeal against an adoption order allowed by any court, the court shall give directions to the Registrar General for Scotland to cancel any entry in the Adopted Children Register, and any marking of an entry in that Register, or the register of births as the case may be, which was effected in pursuance of the order.

(4) If the Registrar General for Scotland is satisfied—

(a) that [a Convention adoption], a Convention adoption order or an overseas adoption has ceased to have effect, whether on annulment or otherwise; or

(b) that any entry or mark was erroneously made in pursuance of paragraph 3 in any register mentioned in that paragraph,

he may cause such alterations to be made in any such register as he considers are required in consequence of the cesser or to correct the error; and where an entry in such a register is amended in pursuance of this sub-paragraph, an extract of the entry shall be deemed to be accurate if and only if it shows the entry as amended but without indicating that it has been amended.

Marking of entries on re-registration of birth

5. Without prejudice to any other provision of this Act where, after an entry in the register of births has been marked in accordance with paragraph 2 or 3, the birth is re-registered under section 20(1) of the Registration of Births, Deaths and Marriages (Scotland) Act 1965 (re-registration of birth in certain cases), the entry made on re-registration shall be marked in the like manner.

Cancellations in registers on legitimation

6. Where an adoption order is revoked under section 46(1) the clerk of the court shall cause the revocation to be communicated in the prescribed manner to the Registrar General for Scotland who shall cause to be cancelled—

(a) the entry in the Adopted Children Register relating to the adopted person; and

(b) the marking with the word 'Adopted' (or, as the case may be, with that word and the word '(England)') of any entry relating to him in the register of births;

and an extract of an entry in any register, being an entry the marking of which is cancelled under this paragraph shall be deemed to be accurate if and only if both the marking and the cancellation are omitted therefrom.

7. In this Schedule, 'Registrar General' means the Registrar General for England and Wales.

SCHEDULE 2
TRANSITIONAL PROVISIONS AND SAVINGS

Section 66

General

1.   In so far as anything done under an enactment repealed by this Act could have been done under a corresponding provision of this Act it shall not be invalidated by the repeal but shall have effect as if done under that provision.

2.   Where any period of time specified in an enactment repealed by this Act is current at the commencement of this Act, this Act shall have effect as if the corresponding provision thereof had been in force when that period began to run.

3.   Nothing in this Act shall affect the enactments repealed by this Act in their operation in relation to offences committed before the commencement of this Act.

4.   Any reference in any enactment or document, whether express or implied, to an enactment repealed by this Act shall, unless the context otherwise requires, be construed as a reference to the corresponding enactment in this Act.

Existing adoption orders

5.—(1)   Without prejudice to paragraph 1, an adoption order made under an enactment at any time before this Act comes into force shall not cease to have effect by virtue only of a repeal effected by this Act.

(2)   Paragraph 4(1) and (2) of Schedule 1 shall apply in relation to an adoption order made before this Act came into force as if the order had been made under section 12, but as if, in sub-paragraph (1)(b) of the said paragraph 4, there were substituted for the reference to paragraph 1(5) and (6) a reference—

(a)   in the case of an order under the Adoption Act 1950, to section 20(4) and (5) of that Act,

(b)   in the case of an order under the Adoption Act 1958, to section 23(4) and (5) of that Act.

(3)   The power of the court under the said paragraph 4(1) to amend an order includes power, in relation to an order made before 1st April 1959, to make on the application of the adopter or adopted person any such amendment of the particulars contained in the order as appears to be required to bring the order into the form in which it would have been made if paragraph 1 of Schedule 1 had applied to the order.

(4)   Section 46(1) and paragraph 6 of Schedule 1 shall apply in relation to an adoption order made under an enactment at any time before this Act came into force as they apply in relation to an adoption order made under this Act.

Payments relating to adoptions

6.   Section 51(8), (9) and (10) shall not have effect if, immediately before section 51 comes into force, there is in force in Scotland an order under section 50(8) of the Adoption Act 1958.

Registers of adoptions

7.   Any register or index to a register kept under the Adoption Act 1958, or any register or index deemed to be part of such a register, shall be deemed to be part of the register or index kept under section 45.

Commencement of Act

8.   An order under section 67(2) may make such transitional provision as appears to the Secretary of State to be necessary or expedient in connection with

the provisions thereby brought into force, including such adaptations of those provisions or any provision of this Act then in force or any provision of the Adoption
Act 1958 or the Children Act 1975 as appear to him to be necessary or expedient in
consequence of the partial operation of this Act.

MATRIMONIAL HOMES (FAMILY PROTECTION) (SCOTLAND) ACT 1981
(1981, c 59)

Protection of occupancy rights of one spouse against the other

1   Right of spouse without title to occupy matrimonial home

(1)   Where, apart from the provisions of this Act, one spouse is entitled, or permitted by a third party, to occupy a matrimonial home (an 'entitled spouse') and
the other spouse is not so entitled or permitted (a 'non-entitled spouse'), the non-
entitled spouse shall, subject to the provisions of this Act, have the following
rights—

     (a)   if in occupation, a right [. . .] to [continue to occupy] the matrimonial
home or any part of it by the entitled spouse;

     (b)   if not in occupation, a right to enter into and occupy the matrimonial
home.

[(1A)   The rights conferred by subsection (1) above to continue to occupy or, as
the case may be, to enter and occupy the matrimonial home include, without prejudice to their generality, the right to do so together with any child of the family.]

(2)   In subsection (1) above, an 'entitled spouse' includes a spouse who is entitled, or permitted by a third party, to occupy a matrimonial home along with an
individual who is not the other spouse only if that individual has waived his or
her right of occupation in favour of the spouse so entitled or permitted.

(3)   If the entitled spouse refuses to allow the non-entitled spouse to exercise
the right conferred by subsection (1)(b) above, the non-entitled spouse may exercise that right only with the leave of the court under section 3(3) or (4) of this Act.

(4)   In this Act, the rights mentioned in paragraphs (a) and (b) of subsection (1)
above are referred to as occupancy rights.

(5)   A non-entitled spouse may renounce in writing his or her occupancy rights
only—

     (a)   in a particular matrimonial home; or

     (b)   in a particular property which it is intended by the spouses will become
a matrimonial home.

(6)   A renunciation under subsection (5) above shall have effect only if at the
time of making the renunciation, the non-entitled spouse has sworn or affirmed
before a notary public that it was made freely and without coercion of any kind.

[In this subsection, 'notary public' includes any person duly authorised by the
law of the country (other than Scotland) in which the swearing or affirmation takes
place to administer oaths or receive affirmations in that other country.]

2   Subsidiary and consequential rights

(1)   For the purpose of securing the occupancy rights of a non-entitled spouse,
that spouse shall, in relation to a matrimonial home, be entitled without the consent of the entitled spouse—

     (a)   to make any payment due by the entitled spouse in respect of rent, rates,
secured loan instalments, interest or other outgoings (not being outgoings on
repairs or improvements);

     (b)   to perform any other obligation incumbent on the entitled spouse (not
being an obligation in respect of non-essential repairs or improvements);

     (c)   to enforce performance of an obligation by a third party which that third
party has undertaken to the entitled spouse to the extent that the entitled spouse
may enforce such performance;

(d)   to carry out such essential repairs as the entitled spouse may carry out;

(e)   to carry out such non-essential repairs or improvements as may be authorised by an order of the court, being such repairs or improvements as the entitled spouse may carry out and which the court considers to be appropriate for the reasonable enjoyment of the occupancy rights;

(f)   to take such other steps, for the purpose of protecting the occupancy rights of the non-entitled spouse, as the entitled spouse may take to protect the occupancy rights of the entitled spouse.

(2)   Any payment made under subsection (1)(a) above or any obligation performed under subsection (1)(b) above shall have effect in relation to the rights of a third party as if the payment were made or the obligation were performed by the entitled spouse; and the performance of an obligation which has been enforced under subsection (1)(c) above shall have effect as if it had been enforced by the entitled spouse.

(3)   Where there is an entitled and a non-entitled spouse, the court, on the application of either of them, may, having regard in particular to the respective financial circumstances of the spouses, make an order apportioning expenditure incurred or to be incurred by either spouse—

(a)   without the consent of the other spouse, on any of the items mentioned in paragraphs (a) and (d) of subsection (1) above;

(b)   with the consent of the other spouse, on anything relating to a matrimonial home.

(4)   Where both spouses are entitled, or permitted by a third party, to occupy a matrimonial home—

(a)   either spouse shall be entitled, without the consent of the other spouse, to carry out such non-essential repairs or improvements as may be authorised by an order of the court, being such repairs or improvements as the court considers to be appropriate for the reasonable enjoyment of the occupancy rights;

(b)   the court, on the application of either spouse, may, having regard in particular to the respective financial circumstances of the spouses, make an order apportioning expenditure incurred or to be incurred by either spouse, with or without the consent of the other spouse, on anything relating to the matrimonial home.

(5)   Where one spouse owns or hires, or is acquiring under a hire-purchase or conditional sale agreement, furniture and plenishings in a matrimonial home—

(a)   the other spouse may, without the consent of the first mentioned spouse—

(i)   make any payment due by the first mentioned spouse which is necessary, or take any other step which the first mentioned spouse is entitled to take to secure the possession or use of any such furniture and plenishings (and any such payment shall have effect in relation to the rights of a third party as if it were made by the first mentioned spouse); or

(ii)   carry out such essential repairs to the furniture and plenishings as the first mentioned spouse is entitled to carry out;

(b)   the court, on the application of either spouse, may, having regard in particular to the respective financial circumstances of the spouses, make an order apportioning expenditure incurred or to be incurred by either spouse—

(i)   without the consent of the other spouse, in making payments under a hire, hire-purchase or conditional sale agreement, or in paying interest charges in respect of the furniture and plenishings, or in carrying out essential repairs to the furniture and plenishings; or

(ii)   with the consent of the other spouse, on anything relating to the furniture and plenishings.

(6)   An order under subsection (3), (4)(b) or (5)(b) above may require one

spouse to make a payment to the other spouse in implementation of the apportionment.

(7)   Any application under subsection (3), (4)(b) or (5)(b) above shall be made
within five years of the date on which any payment in respect of such incurred
expenditure was made.

(8)   Where—

    (a)   the entitled spouse is a tenant of a matrimonial home; and

    (b)   possession thereof is necessary in order to continue the tenancy; and

    (c)   the entitled spouse abandons such possession,

the tenancy shall be continued by such possession by the non-entitled spouse.

(9)   In this section 'improvements' includes alterations and enlargement.

3   Regulation by court of rights of occupancy of matrimonial home

(1)   Where there is an entitled and a non-entitled spouse, or where both spouses
are entitled, or permitted by a third party, to occupy a matrimonial home, either
spouse may apply to the court for an order—

    (a)   declaring the occupancy rights of the applicant spouse;

    (b)   enforcing the occupancy rights of the applicant spouse;

    (c)   restricting the occupancy rights of the non-applicant spouse;

    (d)   regulating the exercise by either spouse of his or her occupancy rights;

    (e)   protecting the occupancy rights of the applicant spouse in relation to the
other spouse.

(2)   Where one spouse owns or hires, or is acquiring under a hire-purchase or
conditional sale agreement, furniture and plenishings in a matrimonial home, the
other spouse, if he or she has occupancy rights in that home, may apply to the
court for an order granting to the applicant the possession or use in the matrimonial home of any such furniture and plenishings; but, subject to section 2 of this
Act, an order under this subsection shall not prejudice the rights of any third party
in relation to the non-performance of any obligation under such hire-purchase or
conditional sale agreement.

(3)   The court shall grant an application under subsection (1)(a) above if it
appears to the court that the application relates to a matrimonial home; and, on an
application under any of paragraphs (b) to (e) of subsection (1) or under subsection (2) above, the court may make such order relating to the application as
appears to it to be just and reasonable having regard to all the circumstances of the
case including—

    (a)   the conduct of the spouses in relation to each other and otherwise;

    (b)   the respective needs and financial resources of the spouses;

    (c)   the needs of any child of the family;

    (d)   the extent (if any) to which—

      (i)   the matrimonial home; and

      (ii)   in relation only to an order under subsection (2) above, any item of
furniture and plenishings referred to in that subsection,

is used in connection with a trade, business or profession of either spouse; and

    (e)   whether the entitled spouse offers or has offered to make available to the
non-entitled spouse any suitable alternative accommodation.

(4)   Pending the making of an order under subsection (3) above, the court, on
the application of either spouse, may make such interim order as it may consider
necessary or expedient in relation to—

    (a)   the residence of either spouse in the home to which the application
relates;

    (b)   the personal effects of either spouse or of any child of the family; or

    (c)   the furniture and plenishings:

Provided that an interim order may be made only if the non-applicant spouse
has been afforded an opportunity of being heard by or represented before the court.

(5)   The court shall not make an order under subsection (3) or (4) above if it

appears that the effect of the order would be to exclude the non-applicant spouse from the matrimonial home.

(6)   If the court makes an order under subsection (3) or (4) above which requires the delivery to one spouse of anything which has been left in or removed from the matrimonial home, it may also grant a warrant authorising a messenger-at-arms or sheriff officer to enter the matrimonial home or other premises occupied by the other spouse and to search for and take possession of the thing required to be delivered, if need be by opening shut and lockfast places, and to deliver the thing in accordance with the said order:

Provided that a warrant granted under this subsection shall be executed only after expiry of the period of a charge, being such period as the court shall specify in the order for delivery.

(7)   Where it appears to the court—

(a)   on the application of a non-entitled spouse, that that spouse has suffered a loss of occupancy rights or that the quality of the non-entitled spouse's occupation of a matrimonial home has been impaired; or

(b)   on the application of a spouse who has been given the possession or use of furniture and plenishings by virtue of an order under subsection (3) above, that the applicant has suffered a loss of such possession or use or that the quality of the applicant's possession or use of the furniture and plenishings has been impaired,

in consequence of any act or default on the part of the other spouse which was intended to result in such loss or impairment, it may order that other spouse to pay to the applicant such compensation as the court in the circumstances considers just and reasonable in respect of that loss or impairment.

(8)   A spouse may renounce in writing the right to apply under subsection (2) above for the possession or use of any item of furniture and plenishings.

4   Exclusion orders

(1)   Where there is an entitled and a non-entitled spouse, or where both spouses are entitled, or permitted by a third party, to occupy a matrimonial home, either spouse [whether or not that spouse is in occupation at the time of the application] may apply to the court for an order (in this Act referred to as 'an exclusion order') suspending the occupancy rights of the other spouse ('the non-applicant spouse') in a matrimonial home.

(2)   Subject to subsection (3) below, the court shall make an exclusion order if it appears to the court that the making of the order is necessary for the protection of the applicant or any child of the family from any conduct or threatened or reasonably apprehended conduct of the non-applicant spouse which is or would be injurious to the physical or mental health of the applicant or child.

(3)   The court shall not make an exclusion order if it appears to the court that the making of the order would be unjustified or unreasonable—

(a)   having regard to all the circumstances of the case including the matters specified in paragraphs (a) to (e) of section 3(3) of this Act; and

(b)   where the matrimonial home—

(i)   is or is part of an agricultural holding within the meaning of section 1 of the [Agricultural Holdings (Scotland) Act 1991]; or

(ii)   is let, or is a home in respect of which possession is given, to the non-applicant spouse or to both spouses by an employer as an incident of employment,

subject to a requirement that the non-applicant spouse or, as the case may be, both spouses must reside in the matrimonial home, having regard to that requirement and the likely consequences of the exclusion of the non-applicant spouse from the matrimonial home.

(4)   In making an exclusion order the court shall, on the application of the applicant spouse,—

    (a)   grant a warrant for the summary ejection of the non-applicant spouse from the matrimonial home;

✳   (b)   grant an interdict prohibiting the non-applicant spouse from entering the matrimonial home without the express permission of the applicant;

    (c)   grant an interdict prohibiting the removal by the non-applicant spouse, except with the written consent of the applicant or by a further order of the court, of any furniture and plenishings in the matrimonial home;

unless, in relation to paragraph (a) or (c) above, the non-applicant spouse satisfies the court that it is unnecessary for it to grant such a remedy.

(5)   In making an exclusion order the court may—

    (a)   grant an interdict prohibiting the non-applicant spouse from entering or remaining in a specified area in the vicinity of the matrimonial home;

    (b)   where the warrant for the summary ejection of the non-applicant spouse has been granted in his or her absence, give directions as to the preservation of the non-applicant spouse's goods and effects which remain in the matrimonial home;

    (c)   on the application of either spouse, make the exclusion order or the warrant or interdict mentioned in paragraph (a), (b) or (c) of subsection (4) above or paragraph (a) of this subsection subject to such terms and conditions as the court may prescribe;

    (d)   on application as aforesaid, make such other order as it may consider necessary for the proper enforcement of an order made under subsection (4) above or paragraph (a), (b) or (c) of this subsection.

(6)   Pending the making of an exclusion order, the court may, on the application of the applicant spouse, make an interim order suspending the occupancy rights of the non-applicant spouse in the matrimonial home to which the application for the exclusion order relates; and subsections (4) and (5) above shall apply to such interim order as they apply to an exclusion order:

Provided that an interim order may be made only if the non-applicant spouse has been afforded an opportunity of being heard by or represented before the court.

(7)   Without prejudice to subsections (1) and (6) above, where both spouses are entitled, or permitted by a third party, to occupy a matrimonial home, it shall be incompetent for one spouse to bring an action of ejection from the matrimonial home against the other spouse.

5 Duration of orders under ss 3 and 4

(1)   The court may, on the application of either spouse, vary or recall any order made by it under section 3 or 4 of this Act, but, subject to subsection (2) below, any such order shall, unless previously so varied or recalled, cease to have effect—

    (a)   on the termination of the marriage; or

    (b)   subject to section 6(1) of this Act, where there is an entitled and a non-entitled spouse, on the entitled spouse ceasing to be an entitled spouse in respect of the matrimonial home to which the order relates; or

    (c)   where both spouses are entitled, or permitted by a third party, to occupy the matrimonial home, on both spouses ceasing to be so entitled or permitted.

(2)   Without prejudice to the generality of subsection (1) above, an order under section 3(3) or (4) of this Act which grants the possession or use of furniture and plenishings shall cease to have effect if the furniture and plenishings cease to be permitted by a third party to be retained in the matrimonial home.

Occupancy rights in relation to dealings with third parties

6 Continued exercise of occupancy rights after dealing

(1)   Subject to subsection (3) below—

    (a)   the continued exercise of the rights conferred on a non-entitled spouse by the provisions of this Act in respect of a matrimonial home shall not be prejudiced by reason only of any dealing of the entitled spouse relating to that home; and

(b)   a third party shall not by reason only of such a dealing be entitled to occupy that matrimonial home or any part of it.

(2)   In this section and section 7 of this Act—

'dealing' includes the grant of a heritable security and the creation of a trust but does not include a conveyance under section 80 of the Lands Clauses Consolidation (Scotland) Act 1845;

'entitled spouse' does not include a spouse who, apart from the provisions of this Act,—

(a)   is permitted by a third party to occupy a matrimonial home; or

(b)   is entitled to occupy a matrimonial home along with an individual who is not the other spouse, whether or not that individual has waived his or her right of occupation in favour of the spouse so entitled;

and 'non-entitled spouse' shall be construed accordingly.

(3)   This section shall not apply in any case where—

(a)   the non-entitled spouse in writing either—

(i)   consents or has consented to the dealing, and any consent shall be in such form as the Secretary of State may, by regulations made by statutory instrument, prescribe; or

(ii)   renounces or has renounced his or her occupancy rights in relation to the matrimonial home or property to which the dealing relates;

(b)   the court has made an order under section 7 of this Act dispensing with the consent of the non-entitled spouse to the dealing;

(c)   the dealing occurred, or implements, a binding obligation entered into by the entitled spouse before his or her marriage to the non-entitled spouse;

(d)   the dealing occurred, or implements, a binding obligation entered into before the commencement of this Act; . . .

(e)   the dealing comprises [a sale to] a third party who has acted in good faith if, [. . .] there is produced to the third party by the [seller]—

[(i)   an affidavit sworn or affirmed by the seller declaring that the subjects of sale are not or were not at the time of the dealing a matrimonial home in relation to which a spouse of the seller has or had occupancy rights.

For the purposes of this paragraph, the time of the dealing, in the case of the sale of an interest in heritable property, is the date of delivery to the purchaser of the deed transferring title to that interest.]

(ii)   a renunciation of occupancy rights or consent to the dealing which bears to have been properly made or given by the non-entitled spouse; or

(f)   the entitled spouse has permanently ceased to be entitled to occupy the matrimonial home, and at any time thereafter a continuous period of 5 years has elapsed, during which the non-entitled spouse has not occupied the matrimonial home.]

(4)   [*Amends Land Registration (Scotland) Act 1979.*]

7   Dispensation by court with spouse's consent to dealing

(1)   The court may, on the application of an entitled spouse or any other person having an interest, make an order dispensing with the consent of a non-entitled spouse to a dealing which has taken place or a proposed dealing, if—

(a)   such consent is unreasonably withheld;

(b)   such consent cannot be given by reason of physical or mental disability;

(c)   the non-entitled spouse cannot be found after reasonable steps have been taken to trace him or her; or

(d)   the non-entitled spouse is [under legal disability by reason of nonage].

(2)   For the purposes of subsection (1)(a) above, a non-entitled spouse shall have unreasonably withheld consent to a dealing which has taken place or a proposed dealing, where it appears to the court—

(a) that the non-entitled spouse has led the entitled spouse to believe that he or she would consent to the dealing and that the non-entitled spouse would not be prejudiced by any change in the circumstances of the case since such apparent consent was given; or

(b) that the entitled spouse has, having taken all reasonable steps to do so, been unable to obtain an answer to a request for consent.

(3) The court, in considering whether to make an order under subsection (1) above, shall have regard to all the circumstances of the case including the matters specified in paragraphs (a) to (e) of section 3(3) of this Act.

(4) Where—

(a) an application is made for an order under this section; and

(b) an action is or has been raised by a non-entitled spouse to enforce occupancy rights,

the action shall be sisted until the conclusion of the proceedings on the application. [. . .]

8 Interests of heritable creditors

(1) The rights of a third party with an interest in the matrimonial home as a creditor under a secured loan in relation to the non-performance of any obligation under the loan shall not be prejudiced by reason only of the occupancy rights of the non-entitled spouse; but where a non-entitled spouse has or obtains occupation of a matrimonial home and—

(a) the entitled spouse is not in occupation; and

(b) there is a third party with such an interest in the matrimonial home,

the court may, on the application of the third party, make an order requiring the non-entitled spouse to make any payment due by the entitled spouse in respect of the loan.

(2) This section shall not apply [to secured loans in respect of which the security was granted prior to the commencement of section 13 of the Law Reform (Miscellaneous Provisions) (Scotland) Act 1985] unless the third party in granting the secured loan acted in good faith and . . . there was produced to the third party by the entitled spouse—

(a) an affidavit sworn or affirmed by the entitled spouse declaring that there is no non-entitled spouse; or

(b) a renunciation of occupancy rights or consent to the taking of the loan which bears to have been properly made or given by the non-entitled spouse.

[(2A) This section shall not apply to secured loans in respect of which the security was granted after the commencement of section 13 of the Law Reform (Miscellaneous Provisions) (Scotland) Act 1985 unless the third party in granting the secured loan acted in good faith and [. . .] there was produced to the third party by the grantor—

(a) an affidavit sworn or affirmed by the grantor declaring that the security subjects are not or were not at the time of the granting of the security a matrimonial home in relation to which a spouse of the grantor has or had occupancy rights; or

(b) a renunciation of occupancy rights or consent to the granting of the security which bears to have been properly made or given by the non-entitled spouse.

(2B) for the purposes of subsections (2) and (2A) above, the time of granting a security, in the case of a heritable security, is the date of delivery of the deed creating the security.]

9 Provisions where both spouses have title

(1) Subject to subsection (2) below, where, apart from the provisions of this Act, both spouses are entitled to occupy a matrimonial home—

(a) the rights in that home of one spouse shall not be prejudiced by reason only of any dealing of the other spouse; and

(b) a third party shall not by reason only of such a dealing be entitled to occupy that matrimonial home or any part of it.

(2) The definition of 'dealing' in section 6(2) of this Act and sections 6(3) and 7 of this Act shall apply for the purposes of subsection (1) above as they apply for the purposes of section 6(1) of this Act subject to the following modifications—

(a) any reference to the entitled spouse and to the non-entitled spouse shall be construed as a reference to a spouse who has entered into or, as the case may be, proposes to enter into a dealing and to the other spouse respectively; and

(b) in paragraph (b) of section 7(4) the reference to occupancy rights shall be construed as a reference to any rights in the matrimonial home.

[. . .]

11 Poinding

Where [an attachment] has been executed of furniture and plenishings of which the debtor's spouse has the possession or use by virtue of an order under section 3(3) or (4) of this Act, the sheriff, on the application of that spouse within 40 days of the date of execution of [the attachment], may—

(a) declare that [the attachment] is null; or

(b) make such order as he thinks appropriate to protect such possession or use by that spouse,

if he is satisfied that the purpose of the diligence was wholly or mainly to prevent such possession or use.

12 Adjudication

(1) Where a matrimonial home of which there is an entitled spouse and a non-entitled spouse is adjudged, the Court of Session, on the application of the non-entitled spouse within 40 days of the date of the decree of adjudication, may—

(a) order the reduction of the decree; or

(b) make such order as it thinks appropriate to protect the occupancy rights of the non-entitled spouse,

if it is satisfied that the purpose of the diligence was wholly or mainly to defeat the occupancy rights of the non-entitled spouse.

(2) In this section, 'entitled spouse' and 'non-entitled spouse' have the same meanings respectively as in section 6(2) of this Act.

Transfer of tenancy

13 Transfer of tenancy

(1) The court may, on the application of a non-entitled spouse, make an order transferring the tenancy of a matrimonial home to that spouse and providing, subject to subsection (11) below, for the payment by the non-entitled spouse to the entitled spouse of such compensation as seems just and reasonable in all the circumstances of the case.

[(2) In an action—

(a) for divorce, the Court of Session or a sheriff;

(b) for nullity of marriage, the Court of Session,

may, on granting decree or within such period as the court may specify on granting decree, make an order granting an application under subsection (1) above.]

(3) In determining whether to grant an application under subsection (1) above, the court shall have regard to all the circumstances of the case including the matters specified in paragraphs (a) to (e) of section 3(3) of this Act and the suitability of the applicant to become the tenant and the applicant's capacity to perform the obligations under the lease of the matrimonial home.

(4) The non-entitled spouse shall serve a copy of an application under subsection (1) above on the landlord and, before making an order under subsection (1) above, the court shall give the landlord an opportunity of being heard by it.

(5) On the making of an order granting an application under subsection (1)

above, the tenancy shall vest in the non-entitled spouse without intimation to the landlord, subject to all the liabilities under the lease (other than any arrears of rent for the period before the making of the order, which shall remain the liability of the original entitled spouse).

(6)   The clerk of court shall notify the landlord of the making of an order granting an application under subsection (1) above.

(7)   It shall not be competent for a non-entitled spouse to apply for an order under subsection (1) above where the matrimonial home—

(a)   is let to the entitled spouse by his or her employer as an incident of employment, and the lease is subject to a requirement that the entitled spouse must reside therein;

(b)   [is on or pertains to land comprised in an agricultural lease];

(c)   is on or pertains to a croft or the subject of a cottar or the holding of a landholder or a statutory small tenant;

(d)   is let on a long lease;

(e)   is part of the tenancy land of a tenant-at-will.

(8)   In subsection (7) above—

['agricultural lease' means a lease constituting a 1991 Act tenancy within the meaning of the Agricultural Holdings (Scotland) Act 2003 (asp 11) or a lease constituting a limited duration tenancy or a short limited duration tenancy (within the meaning of that Act);]

'cottar' has the same meaning as in section 28(4) of the [Crofters (Scotland) Act 1993];

'croft' has the same meaning as in the [Crofters (Scotland) Act 1993];

'holding', in relation to a landholder and a statutory small tenant, 'landholder' and 'statutory small tenant' have the same meanings respectively as in sections 2(1), 2(2) and 32(1) of the Small Landholders (Scotland) Act 1911;

'long lease' has the same meaning as in section 28(1) of the Land Registration (Scotland) Act 1979;

'tenant-at-will' has the same meaning as in section 20(8) of the Land Registration (Scotland) Act 1979.

(9)   Where both spouses are joint or common tenants of a matrimonial home, the court may, on the application of one of the spouses, make an order vesting the tenancy in that spouse solely and providing, subject to subsection (11) below, for the payment by the applicant to the other spouse of such compensation as seems just and reasonable in the circumstances of the case.

(10)   Subsections (2) to (8) above shall apply for the purposes of an order under subsection (9) above as they apply for the purposes of an order under subsection (1) above subject to the following modifications—

(a)   in subsection (3) for the word 'tenant' there shall substituted the words 'sole tenant';

(b)   in subsection (4) for the words 'non-entitled' there should be substituted the word 'applicant';

(c)   in subsection (5) for the words 'non-entitled' and 'liability of the original entitled spouse' there shall substituted respectively the words 'applicant' and 'joint and several liability of both spouses';

(d)   in subsection (7)—

(i)   for the words 'a non-entitled' there shall substituted the words 'an applicant';

(ii)   for paragraph (a) there shall be substituted the following paragraph—

'(a) is let to both spouses by their employer as an incident of employment, and the lease is subject to a requirement that both spouses must reside there;';

(iii)   paragraphs (c) and (e) shall be omitted.

(11)   Where the matrimonial home is a [Scottish secure tenancy within the meaning of the Housing (Scotland) Act 2001 (asp 10)] no account shall be taken, in

assessing the amount of any compensation to be awarded under subsection (1) or (9) above, of the loss, by virtue of the transfer of the tenancy of the home, of a right to purchase the home under [Part III of the Housing (Scotland) Act 1987 (c 26)].

(12)   In the Tenants' Rights, Etc (Scotland) Act 1980—

(a)   paragraph 6 of Part I of Schedule 2 is repealed.

[. . .]

Matrimonial interdicts

14   Interdict competent where spouses live together

(1)   It shall not be incompetent for the court to entertain an application by a spouse for a matrimonial interdict by reason only that the spouses are living together as man and wife.

(2)   In this section and section 15 of this Act—

'matrimonial interdict' means an interdict including an interim interdict which—

(a)   restrains or prohibits any conduct of one spouse towards the other spouse or a child of the family, or

(b)   prohibits a spouse from entering or remaining in a matrimonial home or in a specified area in the vicinity of the matrimonial home.

15   Attachment of powers of arrest to matrimonial interdicts

(1)   [Subject to subsection (1A) below, the] court shall, on the application of the applicant spouse, attach a power of arrest—

(a)   to any matrimonial interdict which is ancillary to an exclusion order, including an interim order under section 4(6) of this Act;

(b)   to any other matrimonial interdict where the non-applicant spouse has had the opportunity of being heard by or represented before the court, unless it appears to the court that in all the circumstances of the case such a power is unnecessary.

[(1A)   The court may attach a power of arrest to an interdict by virtue of subsection (1) above only if satisfied that attaching the power would not result in the non-applicant spouse being subject, in relation to the interdict, to a power of arrest under both this Act and the Protection from Abuse (Scotland) Act 2001 (asp 14.)

(2)   A power of arrest attached to an interdict by virtue of subsection (1) above shall not have effect until such interdict [together with the attached power of arrest] is served on the non-applicant spouse, and such a power of arrest shall, unless previously recalled, cease to have effect upon the termination of the marriage.

(3)   If, by virtue of subsection (1) above, a power of arrest is attached to an interdict, a constable may arrest without warrant the non-applicant spouse if he has reasonable cause for suspecting that spouse of being in breach of the interdict.

(4)   If, by virtue of subsection (1) above, a power of arrest is attached to an interdict, the applicant spouse shall, as soon as possible after service of the interdict [together with the attached power of arrest] on the non-applicant spouse, ensure that there is delivered—

(a)   to the chief constable of the police area in which the matrimonial home is situated; and

(b)   if the applicant spouse resides in another police area, to the chief constable of that other police area,

a copy of the application for the interdict and of the interlocutor granting the interdict together with a certificate of service of the interdict [and where the application to attach the power of arrest to the interdict was made after the interdict was granted, a copy of that application and of the interlocutor granting it and a certificate of service of the interdict together with the attached power of arrest].

(5)   Where any matrimonial interdict to which, by virtue of subsection (1) above

there is attached a power of arrest, is varied or recalled, the spouse who applied
for the variation or recall shall ensure that there is delivered—
    (a) to the chief constable of the police area in which the matrimonial home is
situated; and
    (b) if the applicant spouse (within the meaning of subsection (6) below)
resides in another police area, to the chief constable of that other police area,
a copy of the application for variation or recall and of the interlocutor granting the
variation or recall.
    (6) In this section and in sections 16 and 17 of this Act—
'applicant spouse' means the spouse who has applied for the interdict; and
'non-applicant spouse' shall be construed accordingly.

16 Police powers after arrest

    (1) Where a person has been arrested under section 15(3) of this Act, the officer
in charge of a police station may—
    (a) if satisfied that there is no likelihood of violence to the applicant spouse
or any child of the family, liberate that person unconditionally; or
    (b) refuse to liberate that person; and such refusal and the detention of that
person until his or her appearance in court by virtue of—
        (i) section 17(2) of this Act; or
        (ii) any provision of the [Criminal Procedure (Scotland) Act 1995],
shall not subject the officer to any claim whatsoever.
    (2) Where a person arrested under section 15(3) of this Act is liberated under
subsection (1) above, the facts and circumstances which gave rise to the arrest shall
be reported forthwith to the procurator fiscal who, if he decides to take no criminal
proceedings in respect of those facts and circumstances, shall at the earliest opportunity take all reasonable steps to intimate his decision to the persons mentioned
in paragraphs (a) and (b) of section 17(4) of this Act.

17 Procedure after arrest

    (1) The provisions of this section shall apply only where—
    (a) the non-applicant spouse has not been liberated under section 16(1) of
this Act; and
    (b) the procurator fiscal decides that no criminal proceedings are to be taken
in respect of the facts and circumstances which gave rise to the arrest.
    (2) The non-applicant spouse who has been arrested under section 15(3) of this
Act shall wherever practicable be brought before the sheriff sitting as a court of
summary criminal jurisdiction for the district in which he or she was arrested not
later than in the course of the first day after the arrest, such day not being a Saturday, a Sunday or a court holiday prescribed for that court under [section 8 of the
Criminal Procedure (Scotland) Act 1995].
    Provided that nothing in this subsection shall prevent the non-applicant spouse
from being brought before the sheriff on a Saturday, a Sunday or such a court holiday where the sheriff is in pursuance of the said section 10 sitting on such day for
the disposal of criminal business.
    (3) [Subsections (1) to (3) of section 15 of the said Act of 1995] (intimation to a
named person) shall apply to a non-applicant spouse who has been arrested under
section 15(3) of this Act as they apply to a person who has been arrested in respect
of any offence.
    (4) The procurator fiscal shall at the earliest opportunity, and in any event
prior to the non-applicant spouse being brought before the sheriff under subsection (2) above, take all reasonable steps to intimate—
    (a) to the applicant spouse; and
    (b) to the solicitor who acted for that spouse when the interdict was granted
or to any other solicitor who the procurator fiscal has reason to believe acts for
the time being for that spouse,
that the criminal proceedings referred to in subsection (1) above will not be taken.

(5)   On the non-applicant spouse being brought before the sheriff under sub-section (2) above, the following procedure shall apply—
  (a)   the procurator fiscal shall present to the court a petition containing—
    (i)   a statement of the particulars of the non-applicant spouse;
    (ii)   a statement of the facts and circumstances which gave rise to the arrest; and
    (iii)   a request that the non-applicant spouse be detained for a further period not exceeding 2 days;
  (b)   if it appears to the sheriff that—
    (i)   the statement referred to in paragraph (a)(ii) above discloses a *prima facie* breach of interdict by the non-applicant spouse;
    (ii)   proceedings for breach of interdict will be taken; and
    (iii)   there is a substantial risk of violence by the non-applicant spouse against the applicant spouse or any child of the family,
he may order the non-applicant spouse to be detained for a further period not exceeding 2 days;
  (c)   in any case to which paragraph (b) above does not apply, the non-applicant spouse shall, unless in custody in respect of any other matter, be released from custody;
and in computing the period of two days referred to in paragraphs (a) and (b) above, no account shall be taken of a Saturday or Sunday or of any holiday in the court in which the proceedings for breach of interdict will require to be raised.

Cohabiting couples

18   Occupancy rights of cohabiting couples

(1)   If a man and a woman are living with each other as if they were man and wife ('a cohabiting couple') in a house which, apart from the provisions of this section—
  (a)   one of them (an 'entitled partner') is entitled, or permitted by a third party, to occupy; and
  (b)   the other (a 'non-entitled partner') is not so entitled or permitted to occupy,
the court may, on the application of the non-entitled partner, if it appears that the man and the woman are a cohabiting couple in that house, grant occupancy rights therein to the applicant for such period, not exceeding [6] months, as the court may specify:
Provided that the court may extend the said period for a further period or periods, no such period exceeding 6 months.
(2)   In determining whether for the purpose of subsection (1) above a man and woman are a cohabiting couple the court shall have regard to all the circumstances of the case including—
  (a)   the time for which it appears they have been living together; and
  (b)   whether there are any children of the relationship.
(3)   While an order granting an application under subsection (1) above or an extension of such an order is in force, or where both partners of a cohabiting couple are entitled, or permitted by a third party, to occupy the house where they are cohabiting, the following provisions of this Act shall subject to any necessary modifications—
  (a)   apply to the cohabiting couple as they apply to parties to a marriage; and
  (b)   have effect in relation to any child residing with the cohabiting couple as they have effect in relation to a child of the family,
  section 2;
  section 3, except subsection (1)(a);
  section 4;
  in section 5(1), the words from the beginning to 'Act' where it first occurs;

sections 13 and 14;

section 15, except the words in subsection (2) from 'and such a power of arrest' to the end;

sections 16 and 17; and

section 22,

and any reference in these provisions to a matrimonial home shall be construed as a reference to a house.

(4)   Any order under section 3 or 4 of this Act as applied to a cohabiting couple by subsection (3) above shall have effect—

(a)   if one of them is a non-entitled partner, for such a period, not exceeding the period or periods which from time to time may be specified in any order under subsection (1) above for which occupancy rights have been granted under that subsection, as may be specified in the order;

(b)   if they are both entitled, or permitted by a third party, to occupy the house, until a further order of the court.

(5)   Nothing in this section shall prejudice the rights of any third party having an interest in the house referred to in subsection (1) above.

(6)   In this section—

'house' includes a caravan, houseboat or other structure in which the couple are cohabiting and any garden or other ground or building attached to, and usually occupied with, or otherwise required for the amenity or convenience of, the house, caravan, houseboat or other structure;

'occupancy rights' means the following rights of a non-entitled partner—

(a)   if in occupation, a right to [continue to occupy] the house [and, without prejudice to the generality of these rights, includes the right to continue to occupy or, as the case may be, to enter and occupy the house together with any child residing with the cohabiting couple];

(b)   if not in occupation, a right to enter into and occupy the house;

'entitled partner' includes a partner who is entitled, or permitted by a third party, to occupy the house along with an individual who is not the other partner only if that individual has waived his or her right of occupation in favour of the partner so entitled or permitted.

Miscellaneous and general

19   Rights of occupancy in relation to division and sale

Where a spouse brings an action for the division and sale of a matrimonial home which the spouses own in common, the court, after having regard to all the circumstances of the case including—

(a)   the matters specified in paragraphs (a) to (d) of section 3(3) of this Act; and

(b)   whether the spouse bringing the action offers or has offered to make available to the other spouse any suitable alternative accommodation,

may refuse to grant decree in that action or may postpone the granting of decree for such period as it may consider reasonable in the circumstances or may grant decree subject to such conditions as it may prescribe.

20   Spouse's consent in relation to calling up of standard securities over matrimonial homes

Section 19(10) of the Conveyancing and Feudal Reform (Scotland) Act 1970 shall have effect as if at the end there were added the following proviso—

'Provided that, without prejudice to the foregoing generality, if the standard security is over a matrimonial home as defined in section 22 of the Matrimonial Homes (Family Protection) (Scotland) Act 1981, the spouse on whom the calling-up notice has been served may not dispense with or shorten the said period without the consent in writing of the other spouse.'.

21   Procedural provision

Section 2(2) of the Law Reform (Husband and Wife) Act 1962 (dismissal by court of delictual proceedings between spouses) shall not apply to any proceedings brought before the court in pursuance of any provision of this Act.

22   Interpretation

In this Act—

'caravan' means a caravan which is mobile or affixed to the land;

'child of the family' includes any child or grandchild of either spouse, and any person who has been brought up or [treated] by either spouse as if he or she were a child of that spouse, whatever the age of such a child, grandchild or person may be;

'the court' means the Court of Session or the sheriff;

'furniture and plenishings' means any article situated in a matrimonial home which—

(a)   is owned or hired by either spouse or is being acquired by either spouse under a hire-purchase agreement or conditional sale agreement; and

(b)   is reasonably necessary to enable the home to be used as a family residence,

but does not include any vehicle, caravan or houseboat, or such other structure as is mentioned in the definition of 'matrimonial home';

'matrimonial home' means any house, caravan, houseboat or other structure which has been provided or has been made available by one or both of the spouses as, or has become, a family residence and includes any garden or other ground or building attached to, and usually occupied with, or otherwise required for the amenity or convenience of, the house, caravan, houseboat or other structure [but does not include a residence provided or made available by one spouse for that spouse to reside in, whether with any child of the family or not, separately from the other spouse];

'occupancy rights' has, subject to section 18(6) of this Act, the meaning assigned by section 1(4) of this Act;

'the sheriff' includes the sheriff having jurisdiction in the district where the matrimonial home is situated;

'tenant' includes sub-tenant and a statutory tenant as defined in section 3 of the Rent (Scotland) Act [1984 and a statutory assured tenant as defined in section 16(1) of the Housing (Scotland) Act 1988] and 'tenancy' shall be construed accordingly;

'entitled spouse' and 'non-entitled spouse', subject to sections 6(2) and 12(2) of this Act, have the meanings respectively assigned to them by section 1 of this Act.

23   Short title, commencement and extent

(1)   This Act may be cited as the Matrimonial Homes (Family Protection) (Scotland) Act 1981.

(2)   This Act (except this section) shall come into operation on such day as the Secretary of State may by order made by statutory instrument appoint, and different days may be so appointed for different provisions and for different purposes.

(3)   This Act extends to Scotland only.

ADMINISTRATION OF JUSTICE ACT 1982
(1982, c 53)

PART I
DAMAGES FOR PERSONAL INJURIES ETC

Abolition of certain claims for damages etc

1 Abolition of right to damages for loss of expectation of life

(1) In an action under the law of England and Wales or the law of Northern Ireland for damages for personal injuries—

(a) no damages shall be recoverable in respect of any loss of expectation of life caused to the injured person by the injuries; but

(b) if the injured person's expectation of life has been reduced by the injuries, the court, in assessing damages in respect of pain and suffering caused by the injuries, shall take account of any suffering caused or likely to be caused to him by awareness that his expectation of life has been so reduced.

(2) The reference in subsection (1)(a) above to damages in respect of loss of expectation of life does not include damages in respect of loss of income.

PART II
DAMAGES FOR PERSONAL INJURIES ETC—SCOTLAND

7 Damages in respect of services

Where a person (in this Part of this Act referred to as 'the injured person')—

(a) has sustained personal injuries, or

(b) has died in consequence of personal injuries sustained,

as a result of an act or omission of another person giving rise to liability in any person (in this Part of this Act referred to as 'the responsible person') to pay damages, the responsible person shall also be liable to pay damages in accordance with the provisions of sections 8 and 9 of this Act.

8 Services rendered to injured person

(1) Where necessary services have been rendered to the injured person by a relative in consequence of the injuries in question, then, unless the relative has expressly agreed in the knowledge that an action for damages has been raised or is in contemplation that no payment should be made in respect of those services, the responsible person shall be liable to pay to the injured person by way of damages such sum as represents reasonable remuneration for those services and repayment of reasonable expenses incurred in connection therewith.

[(2) The injured person shall be under an obligation to account to the relative for any damages recovered from the responsible person under subsection (1) above.

(3) Where, at the date of an award of damages in favour of the injured person, it is likely that necessary services will, after that date, be rendered to him by a relative in consequence of the injuries in question, then, unless the relative has expressly agreed that no payment shall be made in respect of those services, the responsible person shall be liable to pay to the injured person by way of damages such sum as represents—

(a) reasonable remuneration for those services; and

(b) reasonable expenses which are likely to be incurred in connection therewith.

(4) The relative shall have no direct right of action in delict against the responsible person in respect of any services or expenses referred to in this section.]

9 Services to injured person's relative

(1) The responsible person shall be liable to pay to the injured person a reason-

able sum by way of damages in respect of the inability of the injured person to render the personal services referred to in subsection (3) below.

(2)   Where the injured person has died, any relative of his entitled to damages in respect of loss of support under section 1(3) of the Damages (Scotland) Act 1976 shall be entitled to include as a head of damage under that section a reasonable sum in respect of the loss to him of the personal services mentioned in subsection (3) below.

(3)   The personal services referred to in subsections (1) and (2) above are personal services—

(a)   which were or might have been expected to have been rendered by the injured person before the occurrence of the act or omission giving rise to liability,

(b)   of a kind which, when rendered by a person other than a relative, would ordinarily be obtainable on payment, and

(c)   which the injured person but for the injuries in question might have been expected to render gratuitously to a relative.

(4)   Subject to subsection (2) above, the relative shall have no direct right of action in delict against the responsible person in respect of the personal services mentioned in subsection (3) above.

10   Assessment of damages for personal injuries

Subject to any agreement to the contrary, in assessing the amount of damages payable to the injured person in respect of personal injuries there shall not be taken into account so as to reduce that amount—

(a)   any contractual pension or benefit (including any payment by a friendly society or trade union);

(b)   any pension or retirement benefit payable from public funds other than any pension or benefit to which section 2(1) of the Law Reform (Personal Injuries) Act 1948 applies;

(c)   any benefit payable from public funds, in respect of any period after the date of the award of damages, designed to secure to the injured person or any relative of his a minimum level of subsistence;

(d)   any redundancy payment under the [Employment Rights Act 1996], or any payment made in circumstances corresponding to those in which a right to a redundancy payment would have accrued if [section 135] of that Act had applied;

(e)   any payment made to the injured person or to any relative of his by the injured person's employer following upon the injuries in question where the recipient is under an obligation to reimburse the employer in the event of damages being recovered in respect of those injuries;

(f)   subject to paragraph (iv) below, any payment of a benevolent character made to the injured person or to any relative of his by any person following upon the injuries in question;

but there shall be taken into account—

(i)   any remuneration or earnings from employment;

(ii)   any [contribution-based jobseeker's allowance (payable under the Jobseekers' Act 1995);]

(iii)   any benefit referred to in paragraph (c) above payable in respect of any period prior to the date of the award of damages;

(iv)   any payment of a benevolent character made to the injured person or to any relative of his by the responsible person following on the injuries in question, where such a payment is made directly and not through a trust or other fund from which the injured person or his relatives have benefited or may benefit.

13   Supplementary

(1)   In this Part of this Act, unless the context otherwise requires—

'personal injuries' includes any disease or any impairment of a person's physical or mental condition [and injury resulting from defamation or any other verbal injury or other injury to reputation];

'relative', in relation to the injured person, means—

(a)   the spouse or divorced spouse;

[(aa) the civil partner or former civil partner;]

(b)   any person, not being the spouse of the injured person, who was, at the time of the act or omission giving rise to liability in the responsible person, living with the injured person as husband or wife;

(c)   any ascendant or descendant;

(d)   any brother, sister, uncle or aunt; or any issue of any such person;

(e)   any person accepted by the injured person as a child of his family.

In deducing any relationship for the purposes of the foregoing definition—

(a)   any relationship by affinity shall be treated as a relationship by consanguinity; any relationship of the half blood shall be treated as a relationship of the whole blood; and the stepchild of any person shall be treated as his child; and

(b)   [section 1(1) of the Law Reform (Parent and Child) (Scotland) Act 1986 shall apply; and any reference (however expressed) in this Act to a relative shall be construed accordingly].

(2)   Any reference in this Part of this Act to a payment, benefit or pension shall be construed as a reference to any such payment, benefit or pension whether in cash or in kind.

(3)   This Part of this Act binds the Crown.

LAW REFORM (HUSBAND AND WIFE) (SCOTLAND) ACT 1984
(1984, c 15)

Abolition of actions of breach of promise of marriage, adherence and enticement

1   Promise of marriage not an enforceable obligation

(1)   No promise of marriage or agreement between two persons to marry one another shall have effect under the law of Scotland to create any rights or obligations; and no action for breach of any such promise or agreement may be brought in any court in Scotland, whatever the law applicable to the promise or agreement.

(2)   This section shall have effect in relation to any promise made or agreement entered into before it comes into force, but shall not affect any action commenced before it comes into force.

2   Actions of adherence and enticement abolished

(1)   No spouse shall be entitled to apply for a decree from any court in Scotland ordaining the other spouse to adhere.

(2)   No person shall be liable in delict to any person by reason only of having induced the spouse of that person to leave or remain apart from that person.

(3)   This section shall not affect any action commenced before this Act comes into force.

Abolition of miscellaneous rules relating to husband and wife

3   Curatory after marriage

(1)   No married person shall, by reason only of minority, be subject to the curatory of his parent or of any person appointed by his parent.

[. . .]

(3)   Section 2 of the Married Women's Property (Scotland) Act 1920 (husband to be curator to his wife during her minority) is repealed.

4 Abolition of husband's right to choose matrimonial home
Any rule of law entitling the husband, as between husband and wife, to determine where the matrimonial home is to be, shall cease to have effect.

5 Abolition of certain rules relating to antenuptial marriage contracts
(1) In relation to an antenuptial contract of marriage entered into after this Act comes into force—

(a) any rule of law enabling a woman to create an alimentary right in her own favour in respect of any property provided by her shall cease to have effect;

(b) any rule of law whereby the marriage is onerous consideration for any provision of the contract, shall cease to have effect.

(2) Nothing in paragraph (b) of subsection (1) above shall affect the operation of any enactment relating to gifts in consideration of marriage.

6 Abolition of husband's remaining liability for wife's debts incurred before marriage
(1) A husband shall not be liable, by reason only of being her husband, for any debts incurred by his wife before marriage.

(2) Subsection (1) above shall have effect in relation to any such debts, whether incurred before or after this Act comes into force.

(3) Section 4 of the Married Women's Property (Scotland) Act 1877 (liability of husband for wife's antenuptial debts limited to amount of property received through her) is repealed.

7 Abolition of *praepositura*
(1) For the purpose of determining a husband's liability for any obligation incurred by his wife after this Act comes into force, a married woman shall not be presumed as a matter of law to have been placed by her husband in charge of his domestic affairs, and any rule of law to the contrary shall cease to have effect.

(2) No warrant of inhibition or inhibition in whatever form may be granted at the instance of a husband for the purpose of cancelling his wife's authority to incur any obligation on his behalf.

(3) No such inhibition granted before the date this Act comes into force shall be registered on or after that date, and any such inhibition registered before that date shall be treated as discharged on that date.

CHILD ABDUCTION ACT 1984
(1984, c 37)

PART II
OFFENCE UNDER LAW OF SCOTLAND

6 Offence in Scotland of parent, etc taking or sending child out of United Kingdom
(1) Subject to subsections (4) and (5) below, a person connected with a child under the age of sixteen years commits an offence if he takes or sends the child out of the United Kingdom—

(a) without the appropriate consent if there is in respect of the child—

(i) an order of a court in the United Kingdom awarding custody of the child to any person [or naming any person as the person with whom the child is to live; or]

(ii) an order of a court in England, Wales or Northern Ireland making the child a ward of court;

(b) if there is in respect of the child an order of a court in the United Kingdom prohibiting the removal of the child from the United Kingdom or any part of it.

(2)   A person is connected with a child for the purposes of this section if—

(a)   he is a parent or guardian of the child; or

(b)   there is in force an order of a court in the United Kingdom awarding custody of the child to him [or naming him as the person with whom the child is to live] (whether solely or jointly with any other person); or

(c)   in the case of [a child whose parents are not and have never been married to one another], there are reasonable grounds for believing that he is the father of the child.

(3)   In this section, the 'appropriate consent' means—

(a)   in relation to a child to whom subsection (1)(a)(i) above applies—

(i)   the consent of each person

(a)   who is a parent or guardian of the child; or

(b)   to whom custody of the child has been awarded [or who is named as the person with whom the child is to live (whether the award is made, or the person so named is named] solely or jointly with any other person) by an order of a court in the United Kingdom; or

(ii)   the leave of that court;

(b)   in relation to a child to whom subsection (1)(a)(ii) above applies, the leave of the court which made the child a ward of court;

Provided that, in relation to a child to whom more than one order referred to in subsection (1)(a) above applies, the appropriate consent may be that of any court which has granted an order as referred to in the said subsection (1)(a); and where one of these orders is an order referred to in the said subsection (1)(a)(ii) no other person as referred to in paragraph (a)(i) above shall be entitled to give the appropriate consent.

(4)   In relation to a child to whom subsection (1)(a)(i) above applies, a person does not commit an offence by doing anything without the appropriate consent if—

(a)   he does it in the belief that each person referred to in subsection (3)(a)(i) above—

(i)   has consented; or

(ii)   would consent if he was aware of all the relevant circumstances; or

(b)   he has taken all reasonable steps to communicate with such other person but has been unable to communicate with him.

(5)   In proceedings against any person for an offence under this section it shall be a defence for that person to show that at the time of the alleged offence he had no reason to believe that there was in existence an order referred to in subsection (1) above.

(6)   For the purposes of this section—

(a)   a person shall be regarded as taking a child if he causes or induces the child to accompany him or any other person, or causes the child to be taken; and

(b)   a person shall be regarded as sending a child if he causes the child to be sent.

(7)   In this section 'guardian' means a person appointed by deed or will or by order of a court of competent jurisdiction to be the guardian of a child.

7   Power of arrest

A constable may arrest without warrant any person whom he reasonably suspects of committing or having committed an offence under this Part of this Act.

8   Penalties and prosecutions

A person guilty of an offence under this Part of this Act shall be liable—

(a)   on summary conviction, to imprisonment for a term not exceeding three months or to a fine not exceeding the statutory maximum . . ., or both; or

(b)   on conviction on indictment, to imprisonment for a term not exceeding two years or to a fine, or both.

9 Proof and admissibility of certain documents

(1) For the purposes of this Part of this Act, a document duly authenticated which purports to be—

(a) an order or other document issued by a court of the United Kingdom (other than a Scottish court) shall be sufficient evidence of any matter to which it relates;

(b) a copy of such an order or other document shall be deemed without further proof to be a true copy unless the contrary is shown, and shall be sufficient evidence of any matter to which it relates.

(2) A document is duly authenticated for the purposes of—

(a) subsection (1)(a) above if it purports to bear the seal of that court;

(b) subsection (1)(b) above if it purports to be certified by any person in his capacity as a judge, magistrate or officer of that court to be a true copy.

10 Evidence

In any proceedings in relation to an offence under this Part of this Act it shall be presumed, unless the contrary is shown, that the child named in the order referred to in section 6(1) above, or in any copy thereof, is the child in relation to whom the proceedings have been taken.

MATRIMONIAL AND FAMILY PROCEEDINGS ACT 1984
(1984, c 42)

PART IV
FINANCIAL PROVISION IN SCOTLAND AFTER OVERSEAS DIVORCE ETC

28 Circumstances in which a Scottish court may entertain application for financial provision

(1) Where parties to a marriage have been divorced in an overseas country, then, subject to subsection (4) below, if the jurisdictional requirements and the conditions set out in subsections (2) and (3) below respectively are satisfied, the court may entertain an application by one of the parties for an order for financial provision.

(2) The jurisdictional requirements mentioned in subsection (1) above are that—

(a) the applicant was domiciled or habitually resident in Scotland on the date when the application was made; and

(b) the other party to the marriage—

(i) was domiciled or habitually resident in Scotland on the date when the application was made; or

(ii) was domiciled or habitually resident in Scotland when the parties last lived together as husband and wife; or

(iii) on the date when the application was made, was an owner or tenant of, or had a beneficial interest in, property in Scotland which had at some time been a matrimonial home of the parties; and

(c) where the court is the sheriff court, either—

(i) one of the parties was, on the date when the application was made, habitually resident in the sheriffdom; or

(ii) paragraph (b)(iii) above is satisfied in respect of property wholly or partially within the sheriffdom.

(3) The conditions mentioned in subsection (1) above are that—

(a) the divorce falls to be recognised in Scotland;

(b) the other party to the marriage initiated the proceedings for divorce;

(c) the application was made within five years after the date when the divorce took effect;

(d)   a court in Scotland would have had jurisdiction to entertain an action for divorce between the parties if such an action had been brought in Scotland immediately before the foreign divorce took effect;

(e)   the marriage had a substantial connection with Scotland; and

(f)   both parties are living at the time of the application.

(4)   Where the jurisdiction of the court to entertain proceedings under this Part of this Act would fall to be determined by reference to the jurisdictional requirements imposed by virtue of Part I of the Civil Jurisdiction and Judgments Act 1982 (implementation of certain European conventions) [or by virtue of Council Regulation (EC) No 44/2001 of 22nd December 2000 on jurisdiction and the recognition and enforcement of judgments in civil and commercial matters] then—

(a)   satisfaction of the requirements of subsection (2) above shall not obviate the need to satisfy the requirements imposed by virtue of [that Regulation or] Part I of that Act; and

(b)   satisfaction of the requirements imposed by virtue of [that Regulation or] Part I of that Act shall obviate the need to satisfy the requirements of subsection (2) above;

and the court shall entertain or not entertain the proceedings accordingly.

29   Disposal of application in Scotland

(1)   Subject to subsections (2) to (5) below, Scots law shall apply, with any necessary modifications, in relation to an application under section 28 above as it would apply if the application were being made in an action for divorce in Scotland.

(2)   In disposing of an application entertained by it under the said section 28, the court shall exercise its powers so as to place the parties, in so far as it is reasonable and practicable to do so, in the financial position in which they would have been if the application had been disposed of, in an action for divorce in Scotland, on the date on which the foreign divorce took effect.

(3)   In determining what is reasonable and practicable for the purposes of subsection (2) above, the court shall have regard in particular to—

(a)   the parties' resources, present and foreseeable at the date of disposal of the application;

(b)   any order made by a foreign court in or in connection with the divorce proceedings for the making of financial provision in whatever form, or the transfer of property, by one of the parties to the other; and

(c)   subsection (5) below.

(4)   Except where subsection (5) below applies, the court may make an order for an interim award of a periodical allowance where—

(a)   it appears from the applicant's averments that in the disposal of the application an order for financial provision is likely to be made; and

(b)   the court considers that such an interim award is necessary to avoid hardship to the applicant.

(5)   Where but for section 28(2)(b)(iii) above the court would not have jurisdiction to entertain the application, the court may make an order—

(a)   relating to the former matrimonial home or its furniture and plenishings; or

(b)   that the other party to the marriage shall pay to the applicant a capital sum not exceeding the value of that other party's interest in the former matrimonial home and its furniture and plenishings,

but shall not be entitled to make any other order for financial provision.

[29A   Application of Part IV to annulled marriages

This Part of this Act shall apply to an annulment, of whatever nature, of a purported marriage, as it applies to a divorce, and references to marriage and divorce shall be construed accordingly.]

30   Interpretation of Part IV

(1)   In the foregoing provisions of this Part of this Act unless the context otherwise requires—

'the court' means the Court of Session or the sheriff court;

'furniture and plenishings' has the meaning assigned by section 22 of the Matrimonial Homes (Family Protection) (Scotland) Act 1981;

'matrimonial home' has the meaning assigned by the said section 22;

'order for financial provision' means any one or more of the orders specified in [section 8(1) of the Family Law (Scotland) Act 1985] (financial provision) or an order under section 13 of the Matrimonial Homes (Family Protection) (Scotland) Act 1981 (transfer of tenancy of matrimonial home);

'overseas country' means a country or territory outside the British Islands; and

'tenant' has the meaning assigned by the said section 22.

(2)   Any reference in the foregoing provisions of this Part of this Act to a party to a marriage shall include a reference to a party to a marriage which has been terminated.

31   Extension of s 31 of Maintenance Orders (Reciprocal Enforcement) Act 1972

(1)   Section 31(4) of the Maintenance Orders (Reciprocal Enforcement) Act 1972 (recovery of maintenance in Scotland from former spouse on order made in convention country) shall have effect with the following amendments.

(2)   In paragraph (i), for the words 'granted in a convention country' there shall be substituted the words 'obtained in a country or territory outside the United Kingdom'.

(3)   For paragraph (ii) there shall be substituted the following paragraphs—

'(ii)   an order for the payment of maintenance for the benefit of the applicant as a divorced person has, in or by reason of, or subsequent to, the divorce proceedings, been made by a court in a convention country;

(iia)   in a case where the order mentioned in paragraph (ii) above was made by a court of a different country from that in which the divorce was obtained, either the applicant or the said former spouse was resident in that different country at the time the application for the order so mentioned was made; and'.

FAMILY LAW (SCOTLAND) ACT 1985
(1985, c 37)

Aliment

1   Obligation of aliment

(1)   From the commencement of this Act, an obligation of aliment shall be owed by, and only by—

(a)   a husband to his wife;

(b)   a wife to her husband;

[(bb) a partner in a civil partnership to the other partner,]

(c)   a father or mother to his or her child;

(d)   a person to a child (other than a child who has been boarded out with him by a local or other public authority or a voluntary organisation) who has been accepted by him as a child of his family.

(2)   For the purposes of this Act, an obligation of aliment is an obligation to provide such support as is reasonable in the circumstances, having regard to the matters to which a court is required or entitled to have regard under section 4 of this Act in determining the amount of aliment to award in an action for aliment.

(3)   Any obligation of aliment arising under a decree or by operation of law and subsisting immediately before the commencement of this Act shall, except insofar

as consistent with this section, cease to have effect as from the commencement of this Act.

(4) Nothing in this section shall affect any arrears due under a decree at the date of termination or cessation of an obligation of aliment, nor any rule of law by which a person who is owed an obligation of aliment may claim aliment from the executor of a deceased person or from any person enriched by the succession to the estate of a deceased person.

(5) In subsection (1) above—

'child' means a person—

(a) under the age of 18 years; or

(b) over that age and under the age of 25 years who is reasonably and appropriately undergoing instruction at an educational establishment, or training for employment or for a trade, profession or vocation;

'husband' and 'wife' include the parties to a valid polygamous marriage.

2 Actions for aliment

(1) A claim for aliment only (whether or not expenses are also sought) may be made, against any person owing an obligation of aliment, in the Court of Session or the sheriff court.

(2) Unless the court considers it inappropriate in any particular case, a claim for aliment may also be made, against any person owing an obligation of aliment, in proceedings—

(a) for divorce, separation, declarator of marriage or declarator of nullity of marriage;

[(aa) for dissolution of a civil partnership, separation of civil partners or declarator of nullity of a civil partnership,]

(b) relating to orders for financial provision;

[(c) concerning parental responsibilities or parental rights (within the meaning of sections 1(3) and 2(4) respectively of the Children (Scotland) Act 1995) or guardianship in relation to children;]

(d) concerning parentage or legitimacy;

(e) of any other kind, where the court considers it appropriate to include a claim for aliment.

(3) In this Act 'action for aliment' means a claim for aliment in proceedings referred to in subsection (1) or (2) above.

(4) An action for aliment may be brought—

(a) by a person (including a child) to whom the obligation of aliment is owed;

(b) by the curator bonis of an incapax;

(c) on behalf of a child under the age of 18 years, by—

(i) the [parent or guardian] of the child;

[. . .]

[(iii) a person with whom the child lives or who is seeking a residence order (within the meaning of section 11(2)(c) of the Children (Scotland) Act 1995) in respect of the child.]

(5) A woman (whether married or not) may bring an action for aliment on behalf of her unborn child as if the child had been born, but no such action shall be heard or disposed of prior to the birth of the child.

(6) It shall be competent to bring an action for aliment, notwithstanding that the person for or on behalf of whom aliment is being claimed is living in the same household as the defender.

(7) It shall be a defence to an action for aliment brought by virtue of subsection (6) above that the defender is fulfilling the obligation of aliment, and intends to continue doing so.

(8) It shall be a defence to an action for aliment by or on behalf of a person other than a child under the age of 16 years that the defender is making an offer,

which it is reasonable to expect the person concerned to accept, to receive that person into his household and to fulfil the obligation of aliment.

(9)   For the purposes of subsection (8) above, in considering whether it is reasonable to expect a person to accept an offer, the court shall have regard among other things to any conduct, decree or other circumstances which appear to the court to be relevant: but the fact that a husband and wife [or the partners in a civil partnership] have agreed to live apart shall not of itself be regarded as making it unreasonable to expect a person to accept such an offer.

(10)   A person bringing an action for aliment under subsection (4)(c) above may give a good receipt for aliment paid under the decree in the action.

3   Powers of court in action for aliment

(1)   The court may, if it thinks fit, grant decree in an action for aliment, and in granting such decree shall have power—

(a)   to order the making of periodical payments, whether for a definite or an indefinite period or until the happening of a specified event;

(b)   to order the making of alimentary payments of an occasional or special nature, including payments in respect of inlying, funeral or educational expenses;

(c)   to backdate an award of aliment under this Act—

(i)   to the date of the bringing of the action or to such later date as the court thinks fit; or

(ii)   on special cause shown, to a date prior to the bringing of the action;

(d)   to award less than the amount claimed even if the claim is undisputed.

(2)   Nothing in subsection (1) above shall empower the court to substitute a lump sum for a periodical payment.

4   Amount of aliment

(1)   In determining the amount of aliment to award in an action for aliment, the court shall, subject to subsection (3) below, have regard—

(a)   to the needs and resources of the parties;

(b)   to the earning capacities of the parties;

(c)   generally to all the circumstances of the case.

(2)   Where two or more parties owe an obligation of aliment to another person, there shall be no order of liability, but the court, in deciding how much, if any, aliment to award against any of those persons, shall have regard, among the other circumstances of the case, to the obligation of aliment owed by any other person.

(3)   In having regard under subsection (1)(c) above generally to all the circumstances of the case, the court—

(a)   may, if it thinks fit, take account of any support, financial or otherwise, given by the defender to any person whom he maintains as a dependant in his household, whether or not the defender owes an obligation of aliment to that person; and

(b)   shall not take account of any conduct of a party unless it would be manifestly inequitable to leave it out of account.

[(4)   Where a court makes an award of aliment in an action brought by or on behalf of a child under the age of 16 years, it may include in that award such provision as it considers to be in all the circumstances reasonable in respect of the expenses incurred wholly or partly by the person having care of the child for the purpose of caring for the child.]

5   Variation or recall of decree of aliment

(1)   A decree granted in an action for aliment brought before or after the commencement of this Act may, on an application by or on behalf of either party to the action, be varied or recalled by an order of the court if since the date of the decree there has been a material change of circumstances.

[(1A)   Without prejudice to the generality of subsection (1) above, the making of a [maintenance calculation] with respect to a child for whom the decree of aliment was granted is a material change of circumstances for the purposes of that subsection.]

(2)　The provisions of this Act shall apply to applications and orders under subsection (1) above as they apply to actions for aliment and decrees in such actions, subject to any necessary modifications.

(3)　On an application under subsection (1) above, the court may, pending determination of the application, make such interim order as it thinks fit.

(4)　Where the court backdates an order under subsection (1) above, the court may order any sums paid under the decree to be repaid.

6　Interim aliment

(1)　A claim for interim aliment shall be competent—

　　(a)　in an action for aliment, by the [person] who claims aliment against the other [person];

　　(b)　in an action for divorce, separation, declarator of marriage or declarator of nullity of marriage, by either party against the other party,

　　[(c)　in an action for dissolution of a civil partnership, separation of civil partners or declarator of nullity of a civil partnership, by either partner against the other partner,]

on behalf of the claimant and any person on whose behalf he is entitled to act under section 2(4) of this Act.

(2)　Where a claim under subsection (1) above has been made, then, whether or not the claim is disputed, the court may award by way of interim aliment the sum claimed or any lesser sum or may refuse to make such an award.

(3)　An award under subsection (2) above shall consist of an award of periodical payments payable only until the date of the disposal of the action in which the award was made or such earlier date as the court may specify.

(4)　An award under subsection (2) above may be varied or recalled by an order of the court; and the provisions of this section shall apply to an award so varied and the claim therefor as they applied to the original award and the claim therefor.

7　Agreements on aliment

(1)　Any provision in an agreement which purports to exclude future liability for aliment or to restrict any right to bring an action for aliment shall have no effect unless the provision was fair and reasonable in all the circumstances of the agreement at the time it was entered into.

(2)　Where a person who owes an obligation of aliment to another person has entered into an agreement to pay aliment to or for the benefit of the other person, on a material change of circumstances application may be made to the court by or on behalf of either person for variation of the amount payable under the agreement or for termination of the agreement.

[(2A)　Without prejudice to the generality of subsection (2) above, the making of a [maintenance calculation] with respect to a child to whom or for whose benefit aliment is payable under such an agreement is a material change of circumstances for the purposes of that subsection.]

(3)　Subsections (8) and (9) of section 2 of this Act (which afford a defence to an action for aliment in certain circumstances) shall apply to an action to enforce such an agreement as is referred to in subsection (2) above as they apply to an action for aliment.

(4)　In subsection (2) above 'the court' means the court which would have jurisdiction and competence to entertain an action for aliment between the parties to the agreement to which the application under that subsection relates.

(5)　In this section 'agreement' means an agreement entered into before or after the commencement of this Act and includes a unilateral voluntary obligation.

Financial provision on divorce, etc

8   Orders for financial provision

(1)   In an action for divorce, either party to the marriage [and in an action for dissolution of a civil partnership, either partner] may apply to the court for one or more of the following orders—

(a)   an order for the payment of a capital sum [. . .] to him by the other party to the marriage;

[(aa)   an order for the transfer of property to him by the other party to the marriage;]

(b)   an order for the making of a periodical allowance to him by the other party to the marriage;

[(ba)   an order under section 12A(2) or (3) of this Act;

(baa)   a pension sharing order;]

(c)   an incidental order within the meaning of section 14(2) of this Act.

(2)   Subject to sections 12 to 15 of this Act, where an application has been made under subsection (1) above, the court shall make such order, if any, as is—

(a)   justified by the principles set out in section 9 of this Act; and

(b)   reasonable having regard to the resources of the parties.

(3)   An order under subsection (2) above is in this Act referred to as an 'order for financial provision'.

[(4)   The court shall not, in the same proceedings, make both a pension sharing order and an order under section 12A(2) or (3) of this Act in relation to the same pension arrangement.

(5)   Where, as regards a pension arrangement, the parties to a marriage [or the partners in a civil partnership] have in effect a qualifying agreement which contains a term relating to pension sharing, the court shall not—

(a)   make an order under section 12A(2) or (3) of this Act; or

(b)   make a pension sharing order,

relating to the arrangement unless it also sets aside the agreement or term under section 16(1)(b) of this Act.

(6)   The court shall not make a pension sharing order in relation to the rights of a person under a pension arrangement if there is in force an order under section 12A(2) or (3) of this Act which relates to benefits or future benefits to which he is entitled under the pension arrangement.

(7)   In subsection (5) above—

(a)   'term relating to pension sharing' shall be construed in accordance with section 16(2A) of this Act; and

(b)   'qualifying agreement' has the same meaning as in section 28(3) of the Welfare Reform and Pensions Act 1999.]

[8A   Pension sharing orders: apportionment of charges

If a pension sharing order relates to rights under a pension arrangement, the court may include in the order provision about the apportionment between the parties of any charge under section 41 of the Welfare Reform and Pensions Act 1999 (charges in respect of pension sharing costs) or under corresponding Northern Ireland legislation.]

9   Principles to be applied

(1)   The principles which the court shall apply in deciding what order for financial provision, if any, to make are that—

(a)   the net value of the matrimonial property should be shared fairly between the parties to the marriage [or as the case may be the net value of the partnership property should be so shared between the partners in the civil partnership];

(b)   fair account should be taken of any economic advantage derived by either [person] from contributions by the other, and of any economic dis-

advantage suffered by either [person] in the interests of the other [person] or of
the family;

    (c)   any economic burden of caring—

      [(i)] after divorce, for a child of the marriage under the age of 16 years
should be shared fairly between the [persons];

      [(ii)] after dissolution of the civil partnership, for a child under that age
who has been accepted by both partners as a child of the family,]

    (d)   a [person] who has been dependent to a substantial degree on the finan-
cial support of the other [person] should be awarded such financial provision as
is reasonable to enable him to adjust, over a period of not more than three years
from—

      [(i)] the date of the decree of divorce, to the loss of that support on divorce;

      [(ii)] the date of the decree of dissolution of the civil partnership, to the loss
of that support on dissolution,]

    (e)   a [person] who at the time of the divorce [or of the dissolution of the
civil partnership] seems likely to suffer serious financial hardship as a result of
the divorce [or dissolution] should be awarded such financial provision as is
reasonable to relieve him of hardship over a reasonable period.

    (2) In subsection (1)(b) above and section 11(2) of this Act—

'economic advantage' means advantage gained whether before or during the
marriage [or civil partnership] and includes gains in capital, in income and in
earning capacity, and 'economic disadvantage' shall be construed accordingly;

'contributions' means contributions made whether before or during the marriage
[or civil partnership]; and includes indirect and non-financial contributions and, in
particular, any such contribution made by looking after the family home or caring
for the family.

10   Sharing of value of matrimonial property

    (1) In applying the principle set out in section 9(1)(a) of this Act, the net value
of the matrimonial property [or partnership property] shall be taken to be shared
fairly between the [persons] when it is shared equally or in such other proportions
as are justified by special circumstances.

    (2) The net value of the [. . .] property shall be the value of the property at the
relevant date after deduction of any debts incurred by [one or both of the parties
to the marriage or as the case may be of the partners]—

    (a)   before the marriage so far as they relate to the matrimonial property [or
before the registration of the partnership so far as they relate to the partnership
property], and

    (b)   during the marriage [or partnership],

which are outstanding at that date.

    (3) In this section 'the relevant date' means whichever is the earlier of—

    (a)   subject to subsection (7) below, the date on which the [persons] ceased to
cohabit;

    (b)   the date of service of the summons in the action for divorce [or for dis-
solution of the civil partnership].

    (4) Subject to subsection (5) below, in this section and in section 11 of this Act
'the matrimonial property' means all the property belonging to the parties or
either of them at the relevant date which was acquired by them or him (otherwise
than by way of gift or succession from a third party)—

    (a)   before the marriage for use by them as a family home or as furniture or
plenishings for such home; or

    (b)   during the marriage but before the relevant date.

    [(4A) Subject to subsection (5) below, in this section and in section 11 of this
Act 'the partnership property' means all the property belonging to the partners or
either of them at the relevant date which was acquired by them or by one of them
(otherwise than by way of gift or succession from a third party)—

(a)   before the registration of the partnership for use by them as a family home or as furniture or plenishings for such a home, or

(b)   during the partnership but before the relevant date.]

(5)   The proportion of any rights or interests of either [person]—

[(a)]   under a life policy [. . .] or similar arrangement [; and

(b)   in any benefits under a pension arrangement which either [person] has or may have (including such benefits payable in respect of the death of either [person]), and

(c)   in the assets in respect of which either [person] has accrued rights to benefits under a pension scheme,

which is] referable to the period to which subsection (4)(b) above refers shall be taken to form part of the matrimonial property [or partnership property].

[(5A)   In the case of an unfunded pension scheme, the court may not make an order which would allow assets to be removed from the scheme earlier than would otherwise have been the case.]

(6)   In subsection (1) above 'special circumstances', without prejudice to the generality of the words, may include—

(a)   the terms of any agreement between the [persons] on the ownership or division of any of the matrimonial property [or partnership property];

(b)   the source of the funds or assets used to acquire any of the matrimonial property [or partnership property] where those funds or assets were not derived from the income or efforts of the [persons] during the marriage [or partnership];

(c)   any destruction, dissipation or alienation of property by either [person];

(d)   the nature of the matrimonial property [or partnership property], the use made of it (including use for business purposes or as a [family] home) and the extent to which it is reasonable to expect it to be realised or divided or used as security;

(e)   the actual or prospective liability for any expenses of valuation or transfer of property in connection with the divorce [or the dissolution of the civil partnership].

(7)   For the purposes of subsection (3) above no account shall be taken of any cessation of cohabitation where the [persons] thereafter resumed cohabitation, except where the [persons] ceased to cohabit for a continuous period of 90 days or more before resuming cohabitation for a period or periods of less than 90 days in all.

[(8)   The Secretary of State may by regulations make provision about calculation and verification in relation to the valuation for the purposes of this Act of benefits under a pension arrangement or relevant state scheme rights.]

[(8A) Regulations under subsection (8) above may include—

(a)   provision for calculation or verification in accordance with guidance from time to time prepared by a prescribed person; and

(b)   provision by reference to regulations under section 30 or 49(4) of the Welfare Reform and Pensions Act 1999.]

(9)   Regulations under subsection (8) above [may make different provision for different purposes and] shall be made by statutory instrument which shall be subject to annulment in pursuance of a resolution of either House of Parliament.

11   Factors to be taken into account

(1)   In applying the principles set out in section 9 of this Act, the following provisions of this section shall have effect.

(2)   For the purposes of section 9(1)(b) of this Act, the court shall have regard to the extent to which—

(a)   the economic advantages or disadvantages sustained by either [person] have been balanced by the economic advantages or disadvantages sustained by the other [person], and

(b)   any resulting imbalance has been or will be corrected by a sharing of the value of the matrimonial property [or the partnership property] or otherwise.

(3)   For the purposes of section 9(1)(c) of this Act, the court shall have regard to—

(a)   any decree or arrangement for aliment for the child;

(b)   any expenditure or loss of earning capacity caused by the need to care for the child;

(c)   the need to provide suitable accommodation for the child;

(d)   the age and health of the child;

(e)   the educational, financial and other circumstances of the child;

(f)   the availability and cost of suitable child-care facilities or services;

(g)   the needs and resources of the [persons]; and

(h)   all the other circumstances of the case.

(4)   For the purposes of section 9(1)(d) of this Act, the court shall have regard to—

(a)   the age, health and earning capacity of the [person] who is claiming the financial provision;

(b)   the duration and extent of the dependence of that [person prior to divorce or to the dissolution of the civil partnership];

(c)   any intention of that [person] to undertake a course of education or training;

(d)   the needs and resources of the [persons]; and

(e)   all the other circumstances of the case.

(5)   For the purposes of section 9(1)(e) of this Act, the court shall have regard to—

(a)   the age, health and earning capacity of the [person] who is claiming the financial provision;

(b)   the duration of the marriage [or of the civil partnership];

(c)   the standard of living of the [persons] during the marriage [or civil partnership];

(d)   the needs and resources of the [persons]; and

(e)   all the other circumstances of the case.

(6)   In having regard under subsections (3) to (5) above to all the other circumstances of the case, the court may, if it thinks fit, take account of any support, financial or otherwise, given by the [person] who is to make the financial provision to any person whom he maintains as a dependant in his household whether or not he owes an obligation of aliment to that person.

(7)   In applying the principles set out in section 9 of this Act, the court shall not take account of the conduct of either party [to the marriage or as the case may be of either partner] unless—

(a)   the conduct has adversely affected the financial resources which are relevant to the decision of the court on a claim for financial provision; or

(b)   in relation to section 9(1)(d) or (e), it would be manifestly inequitable to leave the conduct out of account.

12   Orders for payment of capital sum or transfer of property

(1)   An order under section 8(2) of this Act for payment of a capital sum or transfer of property may be made—

(a)   on granting decree of divorce [or of dissolution of a civil partnership]; or

(b)   within such period as the court on granting [the decree] may specify.

(2)   The court, on making an order referred to in subsection (1) above, may stipulate that it shall come into effect at a specified future date.

(3)   The court, on making an order under section 8(2) of this Act for payment of a capital sum, may order that the capital sum shall be payable by instalments.

(4)   Where an order referred to in subsection (1) above has been made, the court may, on an application by—

[(a)]   either party to the marriage;
[(b)   either partner,]
on a material change of circumstances, vary the date or method of payment of the capital sum or the date of transfer of property.

[12A   Orders for payment of capital sum: pensions lump sums

(1)   This section applies where the court makes an order under section 8(2) of this Act for payment of a capital sum (a 'capital sum order') by a party to the marriage [or a partner in a civil partnership ('the liable person')] in circumstances where—

(a)   the matrimonial property [or the partnership property] within the meaning of section 10 of this Act includes any rights or interests in benefits under a pension [arrangement] which the liable [person] has or may have (whether such benefits are payable to him or in respect of his death); and

(b)   those benefits include a lump sum payable to him or in respect of his death.

(2)   Where the benefits referred to in subsection (1) above include a lump sum payable to the liable party, the court, on making the capital sum order, may make an order requiring the [person responsible for the pension arrangement] in question to pay the whole or part of that sum, when it becomes due, to the other party to the marriage [or as the case may be to the other partner ('the other person')].

(3)   Where the benefits referred to in subsection (1) above include a lump sum payable in respect of the death of the liable [person], the court, on making the capital sum order, may make an order—

(a)   if the [person responsible for the pension arrangement in question has] power to determine the person to whom the sum, or any part of it, is to be paid, requiring them to pay the whole or part of that sum, when it becomes due, to the other [person];

(b)   if the liable [person] has power to nominate the person to whom the sum, or any part of it, is to be paid, requiring the liable [person] to nominate the other [person] in respect of the whole or part of that sum;

(c)   in any other case, requiring the [person responsible for the pension arrangement] in question to pay the whole or part of that sum, when it becomes due, to the other [person] instead of to the person to whom, apart from the order, it would be paid.

(4)   Any payment by the [person responsible for the pension agreement] under an order under subsection (2) or (3) above—

(a)   shall discharge so much of the [liability of the person responsible for the pension arrangement] to or in respect of the liable [person] as corresponds to the amount of the payment; and

(b)   shall be treated for all purposes as a payment made by the liable [person] in or towards the discharge of his liability under the capital sum order.

(5)   Where the liability of the liable [person] under the capital sum order has been discharged in whole or in part, other than by a payment by the [person responsible for the pension arrangement] under an order under subsection (2) or (3) above, the court may, on an application by any person having an interest, recall any order under either of those subsections or vary the amount specified in such an order, as appears to the court appropriate in the circumstances.

(6)   Where—

(a)   an order under subsection (2) or (3) above imposes any requirement on the [person responsible for a pension arrangement] ('the first [arrangement]') and the liable [person] acquires transfer credits under another [arrangement] ('the new [arrangement]') which are derived (directly or indirectly) from a transfer from the first [arrangement] of all his accrued rights under that [arrangement]; and

(b)   [the person responsible for the new arrangement has] been given notice in accordance with regulations under subsection (8) below,
the order shall have effect as if it had been made instead in respect of the [person responsible for the new arrangement]; and in this subsection 'transfer credits' has the same meaning as in the Pension Schemes Act 1993.

(7)   Without prejudice to subsection (6) above, any court may, on an application by any person having an interest, vary an order under subsection (2) or (3) above by substituting for [the person responsible for the pension arrangement] specified in the order [person responsible for any other pension arrangement] under which any lump sum referred to in subsection (1) above is payable to the liable [person] or in respect of his death.

(8)   The Secretary of State may by regulations—
    (a)   require notices to be given in respect of changes of circumstances relevant to orders under subsection (2) or (3) above.
    [. . .]
(9)   Regulations under subsection (8) above shall be made by statutory instrument which shall be subject to annulment in pursuance of a resolution of either House of Parliament.

[(10)   The definition of 'benefits under a pension scheme' in section 27 of this Act does not apply to this section.]

13   Orders for periodical allowance

(1)   An order under section 8(2) of this Act for a periodical allowance may be made—
    (a)   on granting decree of divorce [or of dissolution of a civil partnership];
    (b)   within such period as the court on granting [the decree] may specify; or
    (c)   after [such decree] where—
        (i)   no such order has been made previously;
        (ii)   application for the order has been made after the date of decree; and
        (iii)   since the date of decree there has been a change of circumstances.
(2)   The court shall not make an order for a periodical allowance under section 8(2) of this Act unless—
    (a)   the order is justified by a principle set out in paragraph (c), (d) or (e) of section 9(1) of this Act; and
    (b)   it is satisfied that an order for payment of a capital sum or for transfer of property [or a pension sharing order] under that section would be inappropriate or insufficient to satisfy the requirements of the said section 8(2).
(3)   An order under section 8(2) of this Act for a periodical allowance may be for a definite or an indefinite period or until the happening of a specified event.
(4)   Where an order for a periodical allowance has been made under section 8(2) of this Act, and since the date of the order there has been a material change of circumstances, the court shall, on an application by or on behalf of either party to the marriage or his executor [, or as the case may be either partner or his executor], have power by subsequent order—
    (a)   to vary or recall the order for a periodical allowance;
    (b)   to backdate such variation or recall to the date of the application therefor or, on cause shown, to an earlier date;
    (c)   to convert the order into an order for payment of a capital sum or for a transfer of property.
[(4A)   Without prejudice to the generality of subsection (4) above, the making of a maintenance [calculation] with respect to a child who has his home with a person to whom the periodical allowance is made (being a child to whom the person making the allowance has an obligation of aliment) is a material change of circumstances for the purposes of that subsection.]
(5)   The provisions of this Act shall apply to applications and orders under sub-

section (4) above as they apply to applications for periodical allowance and orders on such applications.

(6) Where the court backdates an order under subsection (4)(b) above, the court may order any sums paid by way of periodical allowance to be repaid.

(7) An order for a periodical allowance made under section 8(2) of this Act—

(a) shall, if subsisting at the death of the [person] making the payment, continue to operate against that [person's] estate, but without prejudice to the making of an order under subsection (4) above;

[(b) shall cease to have effect on the person receiving payment—

(i) marrying,

(ii) entering into a civil partnership,

(iii) dying,]

except in relation to any arrears due under it.

14 Incidental orders

(1) Subject to subsection (3) below, an incidental order may be made under section 8(2) of this Act before, on or after the granting or refusal of decree of divorce [or of dissolution of a civil partnership].

(2) In this Act, 'an incidental order' means one or more of the following orders—

(a) an order for the sale of property;

(b) an order for the valuation of property;

(c) an order determining any dispute between the parties to the marriage [or as the case may be the partners] as to their respective property rights by means of a declarator thereof or otherwise;

(d) an order regulating the occupation of—

[(i)] the matrimonial home; or

[(ii) the family home of the partnership,]

or the use of furniture and plenishings therein or excluding either [person] from such occupation;

(e) an order regulating liability, as between the [persons], for outgoings in respect of—

[(i)] the matrimonial home; or

(ii) the family home of the partnership,]

or furniture or plenishings therein;

(f) an order that security shall be given for any financial provision;

(g) an order that payments shall be made or property transferred to any curator bonis or trustee or other person for the benefit of the [person] by whom or on whose behalf application has been made under section 8(1) of this Act for an incidental order;

(h) an order setting aside or varying any term in an antenuptial or postnuptial marriage settlement [or in any corresponding settlement in respect of the civil partnership];

(j) an order as to the date from which any interest on any amount awarded shall run;

(k) any ancillary order which is expedient to give effect to the principles set out in section 9 of this Act or to any order made under section 8(2) of this Act.

(3) An incidental order referred to in subsection (2)(d) or (e) above may be made only on or after the granting of [the decree].

(4) An incidental order may be varied or recalled by subsequent order on cause shown.

(5) So long as an incidental order granting a party to a marriage the right to occupy a matrimonial home or the right to use furniture and plenishings therein remains in force then—

(a) section 2(1), (2), (5)(a) and (9) of the Matrimonial Homes (Family Protection) (Scotland) Act 1981 (which confer certain general powers of management on a spouse in relation to a matrimonial home), and

(b)   subject to section 15(3) of this Act, section 12 of the said Act of 1981 and section [41 of the Bankruptcy (Scotland) Act 1985] (which protect the occupancy rights of a spouse against arrangements intended to defeat them),

shall, except to the extent that the order otherwise provides, apply in relation to the order—

(i)   as if that party were a non-entitled spouse and the other party were an entitled spouse within the meaning of section 1(1) or 6(2) of the said Act of 1981 as the case may require;

(ii)   as if the right to occupy a matrimonial home under that order were 'occupancy rights' with the meaning of the said Act of 1981; and

(iii)   with any other necessary modifications; and

subject to section 15(3) of this Act, section 11 of the said Act of 1981 (protection of spouse in relation to furniture and plenishings) shall apply in relation to the order as if that party were a spouse within the meaning of the said section 11 and the order were an order under section 3(3) or (4) of the said Act of 1981.

[(5A)   So long as an incidental order granting a partner in a civil partnership the right to occupy a family home or the right to use furnishings and plenishings therein remains in force then—

(a)   section 102(1), (2), (5)(a) and (9) of the Civil Partnership Act 2004, and

(b)   subject to section 15(3) of this Act, section 111 of that Act,

shall, except to the extent that the order otherwise provides, apply in relation to the order in accordance with subsection (5B).

(5B)   Those provisions apply—

(a) as if that partner were a non-entitled partner and the other partner were an entitled partner within the meaning of section 101 or 106(2) of that Act as the case may require,

(b)   as if the right to occupy a family home under that order were a right specified in paragraph (a) or (b) of section 101(1) of that Act, and

(c)   with any other necessary modification.]

(6)   In subsection (2)(h) above, 'settlement' includes a settlement by way of a policy of assurance to which section 2 of the Married Women's Policies of Assurance (Scotland) Act 1880 relates.

(7)   Notwithstanding subsection (1) above, the Court of Session may by Act of Sederunt make rules restricting the categories of incidental order which may be made under section 8(2) of this Act before the granting of decree of divorce.

15   Rights of third parties

(1)   The court shall not make an order under section 8(2) of this Act for the transfer of property if the consent of a third party which is necessary under any obligation, enactment or rule of law has not been obtained.

(2)   The court shall not make an order under section 8(2) of this Act for the transfer of property subject to security without the consent of the creditor unless he has been given an opportunity of being heard by the court.

(3)   Neither an incidental order, nor any rights conferred by such an order, shall prejudice any rights of any third party insofar as those rights existed immediately before the making of the order.

16   Agreements on financial provision

(1)   Where the parties to a marriage [or the partners in a civil partnership] have entered into an agreement as to financial provision to be made on divorce [or on dissolution of the civil partnership], the court may make an order setting aside or varying—

(a)   any term of the agreement relating to a periodical allowance where the agreement expressly provides for the subsequent setting aside or variation by the court of that term; or

(b)   the agreement or any term of it where the agreement was not fair and reasonable at the time it was entered into.

(2)   The court may make an order—
    (a)   under subsection (1)(a) above at any time after granting decree of divorce; and
    [(b)   under subsection (1)(b) above, if the agreement does not contain a term relating to pension sharing, on granting decree of divorce or within such time as the court may specify, on granting decree of divorce; or
    (c)   under subsection (1)(b) above, if the agreement contains a term relating to pension sharing—
        (i)   where the order sets aside the agreement or sets aside or varies the term relating to pension sharing, on granting decree of divorce; and
        (ii)   where the order sets aside or varies any other term of the agreement, on granting decree of divorce or within such time thereafter as the court may specify on granting decree of divorce.]
    [(2A)   In subsection (2) above, a term relating to pension sharing is a term corresponding to provision which may be made in a pension sharing order and satisfying the requirements set out in section 28(1)(f) or 48(1)(f) of the Welfare Reform and Pensions Act 1999.]
    (3)   Without prejudice to subsections (1) and (2) above, where the parties to a marriage [or the partners in a civil partnership] have entered into an agreement as to financial provision to be made on divorce [or on dissolution of the civil partnership] and—
    (a)   the estate of the [person] by whom any periodical allowance is payable under the agreement has, since the date when the agreement was entered into, been sequestrated, the award of sequestration has not been recalled and the [person] has not been discharged;
    (b)   an analogous remedy within the meaning of section 10(5) of the Bankruptcy (Scotland) Act 1985 has, since that date, come into force and remains in force in respect of that [person's] estate;
    (c)   that [person's] estate is being administered by a trustee acting under a voluntary trust deed granted since that date by the [person] for the benefit of his creditors generally or is subject to an analogous arrangement [; or
    (d)   by virtue of the making of a maintenance calculation, child support maintenance has become payable by either party to the agreement with respect to a child to whom or for whose benefit periodical allowance is paid under that agreement,]
the court may, on or at any time after granting decree of divorce [or of dissolution of the civil partnership], make an order setting aside or varying any term of the agreement relating to the periodical allowance.
    (4)   Any term of an agreement purporting to exclude the right to apply for an order under subsection (1)(b) or (3) above shall be void.
    (5)   In this section, 'agreement' means an agreement entered into before or after the commencement of this Act.

17   Financial provision on declarator of nullity of marriage
    (1)   Subject to the following provisions of this section, the provisions of this Act shall apply to actions for declarator of nullity of marriage [or of a civil partnership] as they apply to actions for divorce [or for dissolution of a civil partnership]; and in this Act, unless the context otherwise requires, 'action for divorce' includes an action for declarator of nullity of marriage [and 'action for dissolution of a civil partnership' includes an action for declarator of nullity of a civil partnership] and, in relation to such an action, 'decree' [, 'divorce' and dissolution of a civil partnership] shall be construed accordingly.
    (2)   In an action for declarator of nullity of marriage [or of nullity of a civil partnership], it shall be competent for either party to claim interim aliment under section 6(1) of this Act notwithstanding that he denies the existence of the marriage [or civil partnership].

(3) Any rule of law by virtue of which either party to an action for declarator of nullity of marriage may require restitution of property upon the granting of such declarator shall cease to have effect.

Supplemental

18 Orders relating to avoidance transactions

(1) Where a claim has been made (whether before or after the commencement of this Act), being—

(a)   an action for aliment,

(b)   a claim for an order for financial provision, or

(c)   an application for variation or recall of a decree in such an action or of an order for financial provision,

the [person] making the claim may, not later than one year from the date of the disposal of the claim, apply to the court for an order—

(i) setting aside or varying any transfer of, or transaction involving, property effected by the other [person] not more than 5 years before the date of the making of the claim; or

(ii) interdicting the other [person] from effecting any such transfer or transaction.

(2) Subject to subsection (3) below, on an application under subsection (1) above for an order the court may, if it is satisfied that the transfer or transaction had the effect of, or is likely to have the effect of, defeating in whole or in part any claim referred to in subsection (1) above, make the order applied for or such other order as it thinks fit.

(3) An order under subsection (2) above shall not prejudice any rights of a third party in or to the property where that third party—

(a)   has in good faith acquired the property or any of it or any rights in relation to it for value; or

(b)   derives title to such property or rights from any person who has done so.

(4) Where the court makes an order under subsection (2) above, it may include in the order such terms and conditions as it thinks fit and may make any ancillary order which it considers expedient to ensure that the order is effective.

19 Inhibition and arrestment

(1) Where a claim has been made, being—

(a)   an action for aliment, or

(b)   a claim for an order for financial provision,

the court shall have power, on cause shown, to grant warrant for inhibition or warrant for arrestment on the dependence of the action in which the claim is made and, if it thinks fit, to limit the inhibition to any particular property or to limit the arrestment to any particular property or to funds not exceeding a specified value.

(2) In subsection (1) above, 'the court' means the Court of Session in relation to a warrant for inhibition and the Court of Session or the sheriff, as the case may require, in relation to a warrant for arrestment on the dependence.

(3) This section is without prejudice to section 1 of the Law Reform (Miscellaneous Provisions) (Scotland) Act 1966 (wages, pensions, etc, to be exempt from arrestment on the dependence of an action).

20 Provision of details of resources

In an action—

(a)   for aliment;

(b)   which includes a claim for an order for financial provision; or

(c)   which includes a claim for interim aliment,

the court may order either party to provide details of his resources or those relating to a child or incapax on whose behalf he is acting.

21 Award of aliment or custody where divorce or separation refused
A court which refuses a decree of divorce [, separation or dissolution of a civil partnership] shall not, by virtue of such refusal, be prevented from making an order for aliment [. . .] or an incidental order determining any dispute between the [persons] as to their respective property rights.

22 Expenses of action
The expenses incurred by a [person] in pursuing or defending—
    (a)   an action for aliment brought [—
        (i)] by either party to the marriage or
       [(ii) by either party in a civil partnership,]
  on his own behalf against the other party;
    (b)   an action for divorce, separation [(whether of the parties to a marriage or the civil partners in a civil partnership)], declarator of marriage or declarator of nullity of marriage;
    [(bb) an action for dissolution of a civil partnership, declarator that a civil partnership exists or declarator of nullity of a civil partnership,]
    (c)   an application made after the commencement of this Act for variation or recall of a decree of aliment or an order for financial provision in an action brought before or after the commencement of this Act,
shall not be regarded as necessaries for which the other party to the marriage [or the other partner in a civil partnership] is liable.

23 Actions for aliment of small amounts
For section 3 of the Sheriff Courts (Civil Jurisdiction and Procedure) (Scotland) Act 1963 there shall be substituted the following section—

   3 'Actions for aliment of small amounts
    (1)   An action under section 2 of the Family Law (Scotland) Act 1985 for aliment only (whether or not expenses are also sought) may be brought before the sheriff as a summary cause if the aliment claimed in the action does not exceed—
        (a)   in respect of a child under the age of 18 years, the sum of £35 per week; and
        (b)   in any other case, the sum of £70 per week;
  and any provision in any enactment limiting the jurisdiction of the sheriff in a summary cause by reference to any amount, or limiting the period for which a decree granted by him shall have effect, shall not apply in relation to such an action.
    (2)   Without prejudice to any other enactment, the sheriff shall have jurisdiction in an action for aliment brought as a summary cause by virtue of subsection (1) above if—
        (a)   the pursuer resides within the jurisdiction of the sheriff, and
        (b)   the action could, by virtue of section 6 of the principal Act (which relates to jurisdiction), have been brought in the sheriff court of another sheriffdom.
    (3)   The Lord Advocate may by order vary the amounts prescribed in paragraphs (a) and (b) of subsection (1) above.
    (4)   The power to make an order under subsection (3) above shall be exercisable by statutory instrument subject to annulment in pursuance of a resolution of either House of Parliament and shall include power to vary or revoke any order made thereunder.'

Matrimonial property, etc

24 Marriage not to affect property rights or legal capacity
    (1)   Subject to the provisions of any enactment (including this Act), marriage [or civil partnership] shall not of itself affect—

(a)   the respective rights of the parties to the marriage [or as the case may be the partners in a civil partnership] in relation to their property;

(b)   the legal capacity of [those parties or partners].

(2)   Nothing in subsection (1) above affects the law of succession.

25   Presumption of equal shares in household goods

(1)   If any question arises (whether during or after a marriage [or civil partnership]) as to the respective rights of ownership of the parties to a marriage [or the partners in a civil partnership] in any household goods obtained in prospect of or during the marriage [or civil partnership] other than by gift or succession from a third party, it shall be presumed, unless the contrary is proved, that each has a right to an equal share in the goods in question.

(2)   For the purposes of subsection (1) above, the contrary shall not be treated as proved by reason only that while [—

(a)]   the parties were married;

[(b)   the partners were in a civil partnership],

and living together the goods in question were purchased from a third party by either party alone or by both in unequal shares.

(3)   In this section 'household goods' means any goods (including decorative or ornamental goods) kept or used at any time during the marriage [or civil partnership in any family] home for the joint domestic purposes of the parties to the marriage [or the partners], other than—

(a)   money or securities;

(b)   any motor car, caravan or other road vehicle;

(c) any domestic animal.

26   Presumption of equal shares in money and property derived from housekeeping allowance

If any question arises (whether during or after a marriage [or civil partnership]) as to the right of a party to a marriage [or as the case may be of a partner in a civil partnership] to money derived from any allowance made by either party [or partner] for their joint household expenses or for similar purposes, or to any property acquired out of such money, the money or property shall, in the absence of any agreement between them to the contrary, be treated as belonging to each party [or partner] in equal shares.

General

27   Interpretation

(1)   In this Act, unless the context otherwise requires—

'action' means an action brought after the commencement of this Act;

'action for aliment' has the meaning assigned to it by section 2(3) of this Act;

'aliment' does not include aliment pendente lite or interim aliment under section 6 of this Act;

['benefits under a pension arrangement' includes any benefits by way of pension, including relevant state scheme rights, whether under a pension arrangement or note;]

'caravan' means a caravan which is mobile or affixed to the land;

'child' includes [a child whether or not his parents have ever been married to one another], and any reference to the child of a marriage (whether or not subsisting) includes a child (other than a child who has been boarded out with the parties, or one of them, by a local or other public authority or a voluntary organisation) who has been accepted by the parties as a child of the family;

['child support maintenance' has the meaning assigned to it by section 3(6) of the Child Support Act 1991;]

['civil partnership', in relation to an action for declarator of nullity of a civil partnership, means purported civil partnership;]

'the court' means the Court of Session or the sheriff, as the case may require;

'decree' in an action for aliment includes an order of the court awarding aliment;

'family' includes a one-parent family [and in relation to a civil partnership means the members of the civil partnership together with any child accepted by them both as a child of the family];

'incidental order' has the meaning assigned to it by section 14(2) of this Act;

['maintenance calculation' has the meaning assigned to it by section 54 of the Child Support Act 1991;]

'marriage', in relation to an action for declarator of nullity of marriage, means purported marriage;

'matrimonial home' has the meaning assigned to it by section 22 of the Matrimonial Homes (Family Protection) (Scotland) Act 1981 [as amended by section 13(10) of the Law Reform (Miscellaneous Provisions) (Scotland) Act 1985];

'needs' means present and foreseeable needs;

'obligation of aliment' shall be construed in accordance with section 1(2) of this Act;

'order for financial provision' means an order under section 8(2) of this Act and, in sections 18(1) and 22(c) of this Act, also includes an order under section 5(2) of the Divorce (Scotland) Act 1976;

['partner', in relation to a civil partnership, includes a person who has a partner in a civil partnership which has been terminated and an ostensible partner in a civil partnership which has been annulled;]

'party to a marriage' and 'party to the marriage' include a party to a marriage which has been terminated or annulled;

['pension arrangement' means—

(a)   any occupational pension scheme within the meaning of the Pension Schemes Act 1993;

(b)   a personal pension scheme within the meaning of that Act;

(c)   a retirement annuity contract;

(d)   an annuity or insurance policy purchased or transferred for the purpose of giving effect to rights under an occupational pension scheme or a personal pension scheme;

(e)   an annuity purchased or entered into for the purpose of discharging liability in respect of a pension credit under section 29(1)(b) of the Welfare Reform and Pensions Act 1999 or under corresponding Northern Ireland legislation;]

['pension sharing order' is an order which—

(a)   provides that one party's—

(i)   shareable rights under a specified pension arrangement, or

(ii)   shareable state scheme rights,

be subject to pension sharing for the benefit of the other party, and

(b)   specifies the percentage value, or the amount, to be transferred;]

['person responsible for a pension arrangement' means—

(a)   in the case of an occupational pension scheme or a personal pension scheme, the trustees or managers of the scheme;

(b)   in the case of a retirement annuity contract or an annuity falling within paragraph (d) or (e) of the definition of 'pension arrangement' above, the provider of their annuity;

(c)   in the case of an insurance policy falling within paragraph (d) of the definition of that expression, the insurer;]

'property' in sections 8, 12, 13 and 15 of this Act does not include a tenancy transferable under section 13 of the Matrimonial Homes (Family Protection) (Scotland) Act 1981;

['relevant state scheme rights' means—

(a)   entitlement, or prospective entitlement, to a Category A retirement pension by virtue of section 44(3)(b) of the Social Security Contributions and Benefits Act 1992 or under corresponding Northern Ireland legislation; and

(b)   entitlement, or prospective entitlement, to a pension under section 55A of the Social Security Contributions and Benefits Act 1992 (shared additional pension) or under corresponding Northern Ireland legislation;]

'resources' means present and foreseeable resources;

['retirement annuity contract' means a contract or scheme approved under Chapter III of Part XIV of the Income and Corporation Taxes Act 1988;]

['trustees or managers' in relation to an occupational pension scheme or a personal pension scheme means—

(a)   in the case of a scheme established under a trust, the trustees of the scheme; and

(b)   in any other case, the managers of the scheme;]

'voluntary organisation' means a body, other than a local or other public authority, the activities of which are not carried on for profit.

[(1A)   In subsection (1), in the definition of 'pension sharing order'—

(a)   the reference to shareable rights under a pension arrangement is to rights in relation to which pension sharing is available under Chapter I of Part IV of the Welfare Reform and Pensions Act 1999, or under corresponding Northern Ireland legislation, and

(b)   the reference to shareable state scheme rights is to rights in relation to which pension sharing is available under Chapter II of Part IV of the Welfare Reform and Pensions Act 1999, or under corresponding Northern Ireland legislation.]

(2)   For the purposes of this Act, the parties to a marriage shall be held to cohabit with one another only when they are in fact living together as man and wife.

28   Amendments, repeals and savings

(1)   The enactments specified in Schedule 1 to this Act shall have effect subject to the amendments set out therein.

(2)   The enactments specified in columns 1 and 2 of Schedule 2 to this Act are repealed to the extent specified in column 3 of that Schedule.

(3)   Nothing in subsection (2) above shall affect the operation of section 5 (orders for financial provision) of the Divorce (Scotland) Act 1976 in relation to an action for divorce brought before the commencement of this Act; but in the continued operation of that section the powers of the court—

(a)   to make an order for payment of periodical allowance under subsection (2) thereof; and

(b)   to vary such an order under subsection (4) thereof,

shall include power to make such an order for a definite or an indefinite period or until the happening of a specified event.

29   Citation, commencement and extent

(1)   This Act may be cited as the Family Law (Scotland) Act 1985.

(2)   This Act shall come into operation on such day as the Secretary of State may appoint by order made by statutory instrument, and different days may be appointed for different purposes.

(3)   An order under subsection (2) above may contain such transitional provisions and savings as appear to the Secretary of State necessary or expedient in connection with the provisions brought into force (whether wholly or partly) by the order.

(4)   So much of section 28 of, and Schedule 1 to, this Act as affects the operation of the Maintenance Orders Act 1950 and the Maintenance Orders (Reciprocal Enforcement) Act 1972 shall extend to England and Wales and to Northern Ireland as well as to Scotland, but save as aforesaid this Act shall extend to Scotland only.

CHILD ABDUCTION AND CUSTODY ACT 1985
(1985, c 60)

PART I
INTERNATIONAL CHILD ABDUCTION

1 The Hague Convention

(1) In this Part of this Act 'the Convention' means the Convention on the Civil Aspects of International Child Abduction which was signed at The Hague on 25th October 1980.

(2) Subject to the provisions of this Part of this Act, the provisions of that Convention set out in Schedule 1 to this Act shall have the force of law in the United Kingdom.

[(3) But—

    (a) those provisions of the Convention;

    (b) this Part of this Act; and

    (c) rules of court under section 10 of this Act,

are subject to Article 60 of the Council Regulation (by virtue of which the Regulation takes precedence over the Convention, in so far as it concerns matters governed by the Regulation).

(4) The 'Council Regulation' means Council Regulation (EC) No 2201/2003 of 27th November 2003 concerning jurisdiction and the recognition and enforcement of judgments in matrimonial matters and matters of parental responsibility.]

2 Contracting States

(1) For the purposes of the Convention as it has effect under this Part of this Act the Contracting States other than the United Kingdom shall be those for the time being specified by an Order in Council under this section.

(2) An Order in Council under this section shall specify the date of the coming into force of the Convention as between the United Kingdom and any State specified in the Order; and, except where the Order otherwise provides, the Convention shall apply as between the United Kingdom and that State only in relation to wrongful removals or retentions occurring on or after that date.

(3) Where the Convention applies, or applies only, to a particular territory or particular territories specified in a declaration made by a Contracting State under Article 39 or 40 of the Convention references to that State in subsections (1) and (2) above shall be construed as references to that territory or those territories.

3 Central Authorities

(1) Subject to subsection (2) below, the functions under the Convention of a Central Authority shall be discharged—

    (a) in England and Wales and in Northern Ireland by the Lord Chancellor; and

    (b) in Scotland by the Secretary of State.

(2) Any application made under the Convention by or on behalf of a person outside the United Kingdom may be addressed to the Lord Chancellor as the Central Authority in the United Kingdom,

(3) Where any such application relates to a function to be discharged under subsection (1) above by the Secretary of State it shall be transmitted by the Lord Chancellor to the Secretary of State and where such an application is addressed to the Secretary of State but relates to a function to be discharged under subsection (1) above by the Lord Chancellor the Secretary of State shall transmit it to the Lord Chancellor.

4 Judicial authorities

The courts having jurisdiction to entertain applications under the Convention shall be—

    (a) in England and Wales or in Northern Ireland the High Court; and

    (b) in Scotland the Court of Session.

5   Interim powers

Where an application has been made to a court in the United Kingdom under the Convention, the court may, at any time before the application is determined, give such interim directions as it thinks fit for the purpose of securing the welfare of the child concerned or of preventing changes in the circumstances relevant to the determination of the application.

6   Reports

Where the Lord Chancellor or the Secretary of State is requested to provide information relating to a child under Article 7(d) of the Convention he may—

    (a)   request a local authority or [an officer of the service] to make a report to him in writing with respect to any matter which appears to him to be relevant;

    (b)   request the Department of Health and Social Services for Northern Ireland to arrange for a suitably qualified person to make such a report to him;

    (c)   request any court to which a written report relating to the child has been made to send him a copy of the report;

and such a request shall be duly complied with.

7   Proof of documents and evidence

(1)   For the purposes of Article 14 of the Convention a decision or determination of a judicial or administrative authority outside the United Kingdom may be proved by a duly authenticated copy of the decision or determination; and any document purporting to be such a copy shall be deemed to be a true copy unless the contrary is shown.

(2)   For the purposes of subsection (1) above a copy is duly authenticated if it bears the seal, or is signed by a judge or officer, of the authority in question.

(3)   For the purposes of Articles 14 and 30 of the Convention any such document as is mentioned in Article 8 of the Convention, or a certified copy of any such document, shall be sufficient evidence of anything stated in it.

8   Declarations by United Kingdom courts

The High Court or Court of Session may, on an application made for the purposes of Article 15 of the Convention by any person appearing to the court to have an interest in the matter, make a declaration or declarator that the removal of any child from, or his retention outside, the United Kingdom was wrongful within the meaning of Article 3 of the Convention.

9   Suspension of court's powers in cases of wrongful removal

The reference in Article 16 of the Convention to deciding on the merits of rights of custody shall be construed as a reference to—

    (a)   making, varying or revoking a custody order, or [a supervision order under section 31 of the Children Act 1989 or Article 50 of the Children (Northern Ireland) Order 1995]

    [(aa) enforcing under section 29 of the Family Law Act 1986 a custody order within the meaning of Chapter V of Part I of that Act;]

    (b)   registering or enforcing a decision under Part II of this Act;

    [. . .]

    [(d) making, varying or discharging an order under section 86 of the Children (Scotland) Act 1995].

    [. . .]

10   Rules of court

(1)   An authority having power to make rules of court may make such provision for giving effect to this Part of this Act as appears to that authority to be necessary or expedient.

(2)   Without prejudice to the generality of subsection (1) above, rules of court may make provision—

    (a)   with respect to the procedure on applications for the return of a child and with respect to the documents and information to be furnished and the notices to be given in connection with any such application;

(b)   for the transfer of any such application between the appropriate courts in the different parts of the United Kingdom;

(c)   for the giving of notices by or to a court for the purposes of the provisions of Article 16 of the Convention and section 9 above and generally as respects proceedings to which those provisions apply;

(d)   for enabling a person who wishes to make an application under the Convention in a Contracting State other than the United Kingdom to obtain from any court in the United Kingdom an authenticated copy of any decision of that court relating to the child to whom the application is to relate.

11   Cost of applications

The United Kingdom having made such a reservation as is mentioned in the third paragraph of Article 26 of the Convention, the costs mentioned in that paragraph shall not be borne by any Minister or other authority in the United Kingdom except so far as they fall to be so borne [by virtue of—

(a)   the provision of any service funded by the Legal Services Commission as part of the Community Legal Service, or

(b)   the grant of legal aid or legal advice and assistance under] the Legal Aid (Scotland) Act 1967, Part I of the Legal Advice and Assistance Act 1972 or the Legal Aid Advice and Assistance (Northern Ireland) Order 1981.

PART II
RECOGNITION AND ENFORCEMENT OF CUSTODY DECISIONS

12   The European Convention

(1)   In this Part of this Act 'the Convention' means the European Convention on Recognition and Enforcement of Decisions concerning Custody of Children and on the Restoration of Custody of Children which was signed in Luxembourg on 20th May 1980.

(2)   Subject to the provisions of this Part of this Act, the provisions of that Convention set out in Schedule 2 to this Act (which include Articles 9 and 10 as they have effect in consequence of a reservation made by the United Kingdom under Article 17) shall have the force of law in the United Kingdom.

[(3)   But—

(a)   those provisions of the Convention;

(b)   this Part of this Act; and

(c)   rules of court under section 24 of this Act,

are subject to Article 60 of the Council Regulation (by virtue of which the Regulation takes precedence over the Convention, in so far as it concerns matters governed by the Regulation).

(4)   The 'Council Regulation' means Council Regulation (EC) No 2201/2003 of 27th November 2003 concerning jurisdiction and the recognition and enforcement of judgments in matrimonial matters and matters of parental responsibility.]

13   Contracting States

(1)   For the purposes of the Convention as it has effect under this Part of this Act the Contracting States other than the United Kingdom shall be those for the time being specified by an Order in Council under this section.

(2)   An Order in Council under this section shall specify the date of the coming into force of the Convention as between the United Kingdom and any State specified in the Order.

(3)   Where the Convention applies, or applies only, to a particular territory or particular territories specified by a Contracting State under Article 24 or 25 of the Convention references to that State in subsections (1) and (2.) above shall be construed as references to that territory or those territories.

14 Central Authorities

(1) Subject to subsection (2) below, the functions under the Convention of a Central Authority shall be discharged—

(a) in England and Wales and in Northern Ireland by the Lord Chancellor; and

(b) in Scotland by the Secretary of State.

(2) Any application made under the Convention by or on behalf of a person outside the United Kingdom may be addressed to the Lord Chancellor as the Central Authority in the United Kingdom.

(3) Where any such application relates to a function to be discharged under subsection (1) above by the Secretary of State it shall be transmitted by the Lord Chancellor to the Secretary of State and where such an application is addressed to the Secretary of State but relates to a function to be discharged under subsection (1) above by the Lord Chancellor the Secretary of State shall transmit it to the Lord Chancellor.

15 Recognition of decisions

(1) Articles 7 and 12 of the Convention shall have effect in accordance with this section.

(2) A decision to which either of those Articles applies which was made in a Contracting State other than the United Kingdom shall be recognised in each part of the United Kingdom as if made by a court having jurisdiction to make it in that part but—

(a) the appropriate court in any part of the United Kingdom may, on the application of any person appearing to it to have an interest in the matter, declare on any of the grounds specified in Article 9 or 10 of the Convention that the decision is not to be recognised in any part of the United Kingdom; and

(b) the decision shall not be enforceable in any part of the United Kingdom unless registered in the appropriate court under section 16 below.

(3) The references in Article 9(1)(c) of the Convention to the removal of the child are to his improper removal within the meaning of the Convention.

16 Registration of decisions

(1) A person on whom any rights are conferred by a decision relating to custody made by an authority in a Contracting State other than the United Kingdom may make an application for the registration of the decision in an appropriate court in the United Kingdom.

(2) The Central Authority in the United Kingdom shall assist such a person in making such an application if a request for such assistance is made by him or on his behalf by the Central Authority of the Contracting State in question.

(3) An application under subsection (1) above or a request under subsection (2) above shall be treated as a request for enforcement for the purposes of Articles 10 and 13 of the Convention.

(4) The High Court or Court of Session shall refuse to register a decision if—

(a) the court is of the opinion that on any of the grounds specified in Article 9 or 10 of the Convention the decision should not be recognised in any part of the United Kingdom;

(b) the court is of the opinion that the decision is not enforceable in the Contracting State where it was made and is not a decision to which Article 12 of the Convention applies; or

(c) an application in respect of the child under Part I of this Act is pending.

(5) Where the Lord Chancellor is requested to assist in making an application under this section to the Court of Session he shall transmit the request to the Secretary of State and the Secretary of State shall transmit to the Lord Chancellor any such request to assist in making an application to the High Court.

(6) In this section 'decision relating to custody' has the same meaning as in the Convention.

17 Variation and revocation of registered decisions

(1) Where a decision which has been registered under section 16 above is varied or revoked by an authority in the Contracting State in which it was made, the person on whose behalf the application for registration of the decision was made shall notify the court in which the decision is registered of the variation or revocation.

(2) Where a court is notified under subsection (1) above of the revocation of a decision, it shall—

(a) cancel the registration, and

(b) notify such persons as may be prescribed by rules of court of the cancellation,

(3) Where a court is notified under subsection (1) above of the variation of a decision, it shall—

(a) notify such persons as may be prescribed by rules of court of the variation, and

(b) subject to any conditions which may be so prescribed, vary the registration.

(4) The court in which a decision is registered under section 16 above may also, on the application of any person appearing to the court to have an interest in the matter, cancel or vary the registration if it is satisfied that the decision has been revoked or, as the case may be, varied by an authority in the Contracting State in which it was made.

18 Enforcement of decisions

Where a decision relating to custody has been registered under section 16 above, the court in which it is registered shall have the same powers for the purpose of enforcing the decision as if it had been made by that court; and proceedings for or with respect to enforcement may be taken accordingly.

19 Interim powers

Where an application has been made to a court for the registration of a decision under section 16 above or for the enforcement of such a decision, the court may, at any time before the application is determined, give such interim directions as it thinks fit for the purpose of securing the welfare of the child concerned or of preventing changes in the circumstances relevant to the determination of the application or, in the case of an application for registration, to the determination of any subsequent application for the enforcement of the decision.

20 Suspension of court's powers

(1) Where it appears to any court in which such proceedings as are mentioned in subsection (2) below are pending in respect of a child that—

(a) an application has been made for the registration of a decision in respect of the child under section 16 above (other than a decision mentioned in subsection (3) below) or that such a decision is registered; and

(b) the decision was made in proceedings commenced before the proceedings which are pending,

the powers of the court with respect to the child in those proceedings shall be restricted as mentioned in subsection (2) below unless, in the case of an application for registration, the application is refused.

(2) Where subsection (1) above applies the court shall not—

(a) in the case of custody proceedings, make, vary or revoke any custody order, or [a supervision order under section 31 of the Children Act 1989 or article 50 of the Children (Northern Ireland) Order 1995; or

(aa) in the case of proceedings under section 29 of the Family Law Act 1986 for the enforcement of a custody order within the meaning of Chapter V of Part I of that Act, enforce that order.]

[. . .]

[(d) in the case of proceedings for, or for the variation or discharge of, a parental responsibilities order under section 86 of the Children (Scotland) Act 1995, make, vary or discharge any such order;]
    [. . .]
[(2A) Where it appears to the Secretary of State—
    (a) that an application has been made for the registration of a decision in respect of a child under section 16 above (other than a decision mentioned in subsection (3) below); or
    (b) that such a decision is registered,
the Secretary of State shall not make, vary or revoke any custody order in respect of the child unless, in the case of an application for registration, the application is refused.]
    (3) The decision referred to in subsection (1) [or (2A)] above is a decision which is only a decision relating to custody within the meaning of section 16 of this Act by virtue of being a decision relating to rights of access.
    (4) Paragraph (b) of Article 10(2) of the Convention shall be construed as referring to custody proceedings within the meaning of this Act.
    (5) This section shall apply to a children's hearing [(as defined in section 93(1) of the Children (Scotland) Act 1995)].

21 Reports
Where the Lord Chancellor or the Secretary of State is requested to make enquiries about a child under Article 15(1)(b) of the Convention he may—
    (a) request a local authority or [an officer of the service] to make a report to him in writing with respect to any matter relating to the child concerned which appears to him to be relevant;
    (b) request the Department of Health and Social Services for Northern Ireland to arrange for a suitably qualified person to make such a report to him;
    (c) request any court to which a written report relating to the child has been made to send him a copy of the report;
and any such request shall be duly complied with.

22 Proof of documents and evidence
    (1) In any proceedings under this Part of this Act a decision of an authority outside the United Kingdom may be proved by a duly authenticated copy of the decision; and any document purporting to be such a copy shall be deemed to be a true copy unless the contrary is shown.
    (2) For the purposes of subsection (1) above a copy is duly authenticated if it bears the seal, or is signed by a judge or officer, of the authority in question.
    (3) In any proceedings under this Part of this Act any such document as is mentioned in Article 13 of the Convention, or a certified copy of any such document, shall be sufficient evidence of anything stated in it.

23 Decisions of United Kingdom courts
    (1) Where a person on whom any rights are conferred by a decision relating to custody made by a court in the United Kingdom makes an application to the Lord Chancellor or the Secretary of State under Article 4 of the Convention with a view to securing its recognition or enforcement in another Contracting State, the Lord Chancellor or the Secretary of State may require the court which made the decision to furnish him with all or any of the documents referred to in Article 13(1)(b), (c) and (d) of the Convention.
    (2) Where in any custody proceedings a court in the United Kingdom makes a decision relating to a child who has been removed from the United Kingdom, the court may also, on an application made by any person for the purposes of Article 12 of the Convention, declare the removal to have been unlawful if it is satisfied that the applicant has an interest in the matter and that the child has been taken from or sent or kept out of the United Kingdom without the consent of the person

(or, if more than one, all the persons) having the right to determine the child's place of residence under the law of the part of the United Kingdom in which the child was habitually resident.

(3)   In this section 'decision relating to custody' has the same meaning as in the Convention.

24   Rules of court

(1)   An authority having power to make rules of court may make such provision for giving effect to this Part of this Act as appears to that authority to be necessary or expedient.

(2)   Without prejudice to the generality of subsection (1) above, rules of court may make provision—

(a)   with respect to the procedure on applications to a court under any provision of this Part of this Act and with respect to the documents and information to be furnished and the notices to be given in connection with any such application;

(b)   for the transfer of any such application between the appropriate courts in the different parts of the United Kingdom;

(c)   for the giving of directions requiring the disclosure of information about any child who is the subject of proceedings under this Part of this Act and for safeguarding its welfare.

[24A   Power to order disclosure of child's whereabouts

(1)   Where—

(a)   in proceedings for the return of a child under Part I of this Act; or

(b)   on an application for the recognition, registration or enforcement of a decision in respect of a child under Part II of this Act,

there is not available to the court adequate information as to where the child is, the court may order any person who it has reason to believe may have relevant information to disclose it to the court.

(2)   A person shall not be excused from complying with an order under subsection (1) above by reason that to do so may incriminate him or his spouse of an offence; but a statement or admission made in compliance with such an order shall not be admissible in evidence against either of them in proceedings for any offence other than perjury.]

PART III
SUPPLEMENTARY

25   Termination of existing custody orders, etc

(1)   Where—

(a)   an order is made for the return of a child under Part I of this Act; or

(b)   a decision with respect to a child (other than a decision mentioned in subsection (2) below) is registered under section 16 of this Act,

any custody order relating to him shall cease to have effect.

(2)   The decision referred to in subsection (1)(b) above is a decision which is only a decision relating to custody within the meaning of section 16 of this Act by virtue of being a decision relating to rights of access.

[. . .]

26   Expenses

There shall be paid out of money provided by Parliament—

(a)   any expenses incurred by the Lord Chancellor or the Secretary of State by virtue of this Act; and

(b)   any increase attributable to this Act in the sums so payable under any other Act.

27   Interpretation

(1)   In this Act 'custody order' means [(unless the contrary intention appears)] any such order or authorisation as is mentioned in Schedule 3 to this Act and 'custody proceedings' means proceedings in which an order within paragraphs 1, 2, 5, 6, 8 or 9 of that Schedule may be made [. . .] varied or revoked.

(2)   For the purposes of this Act 'part of the United Kingdom' means England and Wales, Scotland or Northern Ireland and 'the appropriate court', in relation to England and Wales or Northern Ireland means the High Court and, in relation to Scotland, the Court of Session.

(3)   In this Act 'local authority' means—

(a)   in relation to England and Wales, the council of a non-metropolitan county, a metropolitan district, a London borough or the Common Council of the City of London; and

(b)   in relation to Scotland, a [. . .] council [constituted under section 2 of the Local Government Etc (Scotland) Act 1994].

[(4)   In this Act a decision relating to rights of access in England and Wales or Scotland or Northern Ireland means a decision as to the contact which a child may, or may not, have with any person.

(5)   In this Act 'officer of the service' has the same meaning as in the Criminal Justice and Court Services Act 2000.]

28   Application as respects British Islands and colonies

(1)   Her Majesty may by Order in Council direct that any of the provisions of this Act specified in the Order shall extend, subject to such modifications as may be specified in the Order, to—

(a)   the Isle of Man,

(b)   any of the Channel Islands, and

(c)   any colony.

(2)   Her Majesty may by Order in Council direct that this Act shall have effect in the United Kingdom as if any reference in this Act, or in any amendment made by this Act, to any order which may be made, or any proceedings which may be brought or any other thing which may be done in, or in any part of, the United Kingdom included a reference to any corresponding order which may be made or, as the case may be, proceedings which may be brought or other thing which may be done in any of the territories mentioned in subsection (1) above.

(3)   An Order in Council under this section may make such consequential, incidental and supplementary provision as Her Majesty considers appropriate.

(4)   An Order in Council under this section shall be subject to annulment in pursuance of a resolution of either House of Parliament.

29   Short title, commencement and extent

(1)   This Act may be cited as the Child Abduction and Custody Act 1985.

(2)   This Act shall come into force on such day as may be appointed by an order made by statutory instrument by the Lord Chancellor and the Lord Advocate; and different days may be so appointed for different provisions.

(3)   This Act extends to Northern Ireland.

SCHEDULES

SCHEDULE 1
CONVENTION ON THE CIVIL ASPECTS OF INTERNATIONAL CHILD
ABDUCTION

Section 1(2)

CHAPTER 1—SCOPE OF THE CONVENTION

Article 3

The removal or the retention of a child is to be considered wrongful where—

(a)   it is in breach of rights of custody attributed to a person, an institution or any other body, either jointly or alone, under the law of the State in which the child was habitually resident immediately before the removal or retention; and

(b)   at the time of removal or retention those rights were actually exercised, either jointly or alone, or would have been so exercised but for the removal or retention.

The rights of custody mentioned in sub-paragraph (a) above may arise in particular by operation of law or by reason of a judicial or administrative decision, or by reason of an agreement having legal effect under the law of that State.

Article 4

The Convention shall apply to any child who was habitually resident in a Contracting State immediately before any breach of custody or access rights. The Convention shall cease to apply when the child attains the age of sixteen years.

Article 5

For the purposes of this Convention—

(a)   'rights of custody' shall include rights relating to the care of the person of the child and, in particular, the right to determine the child's place of residence;

(b)   'rights of access' shall include the right to take a child for a limited period of time to a place other than the child's habitual residence.

CHAPTER II—CENTRAL AUTHORITIES

Article 7

Central Authorities shall co-operate with each other and promote co-operation amongst the competent authorities in their respective States to secure the prompt return of children and to achieve the other objects of this Convention.

In particular, either directly or through any intermediary, they shall take all appropriate measures—

(a)   to discover the whereabouts of a child who has been wrongfully removed or retained;

(b)   to prevent further harm to the child or prejudice to interested parties by taking or causing to be taken provisional measures;

(c)   to secure the voluntary return of the child or to bring about an amicable resolution of the issues;

(d)   to exchange, where desirable, information relating to the social background of the child;

(e)   to provide information of a general character as to the law of their State in connection with the application of the Convention;

(f)   to initiate or facilitate the institution of judicial or administrative proceedings with a view to obtaining the return of the child and, in a proper case, to make arrangements for organizing or securing the effective exercise of rights of access;

(g)   where the circumstances so require, to provide or facilitate the provision of legal aid and advice, including the participation of legal counsel and advisers;

(h)   to provide such administrative arrangements as may be necessary and appropriate to secure the safe return of the child;

(i)   to keep each other informed with respect to the operation of this Convention and, as far as possible, to eliminate any obstacles to its application.

CHAPTER III—RETURN OF CHILDREN

Article 8

Any person, institution or other body claiming that a child has been removed or retained in breach of custody rights may apply either to the Central Authority of the child's habitual residence or to the Central Authority of any other Contracting State for assistance in securing the return of the child.

The application shall contain—

(a)   information concerning the identity of the applicant, of the child and of the person alleged to have removed or retained the child;

(b)   where available, the date of birth of the child;

(c)   the grounds on which the applicant's claim for return of the child is based;

(d)   all available information relating to the whereabouts of the child and the identity of the person with whom the child is presumed to be.

The application may be accompanied or supplemented by—

(e)   an authenticated copy of any relevant decision or agreement;

(f)   a certificate or an affidavit emanating from a Central Authority, or other competent authority of the State of the child's habitual residence, or from a qualified person, concerning the relevant law of that State;

(g)   any other relevant document.

Article 9

If the Central Authority which receives an application referred to in Article 8 has reason to believe that the child is in another Contracting State, it shall directly and without delay transmit the application to the Central Authority of that Contracting State and inform the requesting Central Authority, or the applicant, as the case may be.

Article 10

The Central Authority of the State where the child is shall take or cause to be taken all appropriate measures in order to obtain the voluntary return of the child.

Article 11

The judicial or administrative authorities of Contracting States shall act expeditiously in proceedings for the return of children.

If the judicial or administrative authority concerned has not reached a decision within six weeks from the date of commencement of the proceedings, the applicant or the Central Authority of the requested State, on its own initiative or if asked by the Central Authority of the requesting State, shall have the right to request a statement of the reasons for the delay. If a reply is received by the Central Authority of the requested State, that Authority shall transmit the reply to the Central Authority of the requesting State, or to the applicant, as the case may be.

Article 12

Where a child has been wrongfully removed or retained in terms Article 3 and, at the date of the commencement of the proceedings before the judicial or administrative authority of the Contracting State where the child is, a period of less than one year has elapsed from the date of the wrongful removal or retention, the authority concerned shall order the return of the child forthwith.

The judicial or administrative authority, even where the proceedings have been commenced after the expiration of the period of one year referred to in the preceding paragraph, shall also order the return of the child, unless it is demonstrated that the child is now settled in its new environment.

Where the judicial or administrative authority in the requested state has reason to believe that the child has been taken to another State, it may stay the proceedings or dismiss the application for the return of the child.

Article 13

Notwithstanding the provisions of the preceding Article, the judicial or administrative authority of the requested State is not bound to order the return of the child if the person, institution or other body which opposes its return establishes that—

(a)   the person, institution or other body having the care of the person of the child was not actually exercising the custody rights at the time of removal or retention, or had consented to or subsequently acquiesced in the removal or retention; or

(b)   there is a grave risk that his or her return would expose the child to physical or psychological harm or otherwise place the child in an intolerable situation.

The judicial or administrative authority may also refuse to order the return of the child if it finds that the child objects to being returned and has attained an age and degree of maturity at which it is appropriate to take account of its views.

In considering the circumstances referred to in this Article, the judicial and administrative authorities shall take into account the information relating to the social background of the child provided by the Central Authority or other competent authority of the child's habitual residence.

Article 14

In ascertaining whether there has been a wrongful removal or retention within the meaning of Article 3, the judicial or administrative authorities of the requested State may take notice directly of the law of, and of judicial or administrative decisions, formally recognised or not in the State of the habitual residence of the child, without recourse to the specific procedures for the proof of that law or for the recognition of foreign decisions which would otherwise be applicable.

Article 15

The judicial or administrative authorities of a Contracting State may, prior to the making of an order for the return of the child request that the applicant obtain from the authorities of the State of the habitual residence of the child a decision or other determination that the removal or retention was wrongful within the meaning of Article 3 of the Convention, where such a decision or determination may be obtained in that State. The Central Authorities of the Contracting States shall so far as practicable assist applicants to obtain such a decision or determination.

Article 16

After receiving notice of a wrongful removal or retention of a child in the sense of

Article 3, the judicial or administrative authorities of the Contracting State to which the child has been removed or in which it has been retained shall not decide on the merits of rights of custody until it has been determined that the child is not to be returned under this Convention or unless an application under this Convention is not lodged within a reasonable time following receipt of the notice.

Article 17

The sole fact that a decision relating to custody has been given in or is entitled to recognition in the requested State shall not be a ground for refusing to return a child under this Convention, but the judicial or administrative authorities of the requested State may take account of the reasons for that decision in applying this Convention.

Article 18

The provisions of this Chapter do not limit the power of a judicial or administrative authority to order the return of the child at any time.

Article 19

A decision under this Convention concerning the return of the child shall not be taken to be a determination on the merits of any custody issue.

CHAPTER IV—RIGHTS OF ACCESS

Article 21

An application to make arrangements for organising or securing the effective exercise of rights of access may be presented to the Central Authorities of the Contracting States in the same way as an application for the return of a child.

The Central Authorities are bound by the obligations of co-operation which are set forth in Article 7 to promote the peaceful enjoyment of access rights and the fulfilment of any conditions to which the exercise of those rights may be subject. The Central Authorities shall take steps to remove, as far as possible, all obstacles to the exercise of such rights. The Central Authorities, either directly or through intermediaries, may initiate or assist in the institution of proceedings with a view to organising or protecting these rights and securing respect for the conditions to which the exercise of these rights may be subject.

CHAPTER V—GENERAL PROVISIONS

Article 22

No security, bond or deposit, however described, shall be required to guarantee the payment of costs and expenses in the judicial or administrative proceedings falling within the scope of this Convention.

Article 24

Any application, communication or other document sent to the Central Authority of the requested State shall be in the original language, and shall be accompanied by a translation into the official language or one of the official languages of the requested State or, where that is not feasible, a translation into French or English.

Article 26

Each Central Authority shall bear its own costs in applying this Convention.

Central Authorities and other public services of Contracting States shall not impose any charges in relation to applications submitted under this Convention. In particular, they may not require any payment from the applicant towards the costs and expenses of the proceedings or, where applicable, those arising from the participation of legal counsel or advisers. However, they may require the payment of the expenses incurred or to be incurred in implementing the return of the child.

However, a Contracting State may, by making a reservation in accordance with Article 42, declare that it shall not be bound to assume any costs referred to in the preceding paragraph resulting from the participation of legal counsel or advisers or from court proceedings, except insofar as those costs may be covered by its system of legal aid and advice.

Upon ordering the return of a child or issuing an order concerning rights of access under this Convention, the judicial or administrative authorities may, where appropriate, direct the person who removed or retained the child, or who prevented the exercise of rights of access, to pay necessary expenses incurred by or on behalf of the applicant, including travel expenses, any costs incurred or payments made for locating the child, the costs of legal representation of the applicant, and those of returning the child.

Article 27

When it is manifest that the requirements of this Convention are not fulfilled or that the application is otherwise not well founded, a Central Authority is not bound to accept the application. In that case, the Central Authority shall forthwith inform the applicant or the Central Authority through which the application was submitted, as the case may be, of its reasons.

Article 28

A Central Authority may require that the application be accompanied by a written authorisation empowering it to act on behalf of the applicant, or to designate a representative so to act.

Article 29

This Convention shall not preclude any person, institution or body who claims that there has been a breach of custody or access rights within the meaning of Article 3 or 21 from applying directly to the judicial or administrative authorities of a Contracting State, whether or not under the provisions of this Convention.

Article 30

Any application submitted to the Central Authorities or directly to the judicial or administrative authorities of a Contracting State in accordance with the terms of this Convention, together with documents and any other information appended thereto or provided by a Central Authority, shall be admissible in the courts or administrative authorities of the Contracting States.

Article 31

In relation to a State which in matters of custody of children has two or more systems of law applicable in different territorial units—

(a)   any reference to habitual residence in that State shall be construed as referring to habitual residence in a territorial unit of that State;

(b)   any reference to the law of the State of habitual residence shall be construed as referring to the law of the territorial unit in that State where the child
habitually resides.

Article 32

In relation to a State which in matters of custody of children has two or more
systems of law applicable to different categories of persons, any reference to the
law of that State shall be construed as referring to the legal system specified by the
law of that State.

SCHEDULE 2
EUROPEAN CONVENTION ON RECOGNITION AND ENFORCEMENT ON
DECISIONS CONCERNING CUSTODY OF CHILDREN

Section 12(2)

Article 1

For the purposes of this Convention:

(a)   'child' means a person of any nationality, so long as he is under 16 years of
age and has not the right to decide on his own place of residence under the law of
his habitual residence, the law of his nationality or the internal law of the State
addressed;

(b)   'authority' means a judicial or administrative authority;

(c)   'decision relating to custody' means a decision of an authority in so far as it
relates to the care of the person of the child, including the right to decide on the
place of his residence, or to the right of access to him.

(d)   'improper removal' means the removal of a child across an international
frontier in breach of a decision relating to his custody which has been given in a
Contracting State and which is enforceable in such a State; 'improper removal' also
includes:

(i)   the failure to return a child across an international frontier at the end of a
period of the exercise of the right of access to this child or at the end of any
other temporary stay in a territory other than that where the custody is
exercised;

(ii)   a removal which is subsequently declared unlawful within the meaning
of Article 12.

Article 4

(1)   Any person who has obtained in a Contracting State a decision relating to
the custody of a child and who wishes to have that decision recognised or
enforced in another Contracting State may submit an application for this purpose
to the central authority in any Contracting State.

(2)   The application shall be accompanied by the documents mentioned in
Article 13.

(3)   The central authority receiving the application, if it is not the central
authority in the State addressed, shall send the documents directly and without
delay to that central authority.

(4)   The central authority receiving the application may refuse to intervene
where it is manifestly clear that the conditions laid down by this Convention are
not satisfied.

(5)   The central authority receiving the application shall keep the applicant
informed without delay of the progress of his application.

Article 5

(1)   The central authority in the State addressed shall take or cause to be taken without delay all steps which it considers to be appropriate, if necessary by instituting proceedings before its competent authorities, in order:

(a)   to discover the whereabouts of the child;

(b)   to avoid, in particular by any necessary provisional measures, prejudice to the interests of the child or of the applicant;

(c)   to secure the recognition or enforcement of the decision;

(d)   to secure the delivery of the child to the applicant where enforcement is granted;

(e)   to inform the requesting authority of the measures taken and their results.

(2)   Where the central authority in the State addressed has reason to believe that the child is in the territory of another Contracting State it shall send the documents directly and without delay to the central authority of that State.

(3)   With the exception of the cost of repatriation, each Contracting State undertakes not to claim any payment from an applicant in respect of any measures taken under paragraph (1) of this Article by the central authority of that State on the applicant's behalf, including the costs of proceedings and, where applicable, the costs incurred by the assistance of a lawyer.

(4)   If recognition or enforcement is refused, and if the central authority of the State addressed considers that it should comply with a request by the applicant to bring in that State proceedings concerning the substance of the case, that authority shall use its best endeavours to secure the representation of the applicant in the proceedings under conditions no less favourable than those available to a person who is resident in and a national of that State and for this purpose it may, in particular, institute proceedings before its competent authorities.

Article 7

A decision relating to custody given in a Contracting State shall be recognised and, where it is enforceable in the State of origin, made enforceable in every other Contracting State.

Article 9

(1)   [Recognition and enforcement may be refused] if:

(a)   in the case of a decision given in the absence of the defendant or his legal representative, the defendant was not duly served with the document which instituted the proceedings or an equivalent document in sufficient time to enable him to arrange his defence; but such a failure to effect service cannot constitute a ground for refusing recognition or enforcement where service was not effected because the defendant had concealed his whereabouts from the person who instituted the proceedings in the State of origin;

(b)   in the case of a decision given in the absence of the defendant or his legal representative, the competence of the authority giving the decision was not founded:

(i)   on the habitual residence of the defendant; or

(ii)   on the last common habitual residence of the child's parents, at least one parent being still habitually resident there; or

(iii)   on the habitual residence of the child;

(c)   the decision is incompatible with a decision relating to custody which became enforceable in the State addressed before the removal of the child, unless the child has had his habitual residence in the territory of the requesting State for one year before his removal.

(3) In no circumstances may the foreign decision be reviewed as to its substance.

Article 10

(1) [Recognition and enforcement may also be refused] on any of the following grounds:
  (a) if it is found that the effects of the decision are manifestly incompatible with the fundamental principles of the law relating to the family and children in the State addressed;
  (b) if it is found that by reason of a change in the circumstances including the passage of time but not including a mere change in the residence of the child after an improper removal, the effects of the original decision are manifestly no longer in accordance with the welfare of the child;
  (c) if at the time when the proceedings were instituted in the State of origin:
    (i) the child was a national of the State addressed or was habitually resident there and no such connection existed with the State of origin;
    (ii) the child was a national both of the State of origin and of the State addressed and was habitually resident in the State addressed;
  (d) if the decision is incompatible with a decision given in the State addressed or enforceable in that State after being given in a third State, pursuant to proceedings begun before the submission of the request for recognition or enforcement, and if the refusal is in accordance with the welfare of the child.
(2) Proceedings for recognition or enforcement may be adjourned on any of the following grounds:
  (a) if an ordinary form of review of the original decision has been commenced;
  (b) if proceedings relating to the custody of the child, commenced before the proceedings in the State of origin were instituted, are pending in the State addressed;
  (c) if another decision concerning the custody of the child is the subject of proceedings for enforcement or of any other proceedings concerning the recognition of the decision.

Article 11

(1) Decisions on rights of access and provisions of decisions relating to custody which deal with the rights of access shall be recognised and enforced subject to the same conditions as other decisions relating to custody.
(2) However, the competent authority of the State addressed may fix the conditions for the implementation and exercise of the right of access taking into account, in particular, undertakings given by the parties on this matter.
(3) Where no decision on the right of access has been taken or where recognition or enforcement of the decision relating to custody is refused, the central authority of the State addressed may apply to its competent authorities for a decision on the right of access if the person claiming a right of access so requests.

Article 12

Where, at the time of the removal of a child across an international frontier, there is no enforceable decision given in a Contracting State relating to his custody, the provisions of this Convention shall apply to any subsequent decision, relating to the custody of that child and declaring the removal to be unlawful, given in a Contracting State at the request of any interested person.

Article 13

(1)   A request for recognition or enforcement in another Contracting State of a decision relating to custody shall be accompanied by:

(a)   a document authorising the central authority of the State addressed to act on behalf of the applicant or to designate another representative for that purpose;

(b)   a copy of the decision which satisfies the necessary conditions of authenticity;

(c)   in the case of a decision given in the absence of the defendant or his legal representative, a document which establishes that the defendant was duly served with the document which instituted the proceedings or an equivalent document;

(d)   if applicable, any document which establishes that, in accordance with the law of the State of origin, the decision is enforceable;

(e)   if possible, a statement indicating the whereabouts or likely whereabouts of the child in the State addressed;

(f)   proposals as to how the custody of the child should be restored.

Article 15

(1)   Before reaching a decision under paragraph (1)(b) of Article 10, the authority concerned in the State addressed:

(a)   shall ascertain the child's views unless this is impracticable having regard in particular to his age and understanding; and

(b)   may request that any appropriate enquiries be carried out.

(2)   The cost of enquiries in any Contracting State shall be met by the authorities of the State where they are carried out.

Requests for enquiries and the results of enquiries may be sent to the authority concerned through the central authorities.

Article 16

(1)   In relation to a State which has in matters of custody two or more systems of law of territorial application:

(a)   reference to the law of a person's habitual residence or to the law of a person's nationality shall be construed as referring to the system of law determined by the rules in force in that State or, if there are no such rules, to the system of law with which the person concerned is most closely connected;

(b)   reference to the State of origin or to the State addressed shall be construed as referring, as the case may be, to the territorial unit where the decision was given or to the territorial unit where recognition or enforcement of the decision or restoration of custody is requested.

(2)   Paragraph (1)(a) of this Article also applies mutatis mutandis to States which have in matters of custody two or more systems of law of personal application.

SCHEDULE 3
CUSTODY ORDER

Section 27(1)

PART I
ENGLAND AND WALES

[1.   The following are the orders referred to in section 27(1) of this Act—

(a)   a care order under the Children Act 1989 (as defined by section 31(11) of that Act, read with section 105(1) and Schedule 14);

(b)   a residence order (as defined by section 8 of the Act of 1989); and

(c)   any order made by a court in England and Wales under any of the
following enactments—
     (i)   section 9(1), 10(1)(a) or 11(a) of the Guardianship of Minors Act
1971;
     (ii)   section 42(1) or (2) or 43(1) of the Matrimonial Causes Act 1973;
     (iii)   section 2(2)(b), 4(b) or (5) of the Guardianship Act 1973 as applied by
section 34(5) of the Children Act 1975;
     (iv)   section 8(2)(a), 10(1) or 19(1)(ii) of the Domestic Proceedings and Magis-
trates Courts Act 1978;
     (v)   section 26(1)(b) of the Adoption Act 1976.]
2.   An order made by the High Court in the exercise of its jurisdiction relating
to wardship so far as it gives the care and control of a child to any person.
   [. . .]
4.   An authorisation given by the Secretary of State under section 26(2) of the
Children and Young Persons Act 1969 (except where the relevant order, within the
meaning of that section, was made by virtue of the court which made it being
satisfied that the child was guilty of an offence).

PART II
SCOTLAND

5.   An order made by a court of civil jurisdiction in Scotland under any enactment or rule of law with respect to the [residence,] custody, care or control of a
child [or contact with,] or access to a child, excluding—
     (i)   an order placing a child under the supervision of a local authority;
     (ii)   an adoption order under section 12(1) of the Adoption (Scotland) Act
1978;
     [(iia)   an order freeing a child for adoption made under section 18 of the
Adoption (Scotland) Act 1978;]
     (iii)   an order relating to the [guardianship] of a child;
     (iv)   an order made under section [86 of the Children (Scotland) Act 1995];
     [(v)   an order made, or warrant or authorisation granted, under or by virtue
of Chapter 2 or 3 of Part II of the Children (Scotland) Act 1995 to remove the
child to a place of safety or to secure accommodation, to keep him at such a
place or in such accommodation, or to prevent his removal from a place where
he is being accommodated (or an order varying or discharging any order,
warrant or authorisation so made or granted);].
   [6.   A supervision requirement made by a children's hearing under section 70
of the Children (Scotland) Act 1995 (whether or not continued under section 73 of
that Act) or made by the sheriff under section 51(5)(c)(iii) of that Act and any
order made by a court in England and Wales or in Northern Ireland if it is an
order which, by virtue of section 33(1) of that Act, has effect as if it were such a
supervision requirement.]
   [. . .]

PART III
NORTHERN IRELAND

[8.   The following orders—
     (a)   a care order under the Children (Northern Ireland) Order 1995 (as
defined by Article 49(1) of that Order read with Article 2(2) and Schedule 8);
     (b)   a residence order (as defined by Article 8 of that Order);
     (c)   any order made by a court in Northern Ireland under any of the follow-
ing enactments—

(i) section 5 of the Guardianship of Infants Act 1886 (except so far as it relates to costs);

(ii) section 49 of the Mental Health Act (Northern Ireland) 1961;

(iii) Article 45(1) or (2) or 46 of the Matrimonial Causes (Northern Ireland) Order 1978;

(iv) Article 10(2)(a), 12(1) or 20(1)(ii) of the Domestic Proceedings (Northern Ireland) Order 1980;

(v) Article 27(1)(b) of the Adoption (Northern Ireland) Order 1987.]

9. An order made by the High Court in the exercise of its jurisdiction relating to wardship so far as it gives the care and control of a child to any person.

[. . .]

LAW REFORM (PARENT AND CHILD) (SCOTLAND) ACT 1986
(1986, c 9)

1 Legal equality of children
(1) The fact that a person's parents are not or have not been married to one another shall be left out of account in establishing the legal relationship between the person and any other person; and accordingly any such relationship shall have effect as if the parents were or had been married to one another.

(2) Subject to subsection (4) below, any reference (however expressed) in any enactment or deed to any relative shall, unless the contrary intention appears in the enactment or deed, be construed in accordance with subsection (1) above.

[(3) Subsection (1) above is subject to subsection (4) below, to section 9(1) of this Act and to section 3(1)(b) of the Children (Scotland) Act 1995 (parental responsibilities and parental rights of natural father).]

(4) Nothing in this section shall apply to the construction or effect of—

(a) any enactment passed or made before the commencement of this Act unless the enactment is amended by Schedule 1 to this Act and, as so amended, otherwise provides;

(b) any deed executed before such commencement;

(c) any reference (however expressed) in any deed executed after such commencement to a legitimate or illegitimate person or relationship.

[. . .]

5 Presumptions
(1) A man shall be presumed to be the father of a child—

(a) if he was married to the mother of the child at any time in the period beginning with the conception and ending with the birth of the child;

(b) where paragraph (a) above does not apply, if both he and the mother of the child have acknowledged that he is the father and he has been registered as such in any register kept under section 13 (register of births and still-births) or section 44 (register of corrections, etc) of the Registration of Births, Deaths and Marriages (Scotland) Act 1965 or in any corresponding register kept under statutory authority in any part of the United Kingdom other than Scotland.

(2) Subsection (1)(a) above shall apply in the case of a void, voidable or irregular marriage as it applies in the case of a valid and regular marriage.

(3) Without prejudice to the effect under any rule of law which a decree of declarator in an action to which section 7 of this Act applies may have in relation to the parties, a decree of declarator in such an action shall give rise to a presumption to the same effect as the decree; and any such presumption shall displace any contrary presumption howsoever arising.

(4) Any presumption under this section may be rebutted by proof on a balance of probabilities.

6 Determination of parentage by blood sample

(1) This section applies where, for the purpose of obtaining evidence relating to the determination of parentage in civil proceedings, a [sample of blood or other body fluid or of body tissue] is sought by a party to the proceedings or by a curator *ad litem*.

(2) Where [such] a sample is sought from a child [under the age of 16 years], consent to the taking of the sample may be given by [any person having parential responsibilities (within the meaning of section 1(3) of the Children (Scotland) Act 1995) in relation to him or having] care and control of him.

(3) Where [such] a sample is sought from any person who is incapable of giving consent, the court may consent to the taking of the sample where—

(a) there is no person who is entitled to give such consent, or

(b) there is such a person, but it is not reasonably practicable to obtain his consent in the circumstances, or he is unwilling to accept the responsibility of giving or withholding consent.

(4) The court shall not consent under subsection (3) above to the taking of [such] a sample from any person unless the court is satisfied that the taking of the sample would not be detrimental to the person's health.

7 Actions for declarator

(1) An action for declarator of parentage, non-parentage, legitimacy, legitimation or illegitimacy may be brought in the Court of Session or the sheriff court.

(2) Such an action may be brought in the Court of Session if and only if the child was born in Scotland or the alleged or presumed parent or the child—

(a) is domiciled in Scotland on the date when the action is brought;

(b) was habitually resident in Scotland for not less than one year immediately preceding that date; or

(c) died before that date and either—

(i) was at the date of death domiciled in Scotland; or

(ii) had been habitually resident in Scotland for not less than one year immediately preceding the date of death.

(3) Such an action may be brought in the sheriff court if and only if—

(a) the child was born in the sheriffdom, or

(b) an action could have been brought in the Court of Session under subsection (2) above and the alleged or presumed parent or the child was habitually resident in the sheriffdom on the date when the action is brought or on the date of his death.

[. . .]

(5) Nothing in any rule of law or enactment shall prevent the court making in any proceedings an incidental finding as to parentage, non-parentage, legitimacy, legitimation or illegitimacy for the purposes of those proceedings.

(6) In this section 'the alleged or presumed parent' includes a person who claims or is alleged to be or not to be the parent.

8 Interpretation

In this Act, unless the context otherwise requires, the following expressions shall have the following meanings respectively assigned to them—

'action for declarator' includes an application for declarator contained in other proceedings [but does not include an appeal under section 20(1)(a) or (b) (Appeals) of the Child Support Act 1991 made to the court by virtue of an order made under section 45 (Jurisdiction of the courts in certain proceedings) of that Act];

[. . .]

'the court' means the Court of Session or the sheriff;

[. . .]

'deed' means any disposition, contract, instrument or writing whether *inter vivos* or *mortis causa*;

'non-parentage' means that a person is not or was not the parent, or is not or was not the child, of another person;

'parent' includes natural parent;

'parentage' means that a person is or was the parent, or is or was the child, of another person;

[. . .]

9 Savings and supplementary provisions

(1) Nothing in this Act shall—

(a) affect any rule of law whereby a child born out of wedlock takes the domicile of his mother as a domicile of origin or dependence;

(b) except to the extent that Schedules 1 and 2 to this Act otherwise provide, affect the law relating to adoption of children;

(c) apply to any title, coat of arms, honour or dignity transmissible on the death of the holder thereof or affect the succession thereto or the devolution thereof;

(d) affect the right of legitim out of, or the right of succession to, the estate of any person who died before the commencement of this Act.

(2) The court may at any time vary or recall any order made under section 3 of this Act or consent given by it under section 6 of this Act.

COURT OF SESSION ACT 1988
(1988, c 36)

PART IV
OTHER CAUSES

Consistorial causes

19 Lord Advocate as party to action for nullity of marriage or divorce

(1) The Lord Advocate may enter appearance as a party in any action of declarator of nullity of marriage or for divorce, and he may lead such proof and maintain such pleas as he thinks fit, and the Court shall, whenever it considers it necessary for the proper disposal of any such action, direct that the action shall be brought to the notice of the Lord Advocate in order that he may determine whether he should enter appearance therein.

(2) No expenses shall be claimable by or against the Lord Advocate in any action in which he has entered appearance under this section.

HUMAN FERTILISATION AND EMBRYOLOGY ACT 1990
(1990, c 37)

Principal terms used

1 Meaning of 'embryo', 'gamete' and associated expressions

(1) In this Act, except where otherwise stated—

(a) embryo means alive human embryo where fertilisation is complete, and

(b) references to an embryo include an egg in the process of fertilisation,

and, for this purpose, fertilisation is not complete until the appearance of a two cell zygote.

(2) This Act, so far as it governs bringing about the creation of an embryo, applies only to bringing about the creation of an embryo outside the human body; and in this Act—

(a) references to embryos the creation of which was brought about *in vitro* (in their application to those where fertilisation is complete) are to those where fertilisation began outside the human body whether or not it was completed there, and

(b)	references to embryos taken from a woman do not include embryos whose creation was brought about *in vitro*.

(3)	This Act, so far as it governs the keeping or use of an embryo, applies only to keeping or using an embryo outside the human body.

(4)	References in this Act to gametes, eggs or sperm, except where otherwise stated, are to live human gametes, eggs or sperm but references below in this Act to gametes or eggs do not include eggs in the process of fertilisation.

## 2	Other terms

(1)	In this Act—

'the Authority' means the Human Fertilisation and Embryology Authority established under section 5 of this Act,

'directions' means directions under section 23 of this Act,

'licence' means a licence under Schedule 2 to this Act and, in relation to a licence, 'the person responsible' has the meaning given by section 17 of this Act, and

'treatment services' means medical, surgical or obstetric services provided to the public or a section of the public for the purpose of assisting women to carry children.

(2)	References in this Act to keeping, in relation to embryos or gametes, include keeping while preserved, whether preserved by cryopreservation or in any other way; and embryos or gametes so kept are referred to in this Act as 'stored' (and 'store' and 'storage' are to be interpreted accordingly).

(3)	For the purposes of this Act, a woman is not to be treated as carrying a child until the embryo has become implanted.

Activities governed by the Act

## 3	Prohibitions in connection with embryos

(1)	No person shall—

(a)	bring about the creation of an embryo, or

(b)	keep or use an embryo,

except in pursuance of a licence.

(2)	No person shall place in a woman—

(a)	a live embryo other than a human embryo, or

(b)	any live gametes other than human gametes.

(3)	A licence cannot authorise—

(a)	keeping or using an embryo after the appearance of the primitive streak,

(b)	placing an embryo in any animal,

(c)	keeping or using an embryo in any circumstances in which regulations prohibit its keeping or use, or

(d)	replacing a nucleus of a cell of an embryo with a nucleus taken from a cell of any person, embryo or subsequent development of an embryo.

(4)	For the purposes of subsection (3)(a) above, the primitive streak is to be taken to have appeared in an embryo not later than the end of the period of 14 days beginning with the day when the gametes are mixed, not counting any time during which the embryo is stored.

## [3A	Prohibition in connection with germ cells

(1)	No person shall, for the purpose of providing fertility services for any woman, use female germ cells taken or derived from an embryo or a foetus or use embryos created by using such cells.

(2)	In this section—

'female germ cells' means cells of the female germ line and includes such cells at any stage of maturity and accordingly includes eggs; and 'fertility services' means medical, surgical or obstetric services provided for the purpose of assisting women to carry children.]

4 Prohibitions in connection with gametes
(1) No person shall—
    (a) store any gametes, or
    (b) in the course of providing treatment services for any woman, use the sperm of any man unless the services are being provided for the woman and the man together or use the eggs of any other woman, or
    (c) mix gametes with the live gametes of any animal, except in pursuance of a licence.
(2) A licence cannot authorise storing or using gametes in any circumstances in which regulations prohibit their storage or use.
(3) No person shall place sperm and eggs in a woman in any circumstances specified in regulations except in pursuance of a licence.
(4) Regulations made by virtue of subsection (3) above may provide that, in relation to licences only to place sperm and eggs in a woman in such circumstances, sections 12 to 22 of this Act shall have effect with such modifications as may be specified in the regulations.
(5) Activities regulated by this section or section 3 of this Act are referred to in this Act as 'activities governed by this Act'.

Status

27 Meaning of 'mother'
(1) The woman who is carrying or has carried a child as a result of the placing in her of an embryo or of sperm and eggs, and no other woman, is to be treated as the mother of the child.
(2) Subsection (1) above does not apply to any child to the extent that the child is treated by virtue of adoption as not being the child of any person other than the adopter or adopters.
(3) Subsection (1) above applies whether the woman was in the United Kingdom or elsewhere at the time of the placing in her of the embryo or the sperm and eggs.

28 Meaning of 'father'
(1) [Subject to subsections (5A) to (5I) below, this] section applies in the case of a child who is being or has been carried by a woman as the result of the placing in her of an embryo or of sperm and eggs or her artificial insemination.
(2) If—
    (a) at the time of the placing in her of the embryo or the sperm and eggs or of her insemination, the woman was a party to a marriage, and
    (b) the creation of the embryo carried by her was not brought about with the sperm of the other party to the marriage,
then, subject to subsection (5) below, the other party to the marriage shall be treated as the father of the child unless it is shown that he did not consent to the placing in her of the embryo or the sperm and eggs or to her insemination (as the case may be).
(3) If no man is treated, by virtue of subsection (2) above, as the father of the child but—
    (a) the embryo or the sperm and eggs were placed in the woman, or she was artificially inseminated, in the course of treatment services provided for her and a man together by a person to whom a licence applies, and
    (b) the creation of the embryo carried by her was not brought about with the sperm of that man,
then, subject to subsection (5) below, that man shall be treated as the father of the child.

(4)   Where a person is treated as the father of the child by virtue of subsection (2) or (3) above, no other person is to be treated as the father of the child.

(5)   Subsections (2) and (3) above do not apply—

(a)   in relation to England and Wales and Northern Ireland, to any child who, by virtue of the rules of common law, is treated as the legitimate child of the parties to a marriage,

(b)   in relation to Scotland, to any child who, by virtue of any enactment or other rule of law, is treated as the child of the parties to a marriage, or

(c)   to any child to the extent that the child is treated by virtue of adoption as not being the child of any person other than the adopter or adopters.

[(5A)   If—

(a)   a child has been carried by a woman as the result of the placing in her of an embryo or of sperm and eggs or her artificial insemination,

(b)   the creation of the embryo carried by her was brought about by using the sperm of a man after his death, or the creation of the embryo was brought about using the sperm of a man before his death but the embryo was placed in the woman after his death,

(c)   the woman was a party to a marriage with the man immediately before his death,

(d)   the man consented in writing (and did not withdraw the consent)—

(i) to the use of his sperm after his death which brought about the creation of the embryo carried by the woman or (as the case may be) to the placing in the woman after his death of the embryo which was brought about using his sperm before his death, and

(ii) to being treated for the purpose mentioned in subsection (5I) below as the father of any resulting child,

(e)   the woman has elected in writing not later than the end of the period of 42 days from the day on which the child was born for the man to be treated for the purpose mentioned in subsection (5I) below as the father of the child, and

(f)   no-one else is to be treated as the father of the child by virtue of subsection (2) or (3) above or by virtue of adoption or the child being treated as mentioned in paragraph (a) or (b) of subsection (5) above,

then the man shall be treated for the purpose mentioned in subsection (5I) below as the father of the child.

(5B)   If—

(a)   a child has been carried by a woman as the result of the placing in her of an embryo or of sperm and eggs or her artificial insemination,

(b)   the creation of the embryo carried by her was brought about by using the sperm of a man after his death, or the creation of the embryo was brought about using the sperm of a man before his death but the embryo was placed in the woman after his death,

(c)   the woman was not a party to a marriage with the man immediately before his death but treatment services were being provided for the woman and the man together before his death either by a person to whom a licence applies or outside the United Kingdom,

(d)   the man consented in writing (and did not withdraw the consent)—

(i) to the use of his sperm after his death which brought about the creation of the embryo carried by the woman or (as the case may be) to the placing in the woman after his death of the embryo which was brought about using his sperm before his death, and

(ii) to being treated for the purpose mentioned in subsection (5I) below as the father of any resulting child,

(e)   the woman has elected in writing not later than the end of the period of 42 days from the day on which the child was born for the man to be treated for the purpose mentioned in subsection (5I) below as the father of the child, and

(f)   no-one else is to be treated as the father of the child by virtue of subsection (2) or (3) above or by virtue of adoption or the child being treated as mentioned in paragraph (a) or (b) of subsection (5) above,

then the man shall be treated for the purpose mentioned in subsection (5I) below as the father of the child.

(5C)   If—

(a)   a child has been carried by a woman as the result of the placing in her of an embryo,

(b)   the embryo was created at a time when the woman was a party to a marriage,

(c)   the creation of the embryo was not brought about with the sperm of the other party to the marriage,

(d)   the other party to the marriage died before the placing of the embryo in the woman,

(e)   the other party to the marriage consented in writing (and did not withdraw the consent)—

(i)   to the placing of the embryo in the woman after his death, and

(ii)   to being treated for the purpose mentioned in subsection (5I) below as the father of any resulting child,

(f)   the woman has elected in writing not later than the end of the period of 42 days from the day on which the child was born for the other party to the marriage to be treated for the purpose mentioned in subsection (5I) below as the father of the child, and

(g)   no-one else is to be treated as the father of the child by virtue of subsection (2) or (3) above or by virtue of adoption or the child being treated as mentioned in paragraph (a) or (b) of subsection (5) above,

then the other party to the marriage shall be treated for the purpose mentioned in subsection (5I) below as the father of the child.

(5D)   If—

(a)   a child has been carried by a woman as the result of the placing in her of an embryo,

(b)   the embryo was not created at a time when the woman was a party to a marriage but was created in the course of treatment services provided for the woman and a man together either by a person to whom a licence applies or outside the United Kingdom,

(c)   the creation of the embryo was not brought about with the sperm of that man,

(d)   the man died before the placing of the embryo in the woman,

(e)   the man consented in writing (and did not withdraw the consent)—

(i)   to the placing of the embryo in the woman after his death, and

(ii)   to being treated for the purpose mentioned in subsection (5I) below as the father of any resulting child,

(f)   the woman has elected in writing not later than the end of the period of 42 days from the day on which the child was born for the man to be treated for the purpose mentioned in subsection (5I) below as the father of the child, and

(g)   no-one else is to be treated as the father of the child by virtue of subsection (2) or (3) above or by virtue of adoption or the child being treated as mentioned in paragraph (a) or (b) of subsection (5) above,

then the man shall be treated for the purpose mentioned in subsection (5I) below as the father of the child.

(5E)   In the application of subsections (5A) to (5D) above to Scotland, for any reference to a period of 42 days there shall be substituted a reference to a period of 21 days.

(5F)   The requirement under subsection (5A), (5B), (5C) or (5D) above as to the making of an election (which requires an election to be made either on or before the day on which the child was born or within the period of 42 or, as the case may be, 21 days from that day) shall nevertheless be treated as satisfied if the required election is made after the end of that period but with the consent of the Registrar General under subsection (5G) below.

(5G)   The Registrar General may at any time consent to the making of an election after the end of the period mentioned in subsection (5F) above if, on an application made to him in accordance with such requirements as he may specify, he is satisfied that there is a compelling reason for giving his consent to the making of such an election.

(5H)   In subsections (5F) and (5G) above 'the Registrar General' means the Registrar General for England and Wales, the Registrar General of Births, Deaths and Marriages for Scotland or (as the case may be) the Registrar General for Northern Ireland.

(5I)   The purpose referred to in subsections (5A) to (5D) above is the purpose of enabling the man's particulars to be entered as the particulars of the child's father in (as the case may be) a register of live-births or still-births kept under the Births and Deaths Registration Act 1953 or the Births and Deaths Registration (Northern Ireland) Order 1976 or a register of births or still-births kept under the Registration of Births, Deaths and Marriages (Scotland) Act 1965.]

(6)   Where—

(a)   the sperm of a man who had given such consent as is required by paragraph 5 of Schedule 3 to this Act was used for a purpose for which such consent was required, or

(b)   the sperm of a man, or any embryo the creation of which was brought about with his sperm, was used after his death,

he is not [, subject to subsections (5A) and (5B) above,] to be treated as the father of the child.

(7)   The references in subsection (2) above [and subsections (5A) to (5D) above] to the parties to a marriage at the time there referred to—

(a)   are to the parties to a marriage subsisting at that time, unless a judicial separation was then in force, but

(b)   include the parties to a void marriage if either or both of them reasonably believed at that time that the marriage was valid; and for the purposes of this subsection it shall be presumed, unless the contrary is shown, that one of them reasonably believed at that time that the marriage was valid.

(8)   This section applies whether the woman was in the United Kingdom or elsewhere at the time of the placing in her of the embryo or the sperm and eggs or her artificial insemination.

(9)   In subsection (7)(a) above, 'judicial separation' includes a legal separation obtained in a country outside the British Islands and recognised in the United Kingdom.

29   Effect of sections 27 and 28

(1)   Where by virtue of section 27 or 28 of this Act a person is to be treated as the mother or father of a child, that person is to be treated in law as the mother or, as the case may be, father of the child for all purposes.

(2)   Where by virtue of section 27 or 28 of this Act a person is not to be treated as the mother or father of a child, that person is to be treated in law as not being the mother or, as the case may be, father of the child for any purpose.

(3)   Where subsection (1) or (2) above has effect, references to any relationship between two people in any enactment, deed or other instrument or document (whenever passed or made) are to be read accordingly.

[(3A)   Subsections (1) to (3) above do not apply in relation to the treatment in law of a deceased man in a case to which section 28(5A), (5B), (5C) or (5D) of this Act applies.

(3B)   Where subsection (5A), (5B), (5C) or (5D) of section 28 of this Act applies, the deceased man—

(a)   is to be treated in law as the father of the child for the purpose referred to in that subsection, but

(b)   is to be treated in law as not being the father of the child for any other purpose.

(3C)   Where subsection (3B) above has effect, references to any relationship between two people in any enactment, deed or other instrument or document (whenever passed or made) are to be read accordingly.

(3D)   In subsection (3C) above 'enactment' includes an enactment comprised in, or in an instrument made under, an Act of the Scottish Parliament or Northern Ireland legislation.]

(4)   In relation to England and Wales and Northern Ireland, nothing in the provisions of section 27(1) or 28(2) to (4) [or (5A) to (5I)], read with this section, affects—

(a)   the succession to any dignity or title of honour or renders any person capable of succeeding to or transmitting a right to succeed to any such dignity or title, or

(b)   the devolution of any property limited (expressly or not) to devolve (as nearly as the law permits) along with any dignity or title of honour.

(5)   In relation to Scotland—

(a)   those provisions do not apply to any title, coat of arms, honour or dignity transmissible on the death of the holder thereof or affect the succession thereto or the devolution thereof, and

(b)   where the terms of any deed provide that any property or interest in property shall devolve along with a title, coat of arms, honour or dignity, nothing in those provisions shall prevent that property or interest from so devolving.

30   Parental orders in favour of gamete donors

(1)   The court may make an order providing for a child to be treated in law as the child of the parties to a marriage (referred to in this section as 'the husband' and 'the wife') if—

(a)   the child has been carried by a woman other than the wife as the result of the placing in her of an embryo or sperm and eggs or her artificial insemination,

(b)   the gametes of the husband or the wife, or both, were used to bring about the creation of the embryo, and

(c)   the conditions in subsections (2) to (7) below are satisfied.

(2)   The husband and the wife must apply for the order within six months of the birth of the child or, in the case of a child born before the coming into force of this Act, within six months of such coming into force.

(3)   At the time of the application and of the making of the order—

(a)   the child's home must be with the husband and the wife, and

(b)   the husband or the wife, of both of them, must be domiciled in a part of the United Kingdom or in the Channel Islands or the Isle of Man.

(4)   At the time of the making of the order both the husband and the wife must have attained the age of eighteen.

(5)   The court must be satisfied that both the father of the child (including a person who is the father by virtue of section 28 of this Act), where he is not the husband, and the woman who carried the child have freely, and with full understanding of what is involved, agreed unconditionally to the making of the order.

(6)   Subsection (5) above does not require the agreement of a person who cannot be found or is incapable of giving agreement and the agreement of the woman who carried the child is ineffective for the purposes of that subsection if given by her less than six weeks after the child's birth.

(7)   The court must be satisfied that no money or other benefit (other than for

expenses reasonably incurred) has been given or received by the husband or the wife for or in consideration of—

(a) the making of the order,

(b) any agreement required by subsection (5) above,

(c) the handing over of the child to the husband and the wife, or

(d) the making of any arrangements with a view to the making of the order, unless authorised by the court.

(8) For the purposes of an application under this section—

(a) in relation to England and Wales, section 92(7) to (10) of, and Part I of Schedule 11 to, the Children Act 1989 (jurisdiction of courts) shall apply for the purposes of this section to determine the meaning of 'the court' as they apply for the purposes of that Act and proceedings on the application shall be 'family proceedings' for the purposes of that Act,

(b) in relation to Scotland, 'the court' means the Court of Session or the sheriff court of the sheriffdom within which the child is, and

(c) in relation to Northern Ireland, 'the court' means the High Court or any county court within whose division the child is.

(9) Regulations may provide—

(a) for any provision of the enactments about adoption to have effect, with such modifications (if any) as may be specified in the regulations, in relation to orders under this section, and applications for such orders, as it has effect in relation to adoption, and applications for adoption orders, and

(b) for references in any enactment to adoption, an adopted child or an adoptive relationship to be read (respectively) as references to the effect of an order under this section, a child to whom such an order applies and a relationship arising by virtue of the enactments about adoption, as applied by the regulations, and for similar expressions in connection with adoption to be read accordingly,

and the regulations may include such incidental or supplemental provision as appears to the Secretary of State necessary or desirable in consequence of any provision made by virtue of paragraph (a) or (b) above.

(10) In this section 'the enactments about adoption' means the Adoption Act 1976, the Adoption (Scotland) Act 1978 and the Adoption (Northern Ireland) Order 1987.

(11) Subsection (1)(a) above applies whether the woman was in the United Kingdom or elsewhere at the time of the placing in her of the embryo or the sperm and eggs or her artificial insemination.

Information

31 The Authority's register of information

(1) The Authority shall keep a register which shall contain any information obtained by the Authority which falls within subsection (2) below.

(2) Information falls within this subsection if it relates to—

(a) the provision of treatment services for any identifiable individual, or

(b) the keeping or use of the gametes of any identifiable individual or of an embryo taken from any identifiable woman,

or if it shows that any identifiable individual was, or may have been, born in consequence of treatment services.

(3) A person who has attained the age of eighteen ('the applicant') may by notice to the Authority require the Authority to comply with a request under subsection (4) below, and the Authority shall do so if—

(a) the information contained in the register shows that the applicant was, or may have been, born in consequence of treatment services, and

(b) the applicant has been given a suitable opportunity to receive proper counselling about the implications of compliance with the request.

(4)   The applicant may request the Authority to give the applicant notice stating whether or not the information contained in the register shows that a person other than a parent of the applicant would or might, but for sections 27 to 29 of this Act, be a parent of the applicant and, if it does show that—

(a)   giving the applicant so much of that information as relates to the person concerned as the Authority is required by regulations to give (but no other information), or

(b)   stating whether or not that information shows that, but for sections 27 to 29 of this Act, the applicant, and a person specified in the request as a person whom the applicant proposes to marry, would or might be related.

(5)   Regulations cannot require the Authority to give any information as to the identity of a person whose gametes have been used or from whom an embryo has been taken if a person to whom a licence applied was provided with the information at a time when the Authority could not have been required to give information of the kind in question.

(6)   A person who has not attained the age of eighteen ('the minor') may by notice to the Authority specifying another person ('the intended spouse') as a person whom the minor proposes to marry require the Authority to comply with a request under subsection (7) below, and the Authority shall do so if—

(a)   the information contained in the register shows that the minor was, or may have been, born in consequence of treatment services, and

(b)   the minor has been given a suitable opportunity to receive proper counselling about the implications of compliance with the request.

(7)   The minor may request the Authority to give the minor notice stating whether or not the information contained in the register shows that, but for sections 27 to 29 of this Act, the minor and the intended spouse would or might be related.

32   Information to be provided to Registrar General

(1)   This section applies where a claim is made before the Registrar General that a man is or is not the father of a child and it is necessary or desirable for the purpose of any function of the Registrar General to determine whether the claim is or may be well-founded.

(2)   The Authority shall comply with any request made by the Registrar General by notice to the Authority to disclose whether any information on the register kept in pursuance of section 31 of this Act tends to show that the man may be the father of the child by virtue of section 28 of this Act and, if it does, disclose that information.

(3)   In this section and section 33 of this Act, 'the Registrar General' means the Registrar General for England and Wales, the Registrar General of Births, Deaths and Marriages for Scotland or the Registrar General for Northern Ireland, as the case may be.

33   Restrictions on disclosure of information

(1)   No person who is or has been a member or employee of the Authority shall disclose any information mentioned in subsection (2) below which he holds or has held as such a member or employee.

(2)   The information referred to in subsection (1) above is—

(a)   any information contained or required to be contained in the register kept in pursuance of section 31 of this Act, and

(b)   any other information obtained by any member or employee of the Authority on terms or in circumstances requiring it to be held in confidence.

(3)   Subsection (1) above does not apply to any disclosure of information mentioned in subsection (2)(a) above made—

(a)   to a person as a member or employee of the Authority.

(b)   to a person to whom a licence applies for the purposes of his functions as such,

(c)   so that no individual to whom the information relates can be identified,

(d)   in pursuance of an order of a court under section 34 or 35 of this Act,

(e)   to the Registrar General in pursuance of a request under section 32 of this Act, or

(f)   in accordance with section 31 of this Act.

(4)   Subsection (1) above does not apply to any disclosure of information mentioned in subsection (2)(b) above—

(a)   made to a person as a member or employee of the Authority,

(b)   made with the consent of the person or persons whose confidence would otherwise be protected, or

(c)   which has been lawfully made available to the public before the disclosure is made.

(5)   No person who is or has been a person to whom a licence applies and no person to whom directions have been given shall disclose any information falling within section 31(2) of this Act which he holds or has held as such a person.

(6)   Subsection (5) above does not apply to any disclosure of information made—

(a)   to a person as a member or employee of the Authority,

(b)   to a person to whom a licence applies for the purposes of his functions as such,

(c)   so far as it identifies a person who, but for sections 27 to 29 of this Act, would or might be a parent of a person who instituted proceedings under section 1A of the Congenital Disabilities (Civil Liability) Act 1976, but only for the purpose of defending such proceedings, or instituting connected proceedings for compensation against that parent,

(d)   so that no individual to whom the information relates can be identified,

(e)   in pursuance of directions given by virtue of section 24(5) or (6) of this Act.

[(f)   necessarily—

(i)   for any purpose preliminary to proceedings, or

(ii)   for the purposes of, or in connection with, any proceedings,

(g)   for the purpose of establishing, in any proceedings relating to an application for an order under subsection (1) of section 30 of this Act, whether the condition specified in paragraph (a) or (b) of that subsection is met, or

(h)   under section 3 of the Access to Health Records Act 1990 (right of access to health records).]

[(6A)   Paragraph (f) of subsection (6) above, so far as relating to disclosure for the purposes of, or in connection with, any proceedings, does not apply—

(a)   to disclosure of information enabling a person to be identified as a person whose gametes were used, in accordance with consent given under paragraph 5 of Schedule 3 to this Act, for the purposes of treatment services in consequence of which an identifiable individual was, or may have been, born, or

(b)   to disclosure, in circumstances in which subsection (1) of section 34 of this Act applies, of information relevant to the determination of the question mentioned in that subsection.

(6B)   In the case of information relating to the provision of treatment services for any identifiable individual—

(a)   where one individual is identifiable, subsection (5) above does not apply to disclosure with the consent of that individual;

(b)   where both a woman and a man treated together with her are identifiable, subsection (5) above does not apply—

(i)   to disclosure with the consent of them both, or

(ii)   if disclosure is made for the purpose of disclosing information about the provision of treatment services for one of them, to disclosure with the consent of that individual.

(6C)   For the purposes of subsection (6B) above, consent must be to disclosure to a specific person, except where disclosure is to a person who needs to know—

(a)   in connection with the provision of treatment services, or any other description of medical, surgical or obstetric services, for the individual giving the consent,

(b)   in connection with the carrying out of an audit of clinical practice, or

(c)   in connection with the auditing of accounts.

(6D)   For the purposes of subsection (6B) above, consent to disclosure given at the request of another shall be disregarded unless, before it is given, the person requesting it takes reasonable steps to explain to the individual from whom it is requested the implications of compliance with the request.

(6E)   In the case of information which relates to the provision of treatment services for any identifiable individual, subsection (5) above does not apply to disclosure in an emergency, that is to say, to disclosure made—

(a)   by a person who is satisfied that it is necessary to make the disclosure to avert an imminent danger to the health of an individual with whose consent the information could be disclosed under subsection (6B) above, and

(b)   in circumstances where it is not reasonably practicable to obtain that individual's consent.

(6F)   In the case of information which shows that any identifiable individual was, or may have been, born in consequence of treatment services, subsection (5) above does not apply to any disclosure which is necessarily incidental to disclosure under subsection (6B) or (6E) above.

(6G)   Regulations may provide for additional exceptions from subsection (5) above, but no exception may be made under this subsection—

(a)   for disclosure of a kind mentioned in paragraph (a) or (b) of subsection (6A) above, or

(b)   for disclosure, in circumstances in which section 32 of this Act applies, of information having the tendency mentioned in subsection (2) of that section.]

(7)   This section does not apply to the disclosure to any individual of information which—

(a)   falls within section 31(2) of this Act by virtue of paragraph (a) or (b) of that subsection, and

(b)   relates only to that individual or, in the case of an individual treated together with another, only to that individual and that other.

[. . .]

[(9)   In subsection (6)(f) above, references to proceedings include any formal procedure for dealing with a complaint.]

34   Disclosure in interests of justice

(1)   Where in any proceedings before a court the question whether a person is or is not the parent of a child by virtue of sections 27 to 29 of this Act falls to be determined, the court may on the application of any party to the proceedings make an order requiring the Authority—

(a)   to disclose whether or not any information relevant to that question is contained in the register kept in pursuance of section 31 of this Act, and

(b)   if it is, to disclose so much of it as is specified in the order,

but such an order may not require the Authority to disclose any information falling within section 31(2)(b) of this Act.

(2)   The court must not make an order under subsection (1) above unless it is satisfied that the interests of justice require it to do so, taking into account—

(a)   any representations made by any individual who may be affected by the disclosure, and

(b)   the welfare of the child, if under 18 years old, and of any other person under that age who may be affected by the disclosure.

(3)   If the proceedings before the court are civil proceedings, it—

(a)   may direct that the whole or any part of the proceedings on the application for an order under subsection (2) above shall be heard in camera, and
(b)   if it makes such an order, may then or later direct that the whole or any
part of any later stage of the proceedings shall be heard in camera.
(4)   An application for a direction under subsection (3) above shall be heard in
camera unless the court otherwise directs.

35   Disclosure in interests of justice: congenital disabilities, etc

(1)   Where for the purpose of instituting proceedings under section 1 of the
Congenital Disabilities (Civil Liability) Act 1976 (civil liability to child born disabled) it is necessary to identify a person who would or might be the parent of
a child but for sections 27 to 29 of this Act, the court may, on the application of
the child, make an order requiring the Authority to disclose any information
contained in the register kept in pursuance of section 31 of this Act identifying
that person.
(2)   Where, for the purposes of any action for damages in Scotland (including
any such action which is likely to be brought) in which the damages claimed
consist of or include damages or solatium in respect of personal injury (including any disease and any impairment of physical or mental condition), it is
necessary to identify a person who would or might be the parent of a child but
for sections 27 to 29 of this Act, the court may, on the application of any party
to the action or, if the proceedings have not been commenced, the prospective
pursuer, make an order requiring the Authority to disclose any information contained in the register kept in pursuance of section 31 of this Act identifying that
person.
(3)   Subsections (2) to (4) of section 34 of this Act apply for the purposes of this
section as they apply for the purposes of that.
(4)   After section 4(4) of the Congenital Disabilities (Civil Liability) Act 1976
there is inserted—

'(4A)   In any case where a child carried by a woman as the result of the
placing in her of an embryo or of sperm and eggs or her artificial insemination
is born disabled, any reference in section 1 of this Act to a parent includes a
reference to a person who would be a parent but for sections 27 to 29 of the
Human Fertilisation and Embryology Act 1990.'.

Surrogacy

36   Amendment of Surrogacy Arrangements Act 1985

(1)   After section 1 of the Surrogacy Arrangements Act 1985 there is inserted—

'1A   Surrogacy arrangements unenforceable
No surrogacy arrangement is enforceable by or against any of the persons
making it.'

(2)   In section 1 of that Act (meaning of 'surrogate mother', etc)—
(a)   in subsection (6), for 'or, as the case may be, embryo insertion' there is
substituted 'or of the placing in her of an embryo, of an egg in the process of
fertilisation or of sperm and eggs, as the case may be,', and
(b)   in subsection (9), the words from 'and whether' to the end are repealed.
[. . .]

Conscientious objection

38   Conscientious objection

(1)   No person who has a conscientious objection to participating in any activity
governed by this Act shall be under any duty, however arising, to do so.
(2)   In any legal proceedings the burden of proof of conscientious objection
shall rest on the person claiming to rely on it.

(3)   In any proceedings before a court in Scotland, a statement on oath by any person to the effect that he has a conscientious objection to participating in a particular activity governed by this Act shall be sufficient evidence of that fact for the purpose of discharging the burden of proof imposed by subsection (2) above.

47   Index

The expressions listed in the left-hand column below are respectively defined or (as the case may be) are to be interpreted in accordance with the provisions of this Act listed in the right-hand column in relation to those expressions.

Expression	Relevant provision
Activities governed by this Act	Section 4(5)
Authority	Section 2(1)
Carry, in relation to a child	Section 2(3)
Directions	Section 2(1)
Embryo	Section 1
Gametes, eggs or sperm	Section 1
Keeping, in relation to embryos or gametes	Section 2(2)
Licence	Section 2(1)
Licence committee	Section 9(1)
Nominal licensee	Section 17(3)
Person responsible	Section 17(1)
Person to whom a licence applies	Section 17(2)
Statutory storage period	Section 14(3) to (5)
Store, and similar expressions, in relation to embryos or gametes	Section 2(2)
Treatment services	Section 2(1)

49   Short title, commencement, etc

(1)   This Act may be cited as the Human Fertilisation and Embryology Act 1990.

(2)   This Act shall come into force on such day as the Secretary of State may by order made by statutory instrument appoint and different days may be appointed for different provisions and for different purposes.

(3)   Sections 27 to 29 of this Act shall have effect only in relation to children carried by women as a result of the placing in them of embryos or of sperm and eggs, or of their artificial insemination (as the case may be), after the commencement of those sections.

(4)   Section 27 of the Family Law Reform Act 1987 (artificial insemination) does not have effect in relation to children carried by women as the result of their artificial insemination after the commencement of sections 27 to 29 of this Act.

(5)   Schedule 4 to this Act (which makes minor and consequential amendments) shall have effect.

(6)   An order under this section may make such transitional provision as the Secretary of State considers necessary or desirable and, in particular, may provide that where activities are carried on under the supervision of a particular individual, being activities which are carried on under the supervision of that individual at the commencement of sections 3 and 4 of this Act, those activities are to be treated, during such period as may be specified in or determined in accordance with the order, as authorised by a licence (having, in addition to the conditions required by this Act, such conditions as may be so specified or determined) under which that individual is the person responsible.

(7)   Her Majesty may by Order in Council direct that any of the provisions of

this Act shall extend, with such exceptions, adaptations and modifications (if any) as may be specified in the Order, to any of the Channel Islands.

LAW REFORM (MISCELLANEOUS PROVISIONS) (SCOTLAND) ACT 1990
(1990, c 40)

Blood and other samples in civil proceedings

70 Blood and other samples in civil proceedings

(1) In any civil proceedings to which this section applies, the court may (whether or not on application made to it) request a party to the proceedings—

(a) to provide a sample of blood or other body fluid or of body tissue for the purpose of laboratory analysis;

(b) to consent to the taking of such a sample from a child in relation to whom the party has power to give such consent.

(2) Where a party to whom a request under subsection (1) above has been made refuses or fails—

(a) to provide or, as the case may be, to consent to the taking of, a sample as requested by the court, or

(b) to take any step necessary for the provision or taking of such a sample, the court may draw from the refusal or failure such adverse inference, if any, in relation to the subject matter of the proceedings as seems to it to be appropriate.

(3) In section 6 of the Law Reform (Parent and Child) (Scotland) Act 1986 (determination of parentage by blood sample)—

(a) in subsection (1), for the words 'blood sample' there shall be substituted 'sample of blood or other body fluid or of body tissue'; and

(b) in each of subsections (2), (3) and (4), for the words 'a blood' there shall be substituted 'such a'.

(4) This section applies to any civil proceedings brought in the Court of Session or the sheriff court—

(a) on or after the date of the commencement of this section; or

(b) before the said date in a case where the proof has not by that date begun.

CHILD SUPPORT ACT 1991
(1991, c 48)

The basic principles

1 The duty to maintain

(1) For the purposes of this Act, each parent of a qualifying child is responsible for maintaining him.

(2) For the purposes of this Act, [a non-resident parent] shall be taken to have met his responsibility to maintain any qualifying child of his by making periodical payments of maintenance with respect to the child of such amount, and at such intervals, as may be determined in accordance with the provisions of this Act.

(3) Where a maintenance [calculation] made under this Act requires the making of periodical payments, it shall be the duty of the [non-resident] parent with respect to whom the [calculation] was made to make those payments.

2 Welfare of children: the general principle

Where, in any case which falls to be dealt with under this Act, the Secretary of State [. . .] is considering the exercise of any discretionary power conferred by this Act, he shall have regard to the welfare of any child likely to be affected by his decision.

3 Meaning of certain terms used in this Act

(1) A child is a 'qualifying child' if—

(a)   one of his parents is, in relation to him, [a non-resident parent]; or

(b)   both of his parents are, in relation to him, [non-resident] parents.

(2)   The parent of any child is a '[non-resident parent'], in relation to him, if—

(a)   that parent is not living in the same household with the child; and

(b)   the child has his home with a person who is, in relation to him, a person with care.

(3)   A person is a 'person with care', in relation to any child, if he is a person—

(a)   with whom the child has his home;

(b)   who usually provides day to day care for the child (whether exclusively or in conjunction with any other person); and

(c)   who does not fall within a prescribed category of person.

(4)   The Secretary of State shall not, under subsection (3)(c), prescribe as a category—

(a)   parents;

(b)   guardians;

(c)   persons in whose favour residence orders under section 8 of the Children Act 1989 are in force;

(d)   in Scotland, persons [with whom a child is to live by virtue of a residence order under section 11 of the Children (Scotland) Act 1995].

(5)   For the purposes of this Act there may be more than one person with care in relation to the same qualifying child.

(6)   Periodical payments which are required to be paid in accordance with a [maintenance calculation] are referred to in this Act as 'child support maintenance'.

(7)   Expressions are defined in this section only for the purposes of this Act.

4   Child support maintenance

(1)   A person who is, in relation to any qualifying child or any qualifying children, either the person with care or the [non-resident] parent may apply to the Secretary of State for a [maintenance calculation] to be made under this Act with respect to that child, or any of those children.

(2)   Where a maintenance [calculation] has been made in response to an application under this section the Secretary of State may, if the person with care or [non-resident] parent with respect to whom the [calculation] was made applies to him under this subsection, arrange for—

(a)   the collection of the child support maintenance payable in accordance with the [calculation];

(b)   the enforcement of the obligation to pay child support maintenance in accordance with the [calculation].

(3)   Where an application under subsection (2) for the enforcement of the obligation mentioned in subsection (2)(b) authorises the Secretary of State to take steps to enforce that obligation whenever he considers it necessary to do so, the Secretary of State may act accordingly.

(4)   A person who applies to the Secretary of State under this section shall, so far as that person reasonably can, comply with such regulations as may be made by the Secretary of State with a view to the Secretary of State . . . being provided with the information which is required to enable—

(a)   the [non-resident parent to be identified or] traced (where that is necessary);

(b)   the amount of child support maintenance payable by the [non-resident] parent to be [calculated]; and

(c)   that amount to be recovered from the [non-resident] parent.

(5)   Any person who has applied to the Secretary of State under this section may at any time request him to cease acting under this section.

(6)   It shall be the duty of the Secretary of State to comply with any request

made under subsection (5) (but subject to any regulations made under subsection (8)).

(7)   The obligation to provide information which is imposed by subsection (4)—

(a)   shall not apply in such circumstances as may be prescribed; and

(b)   may, in such circumstances as may be prescribed, be waived by the Secretary of State.

(8)   The Secretary of State may by regulations make such incidental, supplemental or transitional provision as he thinks appropriate with respect to cases in which he is requested to cease to act under this section.

(9)   No application may be made under this section if there is in force with respect to the person with care and [non-resident] parent in question a maintenance [calculation] made in response to an application [treated as made] under section 6.

[(10)   No application may be made at any time under this section with respect to a qualifying child or any qualifying children if—

(a)   there is in force a written maintenance agreement made before 5th April 1993, or a maintenance order [made before a prescribed date] in respect of that child or those children and the person who is, at that time, the [non-resident] parent; or

[(aa)   a maintenance order made on or after the date prescribed for the purposes of paragraph (a) is in force in respect of them, but has been so for less than the period of one year beginning with the date on which it was made; or]

(b)   benefit is being paid to, or in respect of, a parent with care of that child or those children.

(11)   In subsection (10) 'benefit' means any benefit which is mentioned in, or prescribed by regulations under, section 6(1).]

5   Child support maintenance: supplemental provisions

(1)   Where—

(a)   there is more than one person with care of a qualifying child; and

(b)   one or more, but not all, of them have parental responsibility for . . . the child;

no application may be made for a maintenance [calculation] with respect to the child by any of those persons who do not have parental responsibility for . . . the child.

(2)   Where more than one application for a maintenance [calculation] is made with respect to the child concerned, only one of them may be proceeded with.

(3)   The Secretary of State may by regulations make provision as to which of two or more applications for a maintenance [calculation] with respect to the same child is to be proceeded with.

6   Applications by those claiming or receiving benefit

[(1)   This section applies where income support, an income-based jobseeker's allowance or any other benefit of a prescribed kind is claimed by or in respect of, or paid to or in respect of, the parent of a qualifying child who is also a person with care of the child.

(2)   In this section, that person is referred to as 'the parent'.

(3)   The Secretary of State may—

(a)   treat the parent as having applied for a maintenance calculation with respect to the qualifying child and all other children of the non-resident parent in relation to whom the parent is also a person with care; and

(b)   take action under this Act to recover from the non-resident parent, on the parent's behalf, the child support maintenance so determined.

(4)   Before doing what is mentioned in subsection (3), the Secretary of State must notify the parent in writing of the effect of subsections (3) and (5) and section 46.

(5)   The Secretary of State may not act under subsection (3) if the parent asks him not to (a request which need not be in writing).

(6)   Subsection (1) has effect regardless of whether any of the benefits mentioned there is payable with respect to any qualifying child.

(7)   Unless she has made a request under subsection (5), the parent shall, so far as she reasonably can, comply with such regulations as may be made by the Secretary of State with a view to the Secretary of State's being provided with the information which is required to enable—

(a)   the non-resident parent to be identified or traced;

(b)   the amount of child support maintenance payable by him to be calculated; and

(c)   that amount to be recovered from him.

(8)   The obligation to provide information which is imposed by subsection (7)—

(a)   does not apply in such circumstances as may be prescribed; and

(b)   may, in such circumstances as may be prescribed, be waived by the Secretary of State.

(9) If the parent ceases to fall within subsection (1), she may ask the Secretary of State to cease acting under this section, but until then he may continue to do so.

(10)   The Secretary of State must comply with any request under subsection (9) (but subject to any regulations made under subsection (11)).

(11)   The Secretary of State may by regulations make such incidental or transitional provision as he thinks appropriate with respect to cases in which he is asked under subsection (9) to cease to act under this section.

(12)   The fact that a maintenance calculation is in force with respect to a person with care does not prevent the making of a new maintenance calculation with respect to her as a result of the Secretary of State's acting under subsection (3).]

7   Right of child in Scotland to apply for assessment

(1)   A qualifying child who has attained the age of 12 years and who is habitually resident in Scotland may apply to the Secretary of State for a maintenance [calculation] to be made with respect to him if—

(a)   no such application has been made by a person who is with respect to that child, a person with care or an [non-resident] parent; or

[(b)   no parent has been treated under section 6(3) as having applied for a maintenance calculation with respect to the child.]

(2)   An application made under subsection (1) shall authorise the Secretary of State to make a maintenance [calculation] with respect to any other children of the [non-resident] parent who are qualifying children in the care of the same person as the child making the application.

(3)   Where a maintenance [calculation] has been made in response to an application under this section the Secretary of State may, if the person with care, the [non-resident] parent with respect to whom the [calculation] was made or the child concerned applies to him under this subsection, arrange for—

(a)   the collection of the child support maintenance payable in accordance with the [calculation].

(b)   the enforcement of the obligation to pay child support maintenance in accordance with the [calculation].

(4)   Where an application under subsection (3) for the enforcement of the obligation mentioned in subsection (3)(b) authorises the Secretary of State to take steps to enforce that obligation whenever he considers it necessary to do so, the Secretary of State may act accordingly.

(5)   Where a child has asked the Secretary of State to proceed under this section, the person with care of the child, the [non-resident] parent and the child concerned shall, so far as they reasonably can, comply with such regulations as may be made by the Secretary of State with a view to the Secretary of State [. . .] being provided with the information which is required to enable—

(a)   the [non-resident] parent to be traced (where that is necessary);

(b)   the amount of child support maintenance payable by the [non-resident] parent to be [calculated]; and

(c)   that amount to be recovered from the [non-resident] parent.

(6)   The child who has made the application (but not the person having care of him) may at any time request the Secretary of State to cease acting under this section.

(7)   It shall be the duty of the Secretary of State to comply with any request made under subsection (6) (but subject to any regulations made under subsection (9)).

(8)   The obligation to provide information which is imposed by subsection (5)—

(a)   shall not apply in such circumstances as may be prescribed by the Secretary of State; and

(b)   may, in such circumstances as may be so prescribed, be waived by the Secretary of State.

(9)   The Secretary of State may by regulations make such incidental, supplemental or transitional provision as he thinks appropriate with respect to cases in which he is requested to cease to act under this section.

(10)   No application may be made at any time under this section by a qualifying child if—

[(a)] there is in force a written maintenance agreement made before 5th April 1993, or a maintenance order [made before a prescribed date] in respect of that child and the person who is, at that time, the [non-resident parent; or

(b)   a maintenance order made on or after the date prescribed for the purposes of paragraph (a) is in force in respect of them, but has been so for less than the period of one year beginning with the date on which it was made.]

8   Role of the courts with respect to maintenance for children

(1)   This subsection applies in any case where [the Secretary of State] would have jurisdiction to make a maintenance [calculation] with respect to a qualifying child and [a non-resident parent] of his on an application duly made [(or treated as made)] by a person entitled to apply for such [a calculation] with respect to that child.

(2)   Subsection (1) applies even though the circumstances of the case are such that [the Secretary of State] would not make [a calculation] if it were applied for.

(3)   [Except as provided in subsection (3A)] in any case where subsection (1) applies, no court shall exercise any power which it would otherwise have to make, vary, or revive any maintenance order in relation to the child and [non-resident parent] concerned.

[(3A)   Unless a maintenance calculation has been made with respect to the child concerned, subsection (3) does not prevent a court from varying a maintenance order in relation to that child and the non-resident parent concerned—

(a)   if the maintenance order was made on or after the date prescribed for the purposes of section 4(10)(a) or 7(10)(a); or

(b)   where the order was made before then, in any case in which section 4(10) or 7(10) prevents the making of an application for a maintenance calculation with respect to or by that child.]

(4)   Subsection (3) does not prevent a court from revoking a maintenance order.

(5)   The Lord Chancellor or in relation to Scotland the Lord Advocate may by order provide that, in such circumstances as may be specified by the order, this section shall not prevent a court from exercising any power which it has to make a maintenance order in relation to a child if—

(a)   a written agreement (whether or not enforceable) provides for the making, or securing, by [a non-resident parent] of the child of periodical payments to or for the benefit of the child; and

(b)   the maintenance order which the court makes is, in all material respects, in the same terms as that agreement.

(6)   This section shall not prevent a court from exercising any power which it has to make a maintenance order in relation to a child if—

(a)   a maintenance [calculation] is in force with respect to the child;

[(b)   the non-resident parent's net weekly income exceeds the figure referred to in paragraph 10(3) of Schedule 1 (as it has effect from time to time pursuant to regulations made under paragraph 10A(1)(b));]

(c)   the court is satisfied that the circumstances of the case make it appropriate for the [non-resident] parent to make or secure the making of periodical payments under a maintenance order in addition to the child support maintenance payable by him in accordance with the maintenance [calculation].

(7)   This section shall not prevent a court from exercising any power which it has to make a maintenance order in relation to a child if—

(a)   the child is, will be or (if the order were to be made) would be receiving instruction at an educational establishment or undergoing training for a trade, profession or vocation (whether or not while in gainful employment); and

(b)   the order is made solely for the purposes of requiring the person making or securing the making of periodical payments fixed by the order to meet some or all of the expenses incurred in connection with the provision of the instruction or training.

(8)   This section shall not prevent a court from exercising any power which it has to make a maintenance order in relation to a child if—

(a)   a disability living allowance is paid to or in respect of him; or

(b)   no such allowance is paid but he is disabled,

and the order is made solely for the purpose of requiring the person making or securing the making of periodical payments fixed by the order to meet some or all of any expenses attributable to the child's disability.

(9)   For the purposes of subsection (8), a child is disabled if he is blind, deaf or dumb or is substantially and permanently handicapped by illness, injury, mental disorder or congenital deformity or such other disability as may be prescribed.

(10)   This section shall not prevent a court from exercising any power which it has to make a maintenance order in relation to a child if the order is made against a person with care of the child.

(11)   In this Act 'maintenance order', in relation to any child, means an order which requires the making or securing of periodical payments to or for the benefit of the child and which is made under—

(a)   Part II of the Matrimonial Causes Act 1973;

(b)   the Domestic Proceedings and Magistrates' Courts Act 1978;

(c)   Part III of the Matrimonial and Family Proceedings Act 1984;

(d)   the Family Law (Scotland) Act 1985;

(e)   Schedule 1 to the Children Act 1989; or

(f)   any other prescribed enactment,

and includes any order varying or reviving such an order.

9   Agreements about maintenance

(1)   In this section 'maintenance agreement' means any agreement for the making, or for securing the making, of periodical payments by way of maintenance, or in Scotland aliment, to or for the benefit of any child.

(2)   Nothing in this Act shall be taken to prevent any person from entering into a maintenance agreement.

(3)   [Subject to section 4(10)(a) and section 7(10),] the existence of a maintenance agreement shall not prevent any party to the agreement or any other person, from applying for a maintenance [calculation] with respect to any child to or for whose benefit periodical payments are to be made or secured under the agreement.

(4)   Where any agreement contains a provision which purports to restrict the

right of any person to apply for a maintenance [calculation] that provision shall be void.

(5)   Where section 8 would prevent any court from making a maintenance order in relation to a child and [non-resident] parent of his, no court shall exercise any power that it has to vary any agreement so as—

(a)   to insert a provision requiring that [non-resident] parent to make or secure the making of periodical payments by way of maintenance, or in Scotland aliment, to or for the benefit of that child; or

(b)   to increase the amount payable under such a provision.

[(6)   In any case in which section 4(10) or 7(10) prevents the making of an application for a maintenance [calculation] and—

[(a)   no parent has been treated under section 6(3) as having applied for a maintenance calculation with respect to the child; or

(b)   a parent has been so treated but no maintenance calculation has been made,]

subsection (5) shall have effect with the omission of paragraph (b).]

10   Relationship between maintenance assessments and certain court orders and related matters

(1)   Where an order of a kind prescribed for the purposes of this subsection is in force with respect to any qualifying child with respect to whom a maintenance [calculation] is made, the order—

(a)   shall, so far as it relates to the making or securing of periodical payments, cease to have effect to such extent as may be determined in accordance with regulations made by the Secretary of State; or

(b)   where the regulations so provide, shall, so far as it so relates, have effect subject to such modifications as may be so determined.

(2)   Where an agreement of a kind prescribed for the purposes of this subsection is in force with respect to any qualifying child with respect to whom a maintenance [calculation] is made, the agreement—

(a)   shall, so far as it relates to the making or securing of periodical payments, be unenforceable to such extent as may be determined in accordance with regulations made by the Secretary of State; or

(b)   where the regulations so provide, shall, so far as it so relates, have effect subject to such modifications as may be so determined.

(3)   Any regulations under this section may, in particular, make such provision with respect to—

(a)   any case where any person with respect to whom an order or agreement of a kind prescribed for the purposes of subsection (1) or (2) has effect applies to the prescribed court, before the end of the prescribed period, for the order or agreement to be varied in the light of the maintenance [calculation] and of the provisions of this Act;

(b)   the recovery of any arrears under the order or agreement which fell due before the coming into force of the maintenance [calculation]

as the Secretary of State considers appropriate and may provide that, in prescribed circumstances, an application to any court which is made with respect to an order of a prescribed kind relating to the making or securing of periodical payments to or for the benefit of a child shall be treated by the court as an application for the order to be revoked.

(4)   The Secretary of State may by regulations make provision for—

(a)   notification to be given by [the Secretary or State] to the prescribed person in any case where [he] considers that the making of a maintenance [calculation] has affected, or is likely to affect, any order of a kind prescribed for the purposes of this subsection;

(b)   notification to be given by the prescribed person to the Secretary of State in any case where a court makes an order which it considers has affected, or is likely to affect, a maintenance [calculation].

(5)   Rules may be made under section 144 of the Magistrates' Courts Act 1980 (rules of procedure) requiring any person who, in prescribed circumstances, makes an application to a magistrates' court for a maintenance order to furnish the court with a statement in a prescribed form, and signed by [an officer of the Secretary of State] as to whether or not, at the time when the statement is made, there is a maintenance [calculation] in force with respect to that person or the child concerned.

In this subsection—

'maintenance order' means an order of a prescribed kind for the making or securing of periodical payments to or for the benefit of a child; and

'prescribed' means prescribed by the rules.

Special cases

42   Special cases

(1)   The Secretary of State may by regulations provide that in prescribed circumstances a case is to be treated as a special case for the purposes of this Act.

(2)   Those regulations may, for example, provide for the following to be special cases—

(a)   each parent of a child is [a non-resident] parent in relation to the child;

(b)   there is more than one person who is a person with care in relation to the same child;

(c)   there is more than one qualifying child in relation to the same [non-resident] parent but the person who is the person with care in relation to one of those children is not the person who is the person with care in relation to all of them;

(d)   a person is [a non-resident] parent in relation to more than one child and the other parent of each of those children is not the same person;

(e)   the person with care has care of more than one qualifying child and there is more than one [non-resident] parent in relation to those children;

(f)   a qualifying child has his home in two or more separate households.

(3)   The Secretary of State may by regulations make provision with respect to special cases.

(4)   Regulations made under subsection (3) may, in particular—

(a)   modify any provision made by or under this Act, in its application to any special case or any special case falling within a prescribed category;

(b)   make new provision for any such case; or

(c)   provide for any prescribed provision made by or under this Act not to apply to any such case.

43   Recovery of child support maintenance by deduction from benefit

[(1)   This section applies where—

(a)   a non-resident parent is liable to pay a flat rate of child support maintenance (or would be so liable but for a variation having been agreed to), and that rate applies (or would have applied) because he falls within paragraph 4(1)(b) or (c) or 4(2) of Schedule 1; and

(b)   such conditions as may be prescribed for the purposes of this section are satisfied.

(2)   The power of the Secretary of State to make regulations under section 5 of the Social Security Administration Act 1992 by virtue of subsection (1)(p) (deductions from benefits) may be exercised in relation to cases to which this section applies with a view to securing that payments in respect of child support maintenance are made or that arrears of child support maintenance are recovered.

(3)   For the purposes of this section, the benefits to which section 5 of the 1992 Act applies are to be taken as including war disablement pensions and war

widows' pensions (within the meaning of section 150 of the Social Security Contributions and Benefits Act 1992 (interpretation)).]

44 Jurisdiction

(1) [The Secretary of State] shall have jurisdiction to make a maintenance [calculation] with respect to a person who is—
  (a)   a person with care;
  (b)   a [non-resident] parent; or
  (c)   a qualifying child,
only if that person is habitually resident in the United Kingdom [except in the case of a non-resident parent who falls within subsection (2A)].

(2) Where the person with care is not an individual subsection (1) shall have effect as if paragraph (a) were omitted,

[(2A) A non-resident parent falls within this subsection if he is not habitually resident in the United Kingdom, but is—
  (a)   employed in the civil service of the Crown, including Her Majesty's Diplomatic Service and Her Majesty's Overseas Civil Service;
  (b)   a member of the naval, military or air forces of the Crown, including any person employed by an association established for the purposes of Part XI of the Reserve Forces Act 1996;
  (c)   employed by a company of a prescribed description registered under the Companies Act 1985 in England and Wales or in Scotland, or under the Companies (Northern Ireland) Order 1986; or
  (d)   employed by a body of a prescribed description.]

45 Jurisdiction of courts in certain proceedings under this Act

(1) The Lord Chancellor or, in relation to Scotland, the Lord Advocate may by order make such provision as he considers necessary to secure that appeals, or such class of appeals as may be specified in the order—
  (a)   shall be made to a court instead of being made to an appeal tribunal; or
  (b)   shall be so made in such circumstances as may be so specified.

(2) In subsection (1), 'court' means—
  (a)   in relation to England and Wales and subject to any provision made under Schedule 11 to the Children Act 1989 (jurisdiction of courts with respect to certain proceedings relating to children) the High Court, a county court or a magistrates' court; and
  (b)   in relation to Scotland, the Court of Session or the sheriff.

(3)–(5) [*Amend the Children Act 1989.*]

(6) Where the effect of any order under subsection (1) is that there are no longer any appeals which fall to be dealt with by [. . .] appeal tribunals, the Lord Chancellor after consultation with the Lord Advocate may by order provide for the abolition of those tribunals.

(7) Any order under subsection (1) or (6) may make—
  (a)   such modifications of any provision of this Act or of any other enactment; and
  (b)   such transitional provision,
as the Minister making the order considers appropriate in consequence of any provision made by the order.

Miscellaneous and supplemental

46 [Reduced benefit decisions]

[(1) This section applies where any person ('the parent')—
  (a)   has made a request under section 6(5);
  (b)   fails to comply with any regulation made under section 6(7); or
  (c)   having been treated as having applied for a maintenance calculation

under section 6, refuses to take a scientific test (within the meaning of section 27A).

(2) The Secretary of State may serve written notice on the parent requiring her, before the end of a specified period—

(a) in a subsection (1)(a) case, to give him her reasons for making the request;

(b) in a subsection (1)(b) case, to give him her reasons for failing to do so; or

(c) in a subsection (1)(c) case, to give him her reasons for her refusal.

(3) When the specified period has expired, the Secretary of State shall consider whether, having regard to any reasons given by the parent, there are reasonable grounds for believing that—

(a) in a subsection (1)(a) case, if the Secretary of State were to do what is mentioned in section 6(3);

(b) in a subsection (1)(b) case, if she were to be required to comply; or

(c) in a subsection (1)(c) case, if she took the scientific test,

there would be a risk of her, or of any children living with her, suffering harm or undue distress as a result of his taking such action, or her complying or taking the test.

(4) If the Secretary of State considers that there are such reasonable grounds, he shall—

(a) take no further action under this section in relation to the request, the failure or the refusal in question; and

(b) notify the parent, in writing, accordingly.

(5) If the Secretary of State considers that there are no such reasonable grounds, he may, except in prescribed circumstances, make a reduced benefit decision with respect to the parent.

(6) In a subsection (1)(a) case, the Secretary of State may from time to time serve written notice on the parent requiring her, before the end of a specified period—

(a) to state whether her request under section 6(5) still stands; and

(b) if so, to give him her reasons for maintaining her request,

and subsections (3) to (5) have effect in relation to such a notice and any response to it as they have effect in relation to a notice under subsection (2)(a) and any response to it.

(7) Where the Secretary of State makes a reduced benefit decision he must send a copy of it to the parent.

(8) A reduced benefit decision is to take effect on such date as may be specified in the decision.

(9) Reasons given in response to a notice under subsection (2) or (6) need not be given in writing unless the Secretary of State directs in any case that they must.

(10) In this section—

(a) 'comply' means to comply with the requirement or with the regulation in question; and 'complied' and 'complying' are to be construed accordingly;

(b) 'reduced benefit decision' means a decision that the amount payable by way of any relevant benefit to, or in respect of, the parent concerned be reduced by such amount, and for such period, as may be prescribed;

(c) 'relevant benefit' means income support or an income-based jobseeker's allowance or any other benefit of a kind prescribed for the purposes of section 6; and

(d) 'specified', in relation to a notice served under this section, means specified in the notice; and the period to be specified is to be determined in accordance with regulations made by the Secretary of State.]

[46A Finality of decisions

(1) Subject to the provisions of this Act, any decision of the Secretary of State or an appeal tribunal made in accordance with the foregoing provisions of this Act shall be final.

(2)   If and to the extent that regulations so provide, any finding of fact or other determination embodied in or necessary to such a decision, or on which such a decision is based, shall be conclusive for the purposes of—

   (a)   further such decisions;

   (b)   decisions made in accordance with sections 8 to 16 of the Social Security Act 1998, or with regulations under section 11 of that Act; and

   (c)   decisions made under the Vaccine Damage Payments Act 1979.

46B   Matters arising as respects decisions

(1)   Regulations may make provision as respects matters arising pending—

   (a)   any decision of the Secretary of State under section 11, 12 or 17;

   (b)   any decision of an appeal tribunal under section 20; or

   (c)   any decision of a Child Support Commissioner under section 24.

(2)   Regulations may also make provision as respects matters arising out of the revision under section 16, or on appeal, of any such decision as is mentioned in subsection (1).]

47   Fees

(1)   The Secretary of State may by regulations provide for the payment, by the [non-resident] parent or the person with care (or by both), of such fees as may be prescribed in cases where the Secretary of State takes [or proposes to take] any action under section 4 or 6.

(2)   The Secretary of State may by regulations provide for the payment, by the [non-resident] parent, the person with care or the child concerned (or by any or all of them), of such fees as may be prescribed in cases where the Secretary of State takes [or propose to take] any action under section 7.

(3)   Regulations made under this section—

   (a)   may require any information which is needed for the purpose of determining the amount of any such fee to be furnished, in accordance with the regulations, by such person as may be prescribed;

   (b)   shall provide that no such fees shall be payable by any person to or in respect of whom income support, [an income-based jobseeker's allowance, any element of child tax credit other than the family element, working tax credit or] any other benefit of a prescribed kind is paid; and

   (c)   may, in particular, make provision with respect to the recovery by the Secretary of State of any fees payable under the regulations.

[(4)   The provisions of this Act with respect to—

   (a)   the collection of child support maintenance;

   (b)   the enforcement of any obligation to pay child support maintenance,

shall apply equally (with any necessary modifications) to fees payable by virtue of regulations made under this section.]

48   Right of audience

(1)   Any [officer of the Secretary of State who is authorised] by the Secretary of State for the purposes of this section shall have, in relation to any proceedings under this Act before a magistrates' court, a right of audience and the right to conduct litigation.

(2)   In this section 'right of audience' and 'right to conduct litigation' have the same meaning as in section 119 of the Courts and Legal Services Act 1990.

49   Right of audience: Scotland

In relation to any proceedings before the sheriff under any provision of this Act, the power conferred on the Court of Session by section 32 of the Sheriff Courts (Scotland) Act 1971 (power of Court of Session to regulate civil procedure in sheriff court) shall extend to the making of rules permitting a party to such proceedings, in such circumstances as may be specified in the rules, to be represented by a person who is neither an advocate nor a solicitor.

50 Unauthorised disclosure of information

(1)   Any person who is, or has been, employed in employment to which this section applies is guilty of an offence if, without lawful authority, he discloses any information which—

(a)   was acquired by him in the course of that employment; and

(b)   relates to a particular person.

(2)   It is not an offence under this section—

(a)   to disclose information in the form of a summary or collection of information so framed as not to enable information relating to any particular person to be ascertained from it; or

(b)   to disclose information which has previously been disclosed to the public with lawful authority.

(3)   It is a defence for a person charged with an offence under this section to prove that at the time of the alleged offence—

(a)   he believed that he was making the disclosure in question with lawful authority and had no reasonable cause to believe otherwise; or

(b)   he believed that the information in question had previously been disclosed to the public with lawful authority and had no reasonable cause to believe otherwise.

(4)   A person guilty of an offence under this section shall be liable—

(a)   on conviction on indictment, to imprisonment for a term not exceeding two years or a fine or both; or

(b)   on summary conviction, to imprisonment for a term not exceeding six months or a fine not exceeding the statutory maximum or both.

(5)   This section applies to employment as—

(a)   the Chief Child Support Officer;

(b)   any other child support officer;

(c)   any clerk to, or other officer of [an appeal tribunal or] a child support appeal tribunal;

(d)   any member of the staff of such a tribunal;

(e)   a civil servant in connection with the carrying out of any functions under this Act,

and to employment of any other kind which is prescribed for the purposes of this section.

(6)   For the purposes of this section a disclosure is to be regarded as made with lawful authority if, and only if, it is made—

(a)   by a civil servant in accordance with his official duty; or

(b)   by any other person either—

(i)   for the purposes of the function in the exercise of which he holds the information and without contravening any restriction duly imposed by the responsible person; or

(ii)   to, or in accordance with an authorisation duly given by, the responsible person;

(c)   in accordance with any enactment or order of a court;

(d)   for the purpose of instituting, or otherwise for the purposes of, any proceedings before a court or before any tribunal or other body or person mentioned in this Act; or

(e)   with the consent of the appropriate person.

(7)   'The responsible person' means—

(a)   the Lord Chancellor;

(b)   the Secretary of State;

(c)   any person authorised by the Lord Chancellor, or Secretary of State, for the purposes of this subsection; or

(d)   any other prescribed person, or person falling within a prescribed category.

(8)   'The appropriate person' means the person to whom the information in question relates, except that if the affairs of that person are being dealt with—

(a)   under a power of attorney;

(b)   by a receiver appointed under section 99 of the Mental Health Act 1983;

(c)   by a Scottish mental health custodian, that is to say [a guardian or other person entitled to act on behalf of the person under the Adults with Incapacity (Scotland) Act 2000 (asp 4)]; or

(d)   by a mental health appointee, that is to say—

(i)   a person directed or authorised as mentioned in sub-paragraph (a) of rule 41(1) of the Court of Protection Rules 1984; or

(ii)   a receiver *ad interim* appointed under sub-paragraph (b) of that rule;

the appropriate person is the attorney, receiver, custodian or appointee (as the case may be) or, in a case falling within paragraph (a), the person to whom the information relates.

51   Supplementary powers to make regulations

(1)   The Secretary of State may by regulations make such incidental, supplemental and transitional provision as he considers appropriate in connection with any provision made by or under this Act.

(2)   The regulations may, in particular, make provision—

(a)   as to the procedure to be followed with respect to—

(i)   the making of applications for maintenance [calculations];

[(ii)   the making of decisions under section 11;

(iii)   the making of decisions under section 16 or 17;]

[(b)   extending the categories of case to which section 16, 17 or 20 applies;]

(c)   as to the date on which an application for a maintenance [calculation] is to be treated as having been made;

(d)   for attributing payments made under maintenance [calculations] to the payment of arrears;

(e)   for the adjustment, for the purpose of taking account of the retrospective effect of a maintenance [calculation], of amounts payable under the [calculation];

(f)   for the adjustment, for the purpose of taking account of over-payments or under-payments of child support maintenance, of amounts payable under a maintenance [calculation];

(g)   as to the evidence which is to be required in connection with such matters as may be prescribed;

(h)   as to the circumstances in which any official record or certificate is to be conclusive (or in Scotland, sufficient) evidence;

(i)   with respect to the giving of notices or other documents;

(j)   for the rounding up or down of any amounts calculated, estimated or otherwise arrived at in applying any provision made by or under this Act.

(3)   No power to make regulations conferred by any other provision of this Act shall be taken to limit the powers given to the Secretary of State by this section.

52   Regulations and orders

(1)   Any power conferred on the Lord Chancellor, the Lord Advocate or the Secretary of State by this Act to make regulations or orders (other than a deduction from earnings order) shall be exercisable by statutory instrument.

[(2)   No statutory instrument containing (whether alone or with other provisions) regulations made under—

(a)   section 6(1), 12(4) (so far as the regulations make provision for the default rate of child support maintenance mentioned in section 12(5)(b), 28C(2)(b), 28F(2)(b), 30(5A), 41(2), 41A, 41B(6), 43(1), 44(2A)(d), 46 or 47;

(b)   paragraph 3(2) or 10A(1) of Part I of Schedule 1; or

(c)   Schedule 4B,

or an order made under section 45(1) or (6), shall be made unless a draft of the instrument has been laid before Parliament and approved by a resolution of each House of Parliament.]

[(2A)   No statutory instrument containing (whether alone or with other provisions) the first set of regulations made under paragraph 10(1) of Part I of Schedule 1 as substituted by section 1(3) of the Child Support, Pensions and Social Security Act 2000 shall be made unless a draft of the instrument has been laid before Parliament and approved by a resolution of each House of Parliament.]

(3)   Any other statutory instrument made under this Act (except an order made under section 58(2)) shall be subject to annulment in pursuance of a resolution of either House of Parliament.

(4)   Any power of a kind mentioned in subsection (1) may be exercised—

(a)   in relation to all cases to which it extends, in relation to those cases but subject to specified exceptions or in relation to any specified cases or classes of case;

(b)   so as to make, as respects the cases in relation to which it is exercised—

(i)   the full provision to which it extends or any lesser provision (whether by way of exception or otherwise);

(ii)   the same provision for all cases, different provision for different cases or classes of case or different provision as respects the same case or class of case but for different purposes of this Act;

(iii)   provision which is either unconditional or is subject to any specified condition;

(c)   so to provide for a person to exercise a discretion in dealing with any matter.

53   Financial provisions
Any expenses of the Lord Chancellor or the Secretary of State under this Act shall be payable out of money provided by Parliament.

54   Interpretation
In this Act—

'non-resident', has the meaning given in section 3(2);

['appeal tribunal' means an appeal tribunal constituted under Chapter I of Part I of the Social Security Act 1998;]

['application for a variation' means an application under section 28A or 28G;]

'Benefits Acts' means the [Social Security Contributions and Benefits Act 1992 and the Social Security Administration Act 1992];

[. . .]

'child benefit' has the same meaning as in the Child Benefit Act 1975;

[. . .]

'child support maintenance' has the meaning given in section 3(6);

[. . .]

'deduction from earnings order' has the meaning given in section 31(2);

['default maintenance decision' has the meaning given in section 12;]

'disability living allowance' has the same meaning as in the [Benefit Acts];

[. . .]

'general qualification' shall be construed in accordance with section 71 of the Courts and Legal Services Act 1990 (qualification for judicial appointments);

'income support' has the same meaning as in the Benefit Acts;

['income-based jobseeker's allowance' has the same meaning as in the Jobseeker's Act 1995;]

'interim maintenance [decision]' has the meaning given in section 12;

'liability order' has the meaning given in section 33(2);

'maintenance agreement' has the meaning given in section 9(1);

'maintenance [calculation]' means [a calculation] of maintenance made under this Act and, except in prescribed circumstances, includes [a default maintenance decision and an interim maintenance decision];

'maintenance order' has the meaning given in section 8(11);

[. . .]

'parent', in relation to any child, means any person who is in law the mother or father of the child;

['parental responsibility', in the application of this Act—(a) to England and Wales, has the same meaning as in the Children Act 1989; and (b) to Scotland, shall be construed as a reference to 'parental responsibilities' within the meaning given by section 1(3) of the Children (Scotland) Act 1995;]

[. . .]

'parent with care' means a person who is, in relation to a child, both a parent and a person with care;]

'person with care' has the meaning given in section 3(3);

'prescribed' means prescribed by regulations made by the Secretary of State;

'qualifying child' has the meaning given in section 3(1);

['voluntary payment' has the meaning given in section 28J.]

55 Meaning of 'child'

(1) For the purposes of this Act a person is a child if—

(a) he is under the age of 16;

(b) he is under the age of 19 and receiving full-time education (which is not advanced education)—

(i) by attendance at a recognised educational establishment; or

(ii) elsewhere, if the education is recognised by the Secretary of State; or

(c) he does not fall within paragraph (a) or (b) but—

(i) he is under the age of 18, and

(ii) prescribed conditions are satisfied with respect to him.

(2) A person is not a child for the purposes of this Act if he—

(a) is or has been married;

(b) has celebrated a marriage which is void; or

(c) has celebrated a marriage in respect of which a decree of nullity has been granted.

(3) In this section—

'advanced education' means education of a prescribed description; and

'recognised educational establishment' means an establishment recognised by the Secretary of State for the purposes of this section as being, or as comparable to, a university, college or school.

(4) Where a person has reached the age of 16, the Secretary of State may recognise education provided for him otherwise than at a recognised educational establishment only if the Secretary of State is satisfied that education was being so provided for him immediately before he reached the age of 16.

(5) The Secretary of State may provide that in prescribed circumstances education is or is not to be treated for the purposes of this section as being full-time.

(6) In determining whether a person falls within subsection (1)(b), no account shall be taken of such interruptions in his education as may be prescribed.

(7) The Secretary of State may by regulations provide that a person who ceases to fall within subsection (1) shall be treated as continuing to fall within that subsection for a prescribed period.

(8) No person shall be treated as continuing to fall within subsection (1) by virtue of regulations made under subsection (7) after the end of the week in which he reaches the age of 19.

56 Corresponding provision for and co-ordination with Northern Ireland

(1) An Order in Council made under paragraph 1(1)(b) of Schedule 1 to the Northern Ireland Act 1974 which contains a statement that it is made only for purposes corresponding to those of the provisions of this Act, other than provisions which relate to the appointment of Child Support Commissioners for Northern Ireland—

(a) shall not be subject to sub-paragraphs (4) and (5) of paragraph 1 of that Schedule (affirmative resolution of both Houses of Parliament); but

(b) shall be subject to annulment in pursuance of a resolution of either House of Parliament.

[. . .]

57 Application to Crown

(1) The power of the Secretary of State to make regulations under section 14 requiring prescribed persons to furnish information may be exercised so as to require information to be furnished by persons employed in the service of the Crown or otherwise in the discharge of Crown functions.

(2) In such circumstances, and subject to such conditions, as may be prescribed, an inspector appointed under section 15 may enter any Crown premises for the purpose of exercising any powers conferred on him by that section.

(3) Where such an inspector duly enters any Crown premises for those purposes, section 15 shall apply in relation to persons employed in the service of the Crown or otherwise in the discharge of Crown functions as it applies in relation to other persons.

(4) Where a liable person is in the employment of the Crown, a deduction from earnings order may be made under section 31 in relation to that person; but in such a case subsection (8) of section 32 shall apply only in relation to the failure of that person to comply with any requirement imposed on him by regulations made under section 32.

58 Short title, commencement and extent, etc

(1) This Act may be cited as the Child Support Act 1991.

(2) Section 56(1) and subsections (1) to (11) and (14) of this section shall come into force on the passing of this Act but otherwise this Act shall come into force on such date as may be appointed by order made by the Lord Chancellor, the Secretary of State or Lord Advocate, or by any of them acting jointly.

(3) Different dates may be appointed for different provisions of this Act and for different purposes (including, in particular, for different cases or categories of case).

(4) An order under subsection (2) may make such supplemental, incidental or transitional provision as appears to the person making the order to be necessary or expedient in connection with the provisions brought into force by the order, including such adaptations or modifications of—

(a) the provisions so brought into force;

(b) any provisions of this Act then in force; or

(c) any provision of any other enactment,

as appear to him to be necessary or expedient.

(5) Different provision may be made by virtue of subsection (4) with respect to different periods.

(6) Any provision made by virtue of subsection (4) may, in particular, include provision for—

(a) the enforcement of a maintenance [calculation] (including the collection of sums payable under the [calculation] as if the [calculation] were a court order of a prescribed kind;

(b) the registration of maintenance [calculations] with the appropriate court in connection with any provision of a kind mentioned in paragraph (a);

(c) the variation, on application made to a court, of the provisions of a maintenance [calculation] relating to the method of making payments fixed by the [calculation] or the intervals at which such payments are to be made;

(d) a maintenance [calculation], or an order of a prescribed kind relating to one or more children, to be deemed, in prescribed circumstances, to have been validly made for all purposes or for such purposes as may be prescribed.

In paragraph (c) 'court' includes a single justice.

(7) The Lord Chancellor, the Secretary of State or the Lord Advocate may by order make such amendments or repeals in, or such modifications of, such enact-

ments as may be specified in the order, as appear to him to be necessary or expedient in consequence of any provision made by or under this Act (including any provision made by virtue of subsection (4)).

(8) This Act shall, in its application to the Isles of Scilly, have effect subject to such exceptions, adaptations and modifications as the Secretary of State may by order prescribe.

(9) Sections 27, 35, [40] and 48 and paragraph 7 of Schedule 5 do not extend to Scotland.

(10) Sections 7, 28, [40A] and 49 extend only to Scotland.

(11) With the exception of sections 23 and 56(1), subsections (1) to (3) of this section and Schedules 2 and 4, and (in so far as it amends any enactment extending to Northern Ireland) Schedule 5, this Act does not extend to Northern Ireland.

(12) Until Schedule 1 to the Disability Living Allowance and Disability Working Allowance Act 1991 comes into force, paragraph 1(1) of Schedule 3 shall have effect with the omission of the words 'and disability appeal tribunals' and the insertion, after 'social security appeal tribunals', of the word 'and'.

(13) The consequential amendments set out in Schedule 5 shall have effect.

(14) In Schedule 1 to the Children Act 1989 (financial provision for children), paragraph 2(6)(b) (which is spent) is hereby repealed.

AGE OF LEGAL CAPACITY (SCOTLAND) ACT 1991
(1991, c 50)

1 Age of legal capacity

(1) As from the commencement of this Act—

(a) a person under the age of 16 years shall, subject to section 2 below, have no legal capacity to enter into any transaction;

(b) a person of or over the age of 16 years shall have legal capacity to enter into any transaction.

(2) Subject to section 8 below, any reference in any enactment to a pupil (other than in the context of education or training) or to a person under legal disability or incapacity by reason of nonage shall, insofar as it relates to any time after the commencement of this Act, be construed as a reference to a person under the age of 16 years.

(3) Nothing in this Act shall—

(a) apply to any transaction entered into before the commencement of this Act;

(b) confer any legal capacity on any person who is under legal disability or incapacity other than by reason of nonage;

(c) affect the delictual or criminal responsibility of any person;

(d) affect any enactment which lays down an age limit expressed in years for any particular purpose;

(e) prevent any person under the age of 16 years from receiving or holding any right, title or interest;

(f) affect any existing rule of law or practice whereby—

(i) any civil proceedings may be brought or defended, or any step in civil proceedings may be taken in the name of a person under the age of 16 years [in relation to whom there is no person entitled to act as his legal representative (within the meaning of Part I of the Children (Scotland) Act 1995), or where there is such a person] is unable (whether by reason of conflict of interest or otherwise) or refuses to bring or defend such proceedings or take such step;

(ii) the court may, in any civil proceedings, appoint a curator *ad litem* to a person under the age of 16 years;

(iii) the court may, in relation to the approval of an arrangement under section 1 of the Trusts (Scotland) Act 1961, appoint a curator *ad litem* to a person of or over the age of 16 years but under the age of 18 years;

    (iv)　the court may appoint a curator bonis to any person;

    (g)　prevent any person under the age of 16 years from [exercising parental responsibilities and parental rights (within the meaning of sections 1(3) and 2(4) respectively of the Children (Scotland) Act 1995) in relation to any child of his].

(4)　Any existing rule of law relating to the legal capacity of minors and pupils which is inconsistent with the provisions of this Act shall cease to have effect.

(5)　Any existing rule of law relating to reduction of a transaction on the ground of minority and lesion shall cease to have effect.

2　Exceptions to general rule

(1)　A person under the age of 16 years shall have legal capacity to enter into a transaction—

    (a)　of a kind commonly entered into by persons of his age and circumstances, and

    (b)　on terms which are not unreasonable.

(2)　A person of or over the age of 12 years shall have testamentary capacity, including legal capacity to exercise by testamentary writing any power of appointment.

(3)　A person of or over the age of 12 years shall have legal capacity to consent to the making of an adoption order in relation to him; and accordingly—

    (a)　for section 12(8) (adoption orders) of the Adoption (Scotland) Act 1978 there shall be substituted the following subsection—

      '(8)　An adoption order shall not be made in relation to a child of or over the age of 12 years unless with the child's consent; except that, where the court is satisfied that the child is incapable of giving his consent to the making of the order, it may dispense with that consent.'; and

    (b)　for section 18(8) (freeing child for adoption) of that Act there shall be substituted the following subsection—

      '(8)　An order under this section shall not be made in relation to a child of or over the age of 12 years unless with the child's consent; except that where the court is satisfied that the child is incapable of giving his consent to the making of the order, it may dispense with that consent.'

(4)　A person under the age of 16 years shall have legal capacity to consent on his own behalf to any surgical, medical or dental procedure or treatment where, in the opinion of a qualified medical practitioner attending him, he is capable of understanding the nature and possible consequences of the procedure or treatment.

[(4A)　A person under the age of 16 years shall have legal capacity to instruct a solicitor, in connection with any civil matter, where that person has a general understanding of what it means to do so; and without prejudice to the generality of this subsection a person 12 years of age or more shall be presumed to be of sufficient age and maturity to have such understanding.

(4B)　A person who by virtue of subsection (4A) above has legal capacity to instruct a solicitor shall also have legal capacity to sue, or to defend, in any civil proceedings.

(4C)　Subsections (4A) and (4B) above are without prejudice to any question of legal capacity arising in connection with any criminal matter.]

(5)　Any transaction—

    (a)　which a person under the age of 16 years purports to enter into after the commencement of this Act, and

    (b)　in relation to which that person does not have legal capacity by virtue of this section,

shall be void.

3 Setting aside of transactions

(1) A person under the age of 21 years ('the applicant') may make application to the court to set aside a transaction which he entered into while he was of or over the age of 16 years but under the age of 18 years and which is a prejudicial transaction.

(2) In this section 'prejudicial transaction' means a transaction which—

(a) an adult, exercising reasonable prudence, would not have entered into in the circumstances of the applicant at the time of entering into the transaction, and

(b) has caused or is likely to cause substantial prejudice to the applicant.

(3) Subsection (1) above shall not apply to—

(a) the exercise of testamentary capacity;

(b) the exercise by testamentary writing of any power of appointment;

(c) the giving of consent to the making of an adoption order;

(d) the bringing or defending of, or the taking of any step in, civil proceedings;

(e) the giving of consent to any surgical, medical or dental procedure or treatment;

(f) a transaction in the course of the applicant's trade, business or profession;

(g) a transaction into which any other party was induced to enter by virtue of any fraudulent misrepresentation by the applicant as to age or other material fact;

(h) a transaction ratified by the applicant after he attained the age of 18 years and in the knowledge that it could be the subject of an application to the court under this section to set it aside; or

(j) a transaction ratified by the court under section 4 below.

(4) Where an application to set aside a transaction can be made or could have been made under this section by the person referred to in subsection (1) above, such application may instead be made by that person's executor, trustee in bankruptcy, trustee acting under a trust deed for creditors or curator bonis at any time prior to the date on which that person attains or would have attained the age of 21 years.

(5) An application under this section to set aside a transaction may be made—

(a) by an action in the Court of Session or the sheriff court, or

(b) by an incidental application in other proceedings in such court,

and the court may make an order setting aside the transaction and such further order, if any, as seems appropriate to the court in order to give effect to the rights of the parties.

4 Ratification by court of proposed transaction

(1) Where a person of or over the age of 16 years but under the age of 18 years proposes to enter into a transaction which, if completed, could be the subject of an application to the court under section 3 above to set aside, all parties to the proposed transaction may make a joint application to have it ratified by the court.

(2) The court shall not grant an application under this section if it appears to the court that an adult, exercising reasonable prudence and in the circumstances of the person referred to in subsection (1) above, would not enter into the transaction.

(3) An application under this section shall be made by means of a summary application—

(a) to the sheriff of the sheriffdom in which any of the parties to the proposed transaction resides, or

(b) where none of the said parties resides in Scotland, to the sheriff at Edinburgh,

and the decision of the sheriff on such application shall be final.

5 Guardians of persons under 16

(1) Except insofar as otherwise provided in Schedule 1 to this Act, as from the commencement of this Act any reference in any rule of law, enactment or document to the tutor of a pupil child shall be construed as a reference to [a person entitled to act as a child's legal representative (within the meaning of Part I of the Children (Scotland) Act 1995), and any reference to the tutory of such a child shall be construed as a reference to the entitlement to act as a child's legal representative enjoyed by a person by, under or by virtue of the said Part I].

(2) Subject to section 1(3)(f) above, as from the commencement of this Act no guardian of a person under the age of 16 years shall be appointed as such except under [section 7 of the Children (Scotland) Act 1995].

(3) As from the commencement of this Act, no person shall, by reason of age alone, be subject to the curatory of another person.

(4) As from the commencement of this Act, no person shall be appointed as *factor loco tutoris*.

6 Attainment of age

(1) The time at which a person attains a particular age expressed in years shall be taken to be the beginning of the relevant anniversary of the date of his birth.

(2) Where a person has been born on 29th February in a leap year, the relevant anniversary in any year other than a leap year shall be taken to be 1st March.

(3) The provisions of this section shall apply only to a relevant anniversary which occurs after the commencement of this Act.

7 Acquisition of domicile

The time at which a person first becomes capable of having an independent domicile shall be the date at which he attains the age of 16 years.

8 Transitional provision

Where any person referred to in section 6(4)(b), 17(3), 18(3) or 18A(2) of the Prescription and Limitation (Scotland) Act 1973 as having been under legal disability by reason of nonage was of or over the age of 16 years but under the age of 18 years immediately before the commencement of this Act, any period prior to such commencement shall not be reckoned as, or as part of, the period of 5 years, or (as the case may be) 3 years, specified respectively in section 6, 17, 18 or 18A of that Act.

9 Interpretation

In this Act, unless the context otherwise requires—

'existing' means existing immediately before the commencement of this Act;

[. . .]

'transaction' means a transaction having legal effect, and includes—

(a) any unilateral transaction;

(b) the exercise of testamentary capacity;

(c) the exercise of any power of appointment;

(d) the giving by a person of any consent having legal effect;

(e) the bringing or defending of, or the taking of any step in, civil proceedings;

(f) acting as arbiter or trustee;

(g) acting as an instrumentary witness.

10 Amendments and repeals

(1) The enactments mentioned in Schedule 1 to this Act shall have effect subject to the amendments therein specified.

(2) The enactments specified in Schedule 2 to this Act are repealed to the extent specified in the third column of that Schedule.

11 Short title, commencement and extent

(1) This Act may be cited as the Age of Legal Capacity (Scotland) Act 1991.

(2) This Act shall come into force at the end of the period of two months beginning with the date on which it is passed.

(3) This Act shall extend to Scotland only.

CIVIL EVIDENCE (FAMILY MEDIATION) (SCOTLAND) ACT 1995
(1995, c 6)

1 Inadmissibility in civil proceedings of information as to what occurred during family mediation

(1) Subject to section 2 of this Act, no information as to what occurred during family mediation to which this Act applies shall be admissible as evidence in any civil proceedings.

(2) This Act applies to family mediation—

　(a) between two or more individuals relating to—

　　(i) the residence of a child;

　　(ii) the regulation of personal relations and direct contact between a child and any other person;

　　(iii) the control, direction or guidance of a child's upbringing;

　　(iv) the guardianship or legal representation of a child; or

　　(v) any other matter relating to a child's welfare;

　(b) between spouses or former spouses concerning matters arising out of the breakdown or termination of their marriage;

　(c) between parties to a purported marriage concerning matters arising out of the breakdown or annulment of their purported marriage;

　[(cc) between partners in a civil partnership or persons in a purported civil partnership concerning matters arising out of the breakdown or termination of their relationship;]

　(d) between co-habitants or former co-habitants concerning matters arising out of the breakdown or termination of their relationship; or

　(e) of such other description as the Secretary of State may prescribe,

which is conducted by a person accredited as a mediator in family mediation to an organisation which is concerned with such mediation and which is approved for the purposes of this Act by the Lord President of the Court of Session.

(3) The Lord President of the Court of Session may—

　(a) in approving an organisation under subsection (2) above, specify the period for which the approval is granted;

　(b) if he thinks fit, withdraw the approval at any time.

(4) A certificate by the Lord President approving an organisation under subsection (2) above shall be—

　(a) in such form as may be prescribed by Act of Sederunt; and

　(b) admissible as evidence in any civil proceedings and sufficient evidence of the matters contained therein.

(5) A document purporting to be a certificate by the Lord President for the purposes of this Act shall be accepted by the court as such unless the contrary is proved.

(6) The Lord President may, in connection with the performance of any of his functions under this Act, require an organisation which is seeking, or has been granted, approval under subsection (2) above to provide him with such information as he thinks fit.

(7) For the purposes of subsection (2)(d) above, 'co-habitants' means a man and a woman who are not married to each other but who are living together as if they were husband and wife.

(8) In this Act, 'civil proceedings' does not include an arbitration or proceedings before a tribunal or inquiry.

(9) In this section and section 2 of this Act, any reference to what occurred dur-

ing family mediation shall include a reference to what was said, written or observed during such mediation.

2   Exceptions to general rule of inadmissibility

(1)   Nothing in section 1 of this Act shall prevent the admissibility as evidence in civil proceedings—

(a)   of information as to any contract entered into during family mediation or of the fact that no contract was entered into during such mediation;

(b)   where any contract entered into as a result of family mediation is challenged in those civil proceedings, of information as to what occurred during family mediation which relates to the subject matter of that challenge;

(c)   of information as to what occurred during family mediation if every participant (other than the mediator) in that mediation agrees that the information should be admitted as evidence; or

(d)   of information as to what occurred during family mediation if those civil proceedings are proceedings—

(i)   (whether under any enactment or otherwise) relating to a child's care or protection to which a local authority or a voluntary organisation is a party;

(ii)   Under [Chapter 2 or 3 of Part II of the Children (Scotland) Act 1995] before, or relating to, a children's hearing, [before a sheriff or before a justice of the peace];

[(iia)   on any appeal from such proceedings as are mentioned in subparagraph (ii) above];

(iii)   for an adoption order under section 12 of the Adoption (Scotland) Act 1978;

(iv)   for an order under section 18 of the said Act of 1978 declaring a child free for adoption;

(v)   against one of the participants, or the mediator, in a family mediation in respect of damage to property, or personal injury, alleged to have been caused by that participant or, as the case may be, mediator during family mediation; or

(vi)   arising from the family mediation and to which the mediator is a party.

(2)   For the purposes of this section—

(a)   an individual, spouse, former spouse, party to a purported marriage, or co-habitant referred to in section 1(2) of this Act; and

(b)   insofar as the family mediation includes any of the matters mentioned in section 1(2)(a) of this Act, a child who—

(i)   is the subject of such a family mediation; and

(ii)   at the time the family mediation took place was capable of understanding the nature and significance of the matters to which the information which is sought to be admitted as evidence relates,

shall be regarded as a participant in the family mediation.

(3)   Notwithstanding anything in the Age of Legal Capacity (Scotland) Act 1991, any child who is regarded as a participant in family mediation by virtue of subsection (2) above shall have legal capacity to agree that information should be admitted as evidence.

(4)   The Secretary of State may prescribe other persons or classes of person who shall be regarded for the purposes of this section as participants in a family mediation.

3   Short title, construction, commencement and extent

(1)   This Act may be cited as the Civil Evidence (Family Mediation) (Scotland) Act 1995.

(2)   In this Act, 'prescribe', except in relation to an Act of Sederunt, means pre-

scribe by regulations made by statutory instrument subject to annulment in pursuance of a resolution of either House of Parliament.

(3)   This Act shall come into force on such day as the Lord Advocate may by order made by statutory instrument appoint; and such order may include such transitional or incidental provisions as appear to him to be necessary or expedient.

(4)   This Act extends to Scotland only.

CHILDREN (SCOTLAND) ACT 1995
(1995, c 36)

PART I
PARENTS, CHILDREN AND GUARDIANS

Parental responsibilities and parental rights

1   Parental responsibilities

(1)   Subject to section 3(1)(b) and (3) of this Act, a parent has in relation to his child the responsibility—

(a)   to safeguard and promote the child's health, development and welfare;

(b)   to provide, in a manner appropriate to the stage of development of the child—

(i)   direction;

(ii)   guidance,

to the child;

(c)   if the child is not living with the parent, to maintain personal relations and direct contact with the child on a regular basis; and

(d)   to act as the child's legal representative,

but only in so far as compliance with this section is practicable and in the interests of the child.

(2)   'Child' means for the purposes of—

(a)   paragraphs (a), (b)(i), (c) and (d) of subsection (1) above, a person under the age of sixteen years;

(b)   paragraph (b)(ii) of that subsection, a person under the age of eighteen years.

(3)   The responsibilities mentioned in paragraphs (a) to (d) of subsection (1) above are in this Act referred to as 'parental responsibilities'; and the child, or any person acting on his behalf, shall have title to sue, or to defend, in any proceedings as respects those responsibilities.

(4)   The parental responsibilities supersede any analogous duties imposed on a parent at common law; but this section is without prejudice to any other duty so imposed on him or to any duty imposed on him by, under or by virtue of any other provision of this Act or of any other enactment.

2   Parental rights

(1)   Subject to section 3(1)(b) and (3) of this Act, a parent, in order to enable him to fulfil his parental responsibilities in relation to his child, has the right—

(a)   to have the child living with him or otherwise to regulate the child's residence;

(b)   to control, direct or guide, in a manner appropriate to the stage of development of the child, the child's upbringing;

(c)   if the child is not living with him, to maintain personal relations and direct contact with the child on a regular basis; and

(d)   to act as the child's legal representative.

(2)   Subject to subsection (3) below, where two or more persons have a parental right as respects a child, each of them may exercise that right without the consent

of the other or, as the case may be, of any of the others, unless any decree or deed conferring the right, or regulating its exercise, otherwise provides.

(3) Without prejudice to any court order, no person shall be entitled to remove a child habitually resident in Scotland from, or to retain any such child outwith, the United Kingdom without the consent of a person described in subsection (6) below.

(4) The rights mentioned in paragraphs (a) to (d) of subsection (1) above are in this Act referred to as 'parental rights'; and a parent, or any person acting on his behalf, shall have title to sue, or to defend, in any proceedings as respects those rights.

(5) The parental rights supersede any analogous rights enjoyed by a parent at common law; but this section is without prejudice to any other right so enjoyed by him or to any right enjoyed by him by, under or by virtue of any other provision of this Act or of any other enactment.

(6) The description of a person referred to in subsection (3) above is a person (whether or not a parent of the child) who for the time being has and is exercising in relation to him a right mentioned in paragraph (a) or (c) of subsection (1) above; except that, where both the child's parents are persons so described, the consent required for his removal or retention shall be that of them both.

(7) In this section, 'child' means a person under the age of sixteen years.

3 Provisions relating both to parental responsibilities and to parental rights

(1) Notwithstanding section 1(1) of the Law Reform (Parent and Child) (Scotland) Act 1986 (provision for disregarding whether a person's parents are not, or have not been, married to one another in establishing the legal relationship between him and any other person)—

(a) a child's mother has parental responsibilities and parental rights in relation to him whether or not she is or has been married to his father; and

(b) without prejudice to any arrangements which may be made under subsection (5) below and subject to any agreement which may be made under section 4 of this Act, his father has such responsibilities and rights in relation to him only if married to the mother at the time of the child's conception or subsequently.

(2) For the purposes of subsection (1)(b) above, the father shall be regarded as having been married to the mother at any time when he was a party to a purported marriage with her which was—

(a) voidable; or

(b) void but believed by them (whether by error of fact or of law) in good faith at that time to be valid.

(3) Subsection (1) above is without prejudice to any order made under section 11 of this Act or section 3(1) of the said Act of 1986 (provision analogous to the said section 11 but repealed by this Act) or to any other order, disposal or resolution affecting parental responsibilities or parental rights; and nothing in subsection (1) above or in this Part of this Act shall affect any other—

(a) enactment (including any other provision of this Act or of that Act); or

(b) rule of law,

by, under or by virtue of which a person may have imposed on him (or be relieved of) parental responsibilities or may be granted (or be deprived of) parental rights.

(4) The fact that a person has parental responsibilities or parental rights in relation to a child shall not entitle that person to act in any way which would be incompatible with any court order relating to the child or the child's property, or with any supervision requirement made under section 70 of this Act.

(5) Without prejudice to section 4(1) of this Act, a person who has parental responsibilities or parental rights in relation to a child shall not abdicate those responsibilities or rights to anyone else but may arrange for some or all of them to

be fulfilled or exercised on his behalf, and without prejudice to that generality any such arrangement may be made with a person who already has parental responsibilities or parental rights in relation to the child concerned.

(6) The making of an arrangement under subsection (5) above shall not affect any liability arising from a failure to fulfil parental responsibilities; and where any arrangements so made are such that the child is a foster child for the purposes of the Foster Children (Scotland) Act 1984, those arrangements are subject to the provisions of that Act.

4 Acquisition of parental rights and responsibilities by natural father

(1) Where a child's mother has not been deprived of some or all of the parental responsibilities and parental rights in relation to him and, by virtue of subsection (1)(b) of section 3 of this Act, his father has no parental responsibilities or parental rights in relation to him, the father and mother, whatever age they may be, may by agreement provide that, as from the appropriate date, the father shall have the parental responsibilities and parental rights which (in the absence of any order under section 11 of this Act affecting those responsibilities and rights) he would have if married to the mother.

(2) No agreement under subsection (1) above shall have effect unless—

(a)   in a form prescribed by the Secretary of State; and

(b)   registered in the Books of Council and Session while the mother still has the parental responsibilities and parental rights which she had when the agreement was made.

(3) The date on which such registration as is mentioned in subsection (2)(b) above takes place shall be the 'appropriate date' for the purposes of subsection (1) above.

(4) An agreement which has effect by virtue of subsection (2) above shall, subject only to section 11(11) of this Act, be irrevocable.

5 Care or control of child by person without parental responsibilities or parental rights

(1) Subject to subsection (2) below, it shall be the responsibility of a person who has attained the age of sixteen years and who has care or control of a child under that age, but in relation to him either has no parental responsibilities or parental rights or does not have the parental responsibility mentioned in section 1(1)(a) of this Act, to do what is reasonable in all the circumstances to safeguard the child's health, development and welfare; and in fulfilling his responsibility under this section the person may in particular, even though he does not have the parental right mentioned in section 2(1)(d) of this Act, give consent to any surgical, medical or dental treatment or procedure where—

(a)   the child is not able to give such consent on his own behalf, and

(b)   it is not within the knowledge of the person that a parent of the child would refuse to give the consent in question.

(2) Nothing in this section shall apply to a person in so far as he has care or control of a child in a school ('school' having the meaning given by section 135(1) of the Education (Scotland) Act 1980).

6 Views of children

(1) A person shall, in reaching any major decision which involves—

(a)   his fulfilling a parental responsibility or the responsibility mentioned in section 5(1) of this Act; or

(b)   his exercising a parental right or giving consent by virtue of that section, have regard so far as practicable to the views (if he wishes to express them) of the child concerned, taking account of the child's age and maturity, and to those of any other person who has parental responsibilities or parental rights in relation to the child (and wishes to express those views); and without prejudice to the generality of this subsection a child twelve years of age or more shall be presumed to be of sufficient age and maturity to form a view.

(2) A transaction entered into in good faith by a third party and a person acting as legal representative of a child shall not be challengeable on the ground only that the child, or a person with parental responsibilities or parental rights in relation to the child, was not consulted or that due regard was not given to his views before the transaction was entered into.

Guardianship

7 Appointment of guardians

(1) A child's parent may appoint a person to be guardian of the child in the event of the parent's death; but—

(a)   such appointment shall be of no effect unless—

(i)   in writing and signed by the parent; and

(ii)   the parent, at the time of death, was entitled to act as legal representative of the child (or would have been so entitled if he had survived until after the birth of the child); and

(b)   any parental responsibilities or parental rights (or the right to appoint a further guardian under this section) which a surviving parent has in relation to the child shall subsist with those which, by, under or by virtue of this Part of this Act, the appointee so has.

(2) A guardian of a child may appoint a person to take his place as guardian in the event of the guardian's death; but such appointment shall be of no effect unless in writing and signed by the person making it.

(3) An appointment as guardian shall not take effect until accepted, either expressly or impliedly by acts which are not consistent with any other intention.

(4) If two or more persons are appointed as guardians, any one or more of them shall, unless the appointment expressly provides otherwise, be entitled to accept office even if both or all of them do not accept office.

(5) Subject to any order under section 11 or 86 of this Act, a person appointed as a child's guardian under this section shall have, in respect of the child, the responsibilities imposed, and the rights conferred, on a parent by sections 1 and 2 of this Act respectively; and sections 1 and 2 of this Act shall apply in relation to a guardian as they apply in relation to a parent.

(6) Without prejudice to the generality of subsection (1) of section 6 of this Act, a decision as to the appointment of a guardian under subsection (1) or (2) above shall be regarded for the purposes of that section (or of that section as applied by subsection (5) above) as a major decision which involves exercising a parental right.

8 Revocation and other termination of appointment

(1) An appointment made under section 7(1) or (2) of this Act revokes an earlier such appointment (including one made in an unrevoked will or codicil) made by the same person in respect of the same child, unless it is clear (whether as a result of an express provision in the later appointment or by any necessary implication) that the purpose of the later appointment is to appoint an additional guardian.

(2) Subject to subsections (3) and (4) below, the revocation of an appointment made under section 7(1) or (2) of this Act (including one made in an unrevoked will or codicil) shall not take effect unless the revocation is in writing and is signed by the person making the revocation.

(3) An appointment under section 7(1) or (2) of this Act (other than one made in a will or codicil) is revoked if, with the intention of revoking the appointment, the person who made it—

(a)   destroys the document by which it was made; or

(b)   has some other person destroy that document in his presence.

(4) For the avoidance of doubt, an appointment made under section 7(1) or (2) of this Act in a will or codicil is revoked if the will or codicil is revoked.

(5) Once an appointment of a guardian has taken effect under section 7 of this Act, then, unless the terms of the appointment provide for earlier termination, it shall terminate only by virtue of—

(a) the child concerned attaining the age of eighteen years;

(b) the death of the child or the guardian; or

(c) the termination of the appointment by a court order under section 11 of this Act.

Administration of child's property

9 Safeguarding of child's property

(1) Subject to section 13 of this Act, this section applies where—

(a) property is owned by or due to a child;

(b) the property is held by a person other than a parent or guardian of the child; and

(c) but for this section, the property would be required to be transferred to a parent having parental responsibilities in relation to the child or to a guardian for administration by that parent or guardian on behalf of the child.

(2) Subject to subsection (4) below, where this section applies and the person holding the property is an executor or trustee, then—

(a) if the value of the property exceeds £20,000, he shall; or

(b) if that value is not less than £5,000 and does not exceed £20,000, he may,

apply to the Accountant of Court for a direction as to the administration of the property.

(3) Subject to subsection (4) below, where this section applies and the person holding the property is a person other than an executor or trustee, then, if the value of the property is not less than £5,000, that person may apply to the Accountant of Court for a direction as to the administration of the property.

(4) Where the parent or guardian mentioned in subsection (1)(c) above has been appointed a trustee under a trust deed to administer the property concerned, subsections (2) and (3) above shall not apply, and the person holding the property shall transfer it to the parent or guardian.

(5) On receipt of an application under subsection (2) or (3) above, the Accountant of Court may do one, or (in so far as the context admits) more than one, of the following—

(a) apply to the court for the appointment of a judicial factor (whether or not the parent or guardian mentioned in subsection (1)(c) above) to administer all or part of the property concerned and in the event of the court making such an appointment shall direct that the property, or as the case may be part, concerned be transferred to the factor;

(b) direct that all or part of the property concerned be transferred to himself;

(c) direct that all or, in a case where the parent or guardian so mentioned has not been appointed by virtue of paragraph (a) above, part of the property concerned be transferred to the parent or guardian,

to be administered on behalf of the child.

(6) A direction under subsection (5)(c) above may include such conditions as the Accountant of Court considers appropriate, including in particular a condition—

(a) that in relation to the property concerned no capital expenditure shall be incurred without his approval; or

(b) that there shall be exhibited annually to him the securities and bank books which represent the capital of the estate.

(7) A person who has applied under subsection (2) or (3) above for a direction

shall not thereafter transfer the property concerned except in accordance with a direction under subsection (5) above.

(8) The Secretary of State may from time to time prescribe a variation in any sum referred to in subsections (2) and (3) above.

(9) In this section 'child' means a person under the age of sixteen years who is habitually resident in Scotland.

10 Obligations and rights of person administering child's property

(1) A person acting as a child's legal representative in relation to the administration of the child's property—

(a)   shall be required to act as a reasonable and prudent person would act on his own behalf, and

(b)   subject to any order made under section 11 of this Act, shall be entitled to do anything which the child, if of full age and capacity, could do in relation to that property;

and subject to subsection (2) below, on ceasing to act as legal representative, shall be liable to account to the child for his intromissions with the child's property.

(2) No liability shall be incurred by virtue of subsection (1) above in respect of funds which have been used in the proper discharge of the person's responsibility to safeguard and promote the child's health, development and welfare.

Court orders

11 Court orders relating to parental responsibilities etc

(1) In the relevant circumstances in proceedings in the Court of Session or sheriff court, whether those proceedings are or are not independent of any other action, an order may be made under this subsection in relation to—

(a)   parental responsibilities;

(b)   parental rights;

(c)   guardianship; or

(d)   subject to section 14(1) and (2) of this Act, the administration of a child's property.

(2) The court may make such order under subsection (1) above as it thinks fit; and without prejudice to the generality of that subsection may in particular so make any of the following orders—

(a)   an order depriving a person of some or all of his parental responsibilities or parental rights in relation to a child;

(b)   an order—

(i)   imposing upon a person (provided he is at least sixteen years of age or is a parent of the child) such responsibilities; and

(ii)   giving that person such rights;

(c)   an order regulating the arrangements as to—

(i)   with whom; or

(ii)   if with different persons alternately or periodically, with whom during what periods,

a child under the age of sixteen years is to live (any such order being known as a 'residence order');

(d)   an order regulating the arrangements for maintaining personal relations and direct contact between a child under that age and a person with whom the child is not, or will not be, living (any such order being known as a 'contact order');

(e)   an order regulating any specific question which has arisen, or may arise, in connection with any of the matters mentioned in paragraphs (a) to (d) of subsection (1) of this section (any such order being known as a 'specific issue order');

(f)   an interdict prohibiting the taking of any step of a kind specified in the interdict in the fulfillment of parental responsibilities or the exercise of parental rights relating to a child or in the administration of a child's property;

(g)   an order appointing a judicial factor to manage a child's property or remitting the matter to the Accountant of Court to report on suitable arrangements for the future management of the property; or

(h)   an order appointing or removing a person as guardian of the child.

(3)   The relevant circumstances mentioned in subsection (1) above are—

(a)   that application for an order under that subsection is made by a person who—

(i)   not having, and never having had, parental responsibilities or parental rights in relation to the child, claims an interest;

(ii)   has parental responsibilities or parental rights in relation to the child;

(iii)   has had, but for a reason other than is mentioned in subsection (4) below no longer has, parental responsibilities or parental rights in relation to the child; or

(b)   that although no such application has been made, the court (even if it declines to make any other order) considers it should make such an order.

(4)   The reasons referred to in subsection (3)(a)(iii) above are that the parental responsibilities or parental rights have been—

(a)   extinguished on the making of an adoption order;

(b)   transferred to an adoption agency on the making of an order declaring the child free for adoption;

(c)   extinguished by virtue of subsection (9) of section 30 of the Human Fertilisation and Embryology Act 1990 (provision for enactments about adoption to have effect with modifications) on the making of a parental order under subsection (1) of that section; or

(d)   transferred to a local authority by a parental responsibilities order.

(5)   In subsection (3)(a) above 'person' includes (without prejudice to the generality of that subsection) the child concerned; but it does not include a local authority.

(6)   In subsection (4) above—

'adoption agency' and 'adoption order' have the same meanings as they are given, in section 18 of the Adoption (Scotland) Act 1978, by section 65(1) of that Act; and

'parental responsibilities order' has the meaning given by section 86(1) of this Act.

(7)   Subject to subsection (8) below, in considering whether or not to make an order under subsection (1) above and what order to make, the court—

(a)   shall regard the welfare of the child concerned as its paramount consideration and shall not make any such order unless it considers that it would be better for the child that the order be made than that none should be made at all, and

(b)   taking account of the child's age and maturity, shall so far as practicable—

(i)   give him an opportunity to indicate whether he wishes to express his views;

(ii)   if he does so wish, give him an opportunity to express them; and

(iii)   have regard to such views as he may express.

(8)   The court shall, notwithstanding subsection (7) above, endeavour to ensure that any order which it makes, or any determination by it not to make an order, does not adversely affect the position of a person who has, in good faith and for value, acquired any property of the child concerned, or any right or interest in such property.

(9)   Nothing in paragraph (b) of subsection (7) above requires a child to be legally represented, if he does not wish to be, in proceedings in the course of which the court implements that paragraph.

(10)   Without prejudice to the generality of paragraph (b) of subsection (7) above, a child twelve years of age or more shall be presumed to be of sufficient age and maturity to form a view for the purposes both of that paragraph and of subsection (9) above.

(11)   An order under subsection (1) above shall have the effect of depriving a person of a parental responsibility or parental right only in so far as the order expressly so provides and only to the extent necessary to give effect to the order; but in making any such order as is mentioned in paragraph (a) or (b) of subsection (2) above the court may revoke any agreement which, in relation to the child concerned, has effect by virtue of section 4(2) of this Act.

(12)   Where the court makes a residence order which requires that a child live with a person who, immediately before the order is made does not have in relation to the child all the parental responsibilities mentioned in paragraphs (a), (b) and (d) of section 1(1), and the parental rights mentioned in paragraphs (b) and (d) of section 2(1), of this Act (those which he does not so have being in this subsection referred to as the 'relevant responsibilities and rights') that person shall, subject to the provisions of the order or of any other order made under subsection (1) above, have the relevant responsibilities and rights while the residence order remains in force.

(13)   Any reference in this section to an order includes a reference to an interim order or to an order varying or discharging an order.

12   Restrictions on decrees for divorce, separation or annulment affecting children

(1)   In any action for—

[(a)]   divorce, judicial separation or declarator of nullity of marriage, [or

(b)   dissolution or declarator of nullity of a civil partnership or separation of civil partners,]

the court shall, where this section applies, consider (in the light of such information as is before the court as to the arrangements which have been, or are proposed to be, made for the upbringing of each child by virtue of which it applies) whether to exercise with respect to him the powers conferred by section 11 or 54 of this Act.

(2)   Where, in any case to which this section applies, the court is of the opinion that—

(a)   the circumstances of the case require, or are likely to require, it to exercise any power under section 11 or 54 of this Act with respect to the child concerned;

(b)   it is not in a position to exercise that power without giving further consideration to the case; and

(c)   there are exceptional circumstances which make it desirable in the interests of that child that it should not grant decree in the action until it is in a position to exercise such a power,

it shall postpone its decision on the granting of decree in the action until it is in such a position.

(3)   This section applies where a child of the family has not reached the age of sixteen years at the date when the question first arises as to whether the court should give such consideration as is mentioned in subsection (1) above.

(4)   In this section 'child of the family', in relation to—

(a)   the parties to a marriage, means—

[(i)]   a child of both of them; or

[(ii)]   any other child, not being a child who is placed with them as foster parents by a local authority or voluntary organisation, who has been treated by both of them as a child of their family; [or

(b)   the partners in a civil partnership, means a child who has been accepted by both partners as a child of the family which their partnership constitutes.]

13   Awards of damages to children

(1)   Where in any court proceedings a sum of money becomes payable to, or for the benefit of, a child under the age of sixteen years, the court may make such order relating to the payment and management of the sum for the benefit of the child as it thinks fit.

(2)   Without prejudice to the generality of subsection (1) above, the court may in an order under this section—

     (a)   appoint a judicial factor to invest, apply or otherwise deal with the money for the benefit of the child concerned;

     (b)   order the money to be paid—

         (i)   to the sheriff clerk or the Accountant of Court; or

         (ii)   to a parent or guardian of that child,

to be invested, applied or otherwise dealt with, under the directions of the court, for the benefit of that child; or

     (c)   order the money to be paid directly to that child.

(3)   Where payment is made to a person in accordance with an order under this section, a receipt given by him shall be a sufficient discharge of the obligation to make the payment.

Jurisdiction and choice of law

14   Jurisdiction and choice of law in relation to certain matters

(1)   The Court of Session shall have jurisdiction to entertain an application for an order relating to the administration of a child's property if the child is habitually resident in, or the property is situated in, Scotland.

(2)   A sheriff shall have jurisdiction to entertain such an application if the child is habitually resident in, or the property is situated in, the sheriffdom.

(3)   Subject to subsection (4) below, any question arising under this Part of this Act—

     (a)   concerning—

         (i)   parental responsibilities or parental rights; or

         (ii)   the responsibilities or rights of a guardian,

in relation to a child shall, in so far as it is not also a question such as is mentioned in paragraph (b) below, be determined by the law of the place of the child's habitual residence at the time when the question arises;

     (b)   concerning the immediate protection of a child shall be determined by the law of the place where the child is when the question arises; and

     (c)   as to whether a person is validly appointed or constituted guardian of a child shall be determined by the law of the place of the child's habitual residence on the date when the appointment was made (the date of death of the testator being taken to be the date of appointment where an appointment was made by will), or the event constituting the guardianship occurred.

(4)   Nothing in any provision of law in accordance with which, under subsection (3) above, a question which arises in relation to an application for, or the making of, an order under subsection (1) of section 11 of this Act falls to be determined, shall affect the application of subsection (7) of that section.

[(5)   The provisions of sections 9, 11, 13 and this section are subject to Sections 2 and 3 of Chapter II of Council Regulation (EC) No 2201/2003 of 27th November 2003 concerning jurisdiction and the recognition and enforcement of judgments in matrimonial matters and matters of parental responsibility.]

Interpretation

15   Interpretation of Part I

(1)   In this Part of this Act—

'child' means, where the expression is not otherwise defined, a person under the age of eighteen years;

'contact order' has the meaning given by section 11(2)(d) of this Act;

'parent', in relation to any person, means, subject to Part IV of the Adoption (Scotland) Act 1978 and sections 27 to 30 of the Human Fertilisation and Embryology Act 1990 and any regulations made under subsection (9) of the said section 30, someone, of whatever age, who is that person's genetic father or mother;

'parental responsibilities' has the meaning given by section 1(3) of this Act;

'parental rights' has the meaning given by section 2(4) of this Act;

'residence order' has the meaning given by section 11(2)(c) of this Act;

'specific issue order' has the meaning given by section 11(2)(e) of this Act; and

'transaction' has the meaning given by section 9 of the Age of Legal Capacity (Scotland) Act 1991 (except that, for the purposes of subsection (5)(b) below, paragraph (d) of the definition in question shall be disregarded).

(2)   No provision in this Part of this Act shall affect any legal proceedings commenced, or any application made to a court, before that provision comes into effect; except that where, before section 11 of this Act comes into force, there has been final decree in a cause in which, as respects a child, an order for custody or access, or an order which is analogous to any such order as is mentioned in subsection (2) of that section, has been made, any application on or after the date on which the section does come into force for variation or recall of the order shall proceed as if the order had been made under that section.

(3)   In subsection (2) above, the reference to final decree is to a decree or interlocutor which, taken by itself or along with previous interlocutors, disposes of the whole subject matter of the cause.

(4)   Any reference in this Part of this Act to a person—

    (a)   having parental rights or responsibilities;

    (b)   acting as a legal representative; or

    (c)   being appointed a guardian,

is to a natural person only.

(5)   Any reference in this Part of this Act to a person acting as the legal representative of a child is a reference to that person, in the interests of the child—

    (a)   administering any property belonging to the child; and

    (b)   acting in, or giving consent to, any transaction where the child is incapable of so acting or consenting on his own behalf.

(6)   Where a child has legal capacity to sue, or to defend, in any civil proceedings, he may nevertheless consent to be represented in those proceedings by any person who, had the child lacked that capacity, would have had the responsibility to act as his legal representative.

PART II
PROMOTION OF CHILDREN'S WELFARE BY LOCAL AUTHORITIES AND BY CHILDREN'S HEARINGS ETC

CHAPTER 1
SUPPORT FOR CHILDREN AND THEIR FAMILIES

Introductory

16   Welfare of child and consideration of his views

(1)   Where under or by virtue of this Part of this Act, a children's hearing decide, or a court determines, any matter with respect to a child the welfare of that child throughout his childhood shall be their or its paramount consideration.

(2)   In the circumstances mentioned in subsection (4) below, a children's hearing or as the case may be the sheriff, taking account of the age and maturity of the child concerned, shall so far as practicable—

    (a)   give him an opportunity to indicate whether he wishes to express his views;

(b)   if he does so wish, give him an opportunity to express them; and

(c)   have regard to such views as he may express;

and without prejudice to the generality of this subsection a child twelve years of age or more shall be presumed to be of sufficient age and maturity to form a view.

(3)   In the circumstances mentioned in subsection (4)(a)(i) or (ii) or (b) of this section, no requirement or order so mentioned shall be made with respect to the child concerned unless the children's hearing consider, or as the case may be the sheriff considers, that it would be better for the child that the requirement or order be made than that none should be made at all.

(4)   The circumstances to which subsection (2) above refers are that—

(a)   the children's hearing—

(i)   are considering whether to make, or are reviewing, a supervision requirement;

(ii)   are considering whether to grant a warrant under subsection (1) of section 66, or subsection (4) or (7) of section 69, of this Act or to provide under subsection (5) of the said section 66 for the continuation of a warrant;

(iii)   are engaged in providing advice under section 60(10) of this Act; or

(iv)   are drawing up a report under section 73(13) of this Act;

(b)   the sheriff is considering—

(i)   whether to make, vary or discharge a parental responsibilities order, a child assessment order or an exclusion order;

(ii)   whether to vary or discharge a child protection order;

(iii)   whether to grant a warrant under section 67 of this Act; or

(iv)   on appeal, whether to make such substitution as is mentioned in section 51(5)(c)(iii) of this Act; or

(c)   the sheriff is otherwise disposing of an appeal against a decision of a children's hearing.

(5)   If, for the purpose of protecting members of the public from serious harm (whether or not physical harm)—

(a)   a children's hearing consider it necessary to make a decision under or by virtue of this Part of this Act which (but for this paragraph) would not be consistent with their affording paramountcy to the consideration mentioned in subsection (1) above, they may make that decision; or

(b)   a court considers it necessary to make a determination under or by virtue of Chapters 1 to 3 of this Part of this Act which (but for this paragraph) would not be consistent with its affording such paramountcy, it may make that determination.

17   Duty of local authority to child looked after by them

(1)   Where a child is looked after by a local authority they shall, in such manner as the Secretary of State may prescribe—

(a)   safeguard and promote his welfare (which shall, in the exercise of their duty to him be their paramount concern);

(b)   make such use of services available for children cared for by their own parents as appear to the authority reasonable in his case; and

(c)   take such steps to promote, on a regular basis, personal relations and direct contact between the child and any person with parental responsibilities in relation to him as appear to them to be, having regard to their duty to him under paragraph (a) above, both practicable and appropriate.

(2)   The duty under paragraph (a) of subsection (1) above includes, without prejudice to that paragraph's generality, the duty of providing advice and assistance with a view to preparing the child for when he is no longer looked after by a local authority.

(3)   Before making any decision with respect to a child whom they are looking after, or proposing to look after, a local authority shall, so far as is reasonably practicable, ascertain the views of—

(a)   the child;

(b)   his parents;

(c)   any person who is not a parent of his but who has parental rights in relation to him; and

(d)   any other person whose views the authority consider to be relevant, regarding the matter to be decided.

(4)   In making any such decision a local authority shall have regard so far as practicable—

(a)   to the views (if he wishes to express them) of the child concerned, taking account of his age and maturity;

(b)   to such views of any person mentioned in subsection (3)(b) to (d) above as they have been able to ascertain; and

(c)   to the child's religious persuasion, racial origin and cultural and linguistic background.

(5)   If, for the purpose of protecting members of the public from serious harm (whether or not physical harm) a local authority consider it necessary to exercise, in a manner which (but for this paragraph) would not be consistent with their duties under this section, their powers with respect to a child whom they are looking after, they may do so.

(6)   Any reference in this Chapter of this Part to a child who is 'looked after' by a local authority, is to a child—

(a)   for whom they are providing accommodation under section 25 of this Act;

(b)   who is subject to a supervision requirement and in respect of whom they are the relevant local authority;

(c)   who is subject to an order made, or authorisation or warrant granted, by virtue of Chapter 2, 3 or 4 of this Part of this Act, being an order, authorisation or warrant in accordance with which they have responsibilities as respects the child; or

(d)   who is subject to an order in accordance with which, by virtue of regulations made under section 33(1) of this Act, they have such responsibilities.

(7)   Regulations made by the Secretary of State under subsection (1) above may, without prejudice to the generality of that subsection, include—

(a)   provision as to the circumstances in which the child may be cared for by the child's own parents; and

(b)   procedures which shall be followed in the event of the child's death.

18   Duty of persons with parental responsibilities to notify change of address to local authority looking after child

(1)   Where a child is being looked after by a local authority, each natural person who has parental responsibilities in relation to the child shall, without unreasonable delay, inform that authority whenever the person changes his address.

(2)   A person who knowingly fails to comply with the requirement imposed by subsection (1) above shall be liable on summary conviction to a fine of level 1 on the standard scale; but in any proceedings under this section it shall be a defence that—

(a)   the change was to the same address as that to which another person who at that time had parental responsibilities in relation to the child was changing; and

(b)   the accused had reasonable cause to believe that the other person had informed the authority of the change of address of them both.

Provision of services

19   Local authority plans for services for children

(1)   Within such period after the coming into force of this section as the Secre-

tary of State may direct, each local authority shall prepare and publish a plan for
the provision of relevant services for or in respect of children in their area.

(2) References to 'relevant services' in this section are to services provided by a
local authority under or by virtue of—

(a) this Part of this Act; or

(b) any of the enactments mentioned in section 5(1B)(a) to (o) of the Social
Work (Scotland) Act 1968 (enactments in respect of which Secretary of State may
issue directions to local authorities as to the exercise of their functions).

(3) A local authority shall from time to time review the plan prepared by them
under subsection (1) above (as modified, or last substituted, under this subsection)
and may, having regard to that review, prepare and publish—

(a) modifications (or as the case may be further modifications) to the plan
reviewed; or

(b) a plan in substitution for that plan.

(4) The Secretary of State may, subject to subsection (5) below, issue directions
as to the carrying out by a local authority of their functions under subsection (3)
above.

(5) In preparing any plan, or carrying out any review, under this section a local
authority shall consult—

(a) every Health Board and National Health Service trust providing services
under the National Health Service (Scotland) Act 1978 in the area of the authority;

(b) such voluntary organisations as appear to the authority—

(i) to represent the interests of persons who use or are likely to use
relevant services in that area; or

(ii) to provide services in that area which, were they to be provided by the
authority, might be categorised as relevant services;

(c) the Principal Reporter appointed under section 127 of the Local Government etc (Scotland) Act 1994;

(d) the chairman of the children's panel for that area;

(e) such housing associations, voluntary housing agencies and other bodies
as appear to the authority to provide housing in that area; and

(f) such other persons as the Secretary of State may direct.

20   Publication of information about services for children

(1) A local authority shall, within such period after the coming into force of
this section as the Secretary of State may direct, and thereafter from time to time,
prepare and publish information—

(a) about relevant services which are provided by them for or in respect of
children (including, without prejudice to that generality, services for or in
respect of disabled children or children otherwise affected by disability) in their
area or by any other local authority for those children; and

(b) where they consider it appropriate, about services which are provided by
voluntary organisations and by other persons for those children, being services
which the authority have power to provide and which, were they to do so, they
would provide as relevant services.

(2) In subsection (1) above, 'relevant services' has the same meaning as in
section 19 of this Act.

21   Co-operation between authorities

(1) Where it appears to a local authority that an appropriate person could, by
doing certain things, help in the exercise of any of their functions under this Part
of this Act, they may, specifying what those things are, request the help of that
person.

(2) For the purposes of subsection (1) above, persons who are appropriate
are—

(a) any other local authority;

(b) a health board constituted under section 2 of the National Health Service (Scotland) Act 1978;

(c) a national health service trust established under section 12A of that Act; and

(d) any person authorised by the Secretary of State for the purposes of this section;

and an appropriate person receiving such a request shall comply with it provided that it is compatible with their own statutory or other duties and obligations and (in the case of a person not a natural person) does not unduly prejudice the discharge of any of their functions.

22 Promotion of welfare of children in need

(1) A local authority shall—

(a) safeguard and promote the welfare of children in their area who are in need; and

(b) so far as is consistent with that duty, promote the upbringing of such children by their families,

by providing a range and level of services appropriate to the children's needs.

(2) In providing services under subsection (1) above, a local authority shall have regard so far as practicable to each child's religious persuasion, racial origin and cultural and linguistic background.

(3) Without prejudice to the generality of subsection (1) above—

(a) a service may be provided under that subsection—

(i) for a particular child;

(ii) if provided with a view to safeguarding or promoting his welfare, for his family; or

(iii) if provided with such a view, for any other member of his family; and

(b) the services mentioned in that subsection may include giving assistance in kind or, in exceptional circumstances, in cash.

(4) Assistance such as is mentioned in subsection (3)(b) above may be given unconditionally or subject to conditions as to the repayment, in whole or in part, of it or of its value; but before giving it, or imposing such conditions, the local authority shall have regard to the means of the child concerned and of his parents and no condition shall require repayment by a person at any time when in receipt of—

(a) income support or [working families tax] credit payable under the Social Security Contributions and Benefits Act 1992; or

[(aa) any element of child tax credit other than the family element or working tax credit; or]

(b) an income-based jobseeker's allowance payable under the Jobseekers Act 1995.

23 Children affected by disability

(1) Without prejudice to the generality of subsection (1) of section 22 of this Act, services provided by a local authority under that subsection shall be designed—

(a) to minimise the effect on any—

(i) disabled child who is within the authority's area, of his disability; and

(ii) child who is within that area and is affected adversely by the disability of any other person in his family, of that other person's disability; and

(b) to give those children the opportunity to lead lives which are as normal as possible.

(2) For the purposes of this Chapter of this Part a person is disabled if he is chronically sick or disabled or suffers from mental disorder (within the meaning of the Mental Health (Scotland) Act 1984).

(3) Where requested to do so by a child's parent or guardian a local authority

shall, for the purpose of facilitating the discharge of such duties as the authority may have under section 22(1) of this Act (whether or not by virtue of subsection (1) above) as respects the child, carry out an assessment of the child, or of any other person in the child's family, to determine the needs of the child in so far as attributable to his disability or to that of the other person.

[(4) In determining the needs of a child under subsection (3) above, the local authority shall take account—

(a)   where it appears to them that a person ('the carer') provides a substantial amount of care on a regular basis for the child, or for another person in the child's family who is being assessed under that subsection, of such care as is being so provided; and

(b)   in so far as it is reasonable and practicable to do so, of—

(i)   the views of the parent or guardian of the child, and the child; and

(ii) the views of the carer,

provided that the parent, guardian, child or carer in question has a wish, or as the case may be, a capacity, to express a view.]

24   Assessment of ability of carers to provide care for disabled children

[(1)   Subject to subsection (2) below, a person ('the carer') who provides, or intends to provide, a substantial amount of care on a regular basis for a disabled child may, whether or not the carer is a child, request a local authority to make an assessment ('the carer's assessment') of the carer's ability to provide or to continue to provide such care for the child.

(1A)   The local authority to whom the request is made shall—

(a)   comply with the request where it appears to them that the child, or another person in the child's family, is a person for whom they must or may provide services under section 22(1) of this Act; and

(b)   if they then or subsequently make an assessment under section 23(3) of this Act to determine the needs of the child, have regard to the results of the carer's assessment—

(i)   in the assessment of the child; or

(ii) in making a decision as to the discharge by them of any duty they may have as respects the child under section 2(1) of the Chronically Sick and Disabled Persons Act 1970 (c 44) or under section 22(1) of this Act.]

(2)   No request may be made under subsection (1) above by a person who provides or will provide the care in question—

(a)   under or by virtue of a contract of employment or other contract; or

(b)   as a volunteer for a voluntary organisation.

(3)   Where an assessment of a carer's ability to continue to provide, or as the case may be to provide, care for a child is carried out under subsection (1) above, there shall, as respects the child, be no requirement under section 8 of the Disabled Persons (Services, Consultation and Representation) Act 1986 (carer's ability to continue to provide care to be considered in any decision as respects provision of certain services for disabled persons) to have regard to that ability.

(4)   In this section 'person' means a natural person.

[24A   Duty of local authority to provide information to carer of disabled child

Where it appears to a local authority both that—

(a)   a child is a disabled child for whom they must or may provide services under section 22(1) of this Act; and

(b)   a person ('the carer') provides, or intends to provide, a substantial amount of care on a regular basis for the child,

the local authority shall notify the carer that he may be entitled under section 24(1) of this Act to request an assessment of his ability to provide, or to continue to provide, care for the child.]

25 Provision of accommodation for children, etc

(1) A local authority shall provide accommodation for any child who, residing or having been found within their area, appears to them to require such provision because—

(a) no-one has parental responsibility for him;

(b) he is lost or abandoned; or

(c) the person who has been caring for him is prevented, whether or not permanently and for whatever reason, from providing him with suitable accommodation or care.

(2) Without prejudice to subsection (1) above, a local authority may provide accommodation for any child within their area if they consider that to do so would safeguard or promote his welfare.

(3) A local authority may provide accommodation for any person within their area who is at least eighteen years of age but not yet twenty-one, if they consider that to do so would safeguard or promote his welfare.

(4) A local authority providing accommodation under subsection (1) above for a child who is ordinarily resident in the area of another local authority shall notify the other authority, in writing, that such provision is being made; and the other authority may at any time take over the provision of accommodation for the child.

(5) Before providing a child with accommodation under this section, a local authority shall have regard, so far as practicable, to his views (if he wishes to express them), taking account of his age and maturity; and without prejudice to the generality of this subsection a child twelve years of age or more shall be presumed to be of sufficient age and maturity to form a view.

(6) Subject to subsection (7) below—

(a) a local authority shall not provide accommodation under this section for a child if any person who—

(i) has parental responsibilities in relation to him and the parental rights mentioned in section 2(1)(a) and (b) of this Act; and

(ii) is willing and able either to provide, or to arrange to have provided, accommodation for him,

objects; and

(b) any such person may at any time remove the child from accommodation which has been provided by the local authority under this section.

(7) Paragraph (a) of subsection (6) above does not apply—

(a) as respects any child who, being at least sixteen years of age, agrees to be provided with accommodation under this section; or

(b) where a residence order has been made in favour of one or more persons and that person has, or as the case may be those persons have, agreed that the child should be looked after in accommodation provided by, or on behalf of, the local authority;

and paragraph (b) of that subsection does not apply where accommodation has been provided for a continuous period of at least six months (whether by a single local authority or, by virtue of subsection (4) above, by more than one local authority), unless the person removing the child has given the local authority for the time being making such provision at least fourteen days' notice in writing of his intention to remove the child.

(8) In this Part of this Act, accommodation means, except where the context otherwise requires, accommodation provided for a continuous period of more than twenty-four hours.

26 Manner of provision of accommodation to child looked after by local authority

(1) A local authority may provide accommodation for a child looked after by them by—

(a) placing him with—

(i) a family (other than such family as is mentioned in paragraph (a) or (b) of the definition of that expression in section 93(1) of this Act);

(ii) a relative of his; or

(iii) any other suitable person,

on such terms as to payment, by the authority or otherwise, as the authority may determine;

(b) maintaining him in a residential establishment; or

(c) making such other arrangements as appear to them to be appropriate, including (without prejudice to the generality of this paragraph) making use of such services as are referred to in section 17(1)(b) of this Act.

(2) A local authority may arrange for a child whom they are looking after—

(a) to be placed, under subsection (1)(a) above, with a person in England and Wales or in Northern Ireland; or

(b) to be maintained in any accommodation in which—

(i) a local authority in England and Wales could maintain him by virtue of section 23(2)(b) to (e) of the Children Act 1989; or

(ii) an authority within the meaning of the Children (Northern Ireland) Order 1995 could maintain him by virtue of Article 27(2)(b) to (e) of that Order.

27 Day care for pre-school and other children

(1) Each local authority shall provide such day care for children in need within their area who—

(a) are aged five or under; and

(b) have not yet commenced attendance at a school,

as is appropriate; and they may provide such day care for children within their area who satisfy the conditions mentioned in paragraphs (a) and (b) but are not in need.

(2) A local authority may provide facilities (including training, advice, guidance and counselling) for those—

(a) caring for children in day care; or

(b) who at any time accompany such children while they are in day care.

(3) Each local authority shall provide for children in need within their area who are in attendance at a school such care—

(a) outside school hours; or

(b) during school holidays,

as is appropriate; and they may provide such care for children within their area who are in such attendance but are not in need.

(4) In this section—

'day care' means any form of care provided for children during the day, whether or not it is provided on a regular basis; and

'school' has the meaning given by section 135(1) of the Education (Scotland) Act 1980.

28 Removal of power to arrange for emigration of children

Section 23 of the Social Work (Scotland) Act 1968 (which provides a power for local authorities and voluntary associations, with the consent of the Secretary of State, to make arrangements for the emigration of children in their care) shall cease to have effect.

Advice and assistance for young persons formerly looked after by local authorities

29 After-care

(1) A local authority shall, unless they are satisfied that his welfare does not require it, advise, guide and assist any person in their area over school age but not yet nineteen years of age who, at the time when he ceased to be of school age or at any subsequent time was, but who is no longer, looked after by a local authority.

(2) If a person within the area of a local authority is at least nineteen, but is less than twenty-one, years of age and is otherwise a person such as is described in subsection (1) above, he may by application to the authority request that they provide him with advice, guidance and assistance; and they may, unless they are satisfied that his welfare does not require it, grant that application.

(3) [Subject to section 73(2) of the Regulation of Care (Scotland) Act 2001 (asp 8)], assistance given under subsection (1) or (2) above may include assistance in kind or in cash.

(4) Where a person—

(a) over school age ceases to be looked after by a local authority; or

(b) described in subsection (1) above is being provided with advice, guidance or assistance by a local authority,

they shall, if he proposes to reside in the area of another local authority, inform that other local authority accordingly provided that he consents to their doing so.

[(5) It is the duty of each local authority, in relation to any person to whom they have a duty under subsection (1) above or who makes an application under subsection (2) above, to carry out an assessment of the person's needs.

(6) Each local authority shall establish a procedure for considering representations (including complaints) made to them by any person mentioned in subsection (1) or (2) above about the discharge of their functions under the provisions of subsections (1) to (5) above.

(7) In subsection (1) above, the reference to having been 'looked after by a local authority' shall be construed as including having been looked after by a local authority in England and Wales, and subsection (4) of section 105 of the Children Act 1989 (c 41) (construction of references to a child looked after by a local authority) shall apply for the purposes of this subsection as it applies for the purposes of that Act ('local authority in England and Wales' being construed in accordance with subsection (1) of that section).]

30 Financial assistance towards expenses of education or training and removal of power to guarantee indentures etc

(1) Without prejudice to section 12 of the Social Work (Scotland) Act 1968 (general social welfare services of local authorities), a local authority may make—

(a) grants to any relevant person in their area to enable him to meet expenses connected with his receiving education or training; and

(b) contributions to the accommodation and maintenance of any such person in any place near where he may be—

(i) employed, or seeking employment; or

(ii) receiving education or training.

(2) Subject to subsection (3) below, a person is a relevant person for the purposes of subsection (1) above if—

(a) he is over school age but not yet twenty-one years of age; and

(b) at the time when he ceased to be of school age or at any subsequent time he was, but he is no longer, looked after by a local authority.

(3) A local authority making grants under paragraph (a), or contributions under paragraph (b)(ii), of subsection (1) above to a person may continue to make them, though he has in the meantime attained the age of twenty-one years, until he completes the course of education or training in question; but if, after he has attained that age, the course is interrupted by any circumstances they may only so continue if he resumes the course as soon as is practicable.

(4) Section 25 of the Social Work (Scotland) Act 1968 (which empowers a local authority to undertake obligations by way of guarantee under any indentures or other deed of apprenticeship or articles of clerkship entered into by a person in their care or under supplemental deeds or articles) shall cease to have effect.

Miscellaneous and general

31 Review of case of child looked after by local authority

(1) Without prejudice to their duty under section 17(1)(a) of this Act, it shall be the duty of a local authority who are looking after a child to review his case at such intervals as may be prescribed by the Secretary of State.

(2) The Secretary of State may prescribe—

(a) different intervals in respect of the first such review and in respect of subsequent reviews;

(b) the manner in which cases are to be reviewed under this section;

(c) the considerations to which the local authority are to have regard in reviewing cases under this section.

32 Removal of child from residential establishment

A local authority, notwithstanding any agreement made in connection with the placing of a child in a residential establishment under this Chapter, or Chapter 4, of this Part of this Act by them—

(a) may, at any time; and

(b) shall, if requested to do so by the person responsible for the establishment,

remove a child so placed.

33 Effect of orders etc made in different parts of the United Kingdom

(1) The Secretary of State may make regulations providing for a prescribed order which is made by a court in England and Wales or in Northern Ireland, if that order appears to him to correspond generally to an order of a kind which may be made under this Part of this Act or to a supervision requirement, to have effect in prescribed circumstances and for prescribed purposes of the law of Scotland as if it were an order of that kind or, as the case may be, as if it were a supervision requirement.

(2) The Secretary of State may make regulations providing—

(a) for a prescribed order made under this Part of this Act by a court in Scotland; or

(b) for a supervision requirement,

if that order or requirement appears to him to correspond generally to an order of a kind which may be made under any provision of law in force in England and Wales or in Northern Ireland, to have effect in prescribed circumstances and for prescribed purposes of the law of England and Wales, or as the case may be of Northern Ireland, as if it were an order of that kind.

(3) Regulations under subsection (1) or (2)(a) above may provide for the order given effect for prescribed purposes to cease to have effect for those purposes, or for the purposes of the law of the place where the order was made, if prescribed conditions are satisfied.

(4) Where a child who is subject to a supervision requirement is lawfully taken to live in England and Wales or in Northern Ireland, the requirement shall cease to have effect if prescribed conditions are satisfied.

(5) Regulations under this section may modify any provision of—

(a) the Social Work (Scotland) Act 1968 or this Act in any application which the Acts may respectively have, by virtue of the regulations, in relation to an order made otherwise than in Scotland;

(b) the Children Act 1989 or the Children and Young Persons Act 1969 [or sections 63 to 67 of and Schedules 6 and 7 to the Powers of Criminal Courts (Sentencing) Act 2000] in any application which those Acts may respectively have, by virtue of the regulations, in relation to an order prescribed under subsection (2)(a) above or to a supervision requirement; or

(c) the Children (Northern Ireland) Order 1995 or the Children and Young Persons Act (Northern Ireland) 1968 in any application which they may respectively have, by virtue of the regulations, in relation to an order so prescribed or to a supervision requirement.

[. . .]

35 Welfare of children in accommodation provided for purposes of school attendance

After section 125 of the Education (Scotland) Act 1980 there shall be inserted—

'Children and young persons in accommodation

125A Welfare of children and young persons in accommodation provided for purposes of school attendance

Where, for the purposes of his being in attendance at a school, a child or young person is provided with residential accommodation, in a place in or outwith that school, by—

(a) an education authority [. . .] or the managers of a grant-aided or independent school; or

(b) by any other person in pursuance of arrangements made by any such authority, [. . .] or managers,

the authority, board of management or managers in question shall have the duty to safeguard and promote the welfare of the child or young person while he is so accommodated; and the powers of inspection exercisable by virtue of section 66(1) of this Act shall include the power to inspect the place to determine whether his welfare is adequately safeguarded and promoted there.'.

36 Welfare of certain children in hospitals and nursing homes etc

(1) Where a child is provided with residential accommodation by a person mentioned in subsection (3) below and it appears to the person that the child either—

(a) has had no parental contact for a continuous period of three months or more; or

(b) is likely to have no parental contact for a period which, taken with any immediately preceding period in which the child has had no such contact, will constitute a continuous period of three months or more,

the person shall (whether or not the child has been, or will be, so accommodated throughout the continuous period) so notify the local authority in whose area the accommodation is provided.

(2) A local authority receiving notification under subsection (1) above shall—

(a) take such steps as are reasonably practicable to enable them to determine whether the child's welfare is adequately safeguarded and promoted while he is so accommodated; and

(b) consider the extent to which (if at all) they should exercise any of their functions under this Act with respect to the child.

(3) The persons are—

(a) any health board constituted under section 2 of the National Health Service (Scotland) Act 1978;

(b) any national health service trust established under section 12A of that Act;

(c) any person carrying on a private hospital registered under Part IV of the Mental Health (Scotland) Act 1984;

[(d) any person providing a care home service (as defined by section 2(3) of the Regulation of Care (Scotland) Act 2001 (asp 8)).]

(4) For the purposes of subsection (1) above, a child has parental contact only when in the presence of a person having parental responsibilities in relation to him.

(5) A person duly authorised by a local authority may in the area of that authority, at all reasonable times, enter for the purposes of subsection (2) above or of

determining whether there has been compliance with subsection (1) above any such place as is mentioned in sub-paragraph (i) or (ii) of subsection (3)(c) above and may for those purposes inspect any records or registers relating to that place; and subsections (2A) to (2D) and (4) of section 6 of the Social Work (Scotland) Act 1968 (exercise of powers of entry and inspection) shall apply in respect of a person so authorised as they apply in respect of a person duly authorised under sub-section (1) of that section.

[. . .]

38   Short-term refuges for children at risk of harm

(1)   Where a child appears—

(a)   to a local authority to be at risk of harm, they may at the child's request—

(i)   provide him with refuge in a residential establishment both controlled or managed by them and designated by them for the purposes of this paragraph; or

(ii)   arrange for a person whose household is approved by virtue of section 5(3)(b) of the Social Work (Scotland) Act 1968 (provision for securing that persons are not placed in any household unless the household has prescribed approval) and is designated by them for the purposes of this paragraph to provide him with refuge in that household,

for a period which does not exceed the relevant period;

(b)   to a person who [provides a care home service (as defined by section 2(3) of the Regulation of Care (Scotland) Act 2001 (asp 8))] or to any person for the time being employed in the management of the accommodation in question, to be at risk of harm, the person to whom the child so appears may at the child's request provide him with refuge, for a period which does not exceed the relevant period, in the accommodation but shall do so only if and to the extent that the local authority within whose area the accommodation is situated have given their approval to the use of the accommodation (or a part of the accommodation) for the purposes of this paragraph.

(2)   The Secretary of State may by regulations make provision as to—

(a)   designation, for the purposes of paragraph (a) of subsection (1) above, of establishments and households;

(b)   application for, the giving of and the withdrawal of, approval under paragraph (b) of subsection (1) above;

(c)   requirements (if any) which must be complied with while any such approval remains in force;

(d)   the performance by a person mentioned in the said paragraph (b) of any-thing to be done by him under that paragraph;

(e)   the performance by a local authority of their functions under this section; and

(f)   the giving, to such persons or classes of person as may be specified in the regulations, of notice as to the whereabouts of a child provided with refuge under this section,

and regulations made under this subsection may include such incidental and sup-plementary provisions as he thinks fit.

(3)   While a child is being provided with refuge under, and in accordance with regulations made under, this section, none of the enactments mentioned in sub-section (4) below shall apply in relation to him unless the commencement of the period of refuge has followed within two days of the termination of a prior period of refuge so provided to him by any person.

(4)   The enactments are—

(a)   section 89 of this Act and, so far as it applies in relation to anything done in Scotland, section 83 of this Act; and

(b)   section 32(3) of the Children and Young Persons Act 1969 (compelling, persuading, inciting or assisting any person to be absent from detention etc), so far as it applies in relation to anything done in Scotland.

(5)   References in this section to the relevant period shall be construed as references either to a period which does not exceed seven days or, in such exceptional circumstances as the Secretary of State may prescribe, to a period which does not exceed fourteen days.

(6)   A child who is provided with refuge for a period by virtue of such arrangements as are mentioned in subsection (1)(a) above shall not be regarded as a foster child for the purposes of the Foster Children (Scotland) Act 1984 by reason only of such provision.

CHAPTER 2
CHILDREN'S HEARINGS

Constitution of children's hearings

39   Formation of children's panel and children's hearings

(1)   For every local government area there shall be a children's panel for the purposes of this Act, and any other enactment conferring powers on a children's hearing (or on such a panel).

(2)   Schedule 1 to this Act shall have effect with respect to the recruitment, appointment, training and expenses of members of a children's panel and the establishment of Children's Panel Advisory Committees and joint advisory committees.

(3)   Sittings of members of the children's panel (to be known as 'children's hearings') shall be constituted from the panel in accordance with subsection (5) below.

(4)   A children's hearing shall be constituted for the performance of the functions given to such a hearing by or by virtue of—

(a)   this Act; or
(b)   any other enactment conferring powers on a children's hearing.

(5)   A children's hearing shall consist of three members, one of whom shall act as chairman; and shall not consist solely of male, or solely of female, members.

Qualifications, employment and duties of reporters

40   Qualification and employment of reporters

(1)   The qualifications of a reporter shall be such as the Secretary of State may prescribe.

(2)   A reporter shall not, without the consent of the Scottish Children's Reporter Administration, be employed by a local authority.

(3)   The Secretary of State may make regulations in relation to the functions of any reporter under this Act and the Criminal Procedure (Scotland) Act [1995].

(4)   The Secretary of State [. . .] may—

(a)   by regulations empower a reporter, whether or not he is an advocate or solicitor, to conduct before a sheriff any proceedings which under this Chapter or Chapter 3 of this Part of this Act are heard by the sheriff;
(b)   prescribe such requirements as they think fit as to qualifications, training or experience necessary for a reporter to be so empowered.

(5)   In this section, 'reporter' means—

(a)   the Principal Reporter; or
(b)   any officer of the Scottish Children's Reporter Administration to whom there is delegated, under section 131(1) of the Local Government etc (Scotland) Act 1994, any of the functions which the Principal Reporter has under this or any other enactment.

Safeguards for children

41 Safeguarding child's interests in proceedings

(1)   Subject to subsection (2) below, in any proceedings under this Chapter or Chapter 3 of this Part of this Act either at a children's hearing or before the sheriff, the hearing or, as the case may be, the sheriff—

(a)   shall consider if it is necessary to appoint a person to safeguard the interests of the child in the proceedings; and

(b)   if they, or he, so consider, shall make such an appointment, on such terms and conditions as appear appropriate.

(2)   Subsection (1) above shall not apply in relation to proceedings under section 57 of this Act.

(3)   Where a children's hearing make an appointment under subsection (1)(b) above, they shall state the reasons for their decision to make that appointment.

(4)   The expenses of a person appointed under subsection (1) above shall—

(a)   in so far as reasonably incurred by him in safeguarding the interests of the child in the proceedings, and

(b)   except in so far as otherwise defrayed in terms of regulations made under section 101 of this Act,

be borne by the local authority—

(i)   for whose area the children's panel from which the relevant children's hearing has been constituted is formed;

(ii)   where there is no relevant children's hearing, within whose area the child resides.

(5)   For the purposes of subsection (4) above, 'relevant children's hearing' means, in the case of proceedings—

(a)   at a children's hearing, that hearing;

(b)   under section 68 of this Act, the children's hearing who have directed the application;

(c)   on an appeal under section 51 of this Act, the children's hearing whose decision is being appealed against.

Conduct of proceedings at and in connection with children's hearing

42 Power of Secretary of State to make rules governing procedure at children's hearing etc

(1)   Subject to the following provisions of this Act, the Secretary of State may make rules for constituting and arranging children's hearings and other meetings of members of the children's panel and for regulating their procedure.

(2)   Without prejudice to the generality of subsection (1) above, rules under that subsection may make provision with respect to—

(a)   the conduct of, and matters which shall or may be determined by, a business meeting arranged under section 64 of this Act;

(b)   notification of the time and place of a children's hearing to the child and any relevant person in relation to the child and to such other persons as may be prescribed;

(c)   how the grounds for referring the case to a children's hearing under section 65(1) of this Act are to be stated, and the right of the child and any such relevant person to dispute those grounds;

(d)   the making available by the Principal Reporter, subject to such conditions as may be specified in the rules, of reports or information received by him to—

(i)   members of the children's hearing;

(ii)   the child concerned;

(iii)   any relevant person; and

(iv)   any other person or class of persons so specified;

(e)   the procedure in relation to the disposal of matters arising under section 41(1) of this Act;

(f) the functions of any person appointed by a children's hearing under section 41(1) of this Act and any right of that person to information relating to the proceedings in question;

(g) the recording in writing of any statement given under section 41(3) of this Act;

(h) the right to appeal to the sheriff under section 51(1)(a) of this Act against a decision of the children's hearing and notification to such persons as may be prescribed of the proceedings before him;

(i) the right of the child and of any such relevant person to be represented at a children's hearing;

(j) the entitlement of the child, of any such relevant person and of any person who acts as the representative of the child or of any such relevant person to the refund of such expenses, incurred by the child or as the case may be the person or representative, as may be prescribed in connection with a children's hearing and with any proceedings arising from the hearing;

(k) persons whose presence shall be permitted at a children's hearing.

43 Privacy of proceedings at and right to attend children's hearing

(1) Subject to subsection (3) below, a children's hearing shall be conducted in private, and, subject to any rules made under section 42 of this Act, no person other than a person whose presence is necessary for the proper consideration of the case which is being heard, or whose presence is permitted by the chairman, shall be present.

(2) The chairman shall take all reasonable steps to ensure that the number of persons present at a children's hearing at any one time is kept to a minimum.

(3) The following persons have the right to attend a children's hearing—

(a) a member of the Council on Tribunals, or of the Scottish Committee of that Council, in his capacity as such; and

(b) subject to subsection (4) below, a *bona fide* representative of a newspaper or news agency.

(4) A children's hearing may exclude a person described in subsection (3)(b) above from any part or parts of the hearing where, and for so long as, they are satisfied that—

(a) it is necessary to do so, in the interests of the child, in order to obtain the child's views in relation to the case before the hearing; or

(b) the presence of that person is causing, or is likely to cause, significant distress to the child.

(5) Where a children's hearing have exercised the power conferred by subsection (4) above to exclude a person, the chairman may, after that exclusion has ended, explain to the person the substance of what has taken place in his absence.

44 Prohibition of publication of proceedings at children's hearing

(1) No person shall publish [any matter in respect of a case about which the Principal Reporter has from any source received information or] any matter in respect of proceedings at a children's hearing, or before a sheriff on an application under section 57, section 60(7), section 65(7) or (9), section 76(1) or section 85(1) of this Act, or on any appeal under this Part of this Act, which is intended to, or is likely to, identify—

(a) [the child concerned in, or any child connected (in any way) with, the case,] proceedings or appeal; or

(b) an address or school as being that of any such child.

(2) Any person who contravenes subsection (1) above shall be guilty of an offence and shall be liable on summary conviction to a fine not exceeding level 4 on the standard scale in respect of each such contravention.

(3) It shall be a defence in proceedings for an offence under this section for the accused to prove that he did not know, and had no reason to suspect, that the

published matter was intended, or was likely, to identify the child or, as the case may be, the address or school.

(4)   In this section 'to publish' includes, without prejudice to the generality of that expression,—

(a)   to publish matter in a programme service, as defined by section 201 of the Broadcasting Act 1990 (definition of programme service); and

(b)   to cause matter to be published.

(5)   The requirements of subsection (1) above may, in the interests of justice, be dispensed with by—

(a)   the sheriff in any proceedings before him;

(b)   the Court of Session in any appeal under section 51(11) of this Act; or

(c)   the Secretary of State in relation to any proceedings at a children's hearing,

to such extent as the sheriff, the Court or the Secretary of State as the case may be considers appropriate.

45   Attendance of child and relevant person at children's hearing

(1)   Where a child has been notified in accordance with rules made under subsection (1) of section 42 of this Act by virtue of subsection (2)(b) of that section that his case has been referred to a children's hearing, he shall—

(a)   have the right to attend at all stages of the hearing; and

(b)   subject to subsection (2) below, be under an obligation to attend those stages in accordance with the notice.

(2)   Without prejudice to subsection (1)(a) above and section 65(4) of this Act, where a children's hearing are satisfied—

(a)   in a case concerned with an offence mentioned in Schedule 1 to the Criminal Procedure (Scotland) Act [1995] that the attendance of the child is not necessary for the just hearing of that case; or

(b)   in any case, that it would be detrimental to the interests of the child for him to be present at the hearing of his case,

they may release the child from the obligation imposed by subsection (1)(b) above.

(3)   Subject to subsection (2) above, the Principal Reporter shall be responsible for securing the attendance of the child at the hearing of his case by a children's hearing (and at any subsequent hearing to which the case is continued under section 69(1)(a) of this Act).

(4)   On the application of the Principal Reporter, a children's hearing, if satisfied on cause shown that it is necessary for them to do so, may issue, for the purposes of subsection (3) above, a warrant under this subsection to find the child, to keep him in a place of safety and to bring him before a children's hearing.

(5)   Where a child has failed to attend a children's hearing in accordance with such notice as is mentioned in subsection (1) above, they may, either on the application of the Principal Reporter or of their own motion, issue a warrant under this subsection, which shall have the same effect as a warrant under subsection (4) above.

(6)   A child who has been taken to a place of safety under a warrant granted under this section shall not be kept there after whichever is the earlier of—

(a)   the expiry of seven days beginning on the day he was first so taken there; or

(b)   the day on which a children's hearing first sit to consider his case in accordance with subsection (7) below.

(7)   Where a child has been found in pursuance of a warrant under this section and he cannot immediately be brought before a children's hearing, the Principal Reporter shall, wherever practicable, arrange a children's hearing to sit on the first working day after the child was so found.

(8)   Subject to section 46 of this Act, a person who is a relevant person as

respects a child shall, where a children's hearing are considering the case of the child—

(a)   have the right to attend at all stages of the hearing; and

(b)   be obliged to attend at all stages of the hearing unless the hearing are satisfied that it would be unreasonable to require his attendance or that his attendance is unnecessary for the proper consideration of the case.

(9)   Any person who fails to attend a hearing which, under subsection (8)(b) above, he is obliged to attend shall be guilty of an offence and shall be liable on summary conviction to a fine not exceeding level 3 on the standard scale.

46   Power to exclude relevant person from children's hearing

(1)   Where a children's hearing are considering the case of a child in respect of whom a person is a relevant person, they may exclude that person, or that person and any representative of his, or any such representative, from any part or parts of the hearing for so long as is necessary in the interests of the child, where they are satisfied that—

(a)   they must do so in order to obtain the views of the child in relation to the case before the hearing; or

(b)   the presence of the person or persons in question is causing, or is likely to cause, significant distress to the child.

(2)   Where a children's hearing exercise the power conferred by subsection (1) above, the chairman of the hearing shall, after that exclusion has ended, explain to any person who was so excluded the substance of what has taken place in his absence.

47   Presumption and determination of age

(1)   Where a children's hearing has been arranged in respect of any person, the hearing—

(a)   shall, at the commencement of the proceedings, make inquiry as to his age and shall proceed with the hearing only if he declares that he is a child or they so determine; and

(b)   may, at any time before the conclusion of the proceedings, accept a declaration by the child, or make a fresh determination, as to his age.

(2)   The age declared to, or determined by, a children's hearing to be the age of a person brought before them shall, for the purposes of this Part of this Act, be deemed to be the true age of that person.

(3)   No decision reached, order continued, warrant granted or requirement imposed by a children's hearing shall be invalidated by any subsequent proof that the age of a person brought before them had not been correctly declared to the hearing or determined by them.

Transfer etc of cases

48   Transfer of case to another children's hearing

(1)   Where a children's hearing are satisfied, in relation to a case which they are hearing, that it could be better considered by a children's hearing constituted from a children's panel for a different local government area, they may at any time during the course of the hearing request the Principal Reporter to arrange for such other children's hearing to dispose of the case.

(2)   Where a case has been transferred in pursuance of subsection (1) above, the grounds of referral accepted or established for the case shall not require to be further accepted or established for the purposes of the children's hearing to which the case has been transferred.

[. . .]

50   Treatment of child's case on remission by court

(1)   Where a court has, under [section 49 of the Criminal Procedure (Scotland) Act 1995], remitted a case to a children's hearing for disposal, a certificate signed

by the clerk of the court stating that the child or person concerned has pled guilty to, or has been found guilty of, the offence to which the remit relates shall be conclusive evidence for the purposes of the remit that the offence has been committed by the child or person.

(2) Where a court has under [subsection (7) of the said section 49] remitted a case to a children's hearing for disposal, the provisions of this Act shall apply to the person concerned as if he were a child.

Appeals

51 Appeal against decision of children's hearing or sheriff

(1) Subject to subsection (15) below, a child or a relevant person (or relevant persons) or both (or all)—

(a) may, within a period of three weeks beginning with the date of any decision of a children's hearing, appeal to the sheriff against that decision; and

(b) where such an appeal is made, shall be heard by the sheriff.

(2) The Principal Reporter shall, in respect of any appeal under subsection (1) above, ensure that all reports and statements available to the hearing, along with the reports of their proceedings and the reasons for the decision, are lodged with the sheriff clerk.

(3) The sheriff may, on appeal under subsection (1) above, hear evidence from, or on behalf of, the parties in relation to the decision; and, without prejudice to that generality, the sheriff may—

(a) examine the Principal Reporter;

(b) examine the authors or compilers of any reports or statements; and

(c) call for any further report which he considers may assist him in deciding the appeal.

(4) Where the sheriff decides that an appeal under this section has failed, he shall confirm the decision of the children's hearing.

(5) Where the sheriff is satisfied that the decision of the children's hearing is not justified in all the circumstances of the case he shall allow the appeal, and—

(a) where the appeal is against a warrant to find and keep or, as the case may be, to keep a child in a place of safety, he shall recall the warrant;

(b) where the child is subject to a supervision requirement containing a [movement restriction condition imposed under subsection (3)(b) of section 70 of this Act or a condition imposed under subsection (9) of that section], he shall direct that the condition shall cease to have effect; and

(c) in any case, he may, as he thinks fit—

(i) remit the case with reasons for his decision to the children's hearing for reconsideration of their decision; or

(ii) discharge the child from any further hearing or other proceedings in relation to the grounds for the referral of the case; or

(iii) substitute for the disposal by the children's hearing any requirement which could be imposed by them under section 70 of this Act.

(6) Where a sheriff imposes a requirement under subsection (5)(c)(iii) above, that requirement shall for the purposes of this Act, except of this section, be treated as a disposal by the children's hearing.

(7) Where the sheriff is satisfied that an appeal under subsection (1) above against the decision of a children's hearing arranged under section 73(8) of this Act is frivolous, he may order that no subsequent appeal against a decision to continue (whether with or without any variation) the supervision requirement in question shall lie until the expiration of twelve months beginning with the date of the order.

(8) An appeal under subsection (1) above in respect of the issue of a warrant by a children's hearing shall be disposed of within three days of the lodging of the appeal; and failing such disposal the warrant shall cease to have effect at the end of that period.

(9)   Where a child or a relevant person appeals under subsection (1) above against a decision of a children's hearing in relation to a supervision requirement, the child or the relevant person may make application to a children's hearing for the suspension of the requirement appealed against.

(10)   It shall be the duty of the Principal Reporter forthwith to arrange a children's hearing to consider the application under subsection (9) above, and that hearing may grant or refuse the application.

(11)   Subject to subsections (13) and (15) below, an appeal shall lie by way of stated case either on a point of law or in respect of any irregularity in the conduct of the case—

(a)   to the sheriff principal from any decision of the sheriff—

(i)   on an appeal under subsection (1) of this section;

(ii)   on an application made under section 65(7) or (9) of this Act; or

(iii)   on an application made under section 85(1) of this Act; and

(b)   to the Court of Session from any decision of the sheriff such as is mentioned in sub-paragraphs (i) to (iii) of paragraph (a) above and, with leave of the sheriff principal, from any decision of the sheriff principal on an appeal under that paragraph; and the decision of the Court of Session in the matter shall be final.

(12)   An appeal under subsection (11) above may be made at the instance of—

(a)   the child or any relevant person, either alone or together; or

(b)   the Principal Reporter on behalf of the children's hearing.

(13)   An application to the sheriff, or as the case may be the sheriff principal, to state a case for the purposes of an appeal under subsection (11)(a) or (b) above shall be made within a period of twenty-eight days beginning with the date of the decision appealed against.

(14)   On deciding an appeal under subsection (11) above the sheriff principal or as the case may be the Court of Session shall remit the case to the sheriff for disposal in accordance with such directions as the court may give.

(15)   No appeal shall lie under this section in respect of—

(a)   a decision of the sheriff on an application under section 57 of this Act; or

(b)   a decision of a children's hearing continuing a child protection order under section 59(4) of this Act.

CHAPTER 3
PROTECTION AND SUPERVISION OF CHILDREN

Children requiring compulsory measures of supervision

52   Children requiring compulsory measures of supervision

(1)   The question of whether compulsory measures of supervision are necessary in respect of a child arises if at least one of the conditions mentioned in subsection (2) below is satisfied with respect to him.

(2)   The conditions referred to in subsection (1) above are that the child—

(a)   is beyond the control of any relevant person;

(b)   is falling into bad associations or is exposed to moral danger;

(c)   is likely—

(i)   to suffer unnecessarily; or

(ii)   be impaired seriously in his health or development,

due to a lack of parental care;

(d)   is a child in respect of whom any of the offences mentioned in [Schedule 1 to the Criminal Procedure (Scotland) Act 1995] (offences against children to which special provisions apply) has been committed;

(e)   is, or is likely to become, a member of the same household as a child in respect of whom any of the offences referred to in paragraph (d) above has been committed;

(f)   is, or is likely to become, a member of the same household as a person who has committed any of the offences referred in paragraph (d) above;

(g)   is, or is likely to become, a member of the same household as a person in respect of whom an offence under [sections 1 and 3 of the Criminal Law (Consolidation) (Scotland) Act 1995] (incest and intercourse with a child by step-parent or person in position of trust) has been committed by a member of that household;

(h)   has failed to attend school regularly without reasonable excuse;

(i)   has committed an offence;

(j)   has misused alcohol or any drug, whether or not a controlled drug within the meaning of the Misuse of Drugs Act 1971;

(k)   has misused a volatile substance by deliberately inhaling its vapour, other than for medicinal purposes;

(l)   is being provided with accommodation by a local authority under section 25, or is the subject of a parental responsibilities order obtained under section 86, of this Act and, in either case, his behaviour is such that special measures are necessary for his adequate supervision in his interest or the interest of others.

[(m)   is a child to whom subsection (2A) below applies.

(2A)   This subsection applies to a child where—

(a)   a requirement is made of the Principal Reporter under section 11(1) of the Antisocial Behaviour etc (Scotland) Act 2004 (asp 8) (power of sheriff to require Principal Reporter to refer case to children's hearing) in respect of the child's case; and

(b)   the child is not subject to a supervision requirement.]

(3)   In this Part of this Act, 'supervision' in relation to compulsory measures of supervision may include measures taken for the protection, guidance, treatment or control of the child.

Preliminary and investigatory measures

53   Provision of information to the Principal Reporter

(1)   Where information is received by a local authority which suggests that compulsory measures of supervision may be necessary in respect of a child, they shall—

(a)   cause inquiries to be made into the case unless they are satisfied that such inquiries are unnecessary; and

(b)   if it appears to them after such inquiries, or after being satisfied that such inquiries are unnecessary, that such measures may be required in respect of the child, give to the Principal Reporter such information about the child as they have been able to discover.

(2)   A person, other than a local authority, who has reasonable cause to believe that compulsory measures of supervision may be necessary in respect of a child—

(a)   shall, if he is a constable, give to the Principal Reporter such information about the child as he has been able to discover;

(b)   in any other case, may give the Principal Reporter that information.

(3)   A constable shall make any report required to be made under paragraph (b) of section 17(1) of the Police (Scotland) Act 1967 (duty to make reports in relation to commission of offences) in relation to a child to the Principal Reporter as well as to the appropriate prosecutor.

(4)   Where an application has been made to the sheriff—

(a)   by the Principal Reporter in accordance with a direction given by a children's hearing under section 65(7) or (9) of this Act; or

(b)   by any person entitled to make an application under section 85 of this Act,

the Principal Reporter may request any prosecutor to supply him with any evidence lawfully obtained in the course of, and held by the prosecutor in connection with, the investigation of a crime or suspected crime, being evidence which may assist the sheriff in determining the application; and, subject to subsection (5) below, it shall be the duty of the prosecutor to comply with such a request.

(5)   A prosecutor may refuse to comply with a request issued under subsection (4) above where he reasonably believes that it is necessary to retain the evidence for the purposes of any proceedings in respect of a crime, whether the proceedings have been commenced or are to be commenced by him.

(6)   The Lord Advocate may direct that in any specified case or class of cases any evidence lawfully obtained in the course of an investigation of a crime or suspected crime shall be supplied, without the need for a request under subsection (4) above, to the Principal Reporter.

(7)   In subsections (3), (4) and (5) above 'crime' and 'prosecutor' have the same meanings respectively given by section [307 of the Criminal Procedure (Scotland) Act 1995].

54   Reference to the Principal Reporter by court

(1)   Where in any relevant proceedings it appears to the court that any of the conditions in section 52(2)(a) to (h), (j), (k) or (1) of this Act is satisfied with respect to a child, it may refer the matter to the Principal Reporter, specifying the condition.

(2)   In this section 'relevant proceedings' means—

(a)   an action for divorce or judicial separation or for declarator of marriage, nullity of marriage, parentage or non-parentage;

[(aa)   an action for dissolution or declarator of nullity of a civil partnership or separation of civil partners;]

(b)   proceedings relating to parental responsibilities or parental rights within the meaning of Part I of this Act;

(c)   proceedings for an adoption order under the Adoption (Scotland) Act 1978 or for an order under section 18 of that Act declaring a child free for adoption; and

(d)   proceedings for an offence against section 35 (failure by parent to secure regular attendance by his child at a public school), 41 (failure to comply with attendance order) or 42(3) (failure to permit examination of child) of the Education (Scotland) Act 1980.

(3)   Where the court has referred a matter to the Principal Reporter under subsection (1) above, he shall—

(a)   make such investigation as he thinks appropriate; and

(b)   if he considers that compulsory measures of supervision are necessary, arrange a children's hearing to consider the case of the child under section 69 of this Act; and subsection (1) of that section shall apply as if the condition specified by the court under subsection (1) above were a ground of referral established in accordance with section 68 of this Act.

55   Child assessment orders

(1)   A sheriff may grant an order under this section for an assessment of the state of a child's health or development, or of the way in which he has been treated (to be known as a 'child assessment order'), on the application of a local authority if he is satisfied that—

(a)   the local authority have reasonable cause to suspect that the child in respect of whom the order is sought is being so treated (or neglected) that he is suffering, or is likely to suffer, significant harm;

(b)   such assessment of the child is required in order to establish whether or not there is reasonable cause to believe that the child is so treated (or neglected); and

(c)   such assessment is unlikely to be carried out, or be carried out satisfactorily, unless the order is granted.

(2) Where—

(a) an application has been made under subsection (1) above; and

(b) the sheriff considers that the conditions for making a child protection order under section 57 of this Act are satisfied,

he shall make such an order under that section as if the application had been duly made by the local authority under that section rather than this section.

(3) A child assessment order shall—

(a) specify the date on which the assessment is to begin;

(b) have effect for such period as is specified in the order, not exceeding seven days beginning with the date specified by virtue of paragraph (a) above;

(c) require any person in a position to produce the child to—

(i) produce him to any authorised person;

(ii) permit that person or any other authorised person to carry out an assessment in accordance with the order; and

(iii) comply with any other conditions of the order; and

(d) be carried out by an authorised person in accordance with the terms of the order.

(4) A child assessment order may—

(a) where necessary, permit the taking of the child concerned to any place for the purposes of the assessment; and

(b) authorise the child to be kept at that place, or any other place, for such period of time as may be specified in the order.

(5) Where a child assessment order makes provision under subsection (4) above, it shall contain such directions as the sheriff considers appropriate as to the contact which the child shall be allowed to have with any other person while the child is in any place to which he has been taken or in which he is being kept under a child assessment order.

(6) In this section 'authorised person' means any officer of the local authority, and any person authorised by the local authority to perform the assessment, or perform any part of it.

56 Initial investigation by the Principal Reporter

(1) Where the Principal Reporter receives information from any source about a case which may require a children's hearing to be arranged he shall, after making such initial investigation as he thinks necessary, proceed with the case in accordance with subsection (4) or (6) below.

(2) For the purposes of making any initial investigation under subsection (1) above, the Principal Reporter may request from the local authority a report on the child and on such circumstances concerning the child as appear to him to be relevant; and the local authority shall supply the report which may contain such information, from any person whomsoever, as the Principal Reporter thinks, or the local authority think, fit.

(3) A report requested under subsection (2) above may contain information additional to that given by the local authority under section 53 of this Act.

(4) The Principal Reporter may decide, after an initial investigation under subsection (1) above, that a children's hearing does not require to be arranged; and where he so decides—

(a) he shall inform the child, any relevant person and the person who brought the case to his notice, or any of those persons, that he has so decided;

(b) he may, if he considers it appropriate, refer the case to a local authority with a view to their making arrangements for the advice, guidance and assistance of the child and his family in accordance with Chapter 1 of this Part of this Act [; and

(c) he may, where it appears to him that—

(i) an education authority have a duty under section 14(3) of the Education (Scotland) Act 1980 (c 44) in relation to the child; and

(ii)   the authority are not complying with that duty,
refer the matter to the Scottish Ministers.

(4A)   A reference made under subsection (4)(c) above shall be in writing.

(4B)   A copy of a reference made under subsection (4)(c) above shall be sent by the Principal Reporter to the education authority in respect of which the reference is made.]

(5)   Where the Principal Reporter has decided under subsection (4) above that a children's hearing does not require to be arranged, he shall not at any other time, on the basis solely of the information obtained during the initial investigation referred to in that subsection, arrange a children's hearing under subsection (6) below.

(6)   Where it appears to the Principal Reporter that compulsory measures of supervision are necessary in respect of the child, he shall arrange a children's hearing to which he shall refer the case for consideration and determination.

(7)   Where the Principal Reporter has arranged a children's hearing in accordance with subsection (6) above, he—

(a)   shall, where he has not previously done so, request a report under subsection (2) above;

(b)   may request from the local authority such information, supplementary or additional to a report requested under subsection (2) above, as he thinks fit;

and the local authority shall supply that report, or as the case may be information, and any other information which they consider to be relevant.

Measures for the emergency protection of children

57   Child protection orders

(1)   Where the sheriff, on an application by any person, is satisfied that—

(a)   there are reasonable grounds to believe that a child—

(i)   is being so treated (or neglected) that he is suffering significant harm; or

(ii)   will suffer such harm if he is not removed to and kept in a place of safety, or if he does not remain in the place where he is then being accommodated (whether or not he is resident there); and

(b)   an order under this section is necessary to protect that child from such harm (or such further harm),

he may make an order under this section (to be known as a 'child protection order').

(2)   Without prejudice to subsection (1) above, where the sheriff on an application by a local authority is satisfied—

(a)   that they have reasonable grounds to suspect that a child is being or will be so treated (or neglected) that he is suffering or will suffer significant harm;

(b)   that they are making or causing to be made enquiries to allow them to decide whether they should take any action to safeguard the welfare of the child; and

(c)   that those enquiries are being frustrated by access to the child being unreasonably denied, the authority having reasonable cause to believe that such access is required as a matter of urgency,

he may make a child protection order.

(3)   Without prejudice to any additional requirement imposed by rules made by virtue of section 91 of this Act, an application for a child protection order shall—

(a)   identify—

(i)   the applicant; and

(ii)   in so far as practicable, the child in respect of whom the order is sought;

(b)   state the grounds on which the application is made; and

(c) be accompanied by such supporting evidence, whether in documentary form or otherwise, as will enable the sheriff to determine the application.

(4) A child protection order may, subject to such terms and conditions as the sheriff considers appropriate, do any one or more of the following—

(a) require any person in a position to do so to produce the child to the applicant;

(b) authorise the removal of the child by the applicant to a place of safety, and the keeping of the child at that place;

(c) authorise the prevention of the removal of the child from any place where he is being accommodated;

(d) provide that the location of any place of safety in which the child is being kept should not be disclosed to any person or class of person specified in the order.

(5) Notice of the making of a child protection order shall be given forthwith by the applicant to the local authority in whose area the child resides (where that authority is not the applicant) and to the Principal Reporter.

(6) In taking any action required or permitted by a child protection order or by a direction under section 58 of this Act the applicant shall only act where he reasonably believes that to do so is necessary to safeguard or promote the welfare of the child.

(7) Where by virtue of a child protection order a child is removed to a place of safety provided by a local authority, they shall, subject to the terms and conditions of that order and of any direction given under section 58 of this Act, have the like duties in respect of the child as they have under section 17 of this Act in respect of a child looked after by them.

58 Directions in relation to contact and exercise of parental responsibilities and parental rights

(1) When the sheriff makes a child protection order, he shall at that time consider whether it is necessary to give a direction to the applicant for the order as to contact with the child for—

(a) any parent of the child;

(b) any person with parental responsibilities in relation to the child; and

(c) any other specified person or class of persons;

and if he determines that there is such a necessity he may give such a direction.

(2) Without prejudice to the generality of subsection (1) above, a direction under that subsection may—

(a) prohibit contact with the child for any person mentioned in paragraphs (a) to (c) of that subsection;

(b) make contact with the child for any person subject to such conditions as the sheriff considers appropriate to safeguard and promote the welfare of the child.

(3) A direction under subsection (1) above may make different provision in relation to different persons or classes of person.

(4) A person applying for a child protection order under section 57(1) or (2) of this Act may at the same time apply to the sheriff for a direction in relation to the exercise or fulfilment of any parental responsibilities or parental rights in respect of the child concerned, if the person considers such a direction necessary to safeguard or promote the welfare of the child.

(5) Without prejudice to the generality of subsection (4) above, a direction under that subsection may be sought in relation to—

(a) any examination as to the physical or mental state of the child;

(b) any other assessment or interview of the child; or

(c) any treatment of the child arising out of such an examination or assessment,

which is to be carried out by any person.

(6)   The sheriff may give a direction sought under subsection (4) above where he considers there is a necessity such as is mentioned in that subsection; and such a direction may be granted subject to such conditions, if any, as the sheriff (having regard in particular to the duration of the child protection order to which it relates) considers appropriate.

(7)   A direction under this section shall cease to have effect when—

(a)   the sheriff, on an application under section 60(7) of this Act, directs that it is cancelled; or

(b)   the child protection order to which it is related ceases to have effect.

59   Initial hearing of case of child subject to child protection order

(1)   This section applies where—

(a)   a child in respect of whom a child protection order has been made—

(i)   has been taken to a place of safety by virtue of section 57(4)(b) of this Act; or

(ii)   is prevented from being removed from any place by virtue of section 57(4)(c) of this Act;

(b)   the Principal Reporter has not exercised his powers under section 60(3) of this Act to discharge the child from the place of safety; and

(c)   the Principal Reporter has not received notice, in accordance with section 60(9) of this Act, of an application under subsection (7) of that section.

(2)   Where this section applies, the Principal Reporter shall arrange a children's hearing to conduct an initial hearing of the child's case in order to determine whether they should, in the interests of the child, continue the child protection order under subsection (4) below.

(3)   A children's hearing arranged under subsection (2) above shall take place on the second working day after that order is implemented.

(4)   Where a children's hearing arranged under subsection (2) above are satisfied that the conditions for the making of a child protection order under section 57 of this Act are established, they may continue the child protection order and any direction given under section 58 of this Act (whether with or without variation of the order or, as the case may be, the direction) until the commencement of a children's hearing in relation to the child arranged in accordance with section 65(2) of this Act.

(5)   In subsection (3) above, section 60 and section 65(2) of this Act any reference, in relation to the calculation of any period, to the time at which a child protection order is implemented shall be construed as a reference—

(a)   in relation to such an order made under paragraph (b) of subsection (4) of section 57 of this Act, to the day on which the child was removed to a place of safety in accordance with the order; and

(b)   in relation to such an order made under paragraph (c) of that subsection, to the day on which the order was made,

and 'implement' shall be construed accordingly.

60   Duration, recall or variation of child protection order

(1)   Where, by the end of twenty-four hours of a child protection order being made (other than by virtue of section 57(4)(c) of this Act), the applicant has made no attempt to implement the order it shall cease to have effect.

(2)   Where an application made under subsection (7) below has not been determined timeously in accordance with subsection (8) below, the order to which the application relates shall cease to have effect.

(3)   A child shall not be—

(a)   kept in a place of safety under a child protection order;

(b)   prevented from being removed from any place by such an order; or

(c)   subject to any term or condition contained in such an order or a direction given under section 58 of this Act,

where the Principal Reporter, having regard to the welfare of the child, considers that, whether as a result of a change in the circumstances of the case or of further information relating to the case having been received by the Principal Reporter, the conditions for the making of a child protection order in respect of the child are no longer satisfied or that the term, condition or direction is no longer appropriate and notifies the person who implemented the order that he so considers.

(4) The Principal Reporter shall not give notice under subsection (3) above where—

(a) proceedings before a children's hearing arranged under section 59(2) of this Act in relation to the child who is subject to the child protection order have commenced; or

(b) the hearing of an application made under subsection (7) of this section has begun.

(5) Where the Principal Reporter has given notice under subsection (3) above, he shall also, in such manner as may be prescribed, notify the sheriff who made the order.

(6) A child protection order shall cease to have effect—

(a) where an initial hearing arranged under section 59(2) of this Act does not continue the order under subsection (4) of that section;

(b) where an application is made to the sheriff under subsection (7) below, on the sheriff recalling such order under subsection (13) below;

(c) on the person who implemented the order receiving notice from the Principal Reporter that he has decided not to refer the case of a child who is subject to the order to a children's hearing arranged in accordance with section 65(2) of this Act;

(d) on the Principal Reporter giving notice in accordance with subsection (3) above in relation to the order that he considers that the conditions for the making of it are no longer satisfied; or

(e) where such order is continued under section 59(4) of this Act or subsection (12)(d) below, on the commencement of a children's hearing arranged under section 65(2) of this Act.

(7) An application to the sheriff to set aside or vary a child protection order made under section 57 of this Act or a direction given under section 58 of this Act or such an order or direction continued (whether with or without variation) under section 59(4) of this Act, may be made by or on behalf of—

(a) the child to whom the order or direction relates;

(b) a person having parental rights over the child;

(c) a relevant person;

(d) any person to whom notice of the application for the order was given by virtue of rules; or

(e) the applicant for the order made under section 57 of this Act.

(8) An application under subsection (7) above shall be made—

(a) in relation to a child protection order made under section 57, or a direction given under section 58, of this Act, before the commencement of a children's hearing arranged in accordance with section 59(2) of this Act; and

(b) in relation to such an order or direction continued (whether with or without variation) by virtue of subsection (4) of the said section 59, within two working days of such continuation,

and any such application shall be determined within three working days of being made.

(9) Where an application has been made under subsection (7) above, the applicant shall forthwith give notice, in a manner and form prescribed by rules, to the Principal Reporter.

(10) At any time which is—

(a) after the giving of the notice required by subsection (9) above; but

(b) before the sheriff has determined the application in accordance with subsection (11) below, the Principal Reporter may arrange a children's hearing the purpose of which shall be to provide any advice they consider appropriate to assist the sheriff in his determination of the application.

(11)   The sheriff shall, after hearing the parties to the application and, if he wishes to make representations, the Principal Reporter, determine whether—

(a)   the conditions for the making of a child protection order under section 57 of this Act are satisfied; or

(b)   where the application relates only to a direction under section 58 of this Act, the direction should be varied or cancelled.

(12)   Where the sheriff determines that the conditions referred to in subsection (11)(a) above are satisfied, he may—

(a)   confirm or vary the order, or any term or condition on which it was granted;

(b)   confirm or vary any direction given, in relation to the order, under section 58 of this Act;

(c)   give a new direction under that section; or

(d)   continue in force the order and any such direction until the commencement of a children's hearing arranged in accordance with section 65(2) of this Act.

(13)   Where the sheriff determines that the conditions referred to in subsection (11)(a) above are not satisfied he shall recall the order and cancel any direction given under section 58 of this Act.

61   Emergency protection of children where child protection order not available

(1)   Where, on the application of any person, a justice of the peace is satisfied—

(a)   both that the conditions laid down for the making of a child protection order in section 57(1) of this Act are satisfied and that it is probable that any such order, if made, would contain an authorisation in terms of paragraph (b) or (c) of subsection (4) of that section; but

(b)   that it is not practicable in the circumstances for an application for such an order to be made to the sheriff or for the sheriff to consider such an application,

he may grant to the applicant an authorisation under this section.

(2)   Where on the application of a local authority a justice of the peace is satisfied—

(a)   both that the conditions laid down for the making of a child protection order in section 57(2) of this Act are satisfied and that it is probable that any such order, if made, would contain an authorisation in terms of paragraph (b) or (c) of subsection (4) of that section; but

(b)   that it is not practicable in the circumstances for an application for such an order to be made to the sheriff or for the sheriff to consider such an application,

he may grant an authorisation under this section.

(3)   An authorisation under this section may—

(a)   require any person in a position to do so to produce the child to the applicant;

(b)   prevent any person from removing a child from a place where he is then being accommodated;

(c)   authorise the applicant to remove the child to a place of safety and to keep him there until the expiration of the authorisation.

(4)   An authorisation under this section shall cease to have effect—

(a)   twelve hours after being made, if within that time—

(i)   arrangements have not been made to prevent the child's removal from any place specified in the authorisation; or

(ii)   he has not been, or is not being, taken to a place of safety; or

(b)   where such arrangements have been made or he has been so taken when—

(i)   twenty-four hours have expired since it was so given; or

(ii)   an application for a child protection order in respect of the child is disposed of,

whichever is the earlier.

(5)   Where a constable has reasonable cause to believe that—

(a)   the conditions for the making of a child protection order laid down in section 57(1) are satisfied;

(b)   that it is not practicable in the circumstances for him to make an application for such an order to the sheriff or for the sheriff to consider such an application; and

(c)   that, in order to protect the child from significant harm (or further such harm), it is necessary for him to remove the child to a place of safety,

he may remove the child to such a place and keep him there.

(6)   The power conferred by subsection (5) above shall not authorise the keeping of a child in a place of safety for more than twenty-four hours from the time when the child is so removed.

(7)   The authority to keep a child in a place of safety conferred by subsection (5) above shall cease on the disposal of an application in relation to the child for a child protection order.

(8)   A child shall not be—

(a)   kept in a place of safety; or

(b)   prevented from being removed from any place,

under this section where the Principal Reporter considers that the conditions for the grant of an authorisation under subsection (1) or (2) above or the exercise of the power conferred by subsection (5) above are not satisfied, or that it is no longer in the best interests of the child that he should be so kept.

62   Regulations in respect of emergency child protection measures

(1)   The Secretary of State may make regulations concerning the duties in respect of a child of any person removing him to, and keeping him in, a place of safety under section 61 above.

(2)   Regulations under this section may make provision requiring—

(a)   notification of the removal of a child to be given to a person specified in the regulations;

(b)   intimation to be given to any person of the place of safety at which a child is being kept;

(c)   notification to be given to any person of the ceasing to have effect, under section 61(4)(a) of this Act, of an authorisation.

Children arrested by the police

63   Review of case of child arrested by police

(1)   Where the Principal Reporter has been informed by a constable, in accordance with section [43(5) of the Criminal Procedure (Scotland) Act 1995], that charges are not to be proceeded with against a child who has been detained in a place of safety in accordance with that section, the Principal Reporter shall, unless he considers that compulsory measures of supervision are not required in relation to the child, arrange a children's hearing to which he shall refer the case.

(2)   A children's hearing arranged under subsection (1) above shall begin not later than the third day after the Principal Reporter received the information mentioned in that subsection.

(3)   Where the Principal Reporter considers that a child of whose detention he has been informed does not require compulsory measures of supervision, he shall direct that the child shall no longer be kept in the place of safety.

(4)   Subject to subsection (3) above, a child who has been detained in a place of

safety may continue to be kept at that place until the commencement of a children's hearing arranged under subsection (1) above.

(5) Subject to subsection (6) below, a children's hearing arranged under subsection (1) above may—

(a)   if they are satisfied that the conditions mentioned in subsection (2) of section 66 of this Act are satisfied, grant a warrant to keep the child in a place of safety; and

(b)   direct the Principal Reporter to arrange a children's hearing for the purposes of section 65(1) of this Act, and subsections (3) to (8) of the said section 66 shall apply to a warrant granted under this subsection as they apply to a warrant granted under subsection (1) of the said section 66.

(6)   A child shall not be kept in a place of safety in accordance with a warrant granted under subsection (5) above where the Principal Reporter, having regard to the welfare of the child, considers that, whether as a result of a change in the circumstances of the case or of further information relating to the case having been received by the Principal Reporter—

(a)   the conditions mentioned in section 66(2) of this Act are no longer satisfied in relation to the child; or

(b)   the child is not in need of compulsory measures of supervision,

and where he does so consider he shall give notice to that effect to the person who is keeping the child in that place in accordance with the warrant.

Business meeting preparatory to children's hearing

64   Business meeting preparatory to children's hearing

(1)   At any time prior to the commencement of proceedings at the children's hearing, the Principal Reporter may arrange a meeting with members of the children's panel from which the children's hearing is to be constituted under section 39(4) of this Act for those proceedings (any such meeting being, in this Part of this Act referred to as a 'business meeting').

(2)   Where a business meeting is arranged under subsection (1) above, the Principal Reporter shall give notice to the child in respect of whom the proceedings are to be commenced and any relevant person in relation to the child—

(a)   of the arrangement of the meeting and of the matters which may be considered and determined by the meeting;

(b)   of their right to make their views on those matters known to the Principal Reporter; and

(c)   of the duty of the Principal Reporter to present those views to the meeting.

(3)   A business meeting, subject to subsection (4) below—

(a)   shall determine such procedural and other matters as may be prescribed by rules under subsection (1) of section 42 of this Act by virtue of subsection (2)(a) of that section; and

(b)   may give such direction or guidance to the Principal Reporter in relation to the performance of his functions in relation to the proceedings as they think appropriate.

(4)   Before a business meeting makes such a determination or gives such direction or guidance to the Principal Reporter, the Principal Reporter shall present, and they shall consider, any views expressed to him by virtue of subsection (2)(b) above.

(5)   Subject to any rules made under section 42(1) of this Act by virtue of subsection (2)(a) of that section and with the exception of sections 44 and, as regards any determination made by the business meeting under subsection (3)(a) above, 51, the provisions of this Act which relate to a children's hearing shall not apply to a business meeting.

Referral to, and disposal of case by, children's hearing

65 Referral to, and proceedings at, children's hearing

(1) The Principal Reporter shall refer to the children's hearing, for consideration and determination on the merits, the case of any child in respect of whom he is satisfied that—

(a) compulsory measures of supervision are necessary, and

(b) at least one of the grounds specified in section 52(2) of this Act is established;

and he shall state such grounds in accordance with rules made under section 42(1) of this Act by virtue of subsection (2)(c) of that section.

[(1A) Where the Principal Reporter is satisfied that the ground specified in section 52(2)(m) of this Act is established in respect of any child, he shall be taken to be satisfied as to the matter mentioned in section 65(1)(a) in respect of the child.]

(2) Where a referral is made in respect of a child who is subject to a child protection order made under section 57, and that order is continued under section 59(4) or 60(12)(d), of this Act, the Principal Reporter shall arrange for the children's hearing under subsection (1) above to take place on the eighth working day after the order was implemented.

(3) Where a referral is made in respect of a child who is subject to a supervision requirement, the children's hearing shall, before disposing of the referral in accordance with section 69(1)(b) or (c) of this Act, review that requirement in accordance with subsections (9) to (12) of section 73 of this Act.

(4) Subject to subsections (9) and (10) below, it shall be the duty of the chairman of the children's hearing to whom a child's case has been referred under subsection (1) above to explain to the child and the relevant person, at the opening of proceedings on the referral, the grounds stated by the Principal Reporter for the referral in order to ascertain whether these grounds are accepted in whole or in part by them.

(5) Where the chairman has given the explanation required by subsection (4) above and the child and the relevant person accept the grounds for the referral, the children's hearing shall proceed in accordance with section 69 of this Act.

(6) Where the chairman has given the explanation required by subsection (4) above and the child and the relevant person accept the grounds in part, the children's hearing may, if they consider it appropriate to do so, proceed in accordance with section 69 of this Act with respect to those grounds which are accepted.

(7) Where the chairman has given the explanation required under subsection (4) above and either or both of the child and the relevant person—

(a) do not accept the grounds for the referral; or

(b) accept the grounds in part, but the children's hearing do not consider it appropriate to proceed with the case under subsection (6) above,

the hearing shall either direct the Principal Reporter to make an application to the sheriff for a finding as to whether such grounds for the referral as are not accepted by the child and the relevant person are established or shall discharge the referral.

(8) Subject to subsection (10) below, it shall be the duty of the chairman to explain to the child and to the relevant person the purpose for which the application to the sheriff is being made and to inform the child that he is under an obligation to attend the hearing before the sheriff.

(9) Where a children's hearing are satisfied that the child—

(a) for any reason will not be capable of understanding the explanation of the grounds for the referral required under subsection (4) above; or

(b) has not understood an explanation given under that subsection,

they shall either direct the Principal Reporter to make an application to the sheriff for a finding as to whether any of the grounds of the referral are established or discharge the referral.

(10)   The acceptance by the relevant person of the grounds of the referral shall not be a requirement for a children's hearing proceeding under this section to consider a case where that person is not present.

66   Warrant to keep child where children's hearing unable to dispose of case

(1)   Without prejudice to any other power enjoyed by them under this Part of this Act and subject to subsection (5) below, a children's hearing—

(a)   arranged to consider a child's case under this Part of this Act; and

(b)   unable to dispose of the case,

may, if they are satisfied that one of the conditions mentioned in subsection (2) below is met, grant a warrant under this subsection.

(2)   The conditions referred to in subsection (1) above are—

(a)   that there is reason to believe that the child may—

(i)   not attend at any hearing of his case; or

(ii)   fail to comply with a requirement under section 69(3) of this Act; or

(b)   that it is necessary that the child should be kept in a place of safety in order to safeguard or promote his welfare.

(3)   A warrant under subsection (1) above may require any person named in the warrant—

(a)   to find and to keep or, as the case may be, to keep the child in a place of safety for a period not exceeding twenty-two days after the warrant is granted;

(b)   to bring the child before a children's hearing at such times as may be specified in the warrant.

(4)   A warrant under subsection (1) above may contain such conditions as appear to the children's hearing to be necessary or expedient, and without prejudice to that generality may—

(a)   subject to section 90 of this Act, require the child to submit to any medical or other examination or treatment; and

(b)   regulate the contact with the child of any specified person or class of persons.

(5)   Subject to subsection (8) below, at any time prior to its expiry, a warrant granted under this section may, on an application to the children's hearing, on cause shown by the Principal Reporter, be continued in force, whether with or without variation of any condition imposed by virtue of subsection (4) above, by the children's hearing for such further period, not exceeding twenty-two days, as appears to them to be necessary.

(6)   Where a children's hearing are satisfied—

[(a)   that one of the conditions mentioned in section 70(10) of this Act is met; and

(b)   that it is necessary to do so],

they may order that, pending the disposal of his case, the child shall be liable to be placed and kept in secure accommodation within a residential establishment at such times as the person in charge of that establishment, with the agreement of the chief social work officer of the relevant local authority, considers necessary.

(7)   Where a children's hearing grant a warrant under subsection (1) above or continue such a warrant under subsection (5) above, they may order that the place of safety at which the child is to be kept shall not be disclosed to any person or class of persons specified in the order.

(8)   A child shall not be kept in a place of safety or secure accommodation by virtue of this section for a period exceeding sixty-six days from the day when he was first taken to a place of safety under a warrant granted under subsection (1) above.

67   Warrant for further detention of child

(1)   Where a child is being kept in a place of safety by virtue of a warrant granted under section 66 of this Act or under this subsection, the Principal Reporter at any time prior to the expiry of that warrant may apply to the sheriff for a

warrant to keep the child in that place after the warrant granted under the said section 66 or, as the case may be, this subsection has expired.

(2)   A warrant under subsection (1) above shall only be granted on cause shown and—

(a)   shall specify the date on which it will expire; and

(b)   may contain any such requirement or condition as may be contained in a warrant granted under the said section 66.

(3)   Where the sheriff grants a warrant under subsection (1) above, he may also make an order under this subsection in such terms as are mentioned in subsection (6) or (7) of the said section 66; and any order under this subsection shall cease to have effect when the warrant expires.

(4)   An application under subsection (1) above may be made at the same time as, or during the hearing of, an application which the Principal Reporter has been directed by a children's hearing to make under section 65(7) or (9) of this Act.

68   Application to sheriff to establish grounds of referral

(1)   This section applies to applications under subsections (7) and (9) of section 65 of this Act and a reference in this section (except in subsection (8)) to 'an application' is a reference to an application under either of those subsections.

(2)   An application shall be heard by the sheriff within twenty-eight days of its being lodged.

(3)   Where one of the grounds for the referral to which an application relates is the condition referred to in section 52(2)(i)—

(a)   the application shall be made to the sheriff who would have jurisdiction if the child were being prosecuted for that offence; and

(b)   in hearing the application in relation to that ground, the standard of proof required in criminal proceedings shall apply.

(4)   A child shall—

(a)   have the right to attend the hearing of an application; and

(b)   subject to subsection (5) below, be under an obligation to attend such hearing;

and without prejudice to the right of each of them to be legally represented, the child and the relevant person may be represented by a person other than a legally qualified person at any diet fixed by the sheriff for the hearing of the application.

(5)   Without prejudice to subsection (4)(a) above, the sheriff may dispense with the obligation imposed by subsection (4)(b) above where he is satisfied—

(a)   in an application in which the ground of referral to be established is a condition mentioned in section 52(2)(d), (e), (f) or (g) of this Act, that the obligation to attend of the child is not necessary for the just hearing of that application; and

(b)   in any application, that it would be detrimental to the interests of the child for him to be present at the hearing of the application.

(6)   Where the child fails to attend the hearing of an application at which his attendance has not been dispensed with under subsection (5) above, the sheriff may grant an order to find and keep the child; and any order under this subsection shall be authority for bringing the child before the sheriff and, subject to subsection (7) below, for keeping him in a place of safety until the sheriff can hear the application.

(7)   The child shall not be kept in a place of safety by virtue of subsection (6) above after whichever is the earlier of—

(a)   the expiry of fourteen days beginning with the day on which the child is found; or

(b)   the disposal of the application by the sheriff.

(8)   Where in the course of the hearing of an application—

(a)   under section 65(7) of this Act, the child and the relevant person accept any of the grounds for referral to which the application relates, the sheriff shall; or

(b)   under section 65(9) of this Act, the relevant person accepts any of the grounds for referral to which the application relates, the sheriff may, if it appears to him reasonable to do so,

dispense with the hearing of evidence relating to that ground and deem the ground to be established for the purposes of the application, unless he is satisfied that, in all the circumstances of the case, the evidence should be heard.

(9)   Where a sheriff decides that none of the grounds for referral in respect of which an application has been made are established, he shall dismiss the application, discharge the referral to the children's hearing in respect of those grounds and recall, discharge or cancel any order, warrant, or direction under this Chapter of this Act which relates to the child in respect of those grounds.

(10)   Where the sheriff, after the hearing of any evidence or on acceptance in accordance with subsection (8) above, finds that any of the grounds for the referral to which the application relates is, or should be deemed to be, established—

(a)   he shall remit the case to the Principal Reporter to make arrangements for a children's hearing to consider and determine the case; and

(b)   he may if he is satisfied that—

(i)   keeping the child in a place of safety is necessary in the child's best interests; or

(ii)   there is reason to believe that the child will run away before the children's hearing sit to consider the case,

issue an order requiring, subject to subsection (12) below, that the child be kept in a place of safety until the children's hearing so sit.

(11)   An order issued under subsection (10) above may, if the sheriff is satisfied—

[(a)   that one of the conditions mentioned in section 70(10) of this Act is met; and

(b)   that it is necessary for the order to do so],

provide that the child shall be liable to be placed and kept in secure accommodation within a residential establishment at such times as the person in charge of the establishment, with the agreement of the chief social work officer of the relevant local authority, considers necessary.

(12)   A child shall not be kept in a place of safety by virtue of subsection (10)(b) above after whichever is the earlier of the following—

(a)   the expiry of three days beginning with the day on which he is first so kept; or

(b)   the consideration of his case by the children's hearing arranged under subsection (10)(a) above.

[68A   Restrictions on evidence in certain cases involving sexual abuse

(1)   This section applies in relation to—

(a)   an application under section 65(7) or (9) of this Act in which the ground of referral to be established is a condition mentioned in—

(i)   paragraph (b) of subsection (2) of section 52 of this Act where that condition is alleged to be satisfied by reference to sexual behaviour engaged in by any person,

(ii)   paragraph (d), (e) or (f) of that subsection where that condition is alleged to be satisfied by reference to a relevant offence, or

(iii)   paragraph (g) of that subsection, or

(b)   an application under section 85 of this Act for a review of a finding that any such ground of referral is established.

(2)   In hearing the application, the sheriff shall not admit, or allow questioning designed to elicit, evidence which shows or tends to show that the child who is the

subject of the application or any other witness giving evidence at the hearing (such child or other witness being referred to in this section and section 68B of this Act as 'the witness')—

(a) is not of good character (whether in relation to sexual matters or otherwise),

(b) has, at any time, engaged in sexual behaviour not forming part of the subject matter of the ground of referral,

(c) has, at any time (other than shortly before, at the same time as or shortly after the acts which form part of the subject matter of the ground of referral), engaged in such behaviour, not being sexual behaviour, as might found the inference that the witness is not a credible or reliable witness, or

(d) has, at any time, been subject to any such condition or predisposition as might found the inference referred to in paragraph (c) above.

(3) In subsection (1)(a)(ii) above, 'relevant offence' means—

(a) an offence mentioned in paragraph 1 or 4 of Schedule 1 (offences against children under the age of 17 to which special provisions apply) to the Criminal Procedure (Scotland) Act 1995 (c 46), or

(b) any other offence mentioned in that Schedule where there is a substantial sexual element in the alleged commission of the offence.

(4) In subsection (2)(b) and (c) above—

(a) 'the subject matter of the ground of referral' means—

(i) in the case of an application in which the ground of referral to be established is the condition referred to in paragraph (a)(i) of subsection (1) above, the sexual behaviour referred to in that paragraph,

(ii) in the case of any other application, the acts or behaviour constituting the offence by reference to which the ground of referral is alleged to be established, and

(b) the reference to engaging in sexual behaviour includes a reference to undergoing or being made subject to any experience of a sexual nature.

68B Exceptions to restrictions under section 68A

(1) The sheriff hearing an application referred to in subsection (1) of section 68A of this Act may, on an application by any party to the proceedings, admit such evidence or allow such questioning as is referred to in subsection (2) of that section if satisfied that—

(a) the evidence or questioning will relate only to a specific occurrence or occurrences of sexual or other behaviour or to specific facts demonstrating—

(i) the character of the witness, or

(ii) any condition or predisposition to which the witness is or has been subject,

(b) that occurrence or those occurrences of behaviour or facts are relevant to establishing the ground of referral, and

(c) the probative value of the evidence sought to be admitted or elicited is significant and is likely to outweigh any risk of prejudice to the proper administration of justice arising from its being admitted or elicited.

(2) In subsection (1) above—

(a) the reference to an occurrence or occurrences of sexual behaviour includes a reference to undergoing or being made subject to any experience of a sexual nature,

(b) 'the proper administration of justice' includes—

(i) appropriate protection of the witness's dignity and privacy, and

(ii) ensuring the facts and circumstances of which the sheriff is made aware are relevant to an issue to be put before the sheriff and commensurate with the importance of that issue to the sheriff's decision on the question whether the ground of referral is established.

(3)   In this section, 'the witness' means the child who is the subject of the application referred to in section 68A(1) or other witness in respect of whom the evidence is sought to be admitted or elicited.]

69   Continuation or disposal of referral by children's hearing

(1)   Where the grounds of referral of the child's case stated by the Principal Reporter are accepted or are established in accordance with section 68 or section 85 of this Act, the children's hearing shall consider those grounds, any report obtained under section 56(7) of this Act and any other relevant information available to them and shall—

(a)   continue the case to a subsequent hearing in accordance with subsection (2) below;

(b)   discharge the referral of the case in accordance with subsection (12) below; or

(c)   make a supervision requirement under section 70 of this Act.

(2)   The children's hearing may continue the case to a subsequent hearing under this subsection where they are satisfied that, in order to complete their consideration of the case, it is necessary to have a further investigation of the case.

(3)   Where a children's hearing continue the case under subsection (2) above, they may, for the purposes of the investigation mentioned by that subsection, require the child to attend, or reside at, any clinic, hospital or other establishment during a period not exceeding twenty-two days.

(4)   Where a child fails to fulfil a requirement made under subsection (3) above, the children's hearing may, either on an application by the Principal Reporter or of their own motion, grant a warrant under this subsection.

(5)   A warrant under subsection (4) above shall be authority—

(a)   to find the child;

(b)   to remove the child to a place of safety and keep him there; and

(c)   where the place of safety is not the clinic, hospital or other establishment referred to in the requirement made under subsection (3) above, to take the child from the place of safety to such clinic, hospital or other establishment for the purposes of the investigation mentioned in subsection (2) above.

(6)   A warrant under subsection (4) above shall be granted for such period as appears to the children's hearing to be appropriate, provided that no warrant shall permit the keeping of a child in a place of safety after whichever is the earlier of—

(a)   the expiry of twenty-two days after the warrant is granted; or

(b)   the day on which the subsequent hearing of the child's case by a children's hearing begins.

(7)   Where a child's case has been continued under subsection (2) above and the children's hearing are satisfied that—

(a)   keeping the child in a place of safety is necessary in the interests of safeguarding or promoting the welfare of the child; or

(b)   there is reason to believe that the child may not attend the subsequent hearing of his case,

they may grant a warrant requiring that the child be taken to and kept in a place of safety.

(8)   A warrant under subsection (7) above shall cease to have effect on whichever is the earlier of—

(a)   the expiry of twenty-two days after the warrant is granted; or

(b)   the day on which the subsequent hearing of the child's case by a children's hearing begins.

(9)   A warrant under subsection (4) or (7) above may contain such conditions as appear to the children's hearing to be necessary or expedient, and without prejudice to that generality may—

(a)   subject to section 90 of this Act, require the child to submit to any medical or other examination or treatment;

(b)   regulate the contact with the child of any specified person or class of persons.

(10)   Where a child is to be kept at a place of safety under a warrant granted under this section or is to attend, or reside at, any place in accordance with a requirement made under subsection (3) above, the children's hearing may order that such place shall not be disclosed to any person or class of persons specified in the order.

(11)   Where a child is to reside in a residential establishment by virtue of a requirement made or warrant granted under this section, the children's hearing may, if satisfied—

[(a)   that one of the conditions mentioned in section 70(10) of this Act is met; and

(b)   that it is necessary to do so,]

order that while the requirement or warrant remains in effect he shall be liable to be placed in secure accommodation within that establishment at such times as the person in charge of the establishment, with the agreement of the chief social work officer of the relevant local authority, considers necessary.

(12)   Where a children's hearing decide not to make a supervision requirement under section 70 of this Act they shall discharge the referral.

(13)   On the discharge of the referral of the child's case any order, direction, or warrant under Chapter 2, or this Chapter, of this Act in respect of the child's case shall cease to have effect.

70   Disposal of referral by children's hearing: supervision requirements, including residence in secure accommodation

(1)   Where the children's hearing to whom a child's case has been referred under section 65(1) of this Act are satisfied that compulsory measures of supervision are necessary in respect of the child they may make a requirement under this section (to be known as a 'supervision requirement').

(2)   A children's hearing, where they decide to make such a requirement, shall consider whether to impose any condition such as is described in subsection (5)(b) below.

(3)   A supervision requirement may require the child—

(a)   to reside at any place or places specified in the requirement; and

(b)   to comply with any condition contained in the requirement.

[(3B)   A children's hearing may, for the purpose of enabling a child to comply with a supervision requirement, impose such duties on the relevant local authority as may be specified in the supervision requirement.

(3C)   The duties imposed under subsection (3B) above may include that of securing or facilitating the provision for the child of services of a kind other than that provided by the relevant local authority.]

(4)   The place or, as the case may be, places specified in a requirement under subsection (3)(a) above may, without prejudice to the generality of that subsection, be a place or places in England or Wales; and a supervision requirement shall be authority for the person in charge of such a place to restrict the child's liberty to such extent as that person may consider appropriate, having regard to the terms of the requirement.

(5)   A condition imposed under subsection (3)(b) above may, without prejudice to the generality of that subsection—

(a)   subject to section 90 of this Act, require the child to submit to any medical or other examination or treatment;

(b)   regulate the contact with the child of any specified person or class of persons.

(6)   A children's hearing may require, when making a supervision requirement, that any place where the child is to reside in accordance with the supervision

requirement shall not be disclosed to any person specified in the requirement under this subsection or class of persons so specified.

(7) A children's hearing who make a supervision requirement may determine that the requirement shall be reviewed at such time during the duration of the requirement as they determine.

[(7A) Where, on a review under subsection (7) above, it appears to the children's hearing that the relevant local authority are in breach of a duty imposed on them under section 71 of this Act, the hearing may direct the Principal Reporter to give the authority notice of an intended application under section 71A(2) of this Act.

(7B) The Principal Reporter shall, at the same time as giving the notice of an intended application under section 71A(2) of this Act, send a copy of the notice to—

(a)   the child to whom the duty referred to in subsection (7A) above relates;

(b)   any person who, in relation to the child, is a relevant person;

(c)   any person appointed under section 41 of this Act to safeguard the interests of the child in any proceedings which are taking place when the notice is given.

(7C) Notice of an intended application under section 71A(2) of this Act is a written notice—

(a)   setting out the respects in which the relevant local authority are in breach of the duty imposed on them under section 71 of this Act; and

(b)   stating that if the authority do not comply with that duty within the period of 21 days beginning with the day on which they received the notice, the Principal Reporter may make an application under section 71A(2) of this Act.

(7D) Where a children's hearing have made a direction under subsection (7A) above, they shall determine that a further review under subsection (7) above take place on or as soon as is reasonably practicable after the expiry of the period of 28 days beginning with the day on which notice was given in pursuance of that direction.

(7E) Where on a further review under subsection (7) above which takes place by virtue of subsection (7D) above, it appears to the children's hearing that the relevant local authority continues to be in breach of the duty referred to in subsection (7A) above, the hearing may authorise the Principal Reporter to make an application under section 71A(2) of this Act.]

(8) A supervision requirement shall be in such form as the Secretary of State may prescribe by rules.

[(9) A children's hearing may exercise a power mentioned in subsection (9A) below in relation to a child if they are satisfied—

(a)   that one of the conditions mentioned in subsection (10) below is met; and

(b)   that it is necessary to exercise the power concerned.

(9A) The powers are—

(a)   that the children's hearing may specify in the supervision requirement that the child shall be liable to be placed and kept in secure accommodation in a residential establishment specified, under subsection (3)(a) above, in the requirement during such period as the person in charge of that establishment, with the agreement of the chief social work officer of the relevant local authority, considers necessary; and

(b)   that the children's hearing may impose, under subsection (3)(b) above, a movement restriction condition.

(10) The conditions are—

(a)   that the child, having previously absconded, is likely to abscond and, if he absconds, it is likely that his physical, mental or moral welfare will be at risk; and

(b)   that the child is likely to injure himself or some other person.

(11)   In this section, 'movement restriction condition' means a condition—

(a)   restricting the child's movements in such way as may be specified in the supervision requirement; and

(b)   requiring the child to comply with such arrangements for monitoring compliance with the restriction mentioned in paragraph (a) above as may be so specified.

(12)   Where a children's hearing impose a condition such as is mentioned in subsection (9A)(b) above, they shall also impose under subsection (3)(b) above such of the conditions prescribed by the Scottish Ministers for the purposes of this section as they consider necessary in the child's case.

(13)   The Scottish Ministers may by regulations make provision as to the arrangements mentioned in subsection (11)(b) above.

(14)   Regulations under subsection (13) above may in particular include provision—

(a)   prescribing what method or methods of monitoring compliance with the restriction mentioned in paragraph (a) of subsection (11) above may be specified in a supervision requirement;

(b)   specifying the devices which may be used for the purpose of that monitoring;

(c)   prescribing the person who may be designated by a children's hearing to carry out that monitoring or the class or description of person from which that person may be drawn;

(d)   requiring a children's hearing who have designated a person in pursuance of paragraph (c) above who is no longer within the provision made under that paragraph to vary the designation accordingly and notify the child of the variation.

(15)   The Scottish Ministers may, by contract or otherwise, secure the services of such persons as they think fit to carry out the monitoring mentioned in subsection (11)(b) above and may do so in a way in which those services are provided differently in relation to different areas or different forms of that monitoring.

(16)   Nothing in any enactment or rule of law prevents the disclosure to a person providing services in pursuance of subsection (15) above of information relating to a child where the disclosure is made for the purposes only of the full and proper provision of the monitoring mentioned in subsection (11)(b) above.

(17)   A children's hearing may include in a supervision requirement a movement restriction condition only if the hearing is constituted from the children's panel for a local government area which is prescribed for the purposes of this section by the Scottish Ministers.]

71   Duties of local authority with respect to supervision requirements

(1)   The relevant local authority shall, as respects a child subject to a supervision requirement, give effect to the requirement.

[(1A)   Where a supervision requirement imposes, under section 70(3A) of this Act, duties on the relevant local authority, the authority shall perform those duties.]

(2)   Where a supervision requirement provides that the child shall reside—

(a)   in relevant accommodation; or

(b)   in any other accommodation not provided by a local authority,

the relevant local authority shall from time to time investigate whether, while the child is so resident, any conditions imposed by the supervision requirement are being fulfilled; and may take such steps as they consider reasonable if they find that such conditions are not being fulfilled.

(3)   In this section, 'relevant accommodation' means accommodation provided by the parents or relatives of the child or by any person associated with them or with the child.

[71A   Enforcement of local authorities' duties under section 71

(1)   The sheriff principal may, on an application under subsection (2) below, make an order requiring a relevant local authority in breach of a duty imposed on them under section 71 of this Act to perform that duty.

(2)   The Principal Reporter, having been so authorised by a children's hearing under section 70(7E) of this Act, may apply for an order under subsection (1) above.

(3)   No such application shall be competent unless—

(a)   the Principal Reporter has, on a direction of the children's hearing made under section 70(7A) of this Act, given the relevant local authority the notice referred to in that provision; and

(b)   the authority have failed to comply, within the period stipulated in the notice, with the duty there referred to.

(4)   In deciding whether to apply under subsection (2) above, the Principal Reporter shall not take into account any factor relating to the adequacy of the means available to the relevant local authority to enable it to comply with the duty.

(5)   An application under subsection (2) above shall be made by summary application.

(6)   The sheriff principal having jurisdiction under this section is the sheriff principal of the sheriffdom in which is situated the principal office of the relevant local authority in breach of the duty referred to in subsection (1) above.

(7)   An order under subsection (1) above shall be final.]

72   Transfer of child subject to supervision requirement in case of necessity

(1)   In any case of urgent necessity, where it is in the interests of—

(a)   a child who is required by a supervision requirement imposed under section 70(3)(a) of this Act to reside in a specific residential establishment or specific other accommodation; or

(b)   other children in that establishment or accommodation,

the chief social work officer of the relevant local authority may direct that, notwithstanding that requirement, the child be transferred to another place.

(2)   Any child transferred under subsection (1) above shall have his case reviewed, in accordance with section 73(8) of this Act, by a children's hearing within seven days of his transfer.

73   Duration and review of supervision requirement

(1)   No child shall continue to be subject to a supervision requirement for any period longer than is necessary in the interests of promoting or safeguarding his welfare.

(2)   Subject to any variation or continuation of a supervision requirement under subsection (9) below, no supervision requirement shall remain in force for a period longer than one year.

(3)   A supervision requirement shall cease to have effect in respect of a child not later than on his attaining the age of eighteen years.

(4)   A relevant local authority shall refer the case of a child who is subject to a supervision requirement to the Principal Reporter where they are satisfied that—

(a)   the requirement in respect of the child ought to cease to have effect or be varied;

(b)   a condition contained in the requirement is not being complied with; or

(c)   the best interests of the child would be served by their—

(i)   applying under section 86 of this Act for a parental responsibilities order;

(ii)   applying under section 18 of the Adoption (Scotland) Act 1978 for an order freeing the child for adoption; or

(iii)   placing the child for adoption,

and they intend to apply for such an order or so place the child.

(5)   Where the relevant local authority are aware that an application has been made and is pending, or is about to be made, under section 12 of the said Act of 1978 for an adoption order in respect of a child who is subject to a supervision requirement, they shall forthwith refer his case to the Principal Reporter.

(6)   A child or any relevant person may require a review of a supervision requirement in respect of the child at any time at least three months after—

(a)   the date on which the requirement is made; or

(b)   the date of the most recent continuation, or variation, by virtue of this section of the requirement.

(7)   Where a child is subject to a supervision requirement and, otherwise than in accordance with that requirement or with an order under section 11 of this Act, a relevant person proposes to take the child to live outwith Scotland, the person shall, not later than twenty-eight days before so taking the child, give notice of that proposal in writing to the Principal Reporter and to the relevant local authority.

(8)   The Principal Reporter shall—

(a)   arrange for a children's hearing to review any supervision requirement in respect of a child where—

(i)   the case has been referred to him under subsection (4) or (5) above;

(ii)   the review has been required under subsection (6) above;

(iii)   the review is required by virtue of section 70(7) or section 72(2) of this Act;

(iv)   he has received in respect of the child such notice as is mentioned in subsection (7) above; or

(v)   in any other case, the supervision requirement will expire within three months;

[(aa)   where—

(i)   a requirement is made of the Principal Reporter under section 11(1) of the Antisocial Behaviour etc (Scotland) Act 2004 (asp 8) (power of sheriff to require Principal Reporter to refer case to children's hearing) in respect of the child's case; and

(ii)   the child is subject to a supervision requirement,

arrange for a children's hearing to review the supervision requirement;]; and

(b)   make any arrangements incidental to [any such] review.

(9)   Where a supervision requirement is reviewed by a children's hearing arranged under subsection (8) above, they may—

(a)   where they are satisfied that in order to complete the review of the supervision requirement it is necessary to have a further investigation of the child's case, continue the review to a subsequent hearing;

(b)   terminate the requirement;

(c)   vary the requirement;

(d)   insert in the requirement any requirement which could have been imposed by them under section 70(3) of this Act; or

(e)   continue the requirement, with or without such variation or insertion.

(10)   Subsections (3) to (10) of section 69 of this Act shall apply to a continuation under paragraph (a) of subsection (9) above of a review of a supervision requirement as they apply to the continuation of a case under subsection (1)(a) of that section.

(11)   Where a children's hearing vary or impose a requirement under subsection (9) above which requires the child to reside in any specified place or places, they may order that such place or places shall not be disclosed to any person or class of persons specified in the requirement.

(12)   Where a children's hearing is arranged under subsection (8)(a)(v) above, they shall consider whether, if the supervision requirement is not continued, the child still requires supervision or guidance; and where a children's hearing consider such supervision or guidance is necessary, it shall be the duty of the local

authority to provide such supervision or guidance as the child is willing to accept.

(13)   Where a children's hearing is arranged by virtue of subsection (4)(c) or (5) above, then irrespective of what the hearing do under subsection (9) above they shall draw up a report which shall provide advice in respect of, as the case may be, the proposed application under section 86 of this Act or under section 18 of the said Act of 1978, or the proposed placing for adoption or the application, or prospective application, under section 12 of that Act, for any court which may subsequently require to come to a decision, in relation to the child concerned, such as is mentioned in subsection (14) below.

(14)   A court which is considering whether, in relation to a child, to grant an application under section 86 of this Act or under section 18 or 12 of the said Act of 1978 and which, by virtue of subsection (13) above, receives a report as respects that child, shall consider the report before coming to a decision in the matter.

74   Further provision as respects children subject to supervision requirements

The Secretary of State may by regulations provide—

(a)   for the transmission of information regarding a child who is subject to a supervision requirement to any person who, by virtue of that requirement, has, or is to have, control over the child;

(b)   or the temporary accommodation, where necessary, of a child so subject; and

(c)   for the conveyance of a child so subject—

(i)   to any place in which, under the supervision requirement, he is to reside;

(ii)   to any place to which he falls to be taken under subsection (1) or (5) of section 82 of this Act; or

(iii)   to any person to whom he falls to be returned under subsection (3) of that section.

75   Powers of Secretary of State with respect to secure accommodation

(1)   The Secretary of State may by regulations make provision with respect to the placing in secure accommodation of any child—

(a)   who is subject to a requirement imposed under section 70(3)(a) of this Act but not subject to a requirement under subsection (9) of that section; or

(b)   who is not subject to a supervision requirement but who is being looked after by a local authority in pursuance of such enactments as may be specified in the regulations.

(2)   Regulations under subsection (1) above may—

(a)   specify the circumstances in which a child may be so placed under the regulations;

(b)   make provision to enable a child who has been so placed or any relevant person to require that the child's case be brought before a children's hearing within a shorter period than would apply under regulations made under subsection (3) below; and

(c)   specify different circumstances for different cases or classes of case.

(3)   Subject to subsection (4) below and without prejudice to subsection (2)(b) above, the Secretary of State may prescribe—

(a)   the maximum period during which a child may be kept under this Act in secure accommodation without the authority of a children's hearing or of the sheriff;

(b)   the period within which a children's hearing shall be arranged to consider the case of a child placed in secure accommodation by virtue of regulations made under this section (and different periods may be so prescribed in respect of different cases or classes of case).

(4) Subsection (8) of section 66 of this Act shall apply in respect of a child placed in secure accommodation under regulations made under this section as if such placing took place by virtue of that section.

(5) The Secretary of State may by regulations vary the period within which a review of a condition imposed under section 70(9) of this Act shall be reviewed under section 73 of this Act.

(6) The Secretary of State may by regulations make provision for the procedures to be applied in placing children in secure accommodation; and without prejudice to the generality of this subsection, such regulations may—

(a) specify the duties of the Principal Reporter in relation to the placing of children in secure accommodation;

(b) make provision for the referral of cases to a children's hearing for review; and

(c) make provision for any person with parental responsibilities in relation to the child to be informed of the placing of the child in secure accommodation.

[Parenting orders

75A Requirement on Principal Reporter to apply for parenting order

(1) Subsection (2) below applies where it appears to—

(a) the children's hearing to whom a child's case has been referred under section 65(1) of this Act; or

(b) a children's hearing arranged, under section 73(8) of this Act, to review a supervision requirement in respect of a child,

that it might be appropriate for a parenting order to be made in respect of a parent of the child under section 102 of the Antisocial Behaviour etc (Scotland) Act 2004 (asp 8) (the '2004 Act').

(2) The hearing may require the Principal Reporter to consider whether to apply, under subsection (3) of that section of the 2004 Act, for such an order.

(3) A requirement under subsection (2) above shall specify—

(a) the parent in respect of whom it might be appropriate for the order to be made; and

(b) by reference to subsections (4) to (6) of that section of the 2004 Act, the condition in respect of which the application might be made.

(4) In subsection (1) above, 'parent' and 'child' have the same meanings as in section 117 of the 2004 Act.]

[Failure to provide education for excluded pupils

75B Failure to provide education for excluded pupils: reference to Scottish Ministers

(1) Where it appears to the children's hearing to whom a child's case has been referred under section 65(1) of this Act that—

(a) an education authority have a duty under section 14(3) of the Education (Scotland) Act 1980 (c 44) in relation to the child; and

(b) the authority are not complying with that duty,

they may require the Principal Reporter to refer the matter to the Scottish Ministers.

(2) The Principal Reporter shall comply with any requirement made under subsection (1) above.

(3) A reference made by virtue of subsection (1) above shall be in writing.

(4) A copy of a reference made by virtue of subsection (1) above shall be sent by the Principal Reporter to the education authority in respect of which the reference is made.]

Exclusion orders

76 Exclusion orders

(1) Subject to subsections (3) to (9) below, where on the application of a local authority the sheriff is satisfied, in relation to a child, that the conditions mentioned in subsection (2) below are met, he may grant an order under this section (to be known as 'an exclusion order') excluding from the child's family home any person named in the order (in this Part of this Act referred to as the 'named person').

(2) The conditions are—

(a) that the child has suffered, is suffering, or is likely to suffer, significant harm as a result of any conduct, or any threatened or reasonably apprehended conduct, of the named person;

(b) that the making of an exclusion order against the named person—

(i) is necessary for the protection of the child, irrespective of whether the child is for the time being residing in the family home; and

(ii) would better safeguard the child's welfare than the removal of the child from the family home; and

(c) that, if an order is made, there will be a person specified in the application who is capable of taking responsibility for the provision of appropriate care for the child and any other member of the family who requires such care and who is, or will be, residing in the family home (in this section, sections 77 to 79 and section 91(3)(f) of this Act referred to as an 'appropriate person').

(3) No application under subsection (1) above for an exclusion order shall be finally determined under this section unless—

(a) the named person has been afforded an opportunity of being heard by, or represented before, the sheriff, and

(b) the sheriff has considered any views expressed by any person on whom notice of the application has been served in accordance with rules making such provision as is mentioned in section 91(3)(d) of this Act.

(4) Where, on an application under subsection (1) above, the sheriff—

(a) is satisfied as mentioned in that subsection; but

(b) the conditions mentioned in paragraphs (a) and (b) of subsection (3) above for the final determination of the application are not fulfilled,

he may grant an interim order, which shall have effect as an exclusion order pending a hearing by the sheriff under subsection (5) below held within such period as may be specified in rules made by virtue of section 91(3)(e) of this Act.

(5) The sheriff shall conduct a hearing under this subsection within such period as may be specified in rules made by virtue of section 91(3)(e) of this Act, and, if satisfied at that hearing as mentioned in subsection (1) above, he may, before finally determining the application, confirm or vary the interim order, or any term or condition on which it was granted, or may recall such order.

(6) Where the conditions mentioned in paragraphs (a) and (b) of subsection (3) above have been fulfilled, the sheriff may, at any point prior to the final determination of the application, grant an interim order.

(7) An order under subsection (5) or (6) above shall have effect as an exclusion order pending the final determination of the application.

(8) Where—

(a) an application is made under subsection (1) above; and

(b) the sheriff considers that the conditions for making a child protection order under section 57 of this Act are satisfied,

he may make an order under that section as if the application had been duly made by the local authority under that rather than under this section.

(9) The sheriff shall not make an exclusion order if it appears to him that to do so would be unjustifiable or unreasonable, having regard to—

(a)   all the circumstances of the case, including without prejudice to the generality of this subsection the matters specified in subsection (10) below; and

(b)   any requirement such as is specified in subsection (11) below and the likely consequences in the light of that requirement of the exclusion of the named person from the family home.

(10)   The matters referred to in subsection (9)(a) above are—

(a)   the conduct of the members of the child's family (whether in relation to each other or otherwise);

(b)   the respective needs and financial resources of the members of that family;

(c)   the extent (if any) to which—

(i)   the family home; and

(ii)   any relevant item in that home,

is used in connection with a trade, business or profession by any member of the family.

(11)   The requirement referred to in subsection (9)(b) above is a requirement that the named person (whether alone or with any other person) must reside in the family home, where that home—

(a)   [is on or comprised in a lease constituting a 1991 Act tenancy within the meaning of the Agricultural Holdings (Scotland) Act 2003 (asp 11) or in a lease constituting a short limited duration tenancy or a limited duration tenancy (within the meaning of that Act)]; or

(b)   is let, or is a home in respect of which possession is given, to the named person (whether alone or with any other person) by an employer as an incident of employment.

(12)   In this Part of this Act—

'caravan' has the meaning given to it by section 29(1) of the Caravan Sites and Control of Development Act 1960;

'exclusion order', includes an interim order granted under subsection (4) above and such an order confirmed or varied under subsection (5) above and an interim order granted under subsection (6) above; except that in subsection (3) above and in section 79 of this Act, it does not include an interim order granted under subsection (4) above;

'family' has the meaning given in section 93(1) of this Act;

'family home' means any house, caravan, houseboat or other structure which is used as a family residence and in which the child ordinarily resides with any person described in subsection (13) below and the expression includes any garden or other ground or building attached to and usually occupied with, or otherwise required for the amenity or convenience of, the house, caravan, houseboat or other structure.

(13)   The description of person referred to in the definition of 'family home' in subsection (12) above, is a person who has parental responsibilities in relation to the child, or who ordinarily (and other than by reason only of his employment) has charge of, or control over him.

77   Effect of, and orders etc ancillary to, exclusion order

(1)   An exclusion order shall, in respect of the home to which it relates, have the effect of suspending the named person's rights of occupancy (if any) and shall prevent him from entering the home, except with the express permission of the local authority which applied for the order.

(2)   The sheriff, on the application of the local authority, may, if and in so far as he thinks fit, when making an exclusion order do any of the things mentioned in subsection (3) below.

(3)   The things referred to in subsection (2) above are—

(a)   grant a warrant for the summary ejection of the named person from the home;

(b)   grant an interdict prohibiting the named person from entering the home without the express permission of the local authority;

(c)   grant an interdict prohibiting the removal by the named person of any relevant item specified in the interdict from the home, except either—

(i)   with the written consent of the local authority, or of an appropriate person; or

(ii)   by virtue of a subsequent order of the sheriff,

(d)   grant an interdict prohibiting the named person from entering or remaining in a specified area in the vicinity of the home;

(e)   grant an interdict prohibiting the taking by the named person of any step of a kind specified in the interdict in relation to the child;

(f)   make an order regulating the contact between the child and the named person,

and the sheriff may make any other order which he considers is necessary for the proper enforcement of a remedy granted by virtue of paragraph (a), (b) or (c) of this subsection.

(4)   No warrant, interdict or order (except an interdict granted by virtue of paragraph (b) of subsection (3) above) shall be granted or made under subsection (2) above if the named person satisfies the sheriff that it is unnecessary to do so.

(5)   Where the sheriff grants a warrant of summary ejection under subsection (2) above in the absence of the named person, he may give directions as to the preservation of any of that person's goods and effects which remain in the family home.

(6)   The sheriff may make an order of the kind specified in subsection (3)(f) above irrespective of whether there has been an application for such an order.

(7)   On the application of either the named person or the local authority, the sheriff may make the exclusion order, or any remedy granted under subsection (2) above, subject to such terms and conditions as he considers appropriate.

(8)   In this Part of this Act references to a 'relevant item' are references to any item within the home which both—

(a)   is owned or hired by any member of the family concerned or an appropriate person or is being acquired by any such member or person under a hire purchase agreement or conditional sale agreement; and

(b)   is reasonably necessary to enable the home to be used as a family residence,

but does not include any such vehicle, caravan or houseboat or such other structure so used as is mentioned in the definition of 'family home' in section 76(12) of this Act.

78   Powers of arrest etc in relation to exclusion order

(1)   The sheriff may, whether or not on an application such as is mentioned in subsection (2) below, attach a power of arrest to any interdict granted under section 77(2) of this Act by virtue of subsection (3) of that section.

(2)   A local authority may at any time while an exclusion order has effect apply for such attachment of a power of arrest as is mentioned in subsection (1) above.

(3)   A power of arrest attached to an interdict by virtue of subsection (1) above shall not have effect until such interdict, together with the attached power of arrest, is served on the named person.

(4)   If, by virtue of subsection (1) above, a power of arrest is attached to an interdict, the local authority shall, as soon as possible after the interdict, together with the attached power of arrest, is served on the named person, ensure that there is delivered—

(a)   to the chief constable of the police area in which the family home is situated; and

(b)   where the interdict was granted by virtue of section 77(3)(e) of this Act, to the chief constable of the area in which the step or conduct which is prevented by the interdict may take place,
a copy of the application for the interdict and of the interlocutor granting the interdict together with a certificate of service of the interdict and, where the application to attach the power of arrest was made after the interdict was granted, a copy of that application and of the interlocutor above granting it and a certificate of service of the interdict together with the attached power of arrest.

(5)   Where any interdict to which a power of arrest is attached by virtue of subsection (1) above is varied or recalled, the person who applied for the variation or recall shall ensure that there is delivered to each chief constable specified in subsection (4) above a copy of the application for such variation or recall and of the interlocutor granting the variation or recall.

(6)   A constable may arrest without warrant the named person if he has reasonable cause for suspecting that person to be in breach of an interdict to which a power of arrest has been attached by virtue of subsection (1) above.

(7)   Where a person has been arrested under subsection (6) above, the constable in charge of a police station may—

(a)   if satisfied there is no likelihood of that person further breaching the interdict to which the power of arrest was attached under subsection (1) above, liberate him unconditionally; or

(b)   refuse to liberate that person.

(8)   Such a refusal to liberate an arrested person as is mentioned in subsection (7)(b) above, and the detention of that person until his appearance in court by virtue of either subsection (11) below, or any provision of the Criminal Procedure (Scotland) Act [1995], shall not subject that constable to any claim whatsoever.

(9)   Where a person has been liberated under subsection (7)(a) above, the facts and circumstances which gave rise to the arrest shall be reported to the procurator fiscal forthwith.

(10)   Subsections (11) to (13) below apply only where—

(a)   the arrested person has not been released under subsection (7)(a) above; and

(b)   the procurator fiscal decides that no criminal proceedings are to be taken in respect of the facts and circumstances which gave rise to the arrest.

(11)   A person arrested under subsection (6) above shall, wherever practicable, be brought before the sheriff sitting as a court of summary criminal jurisdiction for the district in which he was arrested not later than in the course of the first day after the arrest such day not being a Saturday, a Sunday or a court holiday prescribed for that court under [section 8 of the said Act of 1995], on which the sheriff is not sitting for the disposal of criminal business.

(12)   Subsections (1), [(2) and (4) of section 15 of the said Act of 1995] (intimation to a person named by the person arrested) shall apply to a person arrested under subsection (6) above as they apply to a person who has been arrested in respect of an offence.

(13)   Where a person is brought before the sheriff under subsection (11) above—

(a)   the procurator fiscal shall present to the court a petition containing—

(i)   a statement of the particulars of the person arrested under subsection (6) above;

(ii)   a statement of the facts and circumstances which gave rise to that arrest; and

(iii)   a request that the person be detained for a further period not exceeding two days;

(b)   the sheriff, if it appears to him that—

(i)   the statement referred to in paragraph (a)(ii) above discloses a *prima facie* breach of interdict by the arrested person;

(ii) proceedings for breach of interdict will be taken; and

(iii) there is a substantial risk of violence by the arrested person against any member of the family, or an appropriate person, resident in the family home,

may order the arrested person to be detained for a period not exceeding two days; and

(c) the sheriff shall, in any case in which paragraph (b) above does not apply, order the release of the arrested person from custody (unless that person is in custody in respect of some other matter);

and in computing the period of two days referred to in paragraphs (a) and (b) above, no account shall be taken of a Saturday, a Sunday or any holiday in the court in which proceedings for breach of interdict will require to be raised.

(14) Where a person—

(a) is liberated under subsection (7)(a) above; or

(b) is to be brought before the sheriff under subsection (11) above,

the procurator fiscal shall at the earliest opportunity, and, in the case of a person to whom paragraph (b) above applies, before that person is brought before the sheriff, take all reasonable steps to intimate to—

(i) the local authority which made the application for the interdict;

(ii) an appropriate person who will reside in, or who remains in residence in, the family home mentioned in the order; and

(iii) any solicitor who acted for the appropriate person when the interdict was granted or to any other solicitor who the procurator fiscal has reason to believe acts for the time being for that person,

that he has decided that no criminal proceedings should be taken in respect of the facts and circumstances which gave rise to the arrest of the named person.

79 Duration, variation and recall of exclusion order

(1) Subject to subsection (2) below, an exclusion order shall cease to have effect on a date six months after being made.

(2) An exclusion order shall cease to have effect on a date prior to the date mentioned in subsection (1) above where—

(a) the order contains a direction by the sheriff that it shall cease to have effect on that prior date;

(b) the sheriff, on an application under subsection (3) below, recalls the order before the date so mentioned; or

(c) any permission given by a third party to the spouse or partner of the named person, or to an appropriate person, to occupy the home to which the order relates is withdrawn.

(3) The sheriff may, on the application of the local authority, the named person, an appropriate person or the spouse or partner of the named person, if that spouse or partner is not excluded from the family home and is not an appropriate person, vary or recall an exclusion order and any warrant, interdict, order or direction granted or made under section 77 of this Act.

(4) For the purposes of this section, partners are persons who live together in a family home as if they were husband and wife.

80 Exclusion orders: supplementary provisions

(1) The Secretary of State may make regulations with respect to the powers, duties and functions of local authorities in relation to exclusion orders.

(2) An application for an exclusion order, or under section 79(3) of this Act for the variation or recall of such an order or of any thing done under section 77(2) of this Act, shall be made to the sheriff for the sheriffdom within which the family home is situated.

Offences in connection with orders etc for protection of children

81 Offences in connection with orders etc for protection of children

A person who intentionally obstructs—

(a) any person acting under a child protection order;

(b) any person acting under an authorisation granted under section 61(1) or (2) of this Act; or

(c) a constable acting under section 61(5) of this Act,

shall, subject to section 38(3) and (4) of this Act, be guilty of an offence and shall be liable on summary conviction to a fine not exceeding level 3 on the standard scale.

Fugitive children and harbouring

82 Recovery of certain fugitive children

(1) A child who absconds—

(a) from a place of safety in which he is being kept under or by virtue of this Part of this Act;

(b) from a place (in this section referred to as a 'relevant place') which, though not a place of safety such as is mentioned in paragraph (a) above, is a residential establishment in which he is required to reside by virtue of section 70(3)(a) of this Act or a hospital or other institution in which he is temporarily residing while subject to such a requirement; or

(c) from a person who, by virtue of a supervision requirement or of section 74 of this Act, has control over him while he is being taken to, is awaiting being taken to, or (whether or not by reason of being on leave) is temporarily away from, such place of safety or relevant place,

may be arrested without warrant in any part of the United Kingdom and taken to the place of safety or as the case may be the relevant place; and a court which is satisfied that there are reasonable grounds for believing that the child is within any premises may, where there is such power of arrest, grant a warrant authorising a constable to enter those premises and search for the child using reasonable force if necessary.

(2) Without prejudice to the generality of subsection (1) above, a child who at the end of a period of leave from a place of safety or relevant place fails to return there shall, for the purposes of this section, be taken to have absconded.

(3) A child who absconds from a person who, not being a person mentioned in paragraph (c) of subsection (1) above, is a person who has control over him by virtue of a supervision requirement may, subject to the same provisions as those to which an arrest under that subsection is subject, be arrested as is mentioned in that subsection and returned to that person; and the provision in that subsection for a warrant to be granted shall apply as respects such a child as it applies as respects a child mentioned in that subsection.

(4) If a child—

(a) is taken under subsection (1) above to a place of safety or relevant place; or

(b) is returned under subsection (3) above to a person,

but the occupier of that place of safety or of that relevant place, or as the case may be that person, is unwilling or unable to receive him, that circumstance shall be intimated forthwith to the Principal Reporter.

(5) Where intimation is required by subsection (4) above as respects a child, he shall be kept in a place of safety until—

(a) in a case where he is subject to a supervision requirement, he can be brought before a children's hearing for that requirement to be reviewed; or

(b) in any other case, the Principal Reporter has, in accordance with section 56(6) of this Act, considered whether compulsory measures of supervision are required in respect of him.

83 Harbouring
A person who—
    (a) knowingly assists or induces a child to abscond in circumstances which render the child liable to arrest under subsection (1) or (3) of section 82 of this Act;
    (b) knowingly and persistently attempts to induce a child so to abscond;
    (c) knowingly harbours or conceals a child who has so absconded; or
    (d) knowingly prevents a child from returning—
        (i) to a place mentioned in paragraph (a) or (b) of the said subsection (1);
        (ii) to a person mentioned in paragraph (c) of that subsection, or in the said subsection (3),
shall, subject to section 38(3) and (4) of this Act, to section 51(5) and (6) of the Children Act 1989 and to Article 70(5) and (6) of the Children (Northern Ireland) Order 1995 (analogous provision for England and Wales and for Northern Ireland), be guilty of an offence and liable on summary conviction to a fine not exceeding level 5 on the standard scale or to imprisonment for a term not exceeding six months or to both such fine and such imprisonment.

Implementation of authorisations etc

84 Implementation of authorisations etc
Where an order, authorisation or warrant under this Chapter or Chapter 2 of this Part of this Act grants power to find a child and to keep him in a place of safety, such order, authorisation or warrant may be implemented as if it were a warrant for the apprehension of an accused person issued by a court of summary jurisdiction; and any enactment or rule of law applying to such a warrant shall, subject to the provisions of this Act, apply in like manner to the order, authorisation or warrant.

New evidence: review of establishment of grounds of referral

85 Application for review of establishment of grounds of referral
    (1) Subject to subsections (3) and (4) below, where subsection (2) below applies an application may be made to the sheriff for a review of a finding such as is mentioned in section 68(10) of this Act.
    (2) This subsection applies where the sheriff, on an application made by virtue of subsection (7) or (9) of section 65 of this Act (in this section referred to as the 'original application'), finds that any of the grounds of referral is established.
    (3) An application under subsection (1) above may only be made where the applicant claims—
    (a) to have evidence which was not considered by the sheriff on the original application, being evidence the existence or significance of which might materially have affected the determination of the original application;
    (b) that such evidence—
        (i) is likely to be credible and reliable; and
        (ii) would have been admissible in relation to the ground of referral which was found to be established on the original application; and
    (c) that there is a reasonable explanation for the failure to lead such evidence on the original application.
    (4) An application under subsection (1) above may only be made by—
    (a) the child in respect of whom the ground of referral was found to be established; or
    (b) any person who is a relevant person in relation to that child.
    (5) Where the sheriff on an application under subsection (1) above is not satisfied that any of the claims made in the application are established he shall dismiss the application.
    (6) Where the sheriff is satisfied on an application under subsection (1) above

that the claims made in the application are established, he shall consider the evidence and if, having considered it, he is satisfied that—

    (a)   none of the grounds of referral in the original application to which the application relates is established, he shall allow the application, discharge the referral to the children's hearing in respect of those grounds and proceed in accordance with subsection (7) below in relation to any supervision requirement made in respect of the child (whether or not varied under section 73 of this Act) in so far as it relates to any such ground; or

    (b)   any ground of referral in the original application to which the application relates is established, he may proceed in accordance with section 68(10) of this Act.

(7)   Where the sheriff is satisfied as is mentioned in subsection (6)(a) above, he may—

    (a)   order that any supervision requirement so mentioned shall terminate—
        (i) immediately; or
       (ii) on such date as he may specify; or

    (b)   if he is satisfied that there is evidence sufficient to establish any ground of referral, being a ground which was not stated in the original application, find such ground established and proceed in accordance with section 68(10) of this Act in relation to that ground.

(8)   Where the sheriff specifies a date for the termination of a supervision requirement in accordance with subsection (7)(a)(ii) above, he may, before such termination, order a variation of that requirement, of any requirement imposed under subsection (6) of section 70 of this Act, or of any determination made under subsection (7) of that section; and such variation may take effect—

    (a)   immediately; or
    (b)   on such date as he may specify.

(9)   Where the sheriff orders the termination of a supervision requirement in accordance with subsection (7)(a) above, he shall consider whether, after such termination, the child concerned will still require supervision or guidance; and where he considers that such supervision or guidance will be necessary he shall direct a local authority to provide it in accordance with subsection (10) below.

(10)   Where a sheriff has given a direction under subsection (9) above, it shall be the duty of the local authority to comply with that direction; but that duty shall be regarded as discharged where they offer such supervision or guidance to the child and he, being a child of sufficient age and maturity to understand what is being offered, is unwilling to accept it.

CHAPTER 4
PARENTAL RESPONSIBILITIES ORDERS, ETC

Parental responsibilities orders

86 Parental responsibilities order: general

(1)   On the application of a local authority the sheriff may make an order transferring (but only during such period as the order remains in force) the appropriate parental rights and responsibilities relating to a child to them; and any such order shall be known as a 'parental responsibilities order'.

(2)   A parental responsibilities order shall not be made unless the sheriff is satisfied that each relevant person either—

    (a)   freely, and with full understanding of what is involved, agrees unconditionally that the order be made; or

    (b)   is a person who—
        (i) is not known, cannot be found or is incapable of giving agreement;
       (ii) is withholding such agreement unreasonably;
      (iii) has persistently failed, without reasonable cause, to fulfil one or other

of the following parental responsibilities in relation to the child, that is to say the responsibility to safeguard and promote the child's health, development and welfare or, if the child is not living with him, the responsibility to maintain personal relations and direct contact with the child on a regular basis; or

(iv) has seriously ill-treated the child, whose reintegration into the same household as that person is, because of the serious ill-treatment or for other reasons, unlikely.

(3) The reference in subsection (1) above to the appropriate parental rights and responsibilities relating to the child is to all parental rights and responsibilities except any right to agree, or decline to agree—

(a) to the making of an application in relation to the child under section 18 (freeing for adoption) or 55 (adoption abroad) of the Adoption Act 1976, under section 18 or 49 of the Adoption (Scotland) Act 1978 or under Article 17, 18 or 57 of the Adoption (Northern Ireland) Order 1987 (corresponding provision for Scotland and Northern Ireland); or

(b) to the making of an adoption order.

(4) A person is a relevant person for the purposes of this section if he is a parent of the child or a person who for the time being has parental rights in relation to the child.

(5) The sheriff may, in an order under this section, impose such conditions as he considers appropriate; and he may vary or discharge such an order on the application of the local authority, of the child, of any person who immediately before the making of the order is a relevant person or of any other person claiming an interest.

(6) An order under this section shall, if not first discharged by the sheriff, terminate on the occurrence of any of the following—

(a) the child attains the age of eighteen years;

(b) he becomes the subject—

(i) of an adoption order within the meaning of the Adoption (Scotland) Act 1978; or

(ii) of an order under section 18 (freeing for adoption) or 55 (adoption abroad) of the Adoption Act 1976, under section 18 or 49 of the said Act of 1978 or under Article 17, 18 or 57 of the Adoption (Northern Ireland) Order 1987 (corresponding provision for Scotland and Northern Ireland);

(c) an order is made for his return under Part I of the Child Abduction and Custody Act 1985; or

(d) a decision, other than a decision mentioned in section 25(2) of the said Act of 1985 (decisions relating to rights of access), is registered with respect to him under section 16 of that Act.

[86A
The provisions of this Chapter are subject to Sections 2 and 3 of Chapter II of Council Regulation (EC) No 2201/2003 of 27th November 2003 concerning jurisdiction and the recognition and enforcement of judgments in matrimonial matters and matters of parental responsibility.]

87   Further provision as respects parental responsibilities orders

(1) Subject to subsections (2) and (3) below, where a parental responsibilities order is made as respects a child it shall be the duty of the local authority which applied for it (in this section and in section 88 of this Act referred to as the 'appropriate authority') to fulfil the transferred responsibilities while the order remains in force.

(2) Notwithstanding that a parental responsibilities order has been made as respects a child, the appropriate authority may allow, either for a fixed period or until the authority otherwise determine, the child to reside with a parent, guar-

dian, relative or friend of his in any case where it appears to the authority that so to allow would be for the benefit of the child.

(3) Without prejudice to any other provision of this Part of this Act, where by virtue of subsection (2) above a child is residing with a person, the appropriate authority may by notice in writing to the person require him to return the child to them by a time specified in the notice; and service of such notice shall be effected either by the authority leaving it in the person's hands or by their sending it to him, at his and the child's most recent known address, by recorded delivery service.

(4) For the purposes of any application for a parental responsibilities order, rules shall provide for the appointment, in such cases as are prescribed by such rules—

(a) of a person to act as curator *ad litem* to the child in question at the hearing of the application, safeguarding the interests of the child in such manner as may be so prescribed; and

(b) of a person (to be known as a 'reporting officer') to witness agreements to parental responsibilities orders and to perform such other duties as may be so prescribed,

but one person may, as respects the child, be appointed both under paragraph (a) and under paragraph (b) above; so however that, where the applicant is a local authority, no employee of theirs shall be appointed under either or both of those paragraphs.

(5) Rules may provide for a person to be appointed reporting officer before the application in question is made.

88 Parental contact

(1) This section applies where a parental responsibilities order is being made, or as the case may be is in force, as respects a child.

(2) The child shall, subject to subsection (3) below, be allowed reasonable contact by the appropriate authority with—

(a) each person who, immediately before the making of the parental responsibilities order, is a relevant person for the purposes of section 86 of this Act as respects the child; and

(b) where, immediately before that order was made—

(i) a residence order or contact order was in force with respect to the child, the person in whose favour the residence order or contact order was made;

(ii) a person was entitled to have the child residing with him under an order by a court of competent jurisdiction, that person.

(3) Without prejudice to subsection (4) below, on an application made to him by the child, by the appropriate authority or by any person with an interest, the sheriff may make such order as he considers appropriate as to the contact, if any, which is to be allowed between the child and any person specified in the order (whether or not a person described in paragraphs (a) and (b) of subsection (2) above).

(4) A sheriff, on making a parental responsibilities order, or at any time while such an order remains in force as respects a child, may make an order under subsection (3) above as respects the child even where no application has been made to him in that regard.

(5) An order under this section may impose such conditions as the sheriff considers appropriate; and he may vary or discharge such an order on the application of the child, the appropriate authority or any person with an interest.

(6) An order under this section shall, if not first discharged by the sheriff, terminate when the parental responsibilities order to which it is referable does.

89 Offences in relation to parental responsibilities orders

Any person who, knowingly and without lawful authority or reasonable excuse—

    (a)   fails to comply with a notice under section 87(3) of this Act;

    (b)   harbours or conceals a child—

        (i)   as respects whom a parental responsibilities order has been made; and

        (ii) who has run away, or been taken away or whose return is required by such a notice; or

    (c)   induces, assists or incites a child as respects whom any such order has been made to run away, or stay away, from a place where he is looked after or who takes away such a child from that place,

shall be guilty of an offence and liable, on summary conviction, to a fine not exceeding level 5 on the standard scale or to imprisonment for a term not exceeding six months or to both such fine and such imprisonment.

Miscellaneous

90 Consent of child to certain procedures

Nothing in this Part of this Act shall prejudice any capacity of a child enjoyed by virtue of section 2(4) of the Age of Legal Capacity (Scotland) Act 1991 (capacity of child with sufficient understanding to consent to surgical, medical or dental procedure or treatment); and without prejudice to that generality, where a condition contained, by virtue of—

    (a)   section 66(4)(a), section 67(2) or section 69(9)(a) of this Act, in a warrant; or

    (b)   section 70(5)(a) of this Act, in a supervision requirement,

requires a child to submit to any examination or treatment but the child has the capacity mentioned in the said section 2(4), the examination or treatment shall only be carried out if the child consents.

91 Procedural rules in relation to certain applications etc

    (1)   All proceedings to which this section applies are civil proceedings for the purposes of section 32 of the Sheriff Courts (Scotland) Act 1971 (power of Court of Session to regulate civil procedure in the sheriff court).

    (2)   Any reference in this Part of this Act to regulation or prescription by rules in relation to any proceedings to which this section applies shall be construed, unless the context otherwise requires, as a reference to regulation or prescription by rules made under the said section 32.

    (3)   Without prejudice to the generality of the said section 32, rules may make provision as to—

    (a)   the functions of a person appointed by the sheriff under section 41(1) of this Act and any right of that person to information relating to the proceedings;

    (b)   the circumstances in which any person who has been given notice in accordance with such rules of an application for a child assessment order, or any other person specified in the rules, may apply to the court to have that order varied or discharged;

    (c)   the persons to whom notice of the making of a child protection order shall be given by the applicant for that order, and without prejudice to that generality may in making such provision require such notice to be given to either or both of the child and any relevant person in relation to that child;

    (d)   the persons to whom notice of an application for an exclusion order or, under section 79(3) of this Act, for the recall or variation of such an order or of anything done under section 77(2) of this Act shall be given;

    (e)   the period within which a hearing shall be held under subsection (5) of section 76 of this Act after the granting of an order under subsection (4) of that section;

    (f)   the service of any exclusion order on the named person and the appropriate person within such period as may be specified in the rules.

    (4)   In relation to any proceedings to which this section applies, rules may per-

mit a party to such proceedings, in such circumstances as may be specified in the rules, to be represented by a person who is neither an advocate nor a solicitor.

(5)   This section applies to any application made to the sheriff, and any other proceeding before the sheriff (whether on appeal or otherwise), under any provision of this Part of this Act.

Interpretation of Part II

93   Interpretation of Part II

(1)   In this Part of this Act, unless the context otherwise requires,—

'accommodation' shall be construed in accordance with section 25(8) of this Act;

'chief social work officer' means an officer appointed under section 3 of the Social Work (Scotland) Act 1968;

'child assessment order' has the meaning given by section 55(1) of this Act;

'child protection order' has the meaning given by section 57(1) of this Act;

'children's hearing' shall be construed in accordance with section 39(3), but does not include a business meeting arranged under section 64, of this Act;

'compulsory measures of supervision' means, in respect of a child, such measures of supervision as may be imposed upon him by a children's hearing;

'constable' means a constable of a police force within the meaning of the Police (Scotland) Act 1967;

'contact order' has the meaning given by section 11(2)(d) of this Act;

'disabled' has the meaning given by section 23(2) of this Act;

['education authority' has the meaning given by section 135(1) of the Education (Scotland) Act 1980 (c 44);]

'exclusion order' has the meaning given by section 76(12) of this Act;

'family', in relation to a child, includes—

(a)   any person who has parental responsibility for the child; and

(b)   any other person with whom the child has been living;

'local authority' means a council constituted under section 2 of the Local Government etc (Scotland) Act 1994;

'local government area' shall be construed in accordance with section 1 of the said Act of 1994;

'parental responsibilities' has the meaning given by section 1(3) of this Act;

'parental responsibilities order' has the meaning given by section 86(1) of this Act;

'parental rights' has the meaning given by section 2(4) of this Act;

'place of safety', in relation to a child, means—

(a)   a residential or other establishment provided by a local authority;

(b)   a community home within the meaning of section 53 of the Children Act 1989;

(c)   a police station;

[(d)   a hospital, or surgery, the person or body of persons responsible for the management of which is willing temporarily to receive the child;

(e)   the dwelling-house of a suitable person who is so willing; or

(f)   any other suitable place the occupier of which is so willing.]

'the Principal Reporter' means the Principal Reporter appointed under section 127 of the said Act of 1994 or any officer of the Scottish Children's Reporter Administration to whom there is delegated, under section 131(1) of that Act, any function of the Principal Reporter under this Act;

'relevant local authority', in relation to a child who is subject to a warrant granted under this Part of this Act or to a supervision requirement, means the local authority for whose area [there is established] the children's panel from which the children's hearing which granted the warrant or imposed the supervision requirement was [constituted];

'residence order' has the meaning given by section 11(2)(c) of this Act;

'residential establishment'—

(a)   in relation to a place in Scotland, means an establishment (whether man-aged by a local authority, by a voluntary organisation or by any other person) which provides residential accommodation for children for the purposes of this Act or the Social Work (Scotland) Act 1968;

(b)   in relation to a place in England and Wales, means a community home, voluntary home or [private] children's home (within the meaning of the Children Act 1989); and

(c)   in relation to a place in Northern Ireland, means a home provided under Part VIII of the Children (Northern Ireland) Order 1995, or a voluntary home, or a registered children's home (which have respectively the meanings given by that Order);

'school age' shall be construed in accordance with section 31 of the Education (Scotland) Act 1980;

'secure accommodation' means accommodation provided in a residential estab-lishment approved [by the Scottish Ministers in accordance with relations made under section 29(9)(a) of the Regulation of Care (Scotland) Act 2001 (asp 8) or] under [section 22(8)(a) of the Care Standards Act 2000], for the purpose of restrict-ing the liberty of children;

'supervision requirement' has the meaning given by section 70(1) of this Act, and includes any condition contained in such a requirement or related to it;

'voluntary organisation' means a body (other than a public or local authority) whose activities are not carried on for profit; and

'working day' means every day except—

(a)   Saturday and Sunday;

(b)   December 25th and 26th; and

(c)   January 1st and 2nd.

(2)   For the purposes of—

(a)   Chapter 1 and this Chapter (except this section) of this Part [and section 44], 'child' means a person under the age of eighteen years; and

(b)   [Chapter 2 (except section 44) and Chapter 3 (except section 75A)] of this Part—

'child' means—

(i)   a child who has not attained the age of sixteen years;

(ii)   a child over the age of sixteen years who has not attained the age of eighteen years and in respect of whom a supervision requirement is in force; or

(iii)   a child whose case has been referred to a children's hearing by virtue of section 33 of this Act;

and for the purposes of the application of those Chapters to a person who has failed to attend school regularly without reasonable excuse includes a person who is over sixteen years of age but is not over school age; and

'relevant person' in relation to a child means—

(a)   any parent enjoying parental responsibilities or parental rights under Part I of this Act;

(b)   any person in whom parental responsibilities or rights are vested by, under or by virtue of this Act; and

(c)   any person who appears to be a person who ordinarily (and other than by reason only of his employment) has charge of, or control over, the child.

(3)   Where, in the course of any proceedings under Chapter 2 or 3 of this Part, a child ceases to be a child within the meaning of subsection (2) above, the pro-visions of those Chapters of this Part and of any statutory instrument made under those provisions shall continue to apply to him as if he had not so ceased to be a child.

(4)   Any reference in this Part of this Act to a child—

(a)   being 'in need', is to his being in need of care and attention because—

(i) he is unlikely to achieve or maintain, or to have the opportunity of achieving or maintaining, a reasonable standard of health or development unless there are provided for him, under or by virtue of this Part, services by a local authority;

(ii) his health or development is likely significantly to be impaired, or further impaired, unless such services are so provided;

(iii) he is disabled; or

(iv) he is affected adversely by the disability of any other person in his family;

(b) who is 'looked after' by a local authority, shall be construed in accordance with section 17(6) of this Act.

(5) Any reference to any proceedings under this Part of this Act, whether on an application or on appeal, being heard by the sheriff, shall be construed as a reference to such proceedings being heard by the sheriff in chambers.

PART III
ADOPTION

94–98. [*Amend Adoption (Scotland) Act 1978.*]

PART IV
GENERAL AND SUPPLEMENTAL

99   Registration of births by persons who are themselves children

(1) In paragraph (a) of section 14(1) of the Registration of Births, Deaths and Marriages (Scotland) Act 1965 (duty of father and mother to give information of particulars of birth), for the words 'father or mother of the child' substitute 'child's father or mother (whether or not they have attained the age of sixteen years)'.

(2) Where, at any time after the coming into force of the Age of Legal Capacity (Scotland) Act 1991 but before the coming into force of subsection (1) above, a person mentioned in the said paragraph (a) who had not at that time attained the age of sixteen years purported to fulfil the duty mentioned in the said section 14(1), he shall be presumed to have had legal capacity to fulfil that duty.

(3) [*amends Registration of Births, Deaths and Marriages (Scotland) Act 1965*]

(4) Where, at any time after the coming into force of the Age of Legal Capacity (Scotland) Act 1991 but before the coming into force of subsection (3) above, a person who had not at that time attained the age of sixteen years made a request, declaration, statutory declaration or application mentioned in subsection (1) or (2) of the said section 18 in relation to a child in respect of whose birth an entry was consequently made under the said subsection (1) in a register of births, or as the case may be under the said subsection (2) in the Register of Corrections etc, the person shall be presumed to have had legal capacity to make the request, declaration, statutory declaration, or application in question.

100   [*Amends Social Work (Scotland) Act 1968*]

101   Panels for curators *ad litem*, reporting officers and safeguarders

[(1) The Scottish Ministers may by regulations make provision for the establishment of one or more of each of the following—

(a) a panel of persons from which curators *ad litem* may be appointed under section 58 of the Adoption (Scotland) Act 1978 or under section 87(4) of this Act;

(b) a panel of persons from which reporting officers may be appointed under either of those sections; and

(c) a panel of persons from which appointments may be made under section 41(1) of this Act.]

(2)   Regulations under subsection (1) above may provide, without prejudice to the generality of that subsection—
  (a)   for the appointment, qualifications and training of persons who may be appointed to [those panels]; and
  (b)   for the management and organisation of persons available for appointment from [those panels].
  [(3)   Regulations under subsection (1) above may provide—
  (a)   for the defrayment by local authorities of expenses incurred by members of any panel established by virtue of that subsection; and
  (b)   for the payment by local authorities of fees and allowances for such members.
  (4)   Paragraphs 9 and 10(b) of Schedule 1 to this Act shall apply in relation to any panel established by virtue of subsection (1)(c) above as they apply in relation to children's panels.]

102   Removal of duty to report on operation of Children Act 1975
Section 105 of the Children Act 1975 (which among other things provides that every five years there shall be laid before Parliament by the Secretary of State a report on the operation of such sections of that Act as are for the time being in force) shall cease to have effect.

103   Interpretation, rules, regulations and Parliamentary control
  (1)   Any reference in this Act, or in any enactment amended by this Act, to a person having, or to there being vested in him, parental responsibilities or parental rights shall, unless the context otherwise requires, be construed as a reference to his having, or to there being so vested, any of those rights or as the case may be responsibilities.
  (2)   Any reference in this Act to something being 'prescribed' is, unless the context otherwise requires, a reference to its being prescribed by regulations; and any power conferred by this Act on the Secretary of State or the Lord Advocate to make rules or regulations shall be exercisable by statutory instrument which shall be subject to annulment in pursuance of a resolution of either House of Parliament.
  (3)   Rules or regulations made under this Act—
  (a)   may make different provision for different cases or classes of case; and
  (b)   may exclude certain cases or classes of case.

104   Financial provision
There shall be paid out of money provided by Parliament—
  (a)   any expenses of the Secretary of State incurred in consequence of the provisions of this Act; and
  (b)   any increase attributable to this Act in the sums payable out of money so provided under any other enactment.

105   Extent, short title, minor and consequential amendments, repeals and commencement
  (1)   This Act, which subject to subsections (8) to (10) below extends to Scotland only—
  (a)   may be cited as the Children (Scotland) Act 1995; and
  (b)   except for subsections (1), (2) and (6) to (10) of this section, shall come into force on such day as the Secretary of State may by order made by statutory instrument appoint;
and different days may be appointed under paragraph (b) above for different purposes.
  (2)   An order under subsection (1)(b) above may contain such transitional and consequential provisions and savings as appear to the Secretary of State to be necessary or expedient in connection with the provisions brought into force.

(3) The transitional provisions and savings contained in Schedule 3 to this Act shall have effect but are without prejudice to sections 16 and 17 of the Interpretation Act 1978 (effect of repeals).

(4) Schedule 4 to this Act, which contains minor amendments and amendments consequential upon the provisions of this Act, shall have effect.

(5) The enactments mentioned in Schedule 5 to this Act (which include spent provisions) are hereby repealed to the extent specified in the third column of that Schedule.

(6) The Secretary of State may by order made by statutory instrument make such further amendments or repeals, in such enactments as may be specified in the order, as appear to him to be necessary or expedient in consequence of any provision of this Act.

(7) A statutory instrument containing an order under subsection (6) above shall be subject to annulment in pursuance of a resolution of either House of Parliament.

(8) Sections 18, 26(2), 33, 44, 70(4), 74, 82, 83, 93 and 104 of this Act and this section extend to England and Wales, and those sections and this section (except section 70(4)) also extend to Northern Ireland; but—

(a) subsection (4) of this section so extends—

(i) to England and Wales, only in so far as it relates to paragraphs 8, 10, 19, 31, 37, 41(1), (2) and (7) to (9), 48 to 52, 54 and 55 of Schedule 4; and

(ii) to Northern Ireland, only in so far as it relates to paragraphs 31, 37, 41(1); (2) and (7) to (9), 54, 55 and 58 of that Schedule; and

(b) subsection (5) of this section so extends—

(i) to England and Wales, only in so far as it relates to the entries in Schedule 5 in respect of Part V of the Social Work (Scotland) Act 1968, the Maintenance Orders (Reciprocal Enforcement) Act 1972, section 35(4)(c) of the Family Law Act 1986, the Children Act 1989, the Child Support Act 1991 and the Education Act 1993; and

(ii) to Northern Ireland, only in so far as it relates to the entries in that Schedule in respect of Part V of the Social Work (Scotland) Act 1968, the Maintenance Orders (Reciprocal Enforcement) Act 1972 and section 35(4)(c) of the Family Law Act 1986.

(9) This section, so far as it relates to the repeal of Part V of the Social Work (Scotland) Act 1968, also extends to the Channel Islands.

(10) Her Majesty may by Order in Council direct that any of the relevant provisions specified in the Order shall extend, with such exceptions, adaptations and modifications (if any) as may be specified in the Order, to any of the Channel Islands; and in this subsection 'the relevant provisions' means sections 74, 82, 83 and 93 of this Act and any regulations made under section 74 of this Act.

SCHEDULES

SCHEDULE 1
CHILDREN'S PANELS

Appointment

1. The Secretary of State shall, for each local government area, appoint such number of members of children's panels as he considers appropriate and from among that number appoint a chairman and a deputy chairman.

2. A member of a children's panel shall hold office for such period as is specified by the Secretary of State, but may be removed from office by the Secretary of State at any time.

Children's Panel Advisory Committees

3. Subject to paragraph 8 below, each local authority shall form a body (to be known as a 'Children's Panel Advisory Committee') consisting of two members nominated by the local authority and three members nominated by the Secretary of State.

4. The Secretary of State may at the request of the local authority provide for an increase in the membership of the Children's Panel Advisory Committee appointed under paragraph 3 above by such number, not exceeding five, of additional members as the authority specify in relation to their request, the additional members to be nominated as follows—

  (a) the first, and any second or fourth additional member, by the Secretary of State;

  (b) any third or fifth additional member, by the local authority.

5. The chairman of the Children's Panel Advisory Committee shall be appointed by the Secretary of State from among such of the members he has nominated as are resident in the local government area for which the panel is appointed.

6. It shall be the duty of the Children's Panel Advisory Committee—

  (a) to submit names of possible panel members to the Secretary of State;

  (b) to advise the Secretary of State, in so far as he requires advice, on the suitability of persons referred to him as potential panel members; and

  (c) to advise the Secretary of State on such matters relating to the general administration of the panels as he may refer to them.

7. The Children's Panel Advisory Committee shall have power—

  (a) to appoint sub-committees;

  (b) to appoint to any such sub-committee a person who is not a member of the Children's Panel Advisory Committee; and

  (c) to refer all or any of the duties set out in paragraph 6 above to any such sub-committee for their advice.

Joint Advisory Committees

8.—(1) Two or more local authorities may, instead of each acting under paragraph 3 above, make arrangements to form a Children's Panel Advisory Committee for their areas (a 'joint advisory committee').

(2) A joint advisory committee shall not be formed in pursuance of arrangements made under sub-paragraph (1) above unless the authorities concerned have obtained the consent in writing of the Secretary of State.

(3) The Secretary of State may give a direction, in any case where a joint advisory committee has not been formed, to two or more local authorities requiring them to form a joint advisory committee; and they shall comply with any such direction.

(4) Paragraphs 3 to 7, 10(a) and 11(b) of this Schedule shall apply to a joint advisory committee as they apply in respect of a Children's Panel Advisory Committee and, for the purposes of those paragraphs the local authorities acting under sub-paragraph (1) above shall be regarded as a single local authority.

Recruitment and training of panel members

9. The Secretary of State may make such arrangements as he considers appropriate—

  (a) to recruit and train members, or possible members, of the children's panels; [and

  [(b) to train members, or possible members, of the Children's Panel Advisory Committees (or of any sub-committees of any of those committees).]

10. Each local authority shall make such arrangements as they consider appropriate—

(a) to enable the Children's Panel Advisory Committee to obtain names for submission to the Secretary of State as potential panel members; and

(b) to train—

(i) panel members or potential panel members; and

(ii) members or potential members of Children's Panel Advisory Committees (or of any sub-committees of any of those committees)]; and

(c) to any person appointed under paragraph 7 above,

such allowances as may be determined by the Secretary of State; and he may determine differently in relation to different cases or different classes of case.

Publication of list of members of children's panel

12. Each local authority shall publish a list of names and addresses of members of the children's panel for their area, and that list shall be open for public inspection at the principal offices of the local authority, and at any place where an electors list for the local government area is available for inspection.

SCHEDULE 2
AMENDMENTS OF THE ADOPTION (SCOTLAND) ACT 1978

[Incorporated into Adoption (Scotland) Act 1978.]

SCHEDULE 3
TRANSITIONAL PROVISIONS AND SAVINGS

Section 105(3)

1. Where, immediately before the day appointed for the coming into force of section 25 of this Act, a child is by virtue of section 15 of the 1968 Act (duty of local authority to provide for orphans, deserted children etc) in the care of a local authority, the child shall on and after that day be treated as if he had been provided with accommodation under (and within the meaning of) subsection (1) of the said section 25.

2. Sections 29 and 30 of this Act shall apply in respect of a person who, at the time when he ceased to be of school age (as defined in section 31 of the Education (Scotland) Act 1980) or at any subsequent time, was—

(a) in the care of a local authority by virtue of the said section 15 or of section 16 of the 1968 Act (assumption of parental rights and powers); or

(b) subject to a supervision requirement (within the meaning of section 44(1) of the 1968 Act),

as they apply in respect of a person who at such time was looked after (within the meaning of Part II of this Act) by a local authority.

3. Where the parental rights in respect of a child have, by a resolution under the said section 16 or under section 16A of the 1968 Act (duty of local authority in cases of necessity to assume parental rights and powers vested in a voluntary organisation), vested in a local authority and immediately before the day appointed for the coming into force of section 86 of this Act those rights remain so vested, the resolution shall on and after that day have effect as if it were a parental responsibilities order transferring the appropriate parental rights and responsibilities (as defined in subsection (3) of the said section 86) relating to the child to the authority; and any access order made under section 17B of the 1968 Act in relation to the child (with any order made under section 17C of that Act as respects the access order) being (in either case) an order which immediately before that day remains undischarged, shall on and after that day have effect as if it were an order made under section 88(3) of this Act as respects the child.

4.   Where the parental rights in respect of a child have, by a resolution under the said section 16, vested in a voluntary organisation (as defined in section 93 of this Act) and immediately before the day mentioned in paragraph 3 above those rights remain so vested, the resolution shall, notwithstanding the repeal by this Act of the said section 16, continue to have effect until one of the following occurs—

(a)   the child attains the age of eighteen years;

(b)   the resolution is rescinded by the local authority because it appears to them that their doing so would promote the child's welfare;

(c)   the period of six months commencing with that day expires;

(d)   an order is made by virtue of section 11(2)(b), or under section 86(1), of this Act in relation to the child;

(e)   an order is made under section 12 (adoption order) or 18 (order freeing for adoption) of the Adoption (Scotland) Act 1978 in relation to the child.

5.   Where the circumstance by virtue of which a resolution under the said section 16 ceases to have effect is that mentioned in sub-paragraph (c) of paragraph 4 above, the appropriate parental rights and responsibilities (defined as mentioned in paragraph 3 above) in relation to the child shall transfer forthwith to the local authority in whose area he resides; and for the purposes of sections 86(6) and 87 to 89 of this Act the transfer shall be deemed effected by a parental responsibilities order applied for by that authority.

6.   While a resolution continues to have effect by virtue of paragraph 4 above, sections 17(3A) and (6) to (10), 17A, 17B, 17D, 17E and 20(3) of the 1968 Act (together with the code of practice last published under subsection (5) of the said section 17E) shall continue to have effect in relation to the child in question notwithstanding the repeal by this Act of those sections.

7.   Where an order made under—

(a)   section 10 (power of court in actions of divorce etc to commit care of child to local authority) or 12 (power of court to provide for supervision of child) of the Matrimonial Proceedings (Children) Act 1958;

(b)   section 11 of the Guardianship Act 1973 (orders relating to care and custody of children); or

(c)   section 26 of the Adoption (Scotland) Act 1978 (provision for supervision or care where adoption order refused),

committed the care of the child to, or as the case may be placed the child under the supervision of, a local authority and immediately before the repeal by this Act of the section in question (the 'relevant repeal') that order remained undischarged, the order shall continue to have effect notwithstanding the relevant repeal until one of the following occurs—

(i)   the period of six months commencing with the date of the relevant repeal expires;

(ii)   the Court of Session direct, or the sheriff directs, that the order be discharged; or

(iii)   there is an event in consequence of which, but for the provisions (apart from this paragraph) of this Act, the order would have fallen to be discharged.

8.—(1)   Where relevant proceedings in relation to a child have been commenced and on the relevant date have not been concluded, the provisions of Part III of the 1968 Act shall continue to apply to those proceedings until the proceedings are concluded, notwithstanding the repeal of any of those provisions by this Act.

(2)   For the purposes of this paragraph, 'relevant proceedings' means any proceedings at a children's hearing under Part III of the 1968 Act, any application to the sheriff under that Part for a warrant or under section 42(2)(c) of that Act to establish any ground of referral, and any appeal under section 49 or 50 of that Act; and a reference to the commencement, or to the conclusion, of such proceedings

shall be construed in accordance with sub-paragraph (3) or, as the case may be, (4) below.

(3) Relevant proceedings are commenced when one of the following occurs—

(a) a children's hearing is arranged under section 37(4) or section 39(3) of the 1968 Act;

(b) an application under section 42(2)(c) of that Act is lodged;

(c) an appeal to the sheriff under section 49 of that Act is lodged;

(d) an application under section 50(2) of that Act is made.

(4) Relevant proceedings are concluded when one of the following occurs—

(a) the sheriff discharges the referral under section 42(5) of the 1968 Act;

(b) a children's hearing discharge the referral under section 43(2) of that Act;

(c) the period of three weeks after a children's hearing make a supervision requirement under section 44 of that Act or on remission to them under section 49(5) of that Act, expires provided that no appeal has been lodged within that period against that decision under section 49 of that Act;

(d) subject, as respects a decision under section 49(5)(b) of that Act, to head (c) above, the period of twenty-eight days after the sheriff has disposed of an appeal under section 49(4), (5) or (6) of that Act expires provided that no application has been made within that period to him to state a case under section 50(2) of that Act;

(e) the period of twenty-eight days after the sheriff has disposed of a case remitted to him under section 50(3) expires provided that no further application under the said section 50(2) has been made.

9. Where a child has been taken to a place of safety, or is being detained in such a place, in accordance with section 37(2) of the 1968 Act before the relevant date, and the first lawful day for the purposes of subsection (4) of that section is on or after that date, the child's case shall be proceeded with as if that day had been before the relevant date.

CRIMINAL LAW (CONSOLIDATION) (SCOTLAND) ACT 1995
(1995, c 39)

PART I
SEXUAL OFFENCES

Incest and related offences

1 Incest

(1) Any male person who has sexual intercourse with a person related to him in a degree specified in column 1 of the Table set out at the end of this subsection, or any female person who has sexual intercourse with a person related to her in a degree specified in column 2 of that Table, shall be guilty of incest, unless the accused proves that he or she—

(a) did not know and had no reason to suspect that the person with whom he or she had sexual intercourse was related in a degree so specified; or

(b) did not consent to have sexual intercourse, or to have sexual intercourse with that person; or

(c) was married to that person, at the time when the sexual intercourse took place, by a marriage entered into outside Scotland and recognised as valid by Scots law.

Table

Degrees of Relationship

Column 1   Column 2

1. Relationships by consanguinity

Mother	Father
Daughter	Son
Grandmother	Grandfather
Grand-daughter	Grandson
Sister	Brother
Aunt	Uncle
Niece	Nephew
Great grandmother	Great grandfather
Great grand-daughter	Great grandson

2. Relationships by adoption

Adoptive mother or former adoptive mother.	Adoptive father or former adoptive father.
Adopted daughter or former adopted daughter.	Adopted son or former adopted son.

(2)   For the purpose of this section, a degree of relationship exists in the case of a degree specified in paragraph 1 of the Table—

(a)   whether it is of the full blood or the half blood; and

(b)   even where traced through or to any person whose parents are not or have not been married to one another.

(3)   For the avoidance of doubt sexual intercourse between persons who are not related to each other in a degree referred to in subsection (1) above is not incest.

2   Intercourse with step-child

Any step-parent or former step-parent who has sexual intercourse with his or her step-child or former step-child shall be guilty of an offence if that step-child is either under the age of 21 years or has at any time before attaining the age of 18 years lived in the same household and been treated as a child of his or her family, unless the accused proves that he or she—

(a)   did not know and had no reason to suspect that the person with whom he or she had sexual intercourse was a step-child or former step-child; or

(b)   believed on reasonable grounds that that person was of or over the age of 21 years; or

(c)   did not consent to have sexual intercourse, or to have sexual intercourse with that person; or

(d)   was married to that person, at the time when the sexual intercourse took place, by a marriage entered into outside Scotland and recognised as valid by Scots law.

3   Intercourse of person in position of trust with child under 16

(1)   Any person of or over the age of 16 years who—

(a)   has sexual intercourse with a child under the age of 16 years;

(b)   is a member of the same household as that child; and

(c)   is in a position of trust or authority in relation to that child,

shall be guilty of an offence, unless the accused proves that subsection (2) below applies in his or her case.

(2)   This subsection applies where the accused—

(a)   believed on reasonable grounds that the person with whom he or she had sexual intercourse was of or over the age of 16 years; or

(b)   did not consent to have sexual intercourse, or to have sexual intercourse with that person; or

(c)   was married to that person, at the time when the sexual intercourse took place, by a marriage entered into outside Scotland and recognised as valid by Scots law.

[. . .]

Offences against children

5   Intercourse with girl under 16

(1)   [Subject to section 205A of the Criminal Procedure (Scotland) Act 1995 (imprisonment for life on further conviction of certain offences)], any person who has unlawful sexual intercourse with any girl under the age of 13 years shall be liable on conviction on indictment to imprisonment for life.

(2)   Any person who attempts to have unlawful sexual intercourse with any girl under the age of 13 years shall be liable on conviction on indictment to imprisonment for a term not exceeding [ten] years or on summary conviction to imprisonment for a term not exceeding three months.

(3)   Without prejudice to sections 1 to 4 of this Act, any person who has, or attempts to have, unlawful sexual intercourse with any girl of or over the age of 13 years and under the age of 16 years shall be liable on conviction on indictment to imprisonment for a term not exceeding [ten] years or on summary conviction to imprisonment for a term not exceeding three months.

(4)   No prosecution shall be commenced for an offence under subsection (3) above more than one year after the commission of the offence.

(5)   It shall be a defence to a charge under subsection (3) above that the person so charged—

(a)   had reasonable cause to believe that the girl was his wife; or

(b)   being a man under the age of 24 years who had not previously been charged with a like offence, had reasonable cause to believe that the girl was of or over the age of 16 years.

(6)   In subsection (5) above, 'a like offence' means an offence under—

(a)   subsection (3) above; or

(b)   section 4(1) or 10(1) of the Sexual Offences (Scotland) Act 1976 or section 5 or 6 of the Criminal Law Amendment Act 1885 (the enactments formerly creating the offences mentioned in subsection (3) above and section [9(1)] of this Act); or

(c)   section 6 of the Sexual Offences Act 1956 (the provision for England and Wales corresponding to subsection (3) above), or with an attempt to commit such an offence; or

[(cc)   any of sections 9 to 14 of the Sexual Offences Act 2003; or]

(d)   section 9(1) of this Act.

(7)   For the purposes of subsection (4) above, a prosecution shall be deemed to commence on the date on which a warrant to apprehend or to cite the accused is granted, if such warrant is executed without undue delay.

6   Indecent behaviour towards girl between 12 and 16

Any person who uses towards a girl of or over the age of 12 years and under the age of 16 years any lewd, indecent or libidinous practice or behaviour which, if used towards a girl under the age of 12 years, would have constituted an offence at common law shall, whether the girl consented to such practice or behaviour or not, be liable on conviction on indictment to imprisonment for a term not exceeding [ten] years or on summary conviction to imprisonment for a term not exceeding three months.

Procuring, prostitution etc

7 Procuring

(1)   Any person who procures or attempts to procure—

(a)   any woman under 21 years of age or girl to have unlawful sexual intercourse with any other person or persons in any part of the world; or

(b)   any woman or girl to become a common prostitute in any part of the world; or

(c)   any woman or girl to leave the United Kingdom, with intent that she may become an inmate of or frequent a brothel elsewhere; or

(d)   any woman or girl to leave her usual place of abode in the United Kingdom, with intent that she may, for the purposes of prostitution, become an inmate of or frequent a brothel in any part of the world,

shall be liable on conviction on indictment to imprisonment for a term not exceeding two years or on summary conviction to imprisonment for a term not exceeding three months.

(2)   Any person who—

(a)   by threats or intimidation procures or attempts to procure any woman or girl to have any unlawful sexual intercourse in any part of the world; or

(b)   by false pretences or false representations procures any woman or girl to have any unlawful sexual intercourse in any part of the world; or

(c)   applies or administers to, or causes to be taken by, any woman or girl any drug, matter or thing, with intent to stupefy or overpower so as thereby to enable any person to have unlawful sexual intercourse with such woman or girl,

shall be liable on conviction on indictment to imprisonment for a term not exceeding two years or on summary conviction to imprisonment for a term not exceeding three months.

(3)   A man who induces a married woman to permit him to have sexual intercourse with her by impersonating her husband shall be deemed to be guilty of rape.

(4)   A constable may arrest without a warrant any person whom he has good cause to suspect of having committed, or of attempting to commit, any offence under subsection (1) above.

10 Seduction, prostitution, etc, of girl under 16

(1)   If any person having parental responsibilities (within the meaning of section 1(3) of the Children (Scotland) Act 1995), in relation to, or having charge or care of a girl under the age of 16 years causes or encourages—

(a)   the seduction or prostitution of;

(b)   unlawful sexual intercourse with; or

(c)   the commission of an indecent assault upon,

her he shall be liable on conviction on indictment to imprisonment for a term not exceeding two years or on summary conviction to imprisonment for a term not exceeding three months.

(2)   For the purposes of this section, a person shall be deemed to have caused or encouraged the matters mentioned in paragraphs (a) to (c) of subsection (1) above upon a girl who has been seduced or indecently assaulted, or who has had unlawful sexual intercourse or who has become a prostitute, if he has knowingly allowed her to consort with, or to enter or continue in the employment of, any prostitute or person of known immoral character.

(3)   Subsections (1) and (2) above shall apply to a contravention of section 6 of this Act in like manner as they apply to an indecent assault, and any reference to the commission of such an assault or to being indecently assaulted shall be construed accordingly.

(4)   Where on the trial of any offence under this Part of this Act it is proved to the satisfaction of the court that the seduction or prostitution of a girl under the

age of 16 years has been caused, encouraged or favoured by her father, mother or guardian it shall be in the power of the court to divest such person of all authority over her, and to appoint any person or persons willing to take charge of such girl to be her guardian until she has attained the age of 21 years, or such lower age as the court may direct.

(5)   The High Court of Justiciary shall have the power from time to time to rescind or vary an order under subsection (4) above by the appointment of any other person or persons as such guardian, or in any other respect.

11   Trading in prostitution and brothel-keeping

(1)   Every male person who—

(a)   knowingly lives wholly or in part on the earnings of prostitution; or

(b)   in any public place persistently solicits or importunes for immoral purposes,

shall be liable on conviction on indictment to imprisonment for a term not exceeding two years or on summary conviction to imprisonment for a term not exceeding six months.

(2)   If it is made to appear to a court of summary jurisdiction by information on oath that there is reason to suspect that any house or any part of a house is used by a female for purposes of prostitution, and that any male person residing in or frequenting the house is living wholly or in part on the earnings of the prostitute, the court may issue a warrant authorising a constable to enter and search the house and to arrest that male person.

(3)   Where a male person is proved to live with or to be habitually in the company of a prostitute, or is proved to have exercised control, direction or influence over the movements of a prostitute in such a manner as to show that he is aiding, abetting or compelling her prostitution with any other person, or generally, he shall, unless he can satisfy the court to the contrary, be deemed to be knowingly living on the earnings of prostitution.

(4)   Every female who is proved to have, for the purposes of gain, exercised control, direction or influence over the movements of a prostitute in such a manner as to show that she is aiding, abetting or compelling her prostitution with any other person, or generally, shall be liable to the penalties set out in subsection (1) above.

(5)   Any person who—

(a)   keeps or manages or acts or assists in the management of a brothel; or

(b)   being the tenant, lessee, occupier or person in charge of any premises, knowingly permits such premises or any part thereof to be used as a brothel or for the purposes of habitual prostitution; or

(c)   being the lessor or landlord of any premises, or the agent of such lessor or landlord, lets the same or any part thereof with the knowledge that such premises or some part thereof are or is to be used as a brothel, or is wilfully a party to the continued use of such premises or any part thereof as a brothel,

shall be guilty of an offence.

(6)   A person convicted of an offence under subsection (5) above shall be liable—

(a)   in the sheriff court to a fine not exceeding level 4 on the standard scale or to imprisonment for a term not exceeding six months; and

(b)   in the district court to a fine not exceeding level 3 on the standard scale or to imprisonment for a term not exceeding three months,

or, in either case, to both such fine and imprisonment.

12   Allowing child to be in brothel

(1)   If any person having parental responsibilities (within the meaning of section 1(3) of the Children (Scotland) Act 1995), in relation to, or having charge or care of a child who has attained the age of four years and is under the age of 16

years, allows that child to reside in or to frequent a brothel, he shall be liable on conviction on indictment, or on summary conviction, to a fine not exceeding level 2 on the standard scale or alternatively, or in default of payment of such a fine, or in addition thereto, to imprisonment for a term not exceeding six months.

(2)   Nothing in this section shall affect the liability of a person to be indicted under section 9 of this Act, but upon the trial of a person under that section it shall be lawful for the jury, if they are satisfied that he is guilty of an offence under this section, to find him guilty of that offence.

Homosexual offences

13   Homosexual offences

(1)   Subject to the provisions of this section, a homosexual act in private shall not be an offence provided that the parties consent thereto and have attained the age of [16] years.

(2)   An act which would otherwise be treated for the purpose of this Act as being done in private shall not be so treated if done— . . .

   (b)   in a lavatory to which the public have, or are permitted to have, access whether on payment or otherwise.

(3)   A male person who is suffering from mental deficiency which is of such a nature or degree that he is incapable of living an independent life or of guarding himself against serious exploitation cannot in law give any consent which, by virtue of subsection (1) above, would prevent a homosexual act from being an offence; but a person shall not be convicted on account of the incapacity of such a male person to consent, of an offence consisting of such an act if he proves that he did not know and had no reason to suspect that male person to be suffering from such mental deficiency.

(4)   In this section, 'a homosexual act' means sodomy or an act of gross indecency or shameless indecency by one male person with another male person.

(5)   Subject to subsection (3) above, it shall be an offence to commit or to be party to the commission of, or to procure or attempt to procure the commission of a homosexual act—

   (a)   otherwise than in private;
   (b)   without the consent of [the] parties to the act; or
   (c)   with a person under the age of [16] years.

(6)   It shall be an offence to procure or attempt to procure the commission of a homosexual act between two other male persons.

(7)   A person who commits or is party to the commission of an offence under subsection (5) or subsection (6) above shall be liable on conviction on indictment to imprisonment for a term not exceeding two years or to a fine or to both and on summary conviction to imprisonment for a term not exceeding 3 months, or to a fine not exceeding the prescribed sum (within the meaning of section 225(8) of the Criminal Procedure (Scotland) Act 1995).

(8)   It shall be a defence to a charge of committing a homosexual act under subsection (5)(c) above that the person so charged being under the age of 24 years who had not previously been charged with a like offence, had reasonable cause to believe that the other person was of or over the age of [16] years.

[(8A)   A person under the age of 16 years does not commit an offence under subsection (5)(a) or (c) above if he commits or is party to the commission of a homosexual act with a person who has attained that age.]

(9)   A person who knowingly lives wholly or in part on the earnings of another from male prostitution or who solicits or importunes any male person for the purpose of procuring the commission of a homosexual act within the meaning of subsection (4) above shall be liable—

(a)   on summary conviction to imprisonment for a term not exceeding six months; or

(b)   on conviction on indictment to imprisonment for a term not exceeding two years.

(10)   Premises shall be treated for the purposes of sections 11(1) and 12 of this Act as a brothel if people resort to it for the purposes of homosexual acts within the meaning of subsection (4) above in circumstances in which resort thereto for heterosexual practices would have led to its being treated as a brothel for the purposes of those sections.

(11)   No proceedings for—

(a)   the offences mentioned in subsections (5) and (6) above; and

(b)   any offence under subsection (9) above which consists of soliciting or importuning any male person for the purpose of procuring the commission of a homosexual act,

shall be commenced after the expiration of twelve months from the date on which that offence was committed.

[16B   Commission of certain sexual acts outside the United Kingdom

(1)   Subject to subsection (2) below, any act done by a person in a country or territory outside the United Kingdom which—

(a)   constituted an offence under the law in force in that country or territory; and

(b)   would constitute a listed sexual offence if it had been done in Scotland, shall constitute that sexual offence.

(2)   No proceedings shall by virtue of this section be brought against any person unless he was at the commencement of this section, or has subsequently become, a British citizen or resident in the United Kingdom.

(3)   An act punishable under the law in force in any country or territory constitutes an offence under that law for the purposes of subsection (1) above, however it is described in that law.

(4)   Subject to subsection (5) below, the condition in subsection (1)(a) above shall be taken to be satisfied unless, not later than may be prescribed by Act of Adjournal, the accused serves on the prosecutor a notice—

(a)   stating that, on the facts as alleged with respect to the act in question, the condition is not in his opinion satisfied;

(b)   setting out the grounds for that opinion; and

(c)   requiring the prosecutor to prove that it is satisfied.

(5)   The court, if it thinks fit, may permit the accused to require the prosecutor to prove that the condition is satisfied without the prior service of a notice under subsection (4) above.

(6)   In proceedings on indictment, the question whether the condition is satisfied is to be decided by the judge alone.

[(6A)   A person may be proceeded against, indicted, tried and punished for any offence to which this section applies—

(a)   in any sheriff court district in Scotland in which he is apprehended or is in custody; or

(b)   in such sheriff court district as the Lord Advocate may determine, as if the offence had been committed in that district; and the offence shall, for all purposes incidental to or consequential on trial or punishment, be deemed to have been committed in that district.

(6B)   In subsection (6A) above, 'sheriff court district' shall be construed in accordance with section 307(1) (interpretation) of the Criminal Procedure (Scotland) Act 1995 (c 46).]

(7)   Subject to subsection (8) below, in this section 'listed sexual offence' means any of the following—

(a)   rape of a girl under the age of 16;

(b)   indecent assault of a person under the age of 16;

(c)   lewd, indecent or libidinous behaviour or practices;

(d)   shamelessly indecent conduct involving a person under the age of 16;

(e)   sodomy with or against a boy under the age of 16;

(f)   an offence under section 5(1) or (2) of this Act (unlawful sexual inter-course with a girl under the age of 13);

(g)   an offence under section 5(3) of this Act (unlawful sexual intercourse with a girl under the age of 16);

(h)   an offence under section 6 of this Act (indecent behaviour towards a girl between the age of 12 and 16);

(i)   an offence under section 13(5) or (6) of this Act when the homosexual act involves a person under the age of 16 (prohibition on certain homosexual acts); and

(j)   an offence under section 52 of the Civic Government (Scotland) Act 1982 (taking and distribution of indecent images of children).

(8)   'Listed sexual offence' includes—

(a)   any conspiracy or incitement to commit any such offence; and

(b)   any offence under section 293(2) of the Criminal Procedure (Scotland) Act 1995 (aiding and abetting etc the commission of statutory offences) relating to any offence mentioned in subsection (7)(f) to (j) above.]

PRIVATE INTERNATIONAL LAW (MISCELLANEOUS PROVISIONS) ACT 1995
(1995, c 42)

7   Validity and effect in Scots law of potentially polygamous marriages

(1)   A person domiciled in Scotland does not lack capacity to enter into a marriage by reason only that the marriage is entered into under a law which permits polygamy.

(2)   For the avoidance of doubt, a marriage valid by the law of Scotland and entered into—

(a)   under a law which permits polygamy; and

(b)   at a time when neither party to the marriage is already married,

has, so long as neither party marries a second spouse during the subsistence of the marriage, the same effects for all purposes of the law of Scotland as a marriage entered into under a law which does not permit polygamy.

PROTECTION FROM HARASSMENT ACT 1997
(1997, c 40)

Scotland

8   Harassment

(1)   Every individual has a right to be free from harassment and, accordingly, a person must not pursue a course of conduct which amounts to harassment of another and—

(a)   is intended to amount to harassment of that person; or

(b)   occurs in circumstances where it would appear to a reasonable person that it would amount to harassment of that person.

(2)   An actual or apprehended breach of subsection (1) may be the subject of a claim in civil proceedings by the person who is or may be the victim of the course of conduct in question; and any such claim shall be known as an action of harassment.

(3)   For the purposes of this section—

'conduct' includes speech;

'harassment' of a person includes causing the person alarm or distress; and

a course of conduct must involve conduct on at least two occasions.

(4)   It shall be a defence to any action of harassment to show that the course of conduct complained of—

(a)   was authorised by, under or by virtue of any enactment or rule of law;

(b)   was pursued for the purpose of preventing or detecting crime; or

(c)   was, in the particular circumstances, reasonable.

(5)   In an action of harassment the court may, without prejudice to any other remedies which it may grant—

(a)   award damages;

(b)   grant—

(i)   interdict or interim interdict;

(ii)   if it is satisfied that it is appropriate for it to do so in order to protect the person from further harassment, an order, to be known as a 'non-harassment order', requiring the defender to refrain from such conduct in re-lation to the pursuer as may be specified in the order for such period (which includes an indeterminate period) as may be so specified,

but a person may not be subjected to the same prohibitions in an interdict or interim interdict and a non-harassment order at the same time.

(6)   The damages which may be awarded in an action of harassment include damages for any anxiety caused by the harassment and any financial loss resulting from it.

(7)   Without prejudice to any right to seek review of any interlocutor, a person against whom a non-harassment order has been made, or the person for whose protection the order was made, may apply to the court by which the order was made for revocation of or a variation of the order and, on any such application, the court may revoke the order or vary it in such manner as it considers appropriate.

(8)   In section 10(1) of the Damages (Scotland) Act 1976 (interpretation), in the definition of 'personal injuries', after 'to reputation' there is inserted ', or injury resulting from harassment actionable under section 8 of the Protection from Har-assment Act 1997'.

9   Breach of non-harassment order

(1)   Any person who is found to be in breach of a non-harassment order made under section 8 is guilty of an offence and liable—

(a)   on conviction on indictment, to imprisonment for a term not exceeding five years or to a fine, or to both such imprisonment and such fine; and

(b)   on summary conviction, to imprisonment for a period not exceeding six months or to a fine not exceeding the statutory maximum, or to both such im-prisonment and such fine.

(2)   A breach of a non-harassment order shall not be punishable other than in accordance with subsection (1).

[(3)   A constable may arrest without warrant any person he reasonably believes is committing or has committed an offence under subsection (1).

(4)   Subsection (3) is without prejudice to any power of arrest conferred by law apart from that subsection.]

11   Non-harassment order following criminal offence

After section 234 of the Criminal Procedure (Scotland) Act 1995 there is inserted the following section—

Non-harassment orders

234A   Non-harassment order

(1)   Where a person is convicted of an offence involving harassment of a person ('the victim'), the prosecutor may apply to the court to make a non-harassment order against the offender requiring him to refrain from such conduct in relation to the victim as may be specified in the order for such

period (which includes an indeterminate period) as may be so specified, in addition to any other disposal which may be made in relation to the offence.

(2)   On an application under subsection (1) above the court may, if it is satisfied on a balance of probabilities that it is appropriate to do so in order to protect the victim from further harassment, make a non-harassment order.

(3)   A non-harassment order made by a criminal court shall be taken to be a sentence for the purposes of any appeal and, for the purposes of this subsection 'order' includes any variation or revocation of such an order made under subsection (6) below.

(4)   Any person who is found to be in breach of a non-harassment order shall be guilty of an offence and liable—

(a)   on conviction on indictment, to imprisonment for a term not exceeding 5 years or to a fine, or to both such imprisonment and such fine; and

(b)   on summary conviction, to imprisonment for a period not exceeding 6 months or to a fine not exceeding the statutory maximum, or to both such imprisonment and such fine.

(5)   The Lord Advocate, in solemn proceedings, and the prosecutor, in summary proceedings, may appeal to the High Court against any decision by a court to refuse an application under subsection (1) above; and on any such appeal the High Court may make such order as it considers appropriate.

(6)   The person against whom a non-harassment order is made, or the prosecutor at whose instance the order is made, may apply to the court which made the order for its revocation or variation and, in relation to any such application the court concerned may, if it is satisfied on a balance of probabilities that it is appropriate to do so, revoke the order or vary it in such manner as it thinks fit, but not so as to increase the period for which the order is to run.

(7)   For the purposes of this section 'harassment' shall be construed in accordance with section 8 of the Protection from Harassment Act 1997.

CRIMINAL JUSTICE (SCOTLAND) ACT 2003
(2003, asp 7)

PART 7
CHILDREN

51 Physical punishment of children

(1)   Where a person claims that something done to a child was a physical punishment carried out in exercise of a parental right or of a right derived from having charge or care of the child, then in determining any question as to whether what was done was, by virtue of being in such exercise, a justifiable assault a court must have regard to the following factors—

(a)   the nature of what was done, the reason for it and the circumstances in which it took place;

(b)   its duration and frequency;

(c)   any effect (whether physical or mental) which it has been shown to have had on the child;

(d)   the child's age; and

(e)   the child's personal characteristics (including, without prejudice to the generality of this paragraph, sex and state of health) at the time the thing was done.

(2)   The court may also have regard to such other factors as it considers appropriate in the circumstances of the case.

(3)   If what was done included or consisted of—

(a)   a blow to the head;

(b)   shaking; or

(c)   the use of an implement,

the court must determine that it was not something which, by virtue of being in exercise of a parental right or of a right derived as is mentioned in subsection (1), was a justifiable assault; but this subsection is without prejudice to the power of the court so to determine on whatever other grounds it thinks fit.

(4)   In subsection (1), 'child' means a person who had not, at the time the thing was done, attained the age of sixteen years.

(5)   *[amends Children and Young Persons (Scotland) Act 1937]*

[52   Amends Children (Scotland) Act 1995]

53   Provision by Principal Reporter of information to victims

(1)   Where the Principal Reporter has received information about a case in which it appears that an offence has been committed by a child, the Principal Reporter may provide any information about the case as is mentioned in subsection (2) to any person mentioned in subsection (3) if (and only if)—

(a)   the information is requested by the person; and

(b)   the Principal Reporter is satisfied that—

(i)   the provision of the information would not be detrimental to the best interests of the child concerned in, or any other child connected (in any way) with, the case; and

(ii)   it is appropriate in the circumstances of the case to provide the information.

(2)   The information is information as to—

(a)   what action the Principal Reporter has taken in the case; and

(b)   any disposal of the case,

in so far as the information relates to the offence.

(3)   The persons are—

(a)   any person against whom the offence appears to have been committed or, where that person is a child, any relevant person; and

(b)   any other person or class of persons, subject to such conditions, as may be prescribed.

(4)   In this section—

'child' means a person who has not attained the age of eighteen years;

'the Principal Reporter' has the same meaning as it has in Part II of the Children (Scotland) Act 1995 (c 36);

'relevant person' in relation to a child means—

(a)   any parent enjoying parental responsibilities or parental rights under Part I of that Act;

(b)   any person in whom parental responsibilities or rights are vested by, under or by virtue of that Act; and

(c)   any person who appears to be a person who ordinarily (and other than by reason only of that person's employment) has charge of, or control over, the child.

COMMISSIONER FOR CHILDREN AND YOUNG PEOPLE (SCOTLAND) ACT 2003
(2003, asp 17)

The Commissioner

1   Establishment

(1)   There is to be a Commissioner for Children and Young People in Scotland.

(2)   Schedule 1 makes further provision about the Commissioner.

2 Appointment

(1)   The Commissioner is to be an individual appointed by Her Majesty on the nomination of the Parliament.

(2)   A person is disqualified from appointment as the Commissioner if that person is, at the date when the appointment is to take effect, or in the year prior to that date has been—

(a)   a member of the Parliament;

(b)   a member of the House of Commons; or

(c)   a member of the European Parliament.

(3)   The Commissioner is to be appointed for such period, not exceeding five years, as the Parliamentary corporation may determine.

(4)   A person who has been appointed for one period as the Commissioner may be appointed for a second period (whether or not consecutive) but not for any additional period.

3 Removal

(1)   The Commissioner may be removed from office by Her Majesty if—

(a)   the Commissioner so requests; or

(b)   the Parliament has passed a resolution for removal on the ground—

(i)   that the Commissioner has breached the terms of appointment; or

(ii)   that the Parliament has lost confidence in the Commissioner's willingness, ability or suitability to carry out the functions of the office.

(2)   A resolution for removal of the Commissioner, if passed on a division, must be voted for by not less than two thirds of those voting.

Functions

4 Promoting and safeguarding rights

(1)   The general function of the Commissioner is to promote and safeguard the rights of children and young people.

(2)   In exercising that general function the Commissioner is, in particular, to—

(a)   promote awareness and understanding of the rights of children and young people;

(b)   keep under review the law, policy and practice relating to the rights of children and young people with a view to assessing the adequacy and effectiveness of such law, policy and practice;

(c)   promote best practice by service providers; and

(d)   promote, commission, undertake and publish research on matters relating to the rights of children and young people.

5 United Nations Convention and equal opportunities

(1)   In exercising functions under this Act, the Commissioner must comply with subsections (2) to (4).

(2)   The Commissioner must have regard to any relevant provisions of the United Nations Convention on the Rights of the Child.

(3)   The Commissioner must, in particular—

(a)   regard, and encourage others to regard, the best interests of children and young people as a primary consideration; and

(b)   have regard to, and encourage others to have regard to, the views of children and young people on all matters affecting them, due allowance being made for age and maturity.

(4)   The Commissioner must act in a manner which encourages equal opportunities and, in particular, the observance of the equal opportunity requirements.

6 Involving children and young people

(1)   The Commissioner must encourage the involvement of children and young people in the work of the Commissioner.

(2)   The Commissioner must, in particular, take reasonable steps to—

(a) ensure that children and young people are made aware of—
    (i) the functions of the Commissioner;
    (ii) the ways in which they may communicate with the Commissioner; and
    (iii) the ways in which the Commissioner may respond to any issues which they raise;
(b) consult children and young people on the work to be undertaken by the Commissioner; and
(c) consult organisations working with and for children and young people on the work to be undertaken by the Commissioner.

(3) In carrying out the duties under subsections (1) and (2) the Commissioner must pay particular attention to groups of children and young people who do not have other adequate means by which they can make their views known.

(4) The Commissioner must prepare and keep under review a strategy for involving children and young people in the work of the Commissioner in accordance with this section.

7 Carrying out investigations

(1) The Commissioner may carry out an investigation into whether, by what means and to what extent, a service provider has regard to the rights, interests and views of children and young people in making decisions or taking actions that affect those children and young people.

(2) The Commissioner may carry out such an investigation only if the Commissioner, having considered the available evidence on, and any information received about, the matter, is satisfied on reasonable grounds that—
(a) the matter to be investigated raises an issue of particular significance to children and young people generally or to particular groups of children and young people; and
(b) the investigation would not duplicate work that is properly the function of another person.

(3) The Commissioner may not carry out an investigation—
(a) if it would relate to a reserved matter;
(b) if it would relate only to a particular child or young person; or
(c) so far as it would relate to—
    (i) the making of decisions or taking of action in particular legal proceedings before a court or tribunal; or
    (ii) a matter which is the subject of legal proceedings before a court or tribunal.

8 Initiation and conduct of investigation

(1) Before taking any steps in the conduct of an investigation, the Commissioner must—
(a) draw up terms of reference for the investigation; and
(b) publish notice of the investigation and its terms of reference in such manner as appears to the Commissioner appropriate to bring it to the attention of persons likely to be affected by it.

(2) An investigation is to be conducted in public except to the extent that the Commissioner considers that the taking of evidence in private is necessary or appropriate.

9 Investigations: witnesses and documents

(1) The Commissioner may require any person—
(a) to give evidence on any matter within the terms of reference of an investigation; or
(b) to produce documents in the custody or control of that person which have a bearing on any such matter.

(2) The Commissioner may not impose such a requirement on any person whom the Parliament could not require, under section 23 of the Scotland Act, to

attend its proceedings for the purpose of giving evidence or to produce documents.

(3) Schedule 2 makes further provision with respect to witnesses and documents and the sanctions for non-compliance with a requirement under this section.

Reports

10 Annual report

(1) The Commissioner must lay before the Parliament annually a report on the exercise of the Commissioner's functions.

(2) The report must include—

(a) a review of issues identified by the Commissioner in the period covered by the report as being relevant to children and young people;

(b) a review of the Commissioner's activity in that period, including the steps taken to fulfil each of the Commissioner's functions;

(c) any recommendations by the Commissioner arising out of such activity; and

(d) an overview of work to be undertaken by the Commissioner in the year following the period covered by the report, including the strategy for involving children and young people in the work of the Commissioner.

11 Reports on investigations

(1) The Commissioner must, at the conclusion of any investigation, lay before the Parliament a report of the investigation.

(2) The report must contain any recommendations by the Commissioner arising out of the investigation.

(3) A report of an investigation into the activities of a person named in, or identifiable from, the report may be laid before the Parliament only if that person has, where this is reasonable and practicable, been given a copy of the draft report and an opportunity to make representations on it.

12 Other reports to Parliament

The Commissioner may lay before the Parliament such other reports on the exercise of the Commissioner's functions as the Commissioner considers necessary or appropriate.

13 Anonymity for children and young people

The Commissioner must ensure that, so far as reasonable and practicable having regard to the subject matter, a report under this Act does not name or identify any child or young person, or group of children or young people, referred to in it.

14 Publication

(1) The Commissioner must publish any report laid before the Parliament under this Act.

(2) The Commissioner may publish any other report relating to the exercise of the Commissioner's functions.

(3) Where the Commissioner publishes a report which is not specifically designed for children or young people the Commissioner must also publish a child friendly version of the report.

Defamation

15 Protection from actions of defamation

(1) For the purposes of the law of defamation—

(a) any statement made by the Commissioner or any of the Commissioner's staff—

(i) in conducting an investigation under this Act;

(ii) in communicating with any person for the purposes of such an investigation;

(iii) in a report published under this Act,
has absolute privilege;
 (b)   any other statement made by the Commissioner or any of the Commissioner's staff in pursuance of the purposes of this Act has qualified privilege; and
 (c)   any statement made to the Commissioner or any of the Commissioner's staff in pursuance of those purposes has qualified privilege.
(2) In subsection (1), 'statement' has the same meaning as in the Defamation Act 1996 (c 31).

Interpretation, commencement and short title

16 Interpretation

(1) In this Act, unless the context otherwise requires—
'action' includes failure to act and related expressions are to be construed accordingly;
'best practice' means such practice in relation to the rights of children and young people as appears to the Commissioner to be desirable;
'child friendly version', in relation to a report, means a version or summary which is specifically designed to take account, so far as practicable, of the age, understanding and usual language of any children or young people by whom it is intended that the report should be read;
'children and young people' means natural persons in Scotland who are under the age of 18 years or, if they have at any time been in the care of, or looked after by, a local authority or Northern Ireland authority, under the age of 21 years; and related expressions have corresponding meanings;
'Commissioner' means the Commissioner for Children and Young People in Scotland;
'equal opportunities' and 'equal opportunity requirements' have the same meaning as in Section L2 of Part II of Schedule 5 to the Scotland Act;
'local authority' means any council of a county, city, town, burgh, borough, district, island or other local government area in Scotland, England or Wales;
'looked after', in relation to a local authority in Scotland, has the same meaning as in section 17(6) of the Children (Scotland) Act 1995 (c 36), in relation to a local authority in England and Wales, has the same meaning as in section 22(1) of the Children Act 1989 (c 41) and in relation to a Northern Ireland authority, has the same meaning as in article 25(1) of the Children (Northern Ireland) Order 1995 (SI 1995/755);
'Northern Ireland authority' means any authority (including any Health and Social Services Board or trust) in Northern Ireland;
'Scotland Act' means the Scotland Act 1998 (c 46);
'Scottish Law Officer' means the Lord Advocate or the Solicitor General for Scotland;
'service provider' means any person providing services for children and young people but does not include a parent or guardian exercising the responsibilities imposed or the rights conferred by sections 1 and 2 of the Children (Scotland) Act 1995 (c 36); and
'terms' includes conditions.
(2) Any reference in this Act to the United Nations Convention on the Rights of the Child is to that Convention read subject to any reservations, objections or interpretative declarations by the United Kingdom for the time being in force.

17 Commencement and short title

(1) The provisions of this Act, except for—
 (a)   sections 1 to 3 and section 16;

(b)   schedule 1; and
(c)   this section,
come into force at the end of the period of six months beginning with the date of Royal Assent.

(2)   This Act may be cited as the Commissioner for Children and Young People (Scotland) Act 2003.

SCHEDULES

SCHEDULE 1
THE COMMISSIONER FOR CHILDREN AND YOUNG PEOPLE IN SCOTLAND
(introduced by section 1)

Status
1.—(1)   Neither the Commissioner nor any member of the Commissioner's staff is to be regarded as a servant or agent of the Crown or as having any status, immunity or privilege of the Crown.

(2)   The Commissioner's property is not to be regarded as property of, or property held on behalf of, the Crown.

Independence
2.—(1)   The Commissioner is not, except as provided in the provisions of this Act listed in sub-paragraph (2), subject to the direction or control of—
(a)   any member of the Parliament;
(b)   any member of the Scottish Executive; or
(c)   the Parliamentary corporation.
(2)   The listed provisions are sections 2(3) and 3(1)(b), paragraphs 4, 6(3), 7 and 10 of this schedule and paragraph 8 of schedule 2.

Validity of actings
3.   The validity of any actings of the Commissioner is not affected by—
(a)   any defect in the nomination by the Parliament for the Commissioner's appointment; or
(b)   any disqualification from appointment as Commissioner.

Remuneration and terms of appointment
4.—(1)   The Commissioner is entitled to—
(a)   a salary of such amount; and
(b)   such allowances,
as the Parliamentary corporation may determine.
(2)   The appointment of the Commissioner is otherwise on such terms as the Parliamentary corporation may determine.
(3)   The terms may include provision as to the circumstances in which the Commissioner may hold any other office or appointment.

Pensions etc
5.—(1)   The Parliamentary corporation may make arrangements for the payment of pensions, allowances and gratuities to, or in respect of, any person who has ceased to hold the office of Commissioner.
(2)   The Parliamentary corporation may, in particular—
(a)   make contributions or payments towards provision for such pensions, allowances or gratuities; and
(b)   establish and administer one or more pension schemes.

General powers

6.—(1) The Commissioner has a general power to do anything necessary or expedient for the purposes of, or in connection with, the exercise of the Commissioner's functions.

(2) In particular, the Commissioner may enter into contracts and acquire and dispose of property.

(3) The Commissioner may charge for such services as may be specified by the Scottish Ministers, by order made by statutory instrument, as chargeable services for the purposes of this Act.

(4) A statutory instrument containing an order under sub-paragraph (3) is subject to annulment in pursuance of a resolution of the Parliament.

Staff

7.—(1) The Commissioner may, with the consent of the Parliamentary corporation as to numbers, appoint staff to assist in carrying out the Commissioner's functions.

(2) The Commissioner may, with the consent of the Parliamentary corporation, determine the terms of appointment of such staff, including arrangements for the payment of pensions, allowances or gratuities to, or in respect of, any person who has ceased to be a member of staff of the Commissioner.

Delegation of authority

8. The Commissioner may authorise any person to exercise functions on behalf of the Commissioner to the extent specified in the authorisation, but any such delegation of authority does not affect the responsibility of the Commissioner for the exercise of the functions.

Financial provision

9. The Parliamentary corporation is to pay—
(a)   the salary and allowances of the Commissioner; and
(b)   any expenses properly incurred by the Commissioner in the exercise of the Commissioner's functions.

Accountable officer

10.—(1) The Parliamentary corporation is to designate the Commissioner or a member of the Commissioner's staff as the accountable officer for the purposes of this paragraph.

(2) The functions of the accountable officer are—
(a)   signing the accounts of the expenditure and receipts of the Commissioner;
(b)   ensuring the propriety and regularity of the finances of the Commissioner;
(c)   ensuring that the resources of the Commissioner are used economically, efficiently and effectively; and
(d)   where the accountable officer is not the Commissioner, the duty set out in sub-paragraph (4).

(3) The accountable officer is answerable to the Parliament for the exercise of those functions.

(4) The duty referred to in sub-paragraph (2)(d) is a duty, where the accountable officer is required to act in some way but considers that to do so would be inconsistent with the proper performance of the functions specified in sub-paragraph (2)(a) to (c), to—
(a)   obtain written authority from the Commissioner before taking the action; and
(b)   send a copy of that authority as soon as possible to the Auditor General for Scotland.

Accounts and audit

11.—(1) The Commissioner must keep proper accounts at all times and prepare annual accounts in respect of each financial year.

(2) The Commissioner must send a copy of the annual accounts to the Auditor General for Scotland for auditing.

(3) The financial year of the Commissioner is—

(a) the period beginning with the date on which the first Commissioner is appointed and ending with the 31st of March next following that date; and

(b) each successive period of twelve months ending with the 31st of March.

(4) If requested by any person, the Commissioner must make available at any reasonable time, and without charge, in printed or electronic form, the audited accounts, so that they may be inspected by that person.

Appointment of acting Commissioner

12.—(1) Where there is no Commissioner for the time being, or the Commissioner is unable to act, the Parliamentary corporation may appoint a person (whether or not a member of the Commissioner's staff) to discharge the Commissioner's functions until a new Commissioner is appointed or the Commissioner is again able to act; and a person so appointed is referred to in this Act as the 'acting Commissioner'.

(2) A person who is disqualified from appointment as the Commissioner is also disqualified from appointment as acting Commissioner.

(3) While holding office as such, the acting Commissioner is governed by the provisions of this Act, other than paragraphs 3(a) and 5 of this schedule, applying to the Commissioner.

SCHEDULE 2

INVESTIGATIONS: SUPPLEMENTARY PROVISIONS ON WITNESSES AND DOCUMENTS

(introduced by section 9)

Requirement to give evidence or produce documents

1.—(1) A requirement under section 9 is imposed by the Commissioner giving the person in question notice in writing specifying—

(a) the time and place at which the person is to attend before the Commissioner and the particular subjects concerning which that person is required to give evidence; or

(b) the documents, or types of documents, which that person is to produce, the date by which that person is to produce them, and the particular subjects concerning which they are required.

(2) Such notice must be given—

(a) in the case of an individual, by sending it, by registered post or the recorded delivery service, addressed to that person at the person's usual or last known address or, where the person has given an address for service, at that address;

(b) in any other case, by sending it, by registered post or the recorded delivery service, addressed to the person at the person's registered or principal office.

Privileges

2.—(1) A person is not obliged under this Act to answer any question or to produce any document which that person would be entitled to refuse to answer or produce in proceedings in a court in Scotland.

(2) A Scottish Law Officer or a procurator fiscal is not obliged under this Act to answer any question or to produce any document which that officer would be

entitled to decline to answer or to produce in accordance with section 27(3) or, as the case may be, section 23(10) of the Scotland Act.

Evidence on oath

3.—(1) The Commissioner may—

(a) administer an oath to any person giving evidence to the Commissioner; and

(b) require that person to take an oath.

(2) Any person who refuses to take an oath when required to do so under this paragraph is guilty of an offence and liable on summary conviction to a fine not exceeding level 5 on the standard scale or to imprisonment for a period not exceeding three months.

Admissibility of statements in subsequent criminal proceedings

4. Any statement made by a person in answer to any question which that person was obliged under this Act to answer is not admissible in any criminal proceedings against that person, except where the proceedings are in respect of perjury relating to that statement.

Offences

5.—(1) Any person to whom a notice under paragraph 1 has been duly given who, not being privileged under paragraph 2—

(a) refuses or fails to attend before the Commissioner as required by the notice;

(b) refuses or fails, when attending before the Commissioner as required by the notice, to answer any question concerning the subjects specified in the notice;

(c) deliberately alters, suppresses, conceals or destroys any document which that person is required to produce by the notice; or

(d) refuses or fails to produce any such document,

is guilty of an offence.

(2) It is a defence for a person charged with an offence under sub-paragraph (1)(a), (b) or (d) to prove that there was a reasonable excuse for the refusal or failure.

(3) A person guilty of an offence under this paragraph is liable on summary conviction to a fine not exceeding level 5 on the standard scale or to imprisonment for a period not exceeding three months.

Offences by bodies corporate and partnerships

6.—(1) Where an offence under paragraph 5 which has been committed by a body corporate is proved to have been committed with the consent or connivance of, or to be attributable to any neglect on the part of—

(a) a director, manager, secretary or other similar officer of the body corporate; or

(b) any person who was purporting to act in any such capacity,

that person, as well as the body corporate, is guilty of that offence and liable to be proceeded against accordingly.

(2) Where the affairs of a body corporate are managed by its members, sub-paragraph (1) applies in relation to the acts or defaults of a member in connection with the member's functions of management as if the member were a director of the body corporate.

(3) Where an offence under paragraph 5 which has been committed by a partnership is proved to have been committed with the consent or connivance of, or to be attributable to any neglect on the part of, a partner, the partner as well as the partnership is guilty of that offence and liable to be proceeded against accordingly.

Producing copies or extracts

7. For the purposes of section 9 and this schedule a person complies with a requirement to produce a document if that person produces a copy of, or an extract of the relevant part of, the document.

Allowances and expenses

8. The Commissioner may pay such allowances and expenses to persons giving evidence before the Commissioner or producing documents which they have been required or requested to produce as the Commissioner may, with the agreement of the Parliamentary corporation, determine.

GENDER RECOGNITION ACT 2004
(2004, c 7)

Applications for gender recognition certificate

1   Applications

(1)   A person of either gender who is aged at least 18 may make an application for a gender recognition certificate on the basis of—

    (a)   living in the other gender, or

    (b)   having changed gender under the law of a country or territory outside the United Kingdom.

(2)   In this Act 'the acquired gender', in relation to a person by whom an application under subsection (1) is or has been made, means—

    (a)   in the case of an application under paragraph (a) of that subsection, the gender in which the person is living, or

    (b)   in the case of an application under paragraph (b) of that subsection, the gender to which the person has changed under the law of the country or territory concerned.

(3)   An application under subsection (1) is to be determined by a Gender Recognition Panel.

(4)   Schedule 1 (Gender Recognition Panels) has effect.

2   Determination of applications

(1)   In the case of an application under section 1(1)(a), the Panel must grant the application if satisfied that the applicant—

    (a)   has or has had gender dysphoria,

    (b)   has lived in the acquired gender throughout the period of two years ending with the date on which the application is made,

    (c)   intends to continue to live in the acquired gender until death, and

    (d)   complies with the requirements imposed by and under section 3.

(2)   In the case of an application under section 1(1)(b), the Panel must grant the application if satisfied—

    (a)   that the country or territory under the law of which the applicant has changed gender is an approved country or territory, and

    (b)   that the applicant complies with the requirements imposed by and under section 3.

(3)   The Panel must reject an application under section 1(1) if not required by subsection (1) or (2) to grant it.

(4)   In this Act 'approved country or territory' means a country or territory prescribed by order made by the Secretary of State after consulting the Scottish Ministers and the Department of Finance and Personnel in Northern Ireland.

3   Evidence

(1)   An application under section 1(1)(a) must include either—

    (a)   a report made by a registered medical practitioner practising in the field of gender dysphoria and a report made by another registered medical practitioner (who may, but need not, practise in that field), or

(b)   a report made by a chartered psychologist practising in that field and a report made by a registered medical practitioner (who may, but need not, practise in that field).

(2)   But subsection (1) is not complied with unless a report required by that subsection and made by—

(a)   a registered medical practitioner, or

(b)   a chartered psychologist,

practising in the field of gender dysphoria includes details of the diagnosis of the applicant's gender dysphoria.

(3)   And subsection (1) is not complied with in a case where—

(a)   the applicant has undergone or is undergoing treatment for the purpose of modifying sexual characteristics, or

(b)   treatment for that purpose has been prescribed or planned for the applicant,

unless at least one of the reports required by that subsection includes details of it.

(4)   An application under section 1(1)(a) must also include a statutory declaration by the applicant that the applicant meets the conditions in section 2(1)(b) and (c).

(5)   An application under section 1(1)(b) must include evidence that the applicant has changed gender under the law of an approved country or territory.

(6)   Any application under section 1(1) must include—

(a)   a statutory declaration as to whether or not the applicant is married [or a civil partner],

(b)   any other information or evidence required by an order made by the Secretary of State, and

(c)   any other information or evidence which the Panel which is to determine the application may require, and may include any other information or evidence which the applicant wishes to include.

(7)   The Secretary of State may not make an order under subsection (6)(b) without consulting the Scottish Ministers and the Department of Finance and Personnel in Northern Ireland.

(8)   If the Panel which is to determine the application requires information or evidence under subsection (6)(c) it must give reasons for doing so.

4   Successful applications

(1)   If a Gender Recognition Panel grants an application under section 1(1) it must issue a gender recognition certificate to the applicant.

(2)   Unless the applicant is married [or a civil partner], the certificate is to be a full gender recognition certificate.

(3)   If the applicant is married [or a civil partner], the certificate is to be an interim gender recognition certificate.

(4)   Schedule 2 (annulment or dissolution of marriage after issue of interim gender recognition certificate) has effect.

(5)   The Secretary of State may, after consulting the Scottish Ministers and the Department of Finance and Personnel in Northern Ireland, specify the content and form of gender recognition certificates.

5   [Issue of full certificates where applicant has been married]

(1)   A court which—

(a)   makes absolute a decree of nullity granted on the ground that an interim gender recognition certificate has been issued to a party to the marriage, or

(b)   (in Scotland) grants a decree of divorce on that ground, must, on doing so, issue a full gender recognition certificate to that party and send a copy to the Secretary of State.

(2)   If an interim gender recognition certificate has been issued to a person and either—

(a)   the person's marriage is dissolved or annulled (otherwise than on the ground mentioned in subsection (1)) in proceedings instituted during the period of six months beginning with the day on which it was issued, or

(b)   the person's spouse dies within that period,

the person may make an application for a full gender recognition certificate at any time within the period specified in subsection (3) (unless the person is again married [or is a civil partner).

(3)   That period is the period of six months beginning with the day on which the marriage is dissolved or annulled or the death occurs.

(4)   An application under subsection (2) must include evidence of the dissolution or annulment of the marriage and the date on which proceedings for it were instituted, or of the death of the spouse and the date on which it occurred.

(5)   An application under subsection (2) is to be determined by a Gender Recognition Panel.

(6)   The Panel—

(a)   must grant the application if satisfied that the applicant [is neither married nor a civil partner], and

(b)   otherwise must reject it.

(7)   If the Panel grants the application it must issue a full gender recognition certificate to the applicant.

[5A   Issue of full certificates where applicant has been a civil partner

(1)   A court which—

(a)   makes final a nullity order made on the ground that an interim gender recognition certificate has been issued to a civil partner, or

(b)   (in Scotland) grants a decree of dissolution on that ground,

must, on doing so, issue a full gender recognition certificate to that civil partner and send a copy to the Secretary of State.

(2)   If an interim gender recognition certificate has been issued to a person and either—

(a)   the person's civil partnership is dissolved or annulled (otherwise than on the ground mentioned in subsection (1)) in proceedings instituted during the period of six months beginning with the day on which it was issued, or

(b)   the person's civil partner dies within that period,

the person may make an application for a full gender recognition certificate at any time within the period specified in subsection (3) (unless the person is again a civil partner or is married).

(3)   That period is the period of six months beginning with the day on which the civil partnership is dissolved or annulled or the death occurs.

(4)   An application under subsection (2) must include evidence of the dissolution or annulment of the civil partnership and the date on which proceedings for it were instituted, or of the death of the civil partner and the date on which it occurred.

(5)   An application under subsection (2) is to be determined by a Gender Recognition Panel.

(6)   The Panel—

(a)   must grant the application if satisfied that the applicant is neither a civil partner nor married, and

(b)   otherwise must reject it.

(7)   If the Panel grants the application it must issue a full gender recognition certificate to the applicant.]

6   Errors in certificates

(1)   Where a gender recognition certificate has been issued to a person, the

person or the Secretary of State may make an application for a corrected certificate
on the ground that the certificate which has been issued contains an error.

(2)   If the certificate was issued by a court the application is to be determined
by the court but in any other case it is to be determined by a Gender Recognition
Panel.

(3)   The court or Panel—

(a)   must grant the application if satisfied that the gender recognition certificate contains an error, and

(b)   otherwise must reject it.

(4)   If the court or Panel grants the application it must issue a corrected gender
recognition certificate to the applicant.

7   Applications: supplementary

(1)   An application to a Gender Recognition Panel under section 1(1), 5(2)
[, 5A(2)] or 6(1) must be made in a form and manner specified by the Secretary of
State after consulting the Scottish Ministers and the Department of Finance and
Personnel in Northern Ireland.

(2)   The applicant must pay to the Secretary of State a non-refundable fee of an
amount prescribed by order made by the Secretary of State unless the application
is made in circumstances in which, in accordance with provision made by the
order, no fee is payable; and fees of different amounts may be prescribed for different circumstances.

8   Appeals etc

(1)   An applicant to a Gender Recognition Panel under section 1(1), 5(2) [,
5A(2)] or 6(1) may appeal to the High Court or Court of Session on a point
of law against a decision by the Panel to reject the application.

(2)   An appeal under subsection (1) must be heard in private if the applicant so
requests.

(3)   On such an appeal the court must—

(a)   allow the appeal and issue the certificate applied for,

(b)   allow the appeal and refer the matter to the same or another Panel for reconsideration, or

(c)   dismiss the appeal.

(4)   If an application under section 1(1) is rejected, the applicant may not make
another application before the end of the period of six months beginning with the
date on which it is rejected.

(5)   If an application under section 1(1), 5(2) [, 5A(2)] or 6(1) is granted but the
Secretary of State considers that its grant was secured by fraud, the Secretary of
State may refer the case to the High Court or Court of Session.

(6)   On a reference under subsection (5) the court—

(a)   must either quash or confirm the decision to grant the application, and

(b)   if it quashes it, must revoke the gender recognition certificate issued on
the grant of the application and may make any order which it considers appropriate in consequence of, or otherwise in connection with, doing so.

Consequences of issue of gender recognition certificate etc

9   General

(1)   Where a full gender recognition certificate is issued to a person, the person's gender becomes for all purposes the acquired gender (so that, if the acquired
gender is the male gender, the person's sex becomes that of a man and, if it is the
female gender, the person's sex becomes that of a woman).

(2)   Subsection (1) does not affect things done, or events occurring, before the
certificate is issued; but it does operate for the interpretation of enactments passed,
and instruments and other documents made, before the certificate is issued (as
well as those passed or made afterwards).

(3)   Subsection (1) is subject to provision made by this Act or any other enactment or any subordinate legislation.

10   Registration

(1)   Where there is a UK birth register entry in relation to a person to whom a full gender recognition certificate is issued, the Secretary of State must send a copy of the certificate to the appropriate Registrar General.

(2)   In this Act 'UK birth register entry', in relation to a person to whom a full gender recognition certificate is issued, means—

    (a)   an entry of which a certified copy is kept by a Registrar General, or

    (b)   an entry in a register so kept,

containing a record of the person's birth or adoption (or, if there would otherwise be more than one, the most recent).

(3)   'The appropriate Registrar General' means whichever of—

    (a)   the Registrar General for England and Wales,

    (b)   the Registrar General for Scotland, or

    (c)   the Registrar General for Northern Ireland,

keeps a certified copy of the person's UK birth register entry or the register containing that entry.

(4)   Schedule 3 (provisions about registration) has effect.

11   Marriage

Schedule 4 (amendments of marriage law) has effect.

12   Parenthood

The fact that a person's gender has become the acquired gender under this Act does not affect the status of the person as the father or mother of a child.

13   Social security benefits and pensions

Schedule 5 (entitlement to benefits and pensions) has effect.

14   Discrimination

Schedule 6 (amendments of Sex Discrimination Act 1975 (c 65) and Sex Discrimination (Northern Ireland) Order 1976 (SI 1976/1042 (NI 15))) has effect.

15   Succession etc

The fact that a person's gender has become the acquired gender under this Act does not affect the disposal or devolution of property under a will or other instrument made before the appointed day.

16   Peerages etc

The fact that a person's gender has become the acquired gender under this Act—

    (a)   does not affect the descent of any peerage or dignity or title of honour, and

    (b)   does not affect the devolution of any property limited (expressly or not) by a will or other instrument to devolve (as nearly as the law permits) along with any peerage or dignity or title of honour unless an intention that it should do so is expressed in the will or other instrument.

17   Trustees and personal representatives

(1)   A trustee or personal representative is not under a duty, by virtue of the law relating to trusts or the administration of estates, to enquire, before conveying or distributing any property, whether a full gender recognition certificate has been issued to any person or revoked (if that fact could affect entitlement to the property).

(2)   A trustee or personal representative is not liable to any person by reason of a conveyance or distribution of the property made without regard to whether a full gender recognition certificate has been issued to any person or revoked if the trustee or personal representative has not received notice of the fact before the conveyance or distribution.

(3)   This section does not prejudice the right of a person to follow the property, or any property representing it, into the hands of another person who has received it unless that person has purchased it for value in good faith and without notice.

18   Orders where expectations defeated

(1)   This section applies where the disposition or devolution of any property under a will or other instrument (made on or after the appointed day) is different from what it would be but for the fact that a person's gender has become the acquired gender under this Act.

(2)   A person may apply to the High Court or Court of Session for an order on the ground of being adversely affected by the different disposition or devolution of the property.

(3)   The court may, if it is satisfied that it is just to do so, make in relation to any person benefiting from the different disposition or devolution of the property such order as it considers appropriate.

(4)   An order may, in particular, make provision for—
  (a)   the payment of a lump sum to the applicant,
  (b)   the transfer of property to the applicant,
  (c)   the settlement of property for the benefit of the applicant,
  (d)   the acquisition of property and either its transfer to the applicant or its settlement for the benefit of the applicant.

(5)   An order may contain consequential or supplementary provisions for giving effect to the order or for ensuring that it operates fairly as between the applicant and the other person or persons affected by it; and an order may, in particular, confer powers on trustees.

19   Sport

(1)   A body responsible for regulating the participation of persons as competitors in an event or events involving a gender-affected sport may, if subsection (2) is satisfied, prohibit or restrict the participation as competitors in the event or events of persons whose gender has become the acquired gender under this Act.

(2)   This subsection is satisfied if the prohibition or restriction is necessary to secure—
  (a)   fair competition, or
  (b)   the safety of competitors,
at the event or events.

(3)   'Sport' means a sport, game or other activity of a competitive nature.

(4)   A sport is a gender-affected sport if the physical strength, stamina or physique of average persons of one gender would put them at a disadvantage to average persons of the other gender as competitors in events involving the sport.

(5)   This section does not affect—
  (a)   section 44 of the Sex Discrimination Act 1975 (c 65) (exception from Parts 2 to 4 of that Act for acts related to sport), or
  (b)   Article 45 of the Sex Discrimination (Northern Ireland) Order 1976 (SI 1976/1042 (NI 15)) (corresponding provision for Northern Ireland).

20   Gender-specific offences

(1)   Where (apart from this subsection) a relevant gender-specific offence could be committed or attempted only if the gender of a person to whom a full gender recognition certificate has been issued were not the acquired gender, the fact that the person's gender has become the acquired gender does not prevent the offence being committed or attempted.

(2)   An offence is a 'relevant gender-specific offence' if—
  (a)   either or both of the conditions in subsection (3) are satisfied, and
  (b)   the commission of the offence involves the accused engaging in sexual activity.

(3)   The conditions are—

(a)   that the offence may be committed only by a person of a particular gender, and

(b)   that the offence may be committed only on, or in relation to, a person of a particular gender,

and the references to a particular gender include a gender identified by reference to the gender of the other person involved.

21   Foreign gender change and marriage

(1)   A person's gender is not to be regarded as having changed by reason only that it has changed under the law of a country or territory outside the United Kingdom.

(2)   Accordingly, a person is not to be regarded as being married by reason of having entered into a foreign post-recognition marriage.

(3)   But if a full gender recognition certificate is issued to a person who has entered into a foreign post-recognition marriage, after the issue of the certificate the marriage is no longer to be regarded as being void on the ground that (at the time when it was entered into) the parties to it were not respectively male and female.

(4)   However, subsection (3) does not apply to a foreign post-recognition marriage if a party to it has entered into a later (valid) marriage [or civil partnership] before the issue of the full gender recognition certificate.

(5)   For the purposes of this section a person has entered into a foreign post-recognition marriage if (and only if)—

(a)   the person has entered into a marriage in accordance with the law of a country or territory outside the United Kingdom,

(b)   before the marriage was entered into the person had changed gender under the law of that or any other country or territory outside the United Kingdom,

(c)   the other party to the marriage was not of the gender to which the person had changed under the law of that country or territory, and

(d)   by virtue of subsection (1) the person's gender was not regarded as having changed under the law of any part of the United Kingdom.

Supplementary

22   Prohibition on disclosure of information

(1)   It is an offence for a person who has acquired protected information in an official capacity to disclose the information to any other person.

(2)   'Protected information' means information which relates to a person who has made an application under section 1(1) and which—

(a)   concerns that application or any application by the person under section 5(2) [, 5A(2)] or 6(1), or

(b)   if the application under section 1(1) is granted, otherwise concerns the person's gender before it becomes the acquired gender.

(3)   A person acquires protected information in an official capacity if the person acquires it—

(a)   in connection with the person's functions as a member of the civil service, a constable or the holder of any other public office or in connection with the functions of a local or public authority or of a voluntary organisation,

(b)   as an employer, or prospective employer, of the person to whom the information relates or as a person employed by such an employer or prospective employer, or

(c)   in the course of, or otherwise in connection with, the conduct of business or the supply of professional services.

(4)   But it is not an offence under this section to disclose protected information relating to a person if—

(a)   the information does not enable that person to be identified,

(b) that person has agreed to the disclosure of the information,

(c) the information is protected information by virtue of subsection (2)(b) and the person by whom the disclosure is made does not know or believe that a full gender recognition certificate has been issued,

(d) the disclosure is in accordance with an order of a court or tribunal,

(e) the disclosure is for the purpose of instituting, or otherwise for the purposes of, proceedings before a court or tribunal,

(f) the disclosure is for the purpose of preventing or investigating crime,

(g) the disclosure is made to the Registrar General for England and Wales, the Registrar General for Scotland or the Registrar General for Northern Ireland,

(h) the disclosure is made for the purposes of the social security system or a pension scheme,

(i) the disclosure is in accordance with provision made by an order under subsection (5), or

(j) the disclosure is in accordance with any provision of, or made by virtue of, an enactment other than this section.

(5) The Secretary of State may by order make provision prescribing circumstances in which the disclosure of protected information is not to constitute an offence under this section.

(6) The power conferred by subsection (5) is exercisable by the Scottish Ministers (rather than the Secretary of State) where the provision to be made is within the legislative competence of the Scottish Parliament.

(7) An order under subsection (5) may make provision permitting—

(a) disclosure to specified persons or persons of a specified description,

(b) disclosure for specified purposes,

(c) disclosure of specified descriptions of information, or

(d) disclosure by specified persons or persons of a specified description.

(8) A person guilty of an offence under this section is liable on summary conviction to a fine not exceeding level 5 on the standard scale.

23 Power to modify statutory provisions

(1) The Secretary of State may by order make provision for modifying the operation of any enactment or subordinate legislation in relation to—

(a) persons whose gender has become the acquired gender under this Act, or

(b) any description of such persons.

(2) The power conferred by subsection (1) is exercisable by the Scottish Ministers (rather than the Secretary of State) where the provision to be made is within the legislative competence of the Scottish Parliament.

(3) The appropriate Northern Ireland department may by order make provision for modifying the operation of any enactment or subordinate legislation which deals with a transferred matter in relation to—

(a) persons whose gender has become the acquired gender under this Act, or

(b) any description of such persons.

(4) In subsection (3)—

'the appropriate Northern Ireland department', in relation to any enactment or subordinate legislation which deals with a transferred matter, means the Northern Ireland department which has responsibility for that matter,

'deals with' is to be construed in accordance with section 98(2) and (3) of the Northern Ireland Act 1998 (c 47), and

'transferred matter' has the meaning given by section 4(1) of that Act.

(5) Before an order is made under this section, appropriate consultation must be undertaken with persons likely to be affected by it.

24 Orders and regulations

(1) Any power of the Secretary of State, the Chancellor of the Exchequer, the Scottish Ministers or a Northern Ireland department to make an order under this

Act includes power to make any appropriate incidental, supplementary, consequential or transitional provision or savings.

(2)   Any power of the Secretary of State, the Chancellor of the Exchequer or the Scottish Ministers to make an order under this Act, and any power of the Registrar General for England and Wales or the Registrar General for Scotland to make regulations under this Act, is exercisable by statutory instrument.

(3)   No order may be made under section 2 or paragraph 11 of Schedule 3 unless a draft of the statutory instrument containing the order has been laid before, and approved by a resolution of, each House of Parliament.

(4)   A statutory instrument containing an order made by the Secretary of State under section 7, 22 or 23 is subject to annulment in pursuance of a resolution of either House of Parliament.

(5)   A statutory instrument containing an order made by the Scottish Ministers under section 22 or 23 is subject to annulment in pursuance of a resolution of the Scottish Parliament.

(6)   Any power of a Northern Ireland department to make an order or regulations under this Act is exercisable by statutory rule for the purposes of the Statutory Rules (Northern Ireland) Order 1979 (SI 1979/1573 (NI 12)).

(7)   Orders and regulations made by a Northern Ireland department under this Act are subject to negative resolution (within the meaning of section 41(6) of the Interpretation Act (Northern Ireland) 1954 (c 33 (NI))).

25   Interpretation

In this Act—

'the acquired gender' is to be construed in accordance with section 1(2),

'approved country or territory' has the meaning given by section 2(4),

'the appointed day' means the day appointed by order under section 26,

'chartered psychologist' means a person for the time being listed in the British Psychological Society's Register of Chartered Psychologists,

'enactment' includes an enactment contained in an Act of the Scottish Parliament or in any Northern Ireland legislation,

'full gender recognition certificate' and 'interim gender recognition certificate' mean the certificates issued as such under section 4 [, 5 or 5A] and 'gender recognition certificate' means either of those sorts of certificate,

'gender dysphoria' means the disorder variously referred to as gender dysphoria, gender identity disorder and transsexualism,

'Gender Recognition Panel' (and 'Panel') is to be construed in accordance with Schedule 1,

'subordinate legislation' means an Order in Council, an order, rules, regulations, a scheme, a warrant, bye-laws or any other instrument made under an enactment, and

'UK birth register entry' has the meaning given by section 10(2).

26   Commencement

Apart from sections 23 to 25, this section and sections 28 and 29, this Act does not come into force until such day as the Secretary of State may appoint by order made after consulting the Scottish Ministers and the Department of Finance and Personnel in Northern Ireland.

27   Applications within two years of commencement

(1)   This section applies where applications are made under section 1(1)(a) during the period of two years beginning with the appointed day ('the initial period').

(2)   Section 2(1)(a) has effect as if there were inserted at the end 'or has undergone surgical treatment for the purpose of modifying sexual characteristics,'.

(3)   In the case of an application which—

(a)   is made during the first six months of the initial period, or

(b)   is made during the rest of the initial period and is based on the applicant having undergone surgical treatment for the purpose of modifying sexual characteristics,

section 2(1)(b) has effect as if for 'two' there were substituted 'six'.

(4)   Subsections (5) and (6) apply in the case of an application to which subsection (3) applies and in the case of an application—

(a)   made during the rest of the initial period,

(b)   based on the applicant having or having had gender dysphoria, and

(c)   including a statutory declaration by the applicant that the applicant has lived in the acquired gender throughout the period of six years ending with the date on which the application is made.

(5)   Section 3 has effect as if for subsections (1) to (3) there were substituted—

'(1)   An application under section 1(1)(a) must include either—

(a)   a report made by a registered medical practitioner, or

(b)   a report made by a chartered psychologist practising in the field of gender dysphoria.

(2)   Where the application is based on the applicant having or having had gender dysphoria—

(a)   the reference in subsection (1) to a registered medical practitioner is to one practising in the field of gender dysphoria, and

(b)   that subsection is not complied with unless the report includes details of the diagnosis of the applicant's gender dysphoria.

(3)   Subsection (1) is not complied with in a case where—

(a)   the applicant has undergone or is undergoing treatment for the purpose of modifying sexual characteristics, or

(b)   treatment for that purpose has been prescribed or planned for the applicant, unless the report required by that subsection includes details of it.'

(6)   Paragraph 4(2) of Schedule 1 has effect with the omission of paragraph (b).

28   Extent

(2)   The following provisions extend only to Scotland—

(a)   section 24(5),

(b)   Part 2 of Schedule 2,

(c)   Part 2 of Schedule 3, and

(d)   Part 2 of Schedule 4.

(3)   The following provisions extend only to England and Wales and Scotland—

(a)   paragraphs 12, 14 and 16 of Schedule 5, and

(b)   Part 1 of Schedule 6.

29   Short title

(1)   This Act may be cited as the Gender Recognition Act 2004.

(2)   Nothing in this Act shall impose any charge on the people or on public funds, or vary the amount or incidence of or otherwise alter any such charge in any manner, or affect the assessment, levying, administration or application of any money raised by any such charge.

SCHEDULES

SCHEDULE 1
GENDER RECOGNITION PANELS

Section 1

List of persons eligible to sit

1.—(1)   The Lord Chancellor must, after consulting the Scottish Ministers and the Department of Finance and Personnel in Northern Ireland, make appointments to a list of persons eligible to sit as members of Gender Recognition Panels.

(2)   The only persons who may be appointed to the list are persons who—
    (a)   have a relevant legal qualification ('legal members'), or
    (b)   are registered medical practitioners or chartered psychologists ('medical members').
(3)   The following have a relevant legal qualification—
    (a)   a person who has a 7 year general qualification within the meaning of section 71 of the Courts and Legal Services Act 1990 (c 41),
    (b)   an advocate or solicitor in Scotland of at least seven years' standing, and
    (c)   a member of the Bar of Northern Ireland or solicitor of the Supreme Court of Northern Ireland of at least seven years' standing.

President
2.—(1)   The Lord Chancellor must, after consulting the Scottish Ministers and the Department of Finance and Personnel in Northern Ireland—
    (a)   appoint one of the legal members to be the President of Gender Recognition Panels ('the President'), and
    (b)   appoint another of the legal members to be the Deputy President of Gender Recognition Panels ('the Deputy President').
(2)   The Deputy President has the functions of the President—
    (a)   if the President is unavailable, and
    (b)   during any vacancy in the office of President.

Tenure of persons appointed to list
3.   Persons on the list—
    (a)   hold and vacate their appointments in accordance with the terms on which they are appointed, and
    (b)   are eligible for re-appointment at the end of their period of appointment.

Membership of Panels
4.—(1)   The President must make arrangements for determining the membership of Panels.
(2)   The arrangements must ensure that a Panel determining an application under section 1(1)(a) includes—
    (a)   at least one legal member, and
    (b)   at least one medical member.
5.   The arrangements must ensure that a Panel determining an application under section 1(1)(b), 5(2) [, 5A(2)] or 6(1) includes at least one legal member.

Procedure
6.—(1)   Where a Panel consists of more than one member, either the President or Deputy President or another legal member nominated by the President must preside.
(2)   Decisions of a Panel consisting of more than one member may be taken by majority vote (and, if its members are evenly split, the member presiding has a casting vote).
(3)   Panels are to determine applications in private.
(4)   A Panel must determine an application without a hearing unless the Panel considers that a hearing is necessary.
(5)   The President may, after consulting the Council on Tribunals, give directions about the practice and procedure of Panels.
(6)   Panels must give reasons for their decisions.
(7)   Where a Panel has determined an application, the Secretary of State must communicate to the applicant the Panel's decision and its reasons for making its decision.

Staff and facilities
    7.   The Secretary of State may make staff and other facilities available to Panels.

Money
    8.—(1)   The Secretary of State may pay sums by way of remuneration, allow-
ances and expenses to members of Panels.
    (2)   The Secretary of State may pay compensation to a person who ceases to be
on the list if the Secretary of State thinks it appropriate to do so because of special
circumstances.

Disqualification
    9.   In Part 3 of Schedule 1 to the House of Commons Disqualification Act
1975 (c 24) (offices disqualifying person from membership of House of Commons),
at the appropriate place insert—
        'Person on the list of those eligible to sit as members of a Gender
        Recognition Panel.'
    10.   In Part 3 of Schedule 1 to the Northern Ireland Assembly Disqualification
Act 1975 (c 25) (offices disqualifying persons from membership of Northern Ireland
Assembly), at the appropriate place insert—
        'Person on the list of those eligible to sit as members of a Gender Recog-
        nition Panel.'

SCHEDULE 2
INTERIM CERTIFICATES: MARRIAGE
Section 4

[Part 2. Scotland amends the Divorce (Scotland) Act 1976]

SCHEDULE 3
REGISTRATION
Section 10

PART 2
SCOTLAND

Introductory
    12.   In this Part—
    'the Registrar General' means the Registrar General for Scotland, and 'the 1965
Act' means the Registration of Births, Deaths and Marriages (Scotland) Act 1965
(c 49).

Gender Recognition Register
    13.—(1)   The Registrar General must maintain, in the General Register Office of
Births, Deaths and Marriages in Scotland, a register to be called the Gender Recognition Register.
    (2)   In this Part 'the Gender Recognition Register' means the register main-
tained under sub-paragraph (1).
    (3)   The form in which the Gender Recognition Register is maintained is to be
determined by the Registrar General.
    (4)   The Gender Recognition Register is not to be open to public inspection or
search.

Entries in Gender Recognition Register
    14.—(1)   If the Registrar General receives under section 10(1) a copy of a full
gender recognition certificate issued to a person, the Registrar General must—
        (a)   make an entry in the Gender Recognition Register containing such parti-

culars as may be prescribed in relation to the person's birth and any other prescribed matter, and

(b)   otherwise than by annotating in any way the birth register, make traceable the connection between the UK birth register entry and the entry in the Gender Recognition Register.

(2)   Sub-paragraph (1) does not apply if the gender recognition certificate was issued after an application under section 6(1) and that sub-paragraph has already been complied with in relation to the person.

(3)   Information kept by the Registrar General for the purposes of subparagraph (1)(b) is not to be open to public inspection or search.

(4)   'Prescribed' means prescribed by regulations made by the Registrar General with the approval of the Scottish Ministers.

Indexing of entries in Gender Recognition Register

15.—(1)   The Registrar General must make arrangements for each entry made in the Gender Recognition Register to be included in an index of such entries kept in the General Register Office of Births, Deaths and Marriages in Scotland.

(2)   Whenever the Registrar General causes a search to be made under subsection (2)(a) of section 38 of the 1965 Act (search of indexes of entries in the registers of births, deaths and marriages) on behalf of any person, he must also, without payment of any fee additional to the fee or fees prescribed under that section—

(a)   cause a search to be made of the index of entries in the Gender Recognition Register on behalf of that person, and

(b)   issue to that person an extract of any such entry provided that (disregarding, for the purposes of subsection (4)(j) of section 22, this paragraph) disclosure of the entry to the person would not constitute an offence under that section.

Extracts of entries in Gender Recognition Register

16.—(1)   This paragraph applies in respect of an extract issued under paragraph 15(2)(b).

(2)   Except as regards the sex and name of the person to whom it relates, the extract must have the form and content it would have had had it been an extract from the register of births of the entry relating to that person.

(3)   The extract must not disclose the fact that the entry is contained in the Gender Recognition Register.

Abbreviated certificates of birth compiled from Gender Recognition Register

17.   Where an abbreviated certificate of birth under section 40 of the 1965 Act is compiled from the Gender Recognition Register, the certificate must not disclose that fact.

Gender Recognition Register: correction, re-registration etc

18.   Section 18A(2) (decrees of parentage and non-parentage), section 20(1) and (3) (re-registration in certain cases), section 42(1) and (5) (correction of errors), section 43(1), (2) and (5) to (9) (recording change of name or surname) and section 44 (Register of Corrections etc) of the 1965 Act apply in relation to the Gender Recognition Register as they apply in relation to the register of births.

Revocation of gender recognition certificate etc

19.—(1)   This paragraph applies if, after an entry has been made in the Gender Recognition Register in relation to a person, the High Court or the Court of Session makes an order under section 8(6) quashing the decision to grant the person's application under section 1(1) [, 5(2) or 5A(2)].

(2)   The High Court or the Court of Session must inform the Registrar General.

(3) Subject to any appeal, the Registrar General must cancel the entry in the Gender Recognition Register.

Authentication and admissibility

20. Section 41 of the 1965 Act (authentication of extracts etc and their admissibility as evidence) applies in relation to the Gender Recognition Register as in relation to the registers kept under the provisions of that Act.

SCHEDULE 4
EFFECT ON MARRIAGE

Section 11

[Part 2. Scotland amends the Marriage (Scotland) Act 1977.]

ANTISOCIAL BEHAVIOUR ETC (SCOTLAND) ACT 2004
(2004, asp 8)

PART 9
PARENTING ORDERS

Applications

102 Applications

(1) The court may make a parenting order in respect of a parent of a child where—

(a) subsection (2) or (3) applies; and

(b) the Scottish Ministers have notified the court that the local authority for the area in which the parent ordinarily resides has made arrangements that would enable the order to be complied with.

(2) This subsection applies where—

(a) the application for the order is made by the appropriate local authority; and

(b) the court is satisfied that—

(i) the behaviour condition; or

(ii) the conduct condition,

is met.

(3) This subsection applies where—

(a) the application for the order is made by the Principal Reporter, and

(b) the court is satisfied that—

(i) the behaviour condition;

(ii) the conduct condition; or

(iii) the welfare condition,

is met.

(4) The behaviour condition is—

(a) that the child has engaged in antisocial behaviour; and

(b) that the making of the order is desirable in the interests of preventing the child from engaging in further such behaviour.

(5) The conduct condition is—

(a) that the child has engaged in criminal conduct; and

(b) that the making of the order is desirable in the interests of preventing the child from engaging in further such conduct.

(6) The welfare condition is that the making of the order is desirable in the interests of improving the welfare of the child.

(7) For the purposes of subsection (5), a child engages in criminal conduct if the child engages in conduct that constitutes a criminal offence (or would do so if the child had attained the age of 8 years).

(8)   An application under this section shall be made by summary application to the sheriff of the sheriffdom where the parent ordinarily resides.

(9)   Before an application is made under this section—
  (a)   by a local authority, it shall consult the Principal Reporter;
  (b)   by the Principal Reporter, the Principal Reporter shall consult the appropriate local authority.

(10)   In this section, 'appropriate local authority' means the local authority for the area where the child ordinarily resides.

Parenting orders

103   Parenting orders

(1)   A parenting order is an order requiring the specified person—
  (a)   to comply, during a specified period—
    (i)   beginning with the making of the order; and
    (ii)   not exceeding 12 months,
with such requirements as are specified; and
  (b)   subject to subsection (2), to attend, during a specified period—
    (i)   falling within the specified period mentioned in paragraph (a); and
    (ii)   not exceeding 3 months,
such counselling or guidance sessions as may be directed by a supervising officer appointed by the relevant local authority.

(2)   Where a parenting order has been made in respect of the person on a previous occasion in the interests of the child in whose interests the order is to be made, the order need not include a requirement under subsection (1)(b).

(3)   The Scottish Ministers may by order amend the number of months mentioned in—
  (a)   subsection (1)(a)(ii); and
  (b)   subsection (1)(b)(ii).

(5)   In subsection (1), 'specified' means specified in the order.

Matters following making of order

104   Notification of making of order

(1)   The clerk of the court by which a parenting order is made shall cause a copy of the order to be—
  (a)   given to the person specified in the order; or
  (b)   sent to the person so specified by registered post or the recorded delivery service.

(2)   A certificate of posting of a letter sent under subsection (1)(b) issued by the postal operator concerned shall be sufficient evidence of the sending of the letter on the day specified in such certificate.

(3)   In subsection (2), 'postal operator' has the meaning given by section 125(1) of the Postal Services Act 2000 (c 26).

105   Review of order

(1)   On the application of a relevant applicant the court that made a parenting order may, if it considers that it would be appropriate to do so—
  (a)   revoke the order; or
  (b)   vary the order by—
    (i)   deleting any of the requirements specified in the order;
    (ii)   adding a new requirement;
    (iii)   altering the period specified for the purpose of section 103(1)(b).

(2)   In subsection (1), 'relevant applicant' means—
  (a)   the person specified in the order;
  (b)   the child in respect of whom the order was made;

(c)   the local authority for the area in which the person specified in the order ordinarily resides.

(3)   Before an application is made under subsection (1) by a local authority, it shall consult the Principal Reporter.

(4)   Where an application under subsection (1) for the revocation or, as the case may be, variation, of a parenting order is refused, another such application by the same applicant under that subsection for revocation or, as the case may be, variation, may be made only with the consent of the court that made the order.

(5)   Where the court that made a parenting order is satisfied that—

(a)   the person specified in the order proposes to change, or has changed, the person's place of ordinary residence; and

(b)   it is appropriate to make an order specifying the sheriff of another sheriffdom as the court that may entertain applications under subsection (1),

it may make such an order; and in such a case, this section shall be read as if references to the court that made the order were references to that sheriff.

106   Appeals

An interlocutor—

(a)   varying, or refusing to vary a parenting order; or

(b)   making a parenting order under section 13,

is an appealable interlocutor.

107   Failure to comply with order

(1)   If the person specified in a parenting order fails without reasonable excuse to comply with—

(a)   any requirement specified in the order; or

(b)   any direction given under the order,

the person shall be guilty of an offence.

(2)   A person guilty of an offence under subsection (1) shall be liable on summary conviction to a fine not exceeding level 3 on the standard scale.

(3)   In determining the sentence to be imposed on a person guilty of an offence under subsection (1) a court shall take into consideration the welfare of any child in respect of whom the person is a parent.

General requirements

108   Procedural requirements

(1)   Before making, varying or revoking a parenting order, a court shall—

(a)   having regard to the age and maturity of the child, so far as practicable—

(i)   give the child an opportunity to indicate whether the child wishes to express views; and

(ii)   if the child so wishes, give the child an opportunity to express those views;

(b)   give the parent the opportunity to be heard;

(c)   obtain information about the family circumstances of the parent and the likely effect of the order on those circumstances.

(2)   Before making a parenting order, the court shall explain in ordinary language—

(a)   the effect of the order and of the requirements proposed to be included in it;

(b)   the consequences of failing to comply with the order;

(c)   the powers the court has under section 81; and

(d)   the entitlement of the parent to appeal against the making of the order.

(3)   Before varying or revoking a parenting order, the court shall explain in ordinary language the effect of the variation or, as the case may be, revocation.

(4)   Subsections (1A) and (1B) apply only where the parent is present in court.

(5)   Failure to comply with subsection (1A) or (1B) shall not affect the validity of the order made.

(6)   Without prejudice to the generality of subsection (1)(a), a child who is at least 12 years of age shall be presumed to be of sufficient age and maturity to form a view.

109   General considerations relating to making, varying and revoking order

(1)   Where a court is determining whether to make, vary or revoke a parenting order its paramount consideration shall be the welfare of the child.

(2)   Where a court is determining whether to make a parenting order it shall have regard to—

(a)   such views as the child has expressed in relation to that matter by virtue of paragraph (a) of subsection (1) of section 108;

(b)   the information obtained in relation to that matter by virtue of paragraph (c) of that subsection;

(c)   whether (and if so the extent to which) the parent has, at any time that appears to the court to be relevant, taken relevant voluntary steps; and

(d)   any other behaviour of the parent that appears to the court to be relevant.

(3)   Where a court is determining whether to vary or revoke a parenting order it shall have regard to—

(a)   such views as the child has expressed in relation to that matter by virtue of paragraph (a) of subsection (1) of section 108;

(b)   the information obtained in relation to that matter by virtue of paragraph (c) of that subsection; and

(c)   any behaviour of the parent that appears to the court to be relevant.

(4)   In subsection (2)(c) 'relevant voluntary steps' means—

(a)   where the court is determining whether to—

(i)   make a parenting order under section 13; or

(ii)   make a parenting order under subsection (1) of section 102 in respect of the condition mentioned in subsection (4) of that section,

voluntary steps intended to be in the interests of preventing the child from engaging in antisocial behaviour;

(b)   where the court is determining whether to make a parenting order under subsection (1) of section 102 in respect of the condition mentioned in subsection (5) of that section, voluntary steps intended to be in the interests of preventing the child from engaging in criminal conduct;

(c)   where the court is determining whether to make a parenting order under subsection (1) of section 102 in respect of the condition mentioned in subsection (6) of that section, voluntary steps intended to be in the interests of improving the welfare of the child.

110   Account to be taken of religion, work and education

(1)   A court shall ensure that the requirements of a parenting order made by it avoid, so far as practicable—

(a)   any conflict with the religious beliefs of the person specified in the order; and

(b)   any interference with times at which that person normally works (or carries out voluntary work) or attends an educational establishment.

(2)   The supervising officer appointed by a local authority in respect of a parenting order shall ensure that the directions given by the officer avoid, so far as practicable, the matters mentioned in subsection (1)(a) and (b).

Miscellaneous

111   Restriction on reporting proceedings relating to parenting orders

(1)   Subject to subsection (2), a person shall be guilty of an offence if the person

publishes, anywhere in the world, any matter in respect of relevant proceedings which is intended, or likely to, identify—

    (a)   the parent concerned in the proceedings (the 'person concerned');

    (b)   any address as being that of the person concerned;

    (c)   the child concerned in the proceedings;

    (d)   any other child—

        (i) who is a member of the same household as the person concerned; or

        (ii) of whom the person concerned is a parent; or

    (e)   any—

        (i) address; or

        (ii) school,

as being that of a child mentioned in paragraph (c) or (d).

(2)   In relevant proceedings, the court may, in the interests of justice, order that subsection (1) shall not apply to the proceedings to such extent as the court considers appropriate.

(3)   A person guilty of an offence under subsection (1) shall be liable on summary conviction to a fine not exceeding level 4 on the standard scale.

(4)   It shall be a defence for a person charged with an offence under subsection (1) to show that the person—

    (a)   did not know; and

    (b)   had no reason to suspect,

that the published matter was intended, or was likely, to identify the person concerned, child, address or school (as the case may be).

(5)   Section 46 of the Children and Young Persons (Scotland) Act 1937 (c 37) shall apply in relation to relevant proceedings only in respect of a person concerned in the proceedings as a witness.

(6)   A child in whose interests a parenting order has been made shall be regarded as a person who falls within subsection (1)(a) of section 47 of the Criminal Procedure (Scotland) Act 1995 (c 46) for the purposes of that section in its application to proceedings in respect of the commission of an offence under section 83(1) in respect of that order.

(7)   In this section—

'programme service' has the meaning given by section 201 of the Broadcasting Act 1990 (c 42);

'publishes' includes—

    (a)   causing to be published; and

    (b)   publishing in a programme service,

and 'published' shall be construed accordingly; and

'relevant proceedings' means—

    (a)   proceedings before a sheriff for the purpose of considering whether to make a parenting order under section 13(1);

    (b)   proceedings before a sheriff on an application for the making of a parenting order under section 102(1);

    (c)   proceedings before a sheriff on an application for the variation, or revocation, of a parenting order under section 105(1);

    (d)   proceedings before a sheriff for the purpose of considering whether to make an order under section 105(5);

    (e)   an appeal arising from proceedings such as are mentioned in paragraphs (a) to (d).

112 Conduct of proceedings by reporters

(1)   The Scottish Ministers may by regulations empower a reporter, whether or not the reporter is an advocate or solicitor, to conduct proceedings—

    (a)   before a sheriff—

        (i) on an application by the Principal Reporter for the making of a parenting order;

(ii) on an application for the variation, or revocation, of a parenting order made on the application of the Principal Reporter, under section 105(1); or

(iii) for the purpose of considering whether to make an order under section 105(5) in respect of a parenting order made on the application of the Principal Reporter; or

(b) before a sheriff principal, on any appeal arising from proceedings such as are mentioned in paragraph (a).

(2) Regulations under subsection (1) may prescribe such requirements as the Scottish Ministers think fit as to—

(a) qualifications;

(b) training; or

(c) experience,

necessary for a reporter to be so empowered.

(3) In this section 'reporter' means—

(a) the Principal Reporter; and

(b) any officer of the Scottish Children's Reporter Administration to whom there is delegated, under section 131(1) of the Local Government etc (Scotland) Act 1994 (c 39), any of the functions which the Principal Reporter has under any enactment.

113   Initial investigations by Principal Reporter

(1) For the purpose of determining whether to make an application for the making of a parenting order under section 102, the Principal Reporter may make such investigations as the Principal Reporter considers appropriate.

(2) On a request made by the Principal Reporter for the purpose mentioned in subsection (1), a local authority shall supply to the Principal Reporter a report on—

(a) the child in relation to whom the Principal Reporter is determining whether to make the application;

(b) the parent in relation to whom the Principal Reporter is determining whether to make the application; and

(c) such circumstances concerning—

(i) the child; and

(ii) the parent,

as appear to the Principal Reporter to be relevant.

114   Power of court to direct reporter to consider application for parenting order

Where, in any proceedings (other than proceedings under section 4 or 102), it appears to a court that it might be appropriate for a parenting order to be made in respect of a parent of a child, the court may require the Principal Reporter to consider whether to apply under section 102 for such an order.

115   Guidance about parenting orders

A person (other than a court) shall, in discharging functions by virtue of section 13 or this Part, have regard to any guidance given by the Scottish Ministers about—

(a) the discharge of those functions; and

(b) matters arising in connection with the discharge of those functions.

116   [Amends Children (Scotland) Act 1995]

Interpretation

117   Interpretation of Part 9

In this Part—

'child' means a person who is under the age of 16 years;

'parent' means any individual who is a relevant person as defined in section 93(2)(b) of the Children (Scotland) Act 1995 (c 36) (the references to a 'person' in that section being read as references to an individual);

'parenting order' has the meaning given by section 103(1).

CIVIL PARTNERSHIP ACT 2004
(2004, c 33)

PART 1
INTRODUCTION

1 Civil partnership
   (1) A civil partnership is a relationship between two people of the same sex
('civil partners')—
      (a) which is formed when they register as civil partners of each other—
         (i)   in England or Wales (under Part 2),
         (ii) in Scotland (under Part 3),
         (iii) in Northern Ireland (under Part 4), or
         (iv) outside the United Kingdom under an Order in Council made under
      Chapter 1 of Part 5 (registration at British consulates etc or by armed forces
      personnel), or
      (b) which they are treated under Chapter 2 of Part 5 as having formed (at
   the time determined under that Chapter) by virtue of having registered an overseas relationship.
   (2) Subsection (1) is subject to the provisions of this Act under or by virtue of
which a civil partnership is void.
   (3) A civil partnership ends only on death, dissolution or annulment.
   (4) The references in subsection (3) to dissolution and annulment are to dissolution and annulment having effect under or recognised in accordance with this
Act.
   (5) References in this Act to an overseas relationship are to be read in accordance with Chapter 2 of Part 5.

PART 3
CIVIL PARTNERSHIP: SCOTLAND

CHAPTER 1
FORMATION AND ELIGIBILITY

85 Formation of civil partnership by registration
   (1) For the purposes of section 1, two people are to be regarded as having
registered as civil partners of each other once each of them has signed the civil
partnership schedule, in the presence of—
      (a) each other,
      (b) two witnesses both of whom have attained the age of 16, and
      (c) the authorised registrar,
(all being present at a registration office or at a place agreed under section 93).
   (2) But the two people must be eligible to be so registered.
   (3) Subsection (1) applies regardless of whether subsection (4) is complied
with.
   (4) After the civil partnership schedule has been signed under subsection (1), it
must also be signed, in the presence of the civil partners and each other by—
      (a) each of the two witnesses, and
      (b) the authorised registrar.

86 Eligibility
   (1) Two people are not eligible to register in Scotland as civil partners of each
other if—
      (a) they are not of the same sex,
      (b) they are related in a forbidden degree,
      (c) either has not attained the age of 16,
      (d) either is married or already in civil partnership, or

    (e)   either is incapable of—
        (i)   understanding the nature of civil partnership, or
        (ii)   validly consenting to its formation.

   (2)   Subject to subsections (3) and (4), a man is related in a forbidden degree to another man if related to him in a degree specified in column 1 of Schedule 10 and a woman is related in a forbidden degree to another woman if related to her in a degree specified in column 2 of that Schedule.

   (3)   A man and any man related to him in a degree specified in column 1 of paragraph 2 of Schedule 10, or a woman and any woman related to her in a degree specified in column 2 of that paragraph, are not related in a forbidden degree if—
    (a)   both persons have attained the age of 21, and
    (b)   the younger has not at any time before attaining the age of 18 lived in the same household as the elder and been treated by the elder as a child of the elder's family.

   (4)   A man and any man related to him in a degree specified in column 1 of paragraph 3 of Schedule 10, or a woman and any woman related to her in a degree specified in column 2 of that paragraph, are not related in a forbidden degree if—
    (a)   both persons have attained the age of 21, and
    (b)   in the case of—
        (i)   a man entering civil partnership with the father of his former wife, both the former wife and the former wife's mother are dead,
        (ii)   a man entering civil partnership with the father of his former civil partner, both the former civil partner and the former civil partner's mother are dead,
        (iii)   a man entering civil partnership with the former husband of his daughter, both the daughter and the daughter's mother are dead,
        (iv)   a man entering civil partnership with the former civil partner of his son, both the son and the son's mother are dead,
        (v)   a woman entering civil partnership with the mother of her former husband, both the former husband and the former husband's father are dead,
        (vi)   a woman entering civil partnership with the mother of her former civil partner, both the former civil partner and the former civil partner's father are dead,
        (vii)   a woman entering civil partnership with the former wife of her son, both the son and the son's father are dead, or
        (viii)   a woman entering civil partnership with the former civil partner of her daughter, both the daughter and the daughter's father are dead.

   (5)   Subsection (4) and paragraphs 2 and 3 of Schedule 10 have effect subject to the modifications specified in subsections (6) and (7) in the case of a person (here the 'relevant person') whose gender has become the acquired gender under the Gender Recognition Act 2004 (c 7).

   (6)   Any reference in subsection (4) or those paragraphs to a former wife or former husband of the relevant person includes (respectively) any former husband or former wife of the relevant person.

   (7)   And the reference—
    (a)   in sub-paragraph (iii) of subsection (4)(b) to the relevant person's daughter's mother is to the relevant person's daughter's father if the relevant person is the daughter's mother,
    (b)   in sub-paragraph (iv) of that subsection to the relevant person's son's mother is to the relevant person's son's father if the relevant person is the son's mother,
    (c)   in sub-paragraph (vii) of that subsection to the relevant person's son's father is to the relevant person's son's mother if the relevant person is the son's father, and
    (d)   in sub-paragraph (viii) of that subsection to the relevant person's

daughter's father is to the relevant person's daughter's mother if the relevant person is the daughter's father.

(8)   References in this section and in Schedule 10 to relationships and degrees of relationship are to be construed in accordance with section 1(1) of the Law Reform (Parent and Child) (Scotland) Act 1986 (c 9).

(9)   For the purposes of this section, a degree of relationship specified in paragraph 1 of Schedule 10 exists whether it is of the full blood or the half blood.

(10)   *[Amends Adoption (Scotland) Act 1978.]*

CHAPTER 2
REGISTRATION

87   Appointment of authorised registrars
For the purpose of affording reasonable facilities throughout Scotland for registration as civil partners, the Registrar General—

(a)   is to appoint such number of district registrars as he thinks necessary, and

(b)   may, in respect of any district for which he has made an appointment under paragraph (a), appoint one or more assistant registrars,

as persons who may carry out such registration (in this Part referred to as 'authorised registrars').

88   Notice of proposed civil partnership
(1)   In order to register as civil partners, each of the intended civil partners must submit to the district registrar a notice, in the prescribed form and accompanied by the prescribed fee, of intention to enter civil partnership (in this Part referred to as a 'notice of proposed civil partnership').

(2)   A notice submitted under subsection (1) must also be accompanied by—

(a)   the birth certificate of the person submitting it,

(b)   if that person has previously been married or in civil partnership and—

(i)   the marriage or civil partnership has been dissolved, a copy of the decree of divorce or dissolution, or

(ii)   the other party to that marriage or civil partnership has died, the death certificate of that other party, and

(c)   if that person has previously ostensibly been married or in civil partnership but decree of annulment has been obtained, a copy of that decree.

(3)   If a person is unable to submit a certificate or decree required by subsection (2) he may instead make a declaration to that effect, stating what the reasons are; and he must provide the district registrar with such—

(a)   information in respect of the matters to which the certificate or document would have related, and

(b)   documentary evidence in support of that information, as the district registrar may require.

(4)   If a document submitted under subsection (2) or (3) is in a language other than English, the person submitting it must attach to the document a translation of it in English, certified by the translator as a correct translation.

(5)   A person submitting a notice under subsection (1) must make and sign the necessary declaration (the form for which must be included in any form prescribed for the notice).

(6)   The necessary declaration is a declaration that the person submitting the notice believes that the intended civil partners are eligible to be in civil partnership with each other.

89   Civil partnership notice book
(1)   On receipt of a notice of proposed civil partnership, the district registrar is to enter in a book (to be known as 'the civil partnership book') supplied to him for

that purpose by the Registrar General such particulars, extracted from the notice, as may be prescribed and the date of receipt by him of that notice.

(2)   The form and content of any page of that book is to be prescribed.

90   Publicisation

(1)   Where notices of a proposed civil partnership are submitted to a district registrar, he must, as soon as practicable after the day on which they are submitted (or, if the two documents are not submitted on the same day, after the day on which the first is submitted), publicise the relevant information and send it to the Registrar General who must also publicise it.

(2)   'The relevant information' means—

(a)   the names of the intended civil partners, and

(b)   the date on which it is intended to register them as civil partners of each other, being a date more than 14 days after publicisation by the district registrar under subsection (1).

(3)   Paragraph (b) of subsection (2) is subject to section 91.

(4)   The manner in which and means by which relevant information is to be publicised are to be prescribed.

91   Early registration

An authorised registrar who receives a request in writing from one or both of two intended civil partners that they should be registered as civil partners of each other on a date specified in the request (being a date 14 days or fewer after publicisation by the district registrar under subsection (1) of section 90) may, provided that he is authorised to do so by the Registrar General, fix that date as the date for registration; and if a date is so fixed, paragraph (b) of subsection (2) of that section is to be construed as if it were a reference to that date.

92   Objections to registration

(1)   Any person may at any time before the registration in Scotland of two people as civil partners of each other submit in writing an objection to such registration to the district registrar.

(2)   But where the objection is that the intended civil partners are not eligible to be in civil partnership with each other because either is incapable of—

(a)   understanding the nature of civil partnership, or

(b)   validly consenting to its formation,

it shall be accompanied by a supporting certificate signed by a registered medical practitioner.

(3)   A person claiming that he may have reason to submit such an objection may, free of charge and at any time when the registration office at which a notice of proposed civil partnership to which the objection would relate is open for public business, inspect any relevant entry in the civil partnership book.

(4)   Where the district registrar receives an objection in accordance with subsection (1) he must—

(a)   in any case where he is satisfied that the objection relates to no more than a misdescription or inaccuracy in a notice submitted under section 88(1)—

(i)   notify the intended civil partners of the nature of the objection and make such enquiries into the matter mentioned in it as he thinks fit, and

(ii)   subject to the approval of the Registrar General, make any necessary correction to any document relating to the proposed civil partnership, or

(b)   in any other case—

(i)   at once notify the Registrar General of the objection, and

(ii)   pending consideration of the objection by the Registrar General, suspend the completion or issue of the civil partnership schedule in respect of the proposed civil partnership.

(5)   If the Registrar General is satisfied, on consideration of an objection of which he has received notification under subsection (4)(b)(i) that—

(a)   there is a legal impediment to registration, he must direct the district registrar not to register the intended civil partners and to notify them accordingly, or

(b)   there is no such impediment, he must inform the district registrar to that effect.

(6)   For the purposes of this section and section 94, there is a legal impediment to registration where the intended civil partners are not eligible to be in civil partnership with each other.

93   Place of registration

(1)   Two people may be registered as civil partners of each other at a registration office or any other place which they and the local registration authority agree is to be the place of registration.

(2)   The place of registration may, if the approval of the Registrar General is obtained, be outwith the district of the authorised registrar carrying out the registration.

(3)   But the place must not be in religious premises, that is to say premises which—

(a)   are used solely or mainly for religious purposes, or

(b)   have been so used and have not subsequently been used solely or mainly for other purposes.

(4)   'Local registration authority' has the meaning given by section 5(3) of the 1965 Act.

94   The civil partnership schedule

Where—

(a)   the district registrar has received a notice of proposed civil partnership in respect of each of the intended civil partners and—

(i)   is satisfied that there is no legal impediment to their registration as civil partners of each other, or

(ii)   as the case may be, is informed under section 92(5)(b) that there is no such impediment,

(b)   the 14 days mentioned in paragraph (b) of section 90(2) have expired (or as the case may be the date which, by virtue of section 91, that paragraph is to be construed as a reference to has been reached), and

(c)   the period which has elapsed since the day of receipt of the notices by him (or, if the two notices were not received on the same day, since the day of receipt of the later) does not exceed 3 months, he is to complete a civil partnership schedule in the prescribed form.

95   Further provision as to registration

(1)   Before the persons present sign in accordance with section 85 the authorised registrar is to require the intended civil partners to confirm that (to the best of their knowledge) the particulars set out in the civil partnership schedule are correct.

(2)   As soon as practicable after the civil partnership schedule has been signed, the authorised registrar must cause those particulars to be entered in a register (to be known as the 'civil partnership register') supplied to him for that purpose by the Registrar General.

(3)   The form and content of any page of that register is to be prescribed.

(4)   A fee payable by the intended civil partners for their registration as civil partners of each other is to be prescribed.

96   Civil partnership with former spouse

(1)   Where an intended civil partner has a full gender recognition certificate issued under section 5(1) of the Gender Recognition Act 2004 (c 7) and the other intended civil partner was the other party in the proceedings in which the certifi-

cate was issued, the procedures for their registration as civil partners of each other may—
(a) if they so elect, and
(b) if each of them submits a notice under section 88(1) within 30 days after the certificate is issued,
be expedited as follows.

(2) The registration may take place on any of the 30 days immediately following—
(a) that on which the notices are submitted, or
(b) (if the two notices are not submitted on the same day) that on which the later is submitted.

(3) And accordingly there are to be disregarded—
(a) in section 90—
(i) in subsection (2)(b), the words from 'being' to the end, and
(ii) subsection (3),
(b) section 91, and
(c) in section 94, paragraph (b).

97 Certificates of no impediment for Part 2 purposes

(1) This section applies where—
(a) two people propose to register as civil partners of each other under Chapter 1 of Part 2, and
(b) one of them ('A') resides in Scotland but the other ('B') resides in England or Wales.

(2) A may submit a notice of intention to register under section 88 as if A and B intended to register as civil partners in the district in which A resides.

(3) If the district registrar is satisfied (after consultation, if he considers it necessary, with the Registrar General) that there is no impediment (in terms of section 92(6)) to A registering as B's civil partner, he must issue a certificate to A in the prescribed form that there is not known to be any such impediment.

(4) But the certificate may not be issued to A earlier than 14 days after the receipt (as entered in the civil partnership notice book) of the notice under subsection (2) unless—
(a) the circumstances are as mentioned in section 96(1), and
(b) A makes an election for the certificate to be issued as soon as possible.

(5) Any person may, at any time before a certificate is issued under subsection (3), submit to the district registrar an objection in writing to its issue.

(6) Any objection made under subsection (5) must be taken into account by the district registrar in deciding whether he is satisfied that there is no legal impediment to A registering as B's civil partner.

98 Application of certain sections of 1965 Act to civil partnership register

Sections 34 (examination of registers by district examiners), 37(1) and (2) (search of indexes kept by registrars), 38(1) and (2) (search of indexes kept by Registrar General) and 44 (Register of Corrections etc) of the 1965 Act apply in relation to the civil partnership register as they apply in relation to the registers of births, deaths and marriages.

99 Correction of errors in civil partnership register

(1) No alteration is to be made in the civil partnership register except as authorised by or under this or any other Act ('Act' including an Act of the Scottish Parliament).

(2) Any clerical error in the register or error in it of a kind prescribed may be corrected by the district registrar.

(3) The Registrar General may authorise district examiners ('district examiner' having the meaning given by section 2(1) of the 1965 Act) to correct any error in

the register of a type specified by him which they discover during an examination under section 34 of the 1965 Act.

100 Offences

(1) A person ('A') commits an offence who registers in Scotland as the civil partner of another person ('B') knowing that either or both—

(a) A is already married to or in civil partnership with a person other than B, or

(b) B is already married to or in civil partnership with a person other than A.

(2) A person commits an offence who knowingly—

(a) falsifies or forges any civil partnership document (that is to say, any document issued or made, or purporting to be issued or made, or required, under this Part),

(b) uses, or gives or sends to any person as genuine, any false or forged civil partnership document,

(c) being an authorised registrar, purports to register two people as civil partners of each other before any civil partnership schedule available to him at the time of registration has been duly completed,

(d) not being an authorised registrar, conducts himself in such a way as to lead intended civil partners to believe that he is authorised to register them as civil partners of each other,

(e) being an authorised registrar, purports to register two people as civil partners of each other without both of them being present, or

(f) being an authorised registrar, purports to register two people as civil partners of each other in a place other than a registration office or a place agreed under section 93.

(3) A person guilty of an offence under subsection (1) or (2) is liable—

(a) on conviction on indictment, to imprisonment for a term not exceeding 2 years or to a fine (or both);

(b) on summary conviction, to imprisonment for a term not exceeding 3 months or to a fine not exceeding level 3 on the standard scale (or both).

(4) Summary proceedings for an offence under subsection (1) or (2) may be commenced at any time within 3 months after evidence sufficient in the opinion of the Lord Advocate to justify the proceedings comes to his knowledge or within 12 months after the offence is committed (whichever period last expires).

(5) Subsection (3) of section 136 of the Criminal Procedure (Scotland) Act 1995 (c 46) (time limits) has effect for the purposes of this section as it has for the purposes of that section.

CHAPTER 3
OCCUPANCY RIGHTS AND TENANCIES

Occupancy rights

101 Occupancy rights

(1) Where, apart from the provisions of this Chapter, one civil partner in a civil partnership is entitled, or permitted by a third party, to occupy a family home of the civil partnership (that civil partner being referred in this Chapter as an 'entitled partner') and the other civil partner is not so entitled or permitted (a 'non-entitled partner'), the non-entitled partner has, subject to the provisions of this Chapter, the following rights—

(a) if in occupation, a right to continue to occupy the family home;

(b) if not in occupation, a right to enter into and occupy the family home.

(2) The rights conferred by subsection (1) to continue to occupy or, as the case may be, to enter and occupy the family home include, without prejudice to their generality, the right to do so together with any child of the family.

(3) In subsection (1), an 'entitled partner' includes a civil partner who is entitled, or permitted by a third party, to occupy the family home along with an individual who is not the other civil partner only if that individual has waived a right of occupation in favour of the civil partner so entitled or permitted.

(4) If the entitled partner refuses to allow the non-entitled partner to exercise the right conferred by subsection (1)(b), the non-entitled partner may exercise that right only with the leave of the Court of Session or the sheriff under section 103(3) or (4).

(5) A non-entitled partner may renounce in writing the rights mentioned in paragraphs (a) and (b) of subsection (1) only—

(a) in a particular family home, or

(b) in a particular property which it is intended by the civil partners will become their family home.

(6) A renunciation under subsection (5) has effect only if, at the time of making the renunciation, the non-entitled partner swears or affirms before a notary public that it is made freely and without coercion of any kind.

(7) In this Part—

'child of the family' means a child under the age of 16 years who has been accepted by both civil partners as a child of the family, and

'family' means the civil partners in the civil partnership, together with any child so accepted by them.

(8) In subsection (6), 'notary public' includes any person duly authorised, by the law of the country other than Scotland in which the swearing or affirmation takes place, to administer oaths or receive affirmations in that other country.

102 Occupancy: subsidiary and consequential rights

(1) For the purpose of securing the occupancy rights of a non-entitled partner, that partner is, in relation to a family home, entitled without the consent of the entitled partner—

(a) to make any payment due by the entitled partner in respect of rent, rates, secured loan instalments, interest or other outgoings (not being outgoings on repairs or improvements);

(b) to perform any other obligation incumbent on the entitled partner (not being an obligation in respect of non-essential repairs or improvements);

(c) to enforce performance of an obligation by a third party which that third party has undertaken to the entitled partner to the extent that the entitled partner may enforce such performance;

(d) to carry out such essential repairs as the entitled partner may carry out;

(e) to carry out such non-essential repairs or improvements as may be authorised by an order of the court, being such repairs or improvements as the entitled partner may carry out and which the court considers to be appropriate for the reasonable enjoyment of the occupancy rights;

(f) to take such other steps, for the purpose of protecting the occupancy rights of the non-entitled partner, as the entitled partner may take to protect the occupancy rights of the entitled partner.

(2) Any payment made under subsection (1)(a) or any obligation performed under subsection (1)(b) has effect in relation to the rights of a third party as if the payment were made or the obligation were performed by the entitled partner; and the performance of an obligation which has been enforced under subsection (1)(c) has effect as if it had been enforced by the entitled partner.

(3) Where there is an entitled and a non-entitled partner, the court, on the application of either of them, may, having regard in particular to the respective financial circumstances of the partners, make an order apportioning expenditure incurred or to be incurred by either partner—

(a) without the consent of the other partner, on any of the items mentioned in paragraphs (a) and (d) of subsection (1);

(b)   with the consent of the other partner, on anything relating to a family home.

(4)   Where both partners are entitled, or permitted by a third party, to occupy a family home—

(a)   either partner is entitled, without the consent of the other partner, to carry out such non-essential repairs or improvements as may be authorised by an order of the court, being such repairs or improvements as the court considers to be appropriate for the reasonable enjoyment of the occupancy rights;

(b)   the court, on the application of either partner, may, having regard in particular to the respective financial circumstances of the partners, make an order apportioning expenditure incurred or to be incurred by either partner, with or without the consent of the other partner, on anything relating to the family home.

(5)   Where one partner ('A') owns or hires, or is acquiring under a hire-purchase or conditional sale agreement, furniture and plenishings in a family home—

(a)   the other partner may, without the consent of A—

(i)   make any payment due by A which is necessary, or take any other step which A is entitled to take, to secure the possession or use of any such furniture and plenishings (and any such payment is to have effect in relation to the rights of a third party as if it were made by A), or

(ii)   carry out such essential repairs to the furniture and plenishings as A is entitled to carry out;

(b)   the court, on the application of either partner, may, having regard in particular to the respective financial circumstances of the partners, make an order apportioning expenditure incurred or to be incurred by either partner—

(i)   without the consent of the other partner, in making payments under a hire, hire-purchase or conditional sale agreement, or in paying interest charges in respect of the furniture and plenishings, or in carrying out essential repairs to the furniture and plenishings, or

(ii)   with the consent of the other partner, on anything relating to the furniture or plenishings.

(6)   An order under subsection (3), (4)(b) or (5)(b) may require one partner to make a payment to the other partner in implementation of the apportionment.

(7)   Any application under subsection (3), (4)(b) or (5)(b) is to be made within 5 years after the date on which any payment in respect of such incurred expenditure was made.

(8)   Where—

(a)   the entitled partner is a tenant of a family home,

(b)   possession of it is necessary in order to continue the tenancy, and

(c)   the entitled partner abandons such possession,

the tenancy is continued by such possession by the non-entitled partner.

(9)   In this section 'improvements' includes alterations and enlargement.

103   Regulation by court of rights of occupancy of family home

(1)   Where there is an entitled and a non-entitled partner, or where both partners are entitled, or permitted by a third party, to occupy a family home, either partner may apply to the court for an order—

(a)   declaring the occupancy rights of the applicant partner;

(b)   enforcing the occupancy rights of the applicant partner;

(c)   restricting the occupancy rights of the non-applicant partner;

(d)   regulating the exercise by either partner of his or her occupancy rights;

(e)   protecting the occupancy rights of the applicant partner in relation to the other partner.

(2)   Where one partner owns or hires, or is acquiring under a hire-purchase or

conditional sale agreement, furniture and plenishings in a family home and the other partner has occupancy rights in that home, that other person may apply to the court for an order granting to the applicant the possession or use in the family home of any such furniture and plenishings; but, subject to section 102, an order under this subsection does not prejudice the rights of any third party in relation to the non-performance of any obligation under such hire-purchase or conditional sale agreement.

(3) The court is to grant an application under subsection (1)(a) if it appears to the court that the application relates to a family home; and, on an application under any of paragraphs (b) to (e) of subsection (1) or under subsection (2), the court may make such order relating to the application as appears to it to be just and reasonable having regard to all the circumstances of the case including—

(a) the conduct of the partners, whether in relation to each other or otherwise,

(b) the respective needs and financial resources of the partners,

(c) the needs of any child of the family,

(d) the extent (if any) to which—

(i) the family home, and

(ii) in relation only to an order under subsection (2), any item of furniture and plenishings referred to in that subsection, is used in connection with a trade, business or profession of either partner, and

(e) whether the entitled partner offers or has offered to make available to the non-entitled partner any suitable alternative accommodation.

(4) Pending the making of an order under subsection (3), the court, on the application of either partner, may make such interim order as it considers necessary or expedient in relation to—

(a) the residence of either partner in the home to which the application relates,

(b) the personal effects of either partner or of any child of the family, or

(c) the furniture and plenishings,

but an interim order may be made only if the non-applicant partner has been afforded an opportunity of being heard by or represented before the court.

(5) The court is not to make an order under subsection (3) or (4) if it appears that the effect of the order would be to exclude the non-applicant partner from the family home.

(6) If the court makes an order under subsection (3) or (4) which requires the delivery to one partner of anything which has been left in or removed from the family home, it may also grant a warrant authorising a messenger-at-arms or sheriff officer to enter the family home or other premises occupied by the other partner and to search for and take possession of the thing required to be delivered, (if need be by opening shut and lockfast places) and to deliver the thing in accordance with the order.

(7) A warrant granted under subsection (6) is to be executed only after expiry of such period as the court is to specify in the order for delivery.

(8) Where it appears to the court—

(a) on the application of a non-entitled partner, that the applicant has suffered a loss of occupancy rights or that the quality of the applicant's occupation of a family home has been impaired, or

(b) on the application of a partner who has been given the possession or use of furniture and plenishings by virtue of an order under subsection (3), that the applicant has suffered a loss of such possession or use or that the quality of the applicant's possession or use of the furniture and plenishings has been impaired, in consequence of any act or default on the part of the other partner which was intended to result in such loss or impairment, it may order that other partner to pay to the applicant such compensation as it considers just and reasonable in respect of that loss or impairment.

(9)   A partner may renounce in writing the right to apply under subsection (2) for the possession or use of any item of furniture and plenishings.

104   Exclusion orders

(1)   Where there is an entitled and non-entitled partner, or where both partners are entitled, or permitted by a third party, to occupy a family home, either partner, whether or not that partner is in occupation at the time of the application, may apply to the court for an order (in this Chapter referred to as 'an exclusion order') suspending the occupancy rights of the other partner ('the non-applicant partner') in a family home.

(2)   Subject to subsection (3), the court is to make an exclusion order if it appears to it that to do so is necessary for the protection of the applicant or any child of the family from any conduct, or threatened or reasonably apprehended conduct, of the non-applicant partner which is or would be injurious to the physical or mental health of the applicant or child.

(3)   The court is not to make an exclusion order if it appears to it that to do so would be unjustified or unreasonable—

    (a)   having regard to all the circumstances of the case including the matters specified in paragraphs (a) to (e) of section 103(3), and

    (b)   where the family home—

        (i)   is, or is part of, an agricultural holding within the meaning of section 1 of the Agricultural Holdings (Scotland) Act 1991 (c 55), or

        (ii)   is let, or is a home in respect of which possession is given, to the non-applicant partner or to both partners by an employer as an incident of employment,

having regard to any requirement that the non-applicant partner, or, as the case may be, both partners must reside in the family home and to the likely consequences of the exclusion of the non-applicant partner from the family home.

(4)   In making an exclusion order the court is, on the application of the applicant partner—

    (a)   to grant a warrant for the summary ejection of the non-applicant partner from the family home unless the non-applicant partner satisfies the court that it is unnecessary for it to grant such a remedy,

    (b)   to grant an interdict prohibiting the non-applicant partner from entering the family home without the express permission of the applicant, and

    (c)   to grant an interdict prohibiting the removal by the non-applicant partner, except with the written consent of the applicant or by a further order of the court, of any furniture and plenishings in the family home unless the non-applicant partner satisfies the court that it is unnecessary for it to grant such a remedy.

(5)   In making an exclusion order the court may—

    (a)   grant an interdict prohibiting the non-applicant partner from entering or remaining in a specified area in the vicinity of the family home;

    (b)   where the warrant for the summary ejection of the non-applicant partner has been granted in that partner's absence, give directions as to the preservation of that partner's goods and effects which remain in the family home;

    (c)   on the application of either partner, make the exclusion order or the warrant or interdict mentioned in paragraph (a), (b) or (c) of subsection (4) or paragraph (a) of this subsection subject to such terms and conditions as the court may prescribe;

    (d)   on the application of either partner, make such other order as it considers necessary for the proper enforcement of an order made under subsection (4) or paragraph (a), (b) or (c).

(6)   Pending the making of an exclusion order, the court may, on the application of the applicant partner, make an interim order suspending the occupancy rights of the non-applicant partner in the family home to which the application for

the exclusion order relates; and subsections (4) and (5) apply to such an interim order as they apply to an exclusion order.

(7) But an interim order may be made only if the non-applicant partner has been afforded an opportunity of being heard by or represented before the court.

(8) Without prejudice to subsections (1) and (6), where both partners are entitled, or permitted by a third party, to occupy a family home, it is incompetent for one partner to bring an action of ejection from the family home against the other partner.

105   Duration of orders under sections 103 and 104

(1) The court may, on the application of either partner, vary or recall any order made by it under section 103 or 104.

(2) Subject to subsection (3), any such order, unless previously so varied or recalled, ceases to have effect—

(a)   on the dissolution of the civil partnership,

(b)   subject to section 106(1), where there is an entitled and non-entitled partner, on the entitled partner ceasing to be an entitled partner in respect of the family home to which the order relates, or

(c)   where both partners are entitled, or permitted by a third party, to occupy the family home, on both partners ceasing to be so entitled or permitted.

(3) Without prejudice to the generality of subsection (2), an order under section 103(3) or (4) which grants the possession or use of furniture and plenishings ceases to have effect if the furniture and plenishings cease to be permitted by a third party to be retained in the family home.

106   Continued exercise of occupancy rights after dealing

(1) Subject to subsection (3)—

(a)   the continued exercise of the rights conferred on a non-entitled partner by the provisions of this Chapter in respect of a family home are not prejudiced by reason only of any dealing of the entitled partner relating to that home, and

(b)   a third party is not by reason only of such a dealing entitled to occupy that home or any part of it.

(2) In this section and section 107—

'dealing' includes the grant of a heritable security and the creation of a trust but does not include a conveyance under section 80 of the Lands Clauses Consolidation Act 1845 (c 18);

'entitled partner' does not include a civil partner who, apart from the provisions of this Chapter—

(a)   is permitted by a third party to occupy a family home, or

(b)   is entitled to occupy a family home along with an individual who is not the other civil partner whether or not that individual has waived a right of occupation in favour of the civil partner so entitled, ('non-entitled partner' being construed accordingly).

(3) This section does not apply in any case where—

(a)   the non-entitled partner in writing either—

(i)   consents or has consented to the dealing (any consent being in such form as the Scottish Ministers may, by regulations made by statutory instrument, prescribe), or

(ii)   renounces or has renounced occupancy rights in relation to the family home or property to which the dealing relates,

(b)   the court has made an order under section 107 dispensing with the consent of the non-entitled partner to the dealing,

(c)   the dealing occurred, or implements a binding obligation entered into by the entitled partner, before the registration of the civil partnership,

(d)   the dealing occurred, or implements a binding obligation entered into, before the commencement of this section,

(e)   the dealing comprises a sale to a third party who has acted in good faith, if there is produced to the third party by the seller—

(i)   an affidavit sworn or affirmed by the seller declaring that the subjects of sale are not, or were not at the time of the dealing, a family home in relation to which a civil partner of the seller has or had occupancy rights,

(ii)   a renunciation of occupancy rights or consent to the dealing which bears to have been properly made or given by the non-entitled partner, or

(f)   the entitled partner has permanently ceased to be entitled to occupy the family home, and at any time after that a continuous period of 5 years has elapsed during which the non-entitled partner has not occupied the family home.

(4)   For the purposes of subsection (3)(e), the time of the dealing, in the case of the sale of an interest in heritable property, is the date of delivery to the purchaser of the deed transferring title to that interest.

107   Dispensation with civil partner's consent to dealing

(1)   The court may, on the application of an entitled partner or any other person having an interest, make an order dispensing with the consent of a non-entitled partner to a dealing which has taken place or a proposed dealing, if—

(a)   such consent is unreasonably withheld,

(b)   such consent cannot be given by reason of physical or mental disability, or

(c)   the non-entitled partner cannot be found after reasonable steps have been taken to trace that partner.

(2)   For the purposes of subsection (1)(a), a non-entitled partner has unreasonably withheld consent to a dealing which has taken place or a proposed dealing, where it appears to the court either—

(a)   that the non-entitled partner—

(i)   has led the entitled partner to believe that the non-entitled partner would consent to the dealing, and

(ii)   would not be prejudiced by any change in the circumstances of the case since the conduct which gave rise to that belief occurred, or

(b)   that the entitled partner has, having taken all reasonable steps to do so, been unable to obtain an answer to a request for consent.

(3)   The court, in considering whether to make an order under subsection (1), is to have regard to all the circumstances of the case including the matters specified in paragraphs (a) to (e) of section 103(3).

(4)   Where—

(a)   an application is made for an order under this section, and

(b)   an action is or has been raised by a non-entitled partner to enforce occupancy rights,

the action is to be sisted until the conclusion of the proceedings on the application.

108   Interests of heritable creditors

(1)   The rights of a third party with an interest in the family home as a creditor under a secured loan in relation to the non-performance of any obligation under the loan are not prejudiced by reason only of the occupancy rights of the non-entitled partner; but where a non-entitled partner has or obtains occupation of a family home and—

(a)   the entitled partner is not in occupation, and

(b)   there is a third party with such an interest in the family home,

the court may, on the application of the third party, make an order requiring the non-entitled partner to make any payment due by the entitled partner in respect of the loan.

(2)   This section does not apply to secured loans in respect of which the security was granted prior to the commencement of section 13 of the Law Reform (Miscellaneous Provisions) (Scotland) Act 1985 (c 73) unless the third

party in granting the secured loan acted in good faith and there was produced to the third party by the entitled partner—

(a)   an affidavit sworn or affirmed by the entitled partner declaring that there is no non-entitled partner, or

(b)   a renunciation of occupancy rights or consent to the taking of the loan which bears to have been properly made or given by the non-entitled partner.

(3)   This section does not apply to secured loans in respect of which the security was granted after the commencement of section 13 of the Law Reform (Miscellaneous Provisions) (Scotland) Act 1985 (c 73) unless the third party in granting the secured loan acted in good faith and there was produced to the third party by the grantor—

(a)   an affidavit sworn or affirmed by the grantor declaring that the security subjects are not or were not at the time of the granting of the security a family home in relation to which a civil partner of the grantor has or had occupancy rights, or

(b)   a renunciation of occupancy rights or consent to the granting of the security which bears to have been properly made or given by the non-entitled partner.

(4)   For the purposes of subsections (2) and (3), the time of granting a security, in the case of a heritable security, is the date of delivery of the deed creating the security.

109   Provisions where both civil partners have title

(1)   Subject to subsection (2), where, apart from the provisions of this Chapter, both civil partners are entitled to occupy a family home—

(a)   the rights in that home of one civil partner are not prejudiced by reason only of any dealing of the other civil partner, and

(b)   a third party is not by reason only of such a dealing entitled to occupy that home or any part of it.

(2)   Sections 106(3) and 107 and the definition of 'dealing' in section 106(2) apply for the purposes of subsection (1) as they apply for the purposes of section 106(1) but subject to the following modifications—

(a)   any reference to the entitled partner and to the non-entitled partner is to be construed as a reference to a civil partner who has entered into, or as the case may be proposes to enter into, a dealing and to the other civil partner respectively, and

(b)   in paragraph (b) of section 107(4) the reference to occupancy rights is to be construed as a reference to any rights in the family home.

110   Rights of occupancy in relation to division and sale

Where a civil partner brings an action for the division and sale of a family home owned in common with the other civil partner, the court, after having regard to all the circumstances of the case including—

(a)   the matters specified in paragraphs (a) to (d) of section 103(3), and

(b)   whether the civil partner bringing the action offers or has offered to make available to the other civil partner any suitable alternative accommodation, may refuse to grant decree in that action or may postpone the granting of decree for such period as it considers reasonable in the circumstances or may grant decree subject to such conditions as it may prescribe.

111   Adjudication

(1)   Where a family home as regards which there is an entitled partner and a non-entitled partner is adjudged, the Court of Session, on the application of the non-entitled partner made within 40 days after the date of the decree of adjudication, may—

(a)   order the reduction of the decree, or

(b)   make such order as it thinks appropriate to protect the occupancy rights
of the non-entitled partner,
if satisfied that the purpose of the diligence was wholly or mainly to defeat the
occupancy rights of the non-entitled partner.

(2)   Section 106(2) applies in construing 'entitled partner' and 'non-entitled
partner' for the purposes of subsection (1).

Transfer of tenancy

112   Transfer of tenancy

(1)   The court may, on the application of a non-entitled partner, make an order
transferring the tenancy of a family home to that partner and providing, subject to
subsection (12), for the payment by the non-entitled partner to the entitled partner
of such compensation as seems to it to be just and reasonable in all the circumstances of the case.

(2)   In an action—
  (a)   for dissolution of a civil partnership, the Court of Session or the sheriff,
  (b)   for declarator of nullity of a civil partnership, the Court of Session,
may, on granting decree or within such period as the court may specify on
granting decree, make an order granting an application under subsection (1).

(3)   In determining whether to grant an application under subsection (1), the
court is to have regard to all the circumstances of the case including the matters
specified in paragraphs (a) to (e) of section 103(3) and the suitability of the applicant to become the tenant and the applicant's capacity to perform the obligations
under the lease of the family home.

(4)   The non-entitled partner is to serve a copy of an application under subsection (1) on the landlord and, before making an order under subsection (1), the
court is to give the landlord an opportunity of being heard by it.

(5)   On the making of an order granting an application under subsection (1), the
tenancy vests in the non-entitled partner without intimation to the landlord, subject to all the liabilities under the lease (other than liability for any arrears of rent
for the period before the making of the order).

(6)   The arrears mentioned in subsection (5) are to remain the liability of the
original entitled partner.

(7)   The clerk of court is to notify the landlord of the making of an order granting an application under subsection (1).

(8)   It is not competent for a non-entitled partner to apply for an order under
subsection (1) where the family home—
  (a)   is let to the entitled partner by the entitled partner's employer as an
  incident of employment, and the lease is subject to a requirement that the
  entitled partner must reside there,
  (b)   is or is part of an agricultural holding,
  (c)   is on, or pertains to—
    (i)   a croft,
    (ii)   the subject of a cottar, or
    (iii)   the holding of a landholder or of a statutory small tenant,
  (d)   is let on a long lease, or
  (e)   is part of the tenancy land of a tenant-at-will.

(9)   In subsection (8)—
'agricultural holding' has the same meaning as in section 1 of the Agricultural
Holdings (Scotland) Act 1991 (c 55),
'cottar' has the same meaning as in section 12(5) of the Crofters (Scotland) Act
1993 (c 44),
'croft' has the same meaning as in that Act of 1993,
'holding', in relation to a landholder and a statutory small tenant,

'landholder' and 'statutory small tenant' have the same meanings respectively as in sections 2(1), 2(2) and 32(1) of the Small Landholders (Scotland) Act 1911 (c 49),

'long lease' has the same meaning as in section 28(1) of the Land Registration (Scotland) Act 1979 (c 33), and

'tenant-at-will' has the same meaning as in section 20(8) of that Act of 1979.

(10)   Where both civil partners are joint or common tenants of a family home, the court may, on the application of one of the civil partners, make an order vesting the tenancy in that civil partner solely and providing, subject to subsection (12), for the payment by the applicant to the other partner of such compensation as seems just and reasonable in the circumstances of the case.

(11)   Subsections (2) to (9) apply for the purposes of an order under subsection (10) as they apply for the purposes of an order under subsection (1) but subject to the following modifications—

(a)   in subsection (3), for 'tenant' there is substituted 'sole tenant';

(b)   in subsection (4), for 'non-entitled' there is substituted 'applicant';

(c)   in subsection (5), for 'non-entitled' there is substituted 'applicant',

(d)   in subsection (6), for 'liability of the original entitled partner' there is substituted 'joint and several liability of both partners';

(e)   in subsection (8)—

(i)   for 'a non-entitled' there is substituted 'an applicant',

(ii)   for paragraph (a) there is substituted—

'(a)   is let to both partners by their employer as an incident of employment, and the lease is subject to a requirement that both partners must reside there;', and

(iii)   paragraphs (c) and (e) are omitted.

(12)   Where the family home is a Scottish secure tenancy within the meaning of the Housing (Scotland) Act 2001 (asp 10), no account is to be taken, in assessing the amount of any compensation to be awarded under subsection (1) or (10), of the loss, by virtue of the transfer of the tenancy of the home, of a right to purchase the home under Part 3 of the Housing (Scotland) Act 1987 (c 26).

CHAPTER 4
INTERDICTS

113   Civil partners: competency of interdict

(1)   It shall not be incompetent for the Court of Session or the sheriff to entertain an application by one civil partner in a civil partnership for a relevant interdict by reason only that the civil partners are living together in civil partnership.

(2)   In subsection (1) and in section 114, 'relevant interdict' means an interdict, including an interim interdict, which—

(a)   restrains or prohibits any conduct of one civil partner towards the other civil partner or a child of the family, or

(b)   prohibits a civil partner from entering or remaining in a family home or in a specified area in the vicinity of a family home.

114   Attachment of powers of arrest to relevant interdicts

(1)   Subject to subsection (2), the court is, on the application of an applicant civil partner, to attach a power of arrest—

(a)   to any relevant interdict which is ancillary to an exclusion order (including an interim order under section 104(6));

(b)   to any other relevant interdict where the non-applicant civil partner has had the opportunity of being heard by or represented before the court, unless it appears to the court that in all the circumstances of the case such a power is unnecessary.

(2)   The court may attach a power of arrest to an interdict by virtue of subsection (1) only if satisfied that attaching the power would not result in the non-applicant civil partner being subject, in relation to the interdict, to a power of

arrest under both this Chapter and the Protection from Abuse (Scotland) Act 2001 (asp 14).

(3)　A power of arrest attached to an interdict by virtue of subsection (1) does not have effect until such interdict together with the attached power of arrest is served on the non-applicant civil partner; and such a power of arrest, unless previously recalled, ceases to have effect upon the dissolution of the civil partnership.

(4)　If, by virtue of subsection (1), a power of arrest is attached to an interdict, a constable may arrest without warrant the non-applicant civil partner if the constable has reasonable cause for suspecting that civil partner of being in breach of the interdict.

(5)　If, by virtue of subsection (1), a power of arrest is attached to an interdict, the applicant civil partner is, as soon as possible after service of the interdict, to ensure that there is delivered—

(a)　to the chief constable of the police area in which the family home is situated, and

(b)　if the applicant civil partner resides in another police area, to the chief constable of that other police area,

a copy of the application for the interdict and of the interlocutor granting the interdict together with a certificate of service of the interdict and, where the application to attach the power of arrest to the interdict was made after the interdict was granted, a copy of that application and of the interlocutor granting it and a certificate of service of the interdict together with the attached power of arrest.

(6)　Where any relevant interdict to which, by virtue of subsection (1), there is attached a power of arrest, is varied or recalled, the civil partner who applied for the variation or recall is to ensure that there is delivered—

(a)　to the chief constable of the police area in which the family home is situated, and

(b)　if the applicant civil partner resides in another police area, to the chief constable of that other police area,

a copy of the application for variation or recall and of the interlocutor granting the variation or recall.

(7)　In this section and in sections 115 and 116—

'applicant civil partner' means the civil partner who has applied for the interdict, and

'non-applicant civil partner' is to be construed accordingly.

115　Police powers after arrest

(1)　Where a person has been arrested under section 114(4), the officer in charge of a police station may—

(a)　if satisfied that there is no likelihood of violence to the applicant civil partner or any child of the family, liberate that person unconditionally, or

(b)　refuse to liberate that person.

(2)　For such refusal and the detention of that person until appearance in court by virtue of section 116(2) or of any provision of the Criminal Procedure (Scotland) Act 1975 (c 21) the officer is not to be subjected to any claim whatsoever.

(3)　Where a person arrested under section 114(4) is liberated under subsection (1), the facts and circumstances which gave rise to the arrest are to be reported forthwith to the procurator fiscal who, if he decides to take no criminal proceedings in respect of those facts and circumstances, is at the earliest opportunity to take all reasonable steps to intimate his decision to the persons mentioned in paragraphs (a) and (b) of section 116(5).

116　Procedure after arrest

(1)　The provisions of this section apply only where—

(a)　the non-applicant civil partner has not been liberated under section 115(1), and

(b)   the procurator fiscal decides that no criminal proceedings are to be taken in respect of the facts and circumstances which gave rise to the arrest.

(2)   The non-applicant civil partner who has been arrested under section 114(4) is wherever practicable to be brought before the sheriff sitting as a court of summary criminal jurisdiction for the district in which that civil partner was arrested not later than in the course of the first day after the arrest, such day not being a Saturday, a Sunday or a court holiday prescribed for that court under section 8 of the Criminal Procedure (Scotland) Act 1995 (c 46).

(3)   Nothing in subsection (2) prevents the non-applicant civil partner being brought before the sheriff on a Saturday, a Sunday or such a court holiday when the sheriff is, in pursuance of that section of that Act, sitting for the disposal of criminal business.

(4)   Subsections (1) to (3) of section 15 of that Act (intimation to a named person) apply to a non-applicant civil partner who has been arrested under section 114(4) as they apply to a person who has been arrested in respect of any offence.

(5)   The procurator fiscal is at the earliest opportunity, and in any event prior to the non-applicant civil partner being brought before the sheriff under subsection (2), to take all reasonable steps to intimate—
(a)   to the applicant civil partner, and
(b)   to the solicitor who acted for that civil partner when the interdict was granted or to any other solicitor who the procurator fiscal has reason to believe acts for the time being for that civil partner,
that the criminal proceedings referred to in subsection (1) will not be taken.

(6)   On the non-applicant civil partner being brought before the sheriff under subsection (2) (as read with subsection (3)), the following procedures apply—
(a)   the procurator fiscal is to present to the court a petition containing—
(i)   a statement of the particulars of the non-applicant civil partner,
(ii)   a statement of the facts and circumstances which gave rise to the arrest, and
(iii)   a request that the non-applicant civil partner be detained for a further period not exceeding 2 days,
(b)   if it appears to the sheriff that—
(i)   the statement referred to in paragraph (a)(ii) ostensibly discloses a breach of interdict by the non-applicant civil partner,
(ii)   proceedings for breach of interdict will be taken, and
(iii)   there is a substantial risk of violence by the non-applicant civil partner against the applicant civil partner or any child of the family,
he may order the non-applicant civil partner to be detained for a further period not exceeding 2 days, and
(c)   in any case to which paragraph (b) does not apply, the non-applicant civil partner is, unless in custody in respect of any other matter, to be released from custody.

(7)   In computing the period of 2 days referred to in paragraphs (a) and (b) of subsection (6), no account is to be taken of a Saturday or Sunday or of any holiday in the court in which the proceedings for breach of interdict will require to be raised.

CHAPTER 5
DISSOLUTION, SEPARATION AND NULLITY

Dissolution and separation

117   Dissolution

(1)   An action for the dissolution of a civil partnership may be brought in the Court of Session or in the sheriff court.

(2)　In such an action the court may grant decree, if, but only if, it is established that—

(a)　the civil partnership has broken down irretrievably, or

(b)　an interim gender recognition certificate under the Gender Recognition Act 2004 (c 7) has, after the date of registration of the civil partnership, been issued to either of the civil partners.

(3)　The irretrievable breakdown of a civil partnership is taken to be established if—

(a)　since the date of registration of the civil partnership the defender has at any time behaved (whether or not as a result of mental abnormality and whether such behaviour has been active or passive) in such a way that the pursuer cannot reasonably be expected to cohabit with the defender,

(b)　the defender has wilfully and without reasonable cause deserted the pursuer and during a continuous period of two years immediately succeeding the defender's desertion—

(i)　there has been no cohabitation between the parties, and

(ii)　the pursuer has not refused a genuine and reasonable offer by the defender to adhere,

(c)　there has been no cohabitation between the civil partners at any time during a continuous period of two years after the date of registration of the civil partnership and immediately preceding the bringing of the action and the defender consents to the granting of decree of dissolution of the civil partnership, or

(d)　there has been no cohabitation between the civil partners at any time during a continuous period of 5 years after that date and immediately preceding the bringing of the action.

(4)　Provision is to be made by act of sederunt—

(a)　for the purpose of ensuring that, in an action to which paragraph (c) of subsection (3) relates, the defender has been given such information as enables that civil partner to understand—

(i)　the consequences of consenting to the granting of decree, and

(ii)　the steps which must be taken to indicate such consent, and

(b)　as to the manner in which the defender in such an action is to indicate such consent, and any withdrawal of such consent,

and where the defender has indicated (and not withdrawn) such consent in the prescribed manner, that indication is sufficient evidence of such consent.

(5)　Provision is to be made by act of sederunt for the purpose of ensuring that, where in an action for the dissolution of a civil partnership the defender is suffering from mental illness, the court appoints a curator ad litem to the defender.

(6)　In an action to which paragraph (d) of subsection (3) relates, even though irretrievable breakdown of the civil partnership is established the court is not bound to grant decree if in its opinion to do so would result in grave financial hardship to the defender.

(7)　For the purposes of subsection (6), hardship includes the loss of the chance of acquiring any benefit.

(8)　In an action for dissolution of a civil partnership the standard of proof required to establish the ground of action is on balance of probability.

118　Encouragement of reconciliation

(1)　At any time before granting decree in an action by virtue of paragraph (a) of section 117(2) for dissolution of a civil partnership, if it appears to the court that there is a reasonable prospect of a reconciliation between the civil partners it must continue, or further continue, the action for such period as it thinks proper to enable attempts to be made to effect such a reconciliation.

(2)　If during any such continuation the civil partners cohabit with one another, no account is to be taken of such cohabitation for the purposes of that action.

119 Effect of resumption of cohabitation

(1) In an action to which paragraph (b) of section 117(3) relates, the irretrievable breakdown of a civil partnership is not to be taken to be established if, after the expiry of the period mentioned in that paragraph—

(a)   the pursuer resumes cohabitation with the defender, and

(b)   cohabits with the defender at any time after the end of a period of 3 months commencing with the date of such resumption.

(2) Subsection (1) is subject to section 118(2).

(3) In considering whether any period mentioned in paragraph (b), (c) or (d) of section 117(3) has been continuous, no account is to be taken of any period or periods not exceeding 6 months in all during which the civil partners cohabited with one another; but no such period or periods during which the civil partners cohabited with one another is to count as part of the period of non-cohabitation required by any of those paragraphs.

120 Separation

(1) An action for the separation of the civil partners in a civil partnership may be brought in the Court of Session or in the sheriff court.

(2) In such an action the court may grant decree if satisfied that the circumstances set out in any of paragraphs (a) to (d) of section 117(3) are established.

121 Dissolution following on decree of separation

(1) The court may grant decree in an action for the dissolution of a civil partnership even though decree of separation has previously been granted to the pursuer on the same, or substantially the same, facts as those averred in support of that action; and in any such action the court may treat an extract decree of separation lodged in process as sufficient proof of the facts under which that decree was granted.

(2) Nothing in this section entitles a court to grant decree of dissolution of a civil partnership without receiving evidence from the pursuer.

122 Registration of dissolution of civil partnership

(1) The Registrar General is to maintain at the General Register Office a register of decrees of dissolution of civil partnership (a register which shall be known as the 'Register of Dissolutions of Civil Partnership').

(2) The Registrar General is to cause to be made and kept at the General Register Office an alphabetical index of the entries in that register.

(3) The register is to be in such form as may be prescribed.

(4) On payment to him of such fee or fees as may be prescribed, the Registrar General must, at any time when the General Register Office is open for that purpose—

(a)   cause a search of the index to be made on behalf of any person or permit any person to search the index himself,

(b)   issue to any person an extract of any entry in the register which that person may require.

(5) An extract of any entry in the register is to be sufficient evidence of the decree of dissolution to which it relates.

(6) The Registrar General may—

(a)   delete,

(b)   amend, or

(c)   substitute another entry for,

any entry in the register.

Nullity

123 Nullity

Where two people register in Scotland as civil partners of each other, the civil partnership is void if, and only if—

(a)   they were not eligible to do so, or

(b)   though they were so eligible, either of them did not validly consent to its formation.

124   Validity of civil partnerships registered outside Scotland

(1)   Where two people register as civil partners of each other in England and Wales—

(a)   the civil partnership is void if it would be void in England and Wales under section 49, and

(b)   the civil partnership is voidable if it would be voidable there under section 50(1)(a), (b), (c) or (e).

(2)   Where two people register as civil partners of each other in Northern Ireland, the civil partnership is—

(a)   void, if it would be void in Northern Ireland under section 173, and

(b)   voidable, if it would be voidable there under section 174(1)(a), (b), (c) or (e).

(3)   Subsection (4) applies where two people register as civil partners of each other under an Order in Council under—

(a)   section 210 (registration at British consulates etc), or

(b)   section 211 (registration by armed forces personnel), ('the relevant section').

(4)   The civil partnership is—

(a)   void, if—

(i)   the condition in subsection (2)(a) or (b) of the relevant section is not met, or

(ii)   a requirement prescribed for the purposes of this paragraph by an Order in Council under the relevant section is not complied with, and

(b)   voidable, if—

(i)   the appropriate part of the United Kingdom is England and Wales and the circumstances fall within section 50(1)(a), (b), (c) or (e), or

(ii)   the appropriate part of the United Kingdom is Northern Ireland and the circumstances fall within section 174(1)(a), (b), (c) or (e).

(5)   The appropriate part of the United Kingdom is the part by reference to which the condition in subsection (2)(b) of the relevant section is met.

(6)   Subsections (7) and (8) apply where two people have registered an apparent or alleged overseas relationship.

(7)   The civil partnership is void if—

(a)   the relationship is not an overseas relationship, or

(b)   (even though the relationship is an overseas relationship), the parties are not treated under Chapter 2 of Part 5 as having formed a civil partnership.

(8)   The civil partnership is voidable if—

(a)   the overseas relationship is voidable under the relevant law,

(b)   where either of the parties was domiciled in England and Wales at the time when the overseas relationship was registered, the circumstances fall within section 50(1)(a), (b), (c) or (e), or

(c)   where either of the parties was domiciled in Northern Ireland at the time when the overseas relationship was registered, the circumstances fall within section 174(1)(a), (b), (c) or (e).

(9)   Section 51 or (as the case may be) section 175 applies for the purposes of—

(a)   subsections (1)(b), (2)(b) and (4)(b),

(b)   subsection (8)(a), in so far as applicable in accordance with the relevant law, and

(c)   subsection (8)(b) and (c).

(10)   In subsections (8)(a) and (9)(b) 'the relevant law' means the law of the country or territory where the overseas relationship was registered (including its rules of private international law).

(11) For the purposes of subsections (8) and (9)(b) and (c), references in sections 50 and 51 or (as the case may be) sections 174 and 175 to the formation of the civil partnership are to be read as references to the registration of the overseas relationship.

Financial provision after overseas proceedings

125 Financial provision after overseas dissolution or annulment
Schedule 11 relates to applications for financial provision in Scotland after a civil partnership has been dissolved or annulled in a country or territory outside the British Islands.

CHAPTER 6
MISCELLANEOUS AND INTERPRETATION

Miscellaneous

126 Regulations
    (1) In this Chapter and in Chapters 2 and 5, 'prescribed' means prescribed by regulations made by the Registrar General.
    (2) Regulations so made may make provision (including provision as to fees) supplementing, in respect of the provision of services by or on behalf of the Registrar General or by local registration authorities (as defined by section 5(3) of the 1965 Act), the provisions of Chapter 2 of this Part.
    (3) Any power to make regulations under subsection (1) or (2) is exercisable by statutory instrument; and no such regulations are to be made except with the approval of the Scottish Ministers.
    (4) A statutory instrument containing regulations under subsection (1) or (2), or regulations under section 106(3)(a)(i), is subject to annulment in pursuance of a resolution of the Scottish Parliament.

127 Attachment
Where an attachment has been executed of furniture and plenishings of which the debtor's civil partner has the possession or use by virtue of an order under section 103(3) or (4), the sheriff, on the application of that civil partner made within 40 days after the execution of the attachment, may—
    (a) declare the attachment null, or
    (b) make such order as he thinks appropriate to protect such possession or use by that civil partner,
if satisfied that the purpose of the attachment was wholly or mainly to prevent such possession or use.

128 Promise or agreement to enter into civil partnership
No promise or agreement to enter into civil partnership creates any rights or obligations under the law of Scotland; and no action for breach of such a promise or agreement may be brought in any court in Scotland, whatever the law applicable to the promise or agreement.

129 Lord Advocate as party to action for nullity or dissolution of civil partnership
    (1) The Lord Advocate may enter appearance as a party in any action—
    (a) of declarator of nullity of a civil partnership, or
    (b) for dissolution of a civil partnership,
and he may lead such proof and maintain such pleas as he thinks fit.
    (2) The Court, whenever it considers it necessary for the proper disposal of any such action, is to direct that the action be brought to the notice of the Lord Advocate for him to determine whether to enter appearance.

(3)   No expenses are claimable by or against the Lord Advocate in any such action in which he enters appearance.

130   Civil partner of accused a competent witness
(1)   The civil partner of an accused may be called as a witness—
    (a)   by the accused, or
    (b)   without the consent of the accused, by a co-accused or by the prosecutor.
(2)   But the civil partner is not a compellable witness for the co-accused or for the prosecutor and is not compelled to disclose any communication made, while the civil partnership subsists, between the civil partners.
(3)   The failure of a civil partner of an accused to give evidence is not to be commented on by the defence or the prosecutor.

131   Succession: legal rights arising by virtue of civil partnership
(1)   Where a person dies survived by a civil partner then, unless the circumstance is as mentioned in subsection (2), the civil partner has right to half of the moveable net estate belonging to the deceased at the time of death.
(2)   That circumstance is that the person is also survived by issue, in which case the civil partner has right to a third of that moveable net estate and those issue have right to another third of it.
(3)   In this section—
'issue' means issue however remote, and
'net estate' has the meaning given by section 36(1) (interpretation) of the Succession (Scotland) Act 1964 (c 41).
(4)   Every testamentary disposition executed after the commencement of this section by which provision is made in favour of the civil partner of the testator and which does not contain a declaration to the effect that the provision so made is in full and final satisfaction of the right to any share in the testator's estate to which the civil partner is entitled by virtue of subsection (1) or (2), has effect (unless the disposition contains an express provision to the contrary) as if it contained such a declaration.
(5)   In section 36(1) of the Succession (Scotland) Act 1964 (c 41), in the definition of 'legal rights', for 'and legitim' substitute 'legitim and rights under section 131 of the Civil Partnership Act 2004'.

132   Assurance policies
Section 2 of the Married Women's Policies of Assurance (Scotland) Act 1880 (c 26) (which provides that a policy of assurance may be effected in trust for a person's spouse, children or spouse and children) applies in relation to a policy of assurance—
    (a)   effected by a civil partner (in this section referred to as 'A') on A's own life, and
    (b)   expressed upon the face of it to be for the benefit of A's civil partner, or of A's children, or of A's civil partner and children,
as it applies in relation to a policy of assurance effected as, and expressed upon the face of it to be for such benefit as, is mentioned in that section.

134   General provisions as to fees
(1)   Subject to such exceptions as may be prescribed, a district registrar may refuse to comply with any application voluntarily made to him under this Part until the appropriate fee, if any, provided for by or under this Part is paid to him; and any such fee, if not prepaid, is recoverable by the registrar to whom it is payable.
(2)   Circumstances, of hardship or otherwise, may be prescribed in which fees provided for by or under this Part may be remitted by the Registrar General.

Interpretation

135   Interpretation of this Part

In this Part, unless the context otherwise requires—

'the 1965 Act' means the Registration of Births, Deaths and Marriages (Scotland) Act 1965 (c 49);

'authorised registrar' has the meaning given by section 87;

'caravan' means a caravan which is mobile or affixed to land;

'child of the family' has the meaning given by section 101(7);

'civil partnership book' has the meaning given by section 89;

'civil partnership register' has the meaning given by section 95(2);

'civil partnership schedule' has the meaning given by section 94;

'the court' means the Court of Session or the sheriff;

'district' means a registration district as defined by section 5(1) of the 1965 Act;

'district registrar' has the meaning given by section 7(12) of the 1965 Act;

'entitled partner' and 'non-entitled partner', subject to sections 106(2) and 111(2), have the meanings respectively assigned to them by section 101(1);

'exclusion order' has the meaning given by section 104(1);

'family' has the meaning given by section 101(7);

'family home' means any house, caravan, houseboat or other structure which has been provided or has been made available by one or both of the civil partners as, or has become, a family residence and includes any garden or other ground or building attached to, and usually occupied with, or otherwise required for the amenity or convenience of, the house, caravan, houseboat or other structure but does not include a residence provided or made available by one civil partner for that civil partner to reside in, whether with any child of the family or not, separately from the other civil partner;

'furniture and plenishings' means any article situated in a family home of civil partners which—

(a)   is owned or hired by either civil partner or is being acquired by either civil partner under a hire-purchase agreement or conditional sale agreement, and

(b)   is reasonably necessary to enable the home to be used as a family residence,

but does not include any vehicle, caravan or houseboat or such other structure as is mentioned in the definition of 'family home';

'notice of proposed civil partnership' has the meaning given by section 88(1);

'occupancy rights' means the rights conferred by section 101(1);

'Registrar General' means the Registrar General of Births, Deaths and Marriages for Scotland;

'registration office' means a registration office provided under section 8(1) of the 1965 Act;

'tenant' includes—

(a)   a sub-tenant,

(b)   a statutory tenant as defined in section 3 of the Rent (Scotland) Act 1984 (c 58), and

(c)   a statutory assured tenant as defined in section 16(1) of the Housing (Scotland) Act 1988 (c 43),

and 'tenancy' is to be construed accordingly.

136   The expression 'relative' in the 1965 Act

In section 56(1) of the 1965 Act (interpretation), in the definition of 'relative', at the end insert ', a civil partner and anyone related to the civil partner of the person as regards whom the expression is being construed'.

PART 5
CIVIL PARTNERSHIP FORMED OR DISSOLVED ABROAD ETC

Jurisdiction of Scottish courts

225 Jurisdiction of Scottish courts

(1) The Court of Session has jurisdiction to entertain an action for the dissolution of a civil partnership or for separation of civil partners if (and only if)—

(a) the court has jurisdiction under section 219 regulations,

(b) no court has, or is recognised as having, jurisdiction under section 219 regulations and either civil partner is domiciled in Scotland on the date when the proceedings are begun, or

(c) the following conditions are met—

(i) the two people concerned registered as civil partners of each other in Scotland,

(ii) no court has, or is recognised as having, jurisdiction under section 219 regulations, and

(iii) it appears to the court to be in the interests of justice to assume jurisdiction in the case.

(2) The sheriff has jurisdiction to entertain an action for the dissolution of a civil partnership or for separation of civil partners if (and only if) the requirements of paragraph (a) or (b) of subsection (1) are met and either civil partner—

(a) was resident in the sheriffdom for a period of 40 days ending with the date when the action is begun, or

(b) had been resident in the sheriffdom for a period of not less than 40 days ending not more than 40 days before that date and has no known residence in Scotland at that date.

(3) The Court of Session has jurisdiction to entertain an action for declarator of nullity of a civil partnership if (and only if)—

(a) the Court has jurisdiction under section 219 regulations,

(b) no court has, or is recognised as having, jurisdiction under section 219 regulations and either of the ostensible civil partners—

(i) is domiciled in Scotland on the date when the proceedings are begun, or

(ii) died before that date and either was at death domiciled in Scotland or had been habitually resident in Scotland throughout the period of 1 year ending with the date of death, or

(c) the following conditions are met—

(i) the two people concerned registered as civil partners of each other in Scotland,

(ii) no court has, or is recognised as having, jurisdiction under section 219 regulations, and

(iii) it appears to the court to be in the interests of justice to assume jurisdiction in the case.

(4) At any time when proceedings are pending in respect of which a court has jurisdiction by virtue of any of subsections (1) to (3) (or this subsection) it also has jurisdiction to entertain other proceedings, in respect of the same civil partnership (or ostensible civil partnership), for dissolution, separation or (but only where the court is the Court of Session) declarator of nullity, even though that jurisdiction would not be exercisable under any of subsections (1) to (3).

226 Sisting of proceedings

(1) Rules of court may make provision in relation to civil partnerships corresponding to the provision made in relation to marriages by Schedule 3 to the Domicile and Matrimonial Proceedings Act 1973 (c 45) (sisting of Scottish consistorial actions).

(2) The rules may in particular make provision—

(a)   for the provision of information by the pursuer and by any other person who has entered appearance in an action where proceedings relating to the same civil partnership (or ostensible civil partnership) are continuing in another jurisdiction, and

(b)   for an action to be sisted where there are concurrent proceedings elsewhere in respect of the same civil partnership (or ostensible civil partnership).

227   Scottish ancillary and collateral orders

(1)   This section applies where after the commencement of this Act an application is competently made to the Court of Session or the sheriff for the making, or the variation or recall, of an order which is ancillary or collateral to an action for—

(a)   the dissolution of a civil partnership,

(b)   the separation of civil partners, or

(c)   declarator of nullity of a civil partnership.

(2)   And the section applies whether the application is made in the same proceedings or in other proceedings and whether it is made before or after the pronouncement of a final decree in the action.

(3)   If the court has or, as the case may be, had jurisdiction to entertain the action, it has jurisdiction to entertain the application unless—

(a)   jurisdiction to entertain the action was under section 219 regulations, and

(b)   to make, vary or recall the order to which the application relates would contravene the regulations.

(4)   Where the Court of Session has jurisdiction by virtue of this section to entertain an application for the variation or recall, as respects any person, of an order made by it and the order is one to which section 8 (variation and recall by the sheriff of certain orders made by the Court of Session) of the Law Reform (Miscellaneous Provisions) (Scotland) Act 1966 (c 19) applies, then for the purposes of any application under that section for the variation or recall of the order in so far as it relates to the person, the sheriff (as defined in that section) has jurisdiction to exercise the power conferred on him by that section.

(5)   The reference in subsection (1) to an order which is ancillary or collateral is to an order relating to children, aliment, financial provision or expenses.

PART 6
RELATIONSHIPS ARISING THROUGH CIVIL PARTNERSHIP

246   Interpretation of statutory references to stepchildren etc

(1)   In any provision to which this section applies, references to a stepchild or step-parent of a person (here, 'A'), and cognate expressions, are to be read as follows—

A's stepchild includes a person who is the child of A's civil partner (but is not A's child);

A's step-parent includes a person who is the civil partner of A's parent (but is not A's parent);

A's stepdaughter includes a person who is the daughter of A's civil partner (but is not A's daughter);

A's stepson includes a person who is the son of A's civil partner (but is not A's son);

A's stepfather includes a person who is the civil partner of A's father (but is not A's parent);

A's stepmother includes a person who is the civil partner of A's mother (but is not A's parent);

A's stepbrother includes a person who is the son of the civil partner of A's parent (but is not the son of either of A's parents);

A's stepsister includes a person who is the daughter of the civil partner of A's parent (but is not the daughter of either of A's parents).

(2)   For the purposes of any provision to which this section applies—

'brother-in-law' includes civil partner's brother,
'daughter-in-law' includes daughter's civil partner,
'father-in-law' includes civil partner's father,
'mother-in-law' includes civil partner's mother,
'parent-in-law' includes civil partner's parent,
'sister-in-law' includes civil partner's sister, and
'son-in-law' includes son's civil partner.

247 Provisions to which section 246 applies: Acts of Parliament etc

(1)   Section 246 applies to—

(a)   any provision listed in Schedule 21 (references to stepchildren, in-laws etc in existing Acts),

(b)   except in so far as otherwise provided, any provision made by a future Act, and

(c)   except in so far as otherwise provided, any provision made by future subordinate legislation.

(2)   A Minister of the Crown may by order—

(a)   amend Schedule 21 by adding to it any provision of an existing Act;

(b)   provide for section 246 to apply to prescribed provisions of existing subordinate legislation.

(3)   The power conferred by subsection (2) is also exercisable—

(a)   by the Scottish Ministers, in relation to a relevant Scottish provision;

(b)   by a Northern Ireland department, in relation to a provision which deals with a transferred matter;

(c)   by the National Assembly for Wales, if the order is made by virtue of subsection (2)(b) and deals with matters with respect to which functions are exercisable by the Assembly.

(4)   Subject to subsection (5), the power to make an order under subsection (2) is exercisable by statutory instrument.

(5)   Any power of a Northern Ireland department to make an order under subsection (2) is exercisable by statutory rule for the purposes of the Statutory Rules (Northern Ireland) Order 1979 (SI 1979/1573 (NI 12)).

(6)   A statutory instrument containing an order under subsection (2) made by a Minister of the Crown is subject to annulment in pursuance of a resolution of either House of Parliament.

(7)   A statutory instrument containing an order under subsection (2) made by the Scottish Ministers is subject to annulment in pursuance of a resolution of the Scottish Parliament.

(8)   A statutory rule containing an order under subsection (2) made by a Northern Ireland department is subject to negative resolution (within the meaning of section 41(6) of the Interpretation Act (Northern Ireland) 1954 (c 33 (NI))).

(9)   In this section—

'Act' includes an Act of the Scottish Parliament;

'existing Act' means an Act passed on or before the last day of the Session in which this Act is passed;

'existing subordinate legislation' means subordinate legislation made before the day on which this section comes into force;

'future Act' means an Act passed after the last day of the Session in which this Act is passed;

'future subordinate legislation' means subordinate legislation made on or after the day on which this section comes into force;

'Minister of the Crown' has the same meaning as in the Ministers of the Crown Act 1975 (c 26);

'prescribed' means prescribed by the order;

'relevant Scottish provision' means a provision that would be within the legislative competence of the Scottish Parliament if it were included in an Act of that Parliament;

'subordinate legislation' has the same meaning as in the Interpretation Act 1978 (c 30) except that it includes an instrument made under an Act of the Scottish Parliament;

'transferred matter' has the meaning given by section 4(1) of the Northern Ireland Act 1998 (c 47) and 'deals with' in relation to a transferred matter is to be construed in accordance with section 98(2) and (3) of the 1998 Act.

PART 7
MISCELLANEOUS

249 Immigration control and formation of civil partnerships
Schedule 23 contains provisions relating to the formation of civil partnerships in the United Kingdom by persons subject to immigration control.

253 Civil partners to have unlimited insurable interest in each other
(1) Where two people are civil partners, each of them is to be presumed for the purposes of section 1 of the Life Assurance Act 1774 (c 48) to have an interest in the life of the other.

(2) For the purposes of section 3 of the 1774 Act, there is no limit on the amount of value of the interest.

PART 8
SUPPLEMENTARY

258 Regulations and orders
(1) This section applies to any power conferred by this Act to make regulations or an order (except a power of a court to make an order).

(2) The power may be exercised so as to make different provision for different cases and different purposes.

(3) The power includes power to make any supplementary, incidental, consequential, transitional, transitory or saving provision which the person making the regulations or order considers expedient.

259 Power to make further provision in connection with civil partnership
(1) A Minister of the Crown may by order make such further provision (including supplementary, incidental, consequential, transitory, transitional or saving provision) as he considers appropriate—

(a) for the general purposes, or any particular purpose, of this Act,

(b) in consequence of any provision made by or under this Act, or

(c) for giving full effect to this Act or any provision of it.

(2) The power conferred by subsection (1) is also exercisable—

(a) by the Scottish Ministers, in relation to a relevant Scottish provision;

(b) by a Northern Ireland department, in relation to a provision which deals with a transferred matter;

(c) by the National Assembly for Wales, in relation to a provision which is made otherwise than by virtue of subsection (3) and deals with matters with respect to which functions are exercisable by the Assembly.

(3) An order under subsection (1) may—

(a) amend or repeal any enactment contained in an Act passed on or before the last day of the Session in which this Act is passed, including an enactment conferring power to make subordinate legislation where the power is limited by reference to persons who are or have been parties to a marriage;

(b) amend, repeal or (as the case may be) revoke any provision contained in Northern Ireland legislation passed or made on or before the last day of the Session in which this Act is passed, including a provision conferring power to make subordinate legislation where the power is limited by reference to persons who are or have been parties to a marriage;

(c)   amend, repeal or (as the case may be) revoke any Church legislation.

(4)   An order under subsection (1) may—

(a)   provide for any provision of this Act which comes into force before another such provision has come into force to have effect, until that other provision has come into force, with such modifications as are specified in the order;

(b)   amend or revoke any subordinate legislation.

(5)   The power to make an order under subsection (1) is not restricted by any other provision of this Act.

(6)   Subject to subsection (7), the power to make an order under subsection (1) is exercisable by statutory instrument.

(7)   Any power of a Northern Ireland department to make an order under this section is exercisable by statutory rule for the purposes of the Statutory Rules (Northern Ireland) Order 1979 (S.I. 1979/1573 (NI 12)).

(8)   An order under subsection (1) which contains any provision (whether alone or with other provisions) made by virtue of subsection (3) may not be made—

(a)   by a Minister of the Crown, unless a draft of the statutory instrument containing the order has been laid before, and approved by a resolution of, each House of Parliament;

(b)   by the Scottish Ministers, unless a draft of the statutory instrument containing the order has been laid before, and approved by a resolution of, the Scottish Parliament;

(c)   by a Northern Ireland department, unless a draft of the statutory rule containing the order has been laid before, and approved by a resolution of, the Northern Ireland Assembly.

(9)   A statutory instrument containing an order under subsection (1) to which subsection (8) does not apply—

(a)   if made by a Minister of the Crown, is subject to annulment in pursuance of a resolution of either House of Parliament;

(b)   if made by the Scottish Ministers, is subject to annulment in pursuance of a resolution of the Scottish Parliament.

(10)   A statutory rule made by a Northern Ireland department and containing an order to which subsection (8) does not apply is subject to negative resolution (within the meaning of section 41(6) of the Interpretation Act (Northern Ireland) 1954 (c 33 (NI))).

(11)   In this section—

'Act' includes an Act of the Scottish Parliament;

'Church legislation' has the same meaning as in section 255;

'Minister of the Crown' has the same meaning as in the Ministers of the Crown Act 1975 (c 26);

'relevant Scottish provision' means a provision that would be within the legislative competence of the Scottish Parliament if it were included in an Act of that Parliament;

'subordinate legislation' has the same meaning as in the Interpretation Act 1978 (c 30) except that it includes any instrument made under an Act of the Scottish Parliament and any instrument within the meaning of section 1(c) of the Interpretation Act (Northern Ireland) 1954 (c 33 (NI));

'transferred matter' has the meaning given by section 4(1) of the Northern Ireland Act 1998 (c 47) and 'deals with' in relation to a transferred matter is to be construed in accordance with section 98(2) and (3) of the 1998 Act.

260   Community obligations and civil partners

(1)   Subsection (2) applies where any person, by Order in Council or regulations under section 2(2) of the European Communities Act 1972 (c 68) (general implementation of Treaties)—

(a)　is making provision for the purpose of implementing, or for a purpose concerning, a Community obligation of the United Kingdom which relates to persons who are or have been parties to a marriage, or

(b)　has made such provision and it has not been revoked.

(2)　The appropriate person may by Order in Council or (as the case may be) by regulations make provision in relation to persons who are or have been civil partners in a civil partnership that is the same or similar to the provision referred to in subsection (1).

(3)　'Marriage' and 'civil partnership' include a void marriage and a void civil partnership respectively.

(4)　'The appropriate person' means—

(a)　if subsection (1)(a) applies, the person making the provision referred to there;

(b)　if subsection (1)(b) applies, any person who would have power to make the provision referred to there if it were being made at the time of the exercise of the power under subsection (2).

(5)　The following provisions apply in relation to the power conferred by subsection (2) to make an Order in Council or regulations as they apply in relation to the power conferred by section 2(2) of the 1972 Act to make an Order in Council or regulations—

(a)　paragraph 2 of Schedule 2 to the 1972 Act (procedure etc in relation to making of Orders in Council and regulations: general);

(b)　paragraph 15(3)(c) of Schedule 8 to the Scotland Act 1998 (c 46) (modifications of paragraph 2 in relation to Scottish Ministers and to Orders in Council made on the recommendation of the First Minister);

(c)　paragraph 3 of Schedule 2 to the 1972 Act (modifications of paragraph 2 in relation to Northern Ireland departments etc) and the Statutory Rules (Northern Ireland) Order 1979 (SI 1979/1573 (NI 12)) (treating the power conferred by subsection (2) as conferred by an Act passed before 1st January 1974 for the purposes of the application of that Order);

(d)　section 29(3) of the Government of Wales Act 1998 (c 38) (modifications of paragraph 2 in relation to the National Assembly for Wales).

261　[Minor and consequential amendments, repeals and revocations]

262　Extent

(2)　Part 3 (civil partnership: Scotland), including Schedules 10 and 11, extends to Scotland only.

(4)　In Part 5 (civil partnerships formed or dissolved abroad etc)—

(b)　sections 225 to 227 extend to Scotland only;

(5)　In Part 6—

(a)　any amendment made by virtue of section 247(1)(a) and Schedule 21 has the same extent as the provision subject to the amendment;

(8)　Schedule 28 extends to Scotland only.

263　[Commencement]

264　Short title

This Act may be cited as the Civil Partnership Act 2004.

SCHEDULE 10
FORBIDDEN DEGREES OF RELATIONSHIP: SCOTLAND
Section 86

Column 1	Column 2
1.—Relationships by consanguinity	
Father	Mother
Son	Daughter
Father's father	Father's mother
Mother's father	Mother's mother
Son's son	Son's daughter
Daughter's son	Daughter's daughter
Brother	Sister
Father's brother	Father's sister
Mother's brother	Mother's sister
Brother's son	Brother's daughter
Sister's son	Sister's daughter
Father's father's father	Father's father's mother
Father's mother's father	Father's mother's mother
Mother's father's father	Mother's father's mother
Mother's mother's father	Mother's mother's mother
Son's son's son	Son's son's daughter
Son's daughter's son	Son's daughter's daughter
Daughter's son's son	Daughter's son's daughter
Daughter's daughter's son	Daughter's daughter's daughter
2.—Relationships by affinity	
Son of former wife	Daughter of former husband
Son of former civil partner	Daughter of former civil partner
Former husband of mother	Former wife of father
Former civil partner of father	Former civil partner of mother
Former husband of father's mother	Former wife of father's father
Former civil partner of father's father	Former civil partner of father's mother
Former husband of mother's mother	Former wife of mother's father
Former civil partner of mother's father	Former civil partner of mother's mother
Son of son of former wife	Daughter of son of former husband
Son of son of former civil partner	Daughter of son of former civil partner
Son of daughter of former wife husband	Daughter of daughter of former
Son of daughter of former civil partner	Daughter of daughter of former civil partner
3.—Further relationships by affinity	
Father of former wife	Mother of former husband
Father of former civil partner	Mother of former civil partner
Former husband of daughter	Former wife of son
Former civil partner of son	Former civil partner of daughter

SCHEDULE 11
FINANCIAL PROVISION IN SCOTLAND AFTER OVERSEAS PROCEEDINGS
Section 125

PART 1
INTRODUCTORY

1 (1)   This Schedule applies where—

(a)   a civil partnership has been dissolved or annulled in a country or territory outside the British Islands by means of judicial or other proceedings (here the 'overseas proceedings'), and

(b)   the dissolution or annulment (here the 'overseas determination') is entitled to be recognised as valid in Scotland.

(2)   This Schedule applies even if the date of the overseas determination is earlier than the date on which this Schedule comes into force.

PART 2
CIRCUMSTANCES IN WHICH COURT MAY ENTERTAIN APPLICATION FOR FINANCIAL PROVISION

2 (1)   Subject to sub-paragraph (4), if the jurisdictional requirements and the conditions set out in sub-paragraphs (2) and (3), respectively, are satisfied, the court may entertain an application by one of the former civil partners or former ostensible civil partners, (here 'A') for an order for financial provision.

(2)   The jurisdictional requirements are—

(a)   that A is domiciled or habitually resident in Scotland when the application is made,

(b)   that the other former civil partner, or former ostensible civil partner, (here 'B')—

(i)   is domiciled or habitually resident in Scotland when the application is made,

(ii)   was domiciled or habitually resident in Scotland when A and B last lived together in civil partnership, or

(iii)   when the application is made is an owner or tenant of, or has a beneficial interest in, property in Scotland which has at some time been a family home of A and B, and

(c)   where the court is the sheriff, that when the application is made either—

(i)   A or B is habitually resident in the sheriffdom, or

(ii)   property mentioned in sub-paragraph (2)(b)(iii) is wholly or partially in the sheriffdom.

(3)   The conditions are that—

(a)   B initiated the overseas proceedings,

(b)   the application is made within 5 years after the overseas determination takes effect,

(c)   the civil partnership (or ostensible civil partnership) had a substantial connection with Scotland,

(d)   A and B are alive when the application is made, and

(e)   (taking Part 3 of this Act to have been in force) a court in Scotland would have had jurisdiction to entertain an action for dissolution or annulment of the civil partnership, if such an action had been brought immediately before the overseas determination took effect.

(4)   Where the jurisdiction of the court to entertain proceedings under this Schedule would fall to be determined by reference to the jurisdictional requirements imposed by virtue of Part 1 of the Civil Jurisdiction and Judgments Act 1982 (c 27) (implementation of certain European conventions) or by virtue of Council

Regulation (EC) No 44/2001 of 22nd December 2000 on jurisdiction and the recognition and enforcement of judgments in civil and commercial matters, then—

(a)   satisfaction of the jurisdictional requirements set out in sub-paragraph (2) does not obviate the need to satisfy those so imposed, and

(b)   satisfaction of those so imposed obviates the need to satisfy those set out in sub-paragraph (2).

PART 3
DISPOSAL OF APPLICATIONS

3 (1)   Subject to sub-paragraphs (2) to (5), Scots law applies in relation to an application made under paragraph 2 as it would apply were the application made in an action in Scotland for, as the case may be, dissolution or annulment of a civil partnership.

(2)   In disposing of an application made under paragraph 2 the court must exercise its powers so as to place A and B, in so far as it is reasonable and practicable to do so, in the financial position in which they would have been had that application been disposed of, in such an action in Scotland, on the date when the overseas determination took effect.

(3)   In determining what is reasonable and practicable for the purposes of sub-paragraph (2), the court must have regard in particular to—

(a)   A and B's respective resources, both present and foreseeable, at the date the application is disposed of,

(b)   any order made by a foreign court in or in connection with the overseas proceedings, being an order—

(i)   for the making of financial provision, in whatever form, by A for B or by B for A, or

(ii)   for the transfer of property from A to B or from B to A.

(4)   Subject to sub-paragraph (5), the court may make an order for an interim award of a periodical allowance where—

(a)   it appears from A's averments that in the disposal of the application an order for financial provision is likely to be made, and

(b)   the court considers that such an interim award is necessary to avoid hardship to A.

(5)   Where but for paragraph 2(2)(b)(iii) the court would not have jurisdiction to entertain the application, the court may make no order for financial provision other than an order—

(a)   relating to the former family home or its furniture and plenishings, or

(b)   that B must pay A a capital sum not exceeding the value of B's interest in the former family home and its furniture and plenishings.

PART 4
THE EXPRESSION 'ORDER FOR FINANCIAL PROVISION'

4   In this Schedule, 'order for financial provision' means any one or more of the orders specified in section 8(1) of the Family Law (Scotland) Act 1985 (c 37) or an order under section 111.

VULNERABLE WITNESSES (SCOTLAND) ACT 2004
(2004, asp 3)

PART 2
CIVIL PROCEEDINGS

Evidence of children and other vulnerable witnesses: special measures

11 Interpretation of this Part

(1)   For the purposes of this Part of this Act, a person who is giving or is to give evidence in or for the purposes of any civil proceedings is a vulnerable witness if—

(a)   the person is under the age of 16 on the date of commencement of the proceedings (such a vulnerable witness being referred to in this Part as a 'child witness'), or

(b)   where the person is not a child witness, there is a significant risk that the quality of the evidence to be given by the person will be diminished by reason of—

(i)   mental disorder (within the meaning of section 328 of the Mental Health (Care and Treatment) (Scotland) Act 2003 (asp 13)), or

(ii)   fear or distress in connection with giving evidence in the proceedings.

(2)   In considering whether a person is a vulnerable witness by virtue of subsection (1)(b) above, the court must take into account—

(a)   the nature and circumstances of the alleged matter to which the proceedings relate,

(b)   the nature of the evidence which the person is likely to give,

(c)   the relationship (if any) between the person and any party to the proceedings,

(d)   the person's age and maturity,

(e)   any behaviour towards the person on the part of—

(i)   any party to the proceedings,

(ii)   members of the family or associates of any such party,

(iii)   any other person who is likely to be a party to the proceedings or a witness in the proceedings, and

(f)   such other matters, including—

(i)   the social and cultural background and ethnic origins of the person,

(ii)   the person's sexual orientation,

(iii)   the domestic and employment circumstances of the person,

(iv)   any religious beliefs or political opinions of the person, and

(v)   any physical disability or other physical impairment which the person has,

as appear to the court to be relevant.

(3)   For the purposes of subsection (1)(a) above, proceedings are taken to have commenced when the petition, summons, initial writ or other document initiating the proceedings is served, and, where the document is served on more than one person, the proceedings shall be taken to have commenced when the document is served on the first person on whom it is served.

(4)   In subsection (1)(b), the reference to the quality of evidence is to its quality in terms of completeness, coherence and accuracy.

(5)   In this Part—

'child witness notice' has the meaning given in section 12(2),

'civil proceedings' includes, in addition to such proceedings in any of the ordinary courts of law, any proceedings to which section 91 (procedural rules in relation to certain applications etc) of the Children (Scotland) Act 1995 (c 36) applies,

'court' is to be construed in accordance with the meaning of 'civil proceedings', 'special measure' means any of the special measures set out in, or prescribed under, section 18,

'vulnerable witness application' has the meaning given in section 12(6)(a).

12 Orders authorising the use of special measures for vulnerable witnesses

(1) Where a child witness is to give evidence in or for the purposes of any civil proceedings, the court must, before the proof or other hearing at which the child is to give evidence, make an order—

(a) authorising the use of such special measure or measures as the court considers to be the most appropriate for the purpose of taking the child witness's evidence, or

(b) that the child witness is to give evidence without the benefit of any special measure.

(2) The party citing or intending to cite a child witness must lodge with the court a notice (referred to in this Part as a 'child witness notice')—

(a) specifying the special measure or measures which the party considers to be the most appropriate for the purpose of taking the child witness's evidence, or

(b) if the party considers that the child witness should give evidence without the benefit of any special measure, stating that fact,

and the court must have regard to the child witness notice in making an order under subsection (1) above.

(3) If a child witness notice specifies any of the following special measures, namely—

(a) the use of a live television link in accordance with section 20 where the place from which the child witness is to give evidence by means of the link is another part of the court building in which the court-room is located,

(b) the use of a screen in accordance with section 21, or

(c) the use of a supporter in accordance with section 22 in conjunction with either of the special measures referred to in paragraphs (a) and (b) above,

that special measure is, for the purposes of subsection (1)(a) above, to be taken to be the most appropriate for the purposes of taking the child witness's evidence.

(4) The court may make an order under subsection (1)(b) above only if satisfied—

(a) that the child witness has expressed a wish to give evidence without the benefit of any special measure and that it is appropriate for the child witness so to give evidence, or

(b) that—

(i) the use of any special measure for the purpose of taking the evidence of the child witness would give rise to a significant risk of prejudice to the fairness of the proceedings or otherwise to the interests of justice, and

(ii) that risk significantly outweighs any risk of prejudice to the interests of the child witness if the order is made.

(5) Subsection (6) below applies in relation to a person other than a child witness who is to give evidence in or for the purpose of any civil proceedings (referred to in this section as 'the witness').

(6) The court may—

(a) on an application (referred to in this Part as a 'vulnerable witness application') made to it by the party citing or intending to cite the witness, and

(b) if satisfied that the witness is a vulnerable witness,

make an order authorising the use of such special measure or measures as the court considers most appropriate for the purpose of taking the witness's evidence.

(7) In deciding whether to make an order under subsection (6) above, the court must—

(a) have regard to—

(i) the possible effect on the witness if required to give evidence without the benefit of any special measure, and

(ii) whether it is likely that the witness would be better able to give evidence with the benefit of a special measure, and

(b) take into account the matters specified in section 11(2)(a) to (f).

13 Review of arrangements for vulnerable witnesses

(1) In any civil proceedings in which a person who is giving or is to give evidence (referred to in this section as 'the witness') appears to the court to be a vulnerable witness, the court may at any stage in the proceedings (whether before or after the commencement of the proof or other hearing at which the witness is giving or is to give evidence or before or after the witness has begun to give evidence)—

(a) on the application of the party citing or intending to cite the witness, or

(b) of its own motion,

review the current arrangements for taking the witness's evidence and make an order under subsection (2) below.

(2) The order which may be made under this subsection is—

(a) where the current arrangements for taking the witness's evidence include the use of a special measure or combination of special measures authorised by an order under section 12 or under this subsection (referred to as the 'earlier order'), an order varying or revoking the earlier order, or

(b) where the current arrangements for taking the witness's evidence do not include any special measure, an order authorising the use of such special measure or measures as the court considers most appropriate for the purpose of taking the witness's evidence.

(3) An order under subsection (2)(a) above varying an earlier order may—

(a) add to or substitute for any special measure authorised by the earlier order such other special measure as the court considers most appropriate for the purpose of taking the witness's evidence, or

(b) where the earlier order authorises the use of a combination of special measures for that purpose, delete any of the special measures so authorised.

(4) The court may make an order under subsection (2)(a) above revoking an earlier order only if satisfied that—

(a) the witness has expressed a wish to give or, as the case may be, continue to give evidence without the benefit of any special measure and that it is appropriate for the witness so to give evidence, or

(b) that—

(i) the use, or continued use, of the special measure for the purpose of taking the witness's evidence would give rise to a significant risk of prejudice to the fairness of the proceedings or otherwise to the interests of justice, and

(ii) that risk significantly outweighs any risk of prejudice to the interests of the witness if the order is made.

(5) Subsection (7) of section 12 applies to the making of an order under subsection (2)(b) of this section as it applies to the making of an order under subsection (6) of that section but as if the references to the witness were to the witness within the meaning of this section.

(6) In this section, 'current arrangements' means the arrangements in place at the time the review under this section is begun.

14 [Amends Court of Session Act 1988.]

15 Vulnerable witnesses: supplementary provision

(1) Subsection (2) below applies where—

(a) a party is considering for the purposes of a child witness notice or a vulnerable witness application which of the special measures is or are the most appropriate for the purpose of taking the evidence of the person to whom the notice or application relates, or

(b) the court is making an order under section 12(1) or (6) or 13(2).

(2)   The party or, as the case may be, the court must—
    (a)   have regard to the best interests of the witness, and
    (b)   take account of any views expressed by—
        (i)   the witness (having regard, where the witness is a child witness, to the witness's age and maturity), and
        (ii)   where the witness is a child witness, the witness's parent.
(3)   For the purposes of subsection (2)(b) above, where the witness is a child witness—
    (a)   the witness is to be presumed to be of sufficient age and maturity to form a view if aged 12 or older, and
    (b)   in the event that any views expressed by the witness are inconsistent with any views expressed by the witness's parent, the views of the witness are to be given greater weight.
(4)   In this section—
'parent', in relation to a child witness, means any person having parental responsibilities within the meaning of section 1(3) of the Children (Scotland) Act 1995 (c 36) in relation to the child witness
'the witness' means—
    (a)   in the case referred to in subsection (1)(a) above, the person to whom the child witness notice or vulnerable witness application relates,
    (b)   in the case referred to in subsection (1)(b) above, the person to whom the order would relate.

16   Party to proceedings as a vulnerable witness

Where a child witness or other person who is giving or is to give evidence in or for the purposes of any civil proceedings (referred to in this section as 'the witness') is a party to the proceedings—
    (a)   sections 12 and 13 have effect in relation to the witness as if references in those sections to the party citing or intending to cite the witness were references to the witness, and
    (b)   section 15 has effect in relation to the witness as if—
        (i)   in subsection (1), paragraph (a) were omitted, and
        (ii)   in subsection (2), the words 'The party or, as the case may be,' were omitted.

17   Crown application and saving provision

(1)   Sections 11 to 15 of this Act apply to the Crown.
(2)   Nothing in section 12 or 13 of this Act affects any power or duty which a court has otherwise than by virtue of those sections to make or authorise any special arrangements for taking the evidence of any person in any civil proceedings.

18   The special measures

(1)   The special measures which may be authorised to be used by virtue of section 12 or 13 of this Act for the purpose of taking the evidence of a vulnerable witness are—
    (a)   taking of evidence by a commissioner in accordance with section 19,
    (b)   use of a live television link in accordance with section 20,
    (c)   use of screen in accordance with section 21,
    (d)   use of a supporter in accordance with section 22, and
    (e)   such other measures as the Scottish Ministers may, by order made by statutory instrument, prescribe.
(2)   An order under subsection (1)(e) above is not to be made unless a draft of the statutory instrument containing the order has been laid before and approved by a resolution of the Scottish Parliament.

19   Taking of evidence by a commissioner

(1)   Where the special measure to be used is taking of evidence by a commis-

sioner, the court must appoint a commissioner to take the evidence of the vulnerable witness in respect of whom the special measure is to be used.

(2)   Proceedings before a commissioner appointed under subsection (1) above must be recorded by video recorder.

(3)   A party to the proceedings—

(a)   must not, except by leave of the court, be present in the room where such proceedings are taking place, but

(b)   is entitled by such means as seem suitable to the court to watch and hear the proceedings.

(4)   The recording of the proceedings made in pursuance of subsection (2) above is to be received in evidence without being sworn to by witnesses.

20   Live television link

(1)   Where the special measure to be used is a live television link, the court must make such arrangements as seem to it appropriate for the vulnerable witness in respect of whom the special measure is to be used to give evidence by means of such a link.

(2)   Where—

(a)   the live television link is to be used in proceedings in a sheriff court, but

(b)   that court lacks accommodation or equipment necessary for the purpose of receiving such a link,

the sheriff may by order transfer the proceedings to any sheriff court in the same sheriffdom which has such accommodation or equipment available.

(3)   An order may be made under subsection (2) above—

(a)   at any stage in the proceedings (whether before or after the commencement of the proof or other hearing at which the vulnerable witness is to give evidence), or

(b)   in relation to a part of the proceedings.

21   Screens

(1)   Where the special measure to be used is a screen, the screen must be used to conceal the parties to the proceedings from the sight of the vulnerable witness in respect of whom the special measure is to be used.

(2)   However, the court must make arrangements to ensure that the parties are able to watch and hear the vulnerable witness giving evidence.

(3)   Subsections (2) and (3) of section 20 apply for the purposes of use of a screen under this section as they apply for the purposes of use of a live television link under that section but as if—

(a)   references to the live television link were references to the screen, and

(b)   the reference to receiving such a link were a reference to the use of a screen.

22   Supporters

(1)   Where the special measure to be used is a supporter, another person ('the supporter') nominated by or on behalf of the vulnerable witness in respect of whom the special measure is to be used may be present alongside the witness for the purpose of providing support whilst the witness is giving evidence.

(2)   Where the person nominated as the supporter is to give evidence in the proceedings, that person may not act as the supporter at any time before giving evidence.

(3)   The supporter must not prompt or otherwise seek to influence the vulnerable witness in the course of giving evidence.

PART II

INTERNATIONAL CONVENTIONS

EUROPEAN CONVENTION FOR THE PROTECTION OF HUMAN RIGHTS AND FUNDAMENTAL FREEDOMS (1950)

Article 6

1. In the determination of his civil rights and obligations or of any criminal charge against him, everyone is entitled to a fair and public hearing within a reasonable time by an independent and impartial tribunal established by law. Judgment shall be pronounced publicly but the press and public may be excluded from all or part of the trial in the interests of morals, public order or national security in a democratic society, where the interests of juveniles or the protection of the private life of the parties so require, or to the extent strictly necessary in the opinion of the court in special circumstances where publicity would prejudice the interests of justice.

2. Everyone charged with a criminal offence shall be presumed innocent until proved guilty according to law.

3. Everyone charged with a criminal offence has the following minimum rights:

> (a) to be informed promptly, in a language which he understands and in detail, of the nature and cause of the accusation against him;
>
> (b) to have adequate time and facilities for the preparation of his defence;
>
> (c) to defend himself in person or through legal assistance of his own choosing or, if he has not sufficient means to pay for legal assistance, to be given it free when the interests of justice so require;
>
> (d) to examine or have examined witnesses against him and to obtain the attendance and examination of witnesses on his behalf under the same conditions as witnesses against him;
>
> (e) to have the free assistance of an interpreter if he cannot understand or speak the language used in court.

Article 8

1. Everyone has the right to respect for his private and family life, his home and his correspondence.

2. There shall be no interference by a public authority with the exercise of this right except such as is in accordance with the law and is necessary in a democratic society in the interests of national security, public safety or the economic well-being of the country, for the prevention of disorder or crime, for the protection of health or morals, or for the protection of the rights and freedoms of others.

Article 12

Men and women of marriageable age have the right to marry and to found a family, according to the national laws governing the exercise of this right.

Article 14

The enjoyment of the rights and freedoms set forth in this Convention shall be secured without discrimination on any ground such as sex, race, colour, language, religion, political or other opinion, national or social origin, association with a national minority, property, birth or other status.

UNITED NATIONS CONVENTION ON THE RIGHTS OF THE CHILD
(1989)

Article 1
For the purposes of the present Convention, a child means every human being below the age of eighteen years unless, under the law applicable to the child, majority is attained earlier.

Article 2
1. States Parties shall respect and ensure the rights set forth in the present Convention to each child within their jurisdiction without discrimination of any kind, irrespective of the child's or his or her parent's or legal guardian's race, colour, sex, language, religion, political or other opinion, national, ethnic or social origin, property, disability, birth or other status.
2. States Parties shall take all appropriate measures to ensure that the child is protected against all forms of discrimination or punishment on the basis of the status, activities, expressed opinions, or beliefs of the child's parents, legal guardians, or family members.

Article 3
1. In all actions concerning children, whether undertaken by public or private social welfare institutions, courts of law, administrative authorities or legislative bodies, the best interests of the child shall be a primary consideration.
2. States Parties undertake to ensure the child such protection and care as is necessary for his or her well-being, taking into account the rights and duties of his or her parents, legal guardians, or other individuals legally responsible for him or her, and to this end, shall take all appropriate legislative and administrative measures.
3. States Parties shall ensure that the institutions, services and facilities responsible for the care or protection of children shall conform with the standards established by competent authorities, particularly in the areas of safety, health, in the number and suitability of their staff, as well as competent supervision.

Article 6
1. States Parties recognise that every child has the inherent right to life.
2. States Parties shall ensure to the maximum extent possible the survival and development of the child.

Article 7
1. The child shall be registered immediately after birth and shall have the right from birth to a name, the right to acquire a nationality and, as far as possible, the right to know and be cared for by his or her parents.
2. States Parties shall ensure the implementation of these rights in accordance with their national law and their obligations under the relevant international instruments in this field, in particular where the child would otherwise be stateless.

Article 9
1. States Parties shall ensure that a child shall not be separated from his or her parents against their will, except when competent authorities subject to judicial review determine, in accordance with applicable law and procedures, that such separation is necessary for the best interests of the child. Such determination may be necessary in a particular case such as one involving abuse or neglect of the child by the parents, or one where the parents are living separately and a decision must be made as to the child's place of residence.
2. In any proceedings pursuant to paragraph 1 of the present article, all interested parties shall be given the opportunity to participate in the proceedings and make their views known.
3. States Parties shall respect the right of the child who is separated from one

or both parents to maintain personal relations and direct contact with both parents on a regular basis, except if it is contrary to the child's best interests.

4. Where such separation results from any action initiated by a State Party, such as the detention, imprisonment, exile, deportation or death (including death arising from any cause while the person is in the custody of the State) of one or both parents or of the child, that State Party shall, upon request, provide the parents, the child or, if appropriate, another member of the family with the essential information concerning the whereabouts of the absent member(s) of the family unless the provision of the information would be detrimental to the well-being of the child. States Parties shall further ensure that the submission of such a request shall of itself entail no adverse consequences for the person(s) concerned.

Article 10

1. In accordance with the obligation of States Parties under article 9, paragraph 1, applications by a child or his or her parents to enter or leave a State Party for the purposes of family reunification shall be dealt with by States Parties in a positive, humane and expeditious manner. States Parties shall further ensure that the submission of such a request shall entail no adverse consequences for the applicants and for the members of their family.

2. A child whose parents reside in different States shall have the right to maintain on a regular basis, save in exceptional circumstances, personal relations and direct contacts with both parents. Towards that end and in accordance with the obligation of States Parties under article 9, paragraph 1, States Parties shall respect the right of the child and his or her parents to leave any country, including their own, and to enter their own country. The right to leave any country shall be subject only to such restrictions as are prescribed by law and which are necessary to protect the national security, public order (*ordre public*), public health or morals or the rights and freedoms of others and are consistent with the other rights recognised in the present Convention.

Article 12

1. States Parties shall assure to the child who is capable of forming his or her own views the right to express those views freely in all matters affecting the child, the views of the child being given due weight in accordance with the age and maturity of the child.

2. For this purpose, the child shall in particular be provided the opportunity to be heard in any judicial and administrative proceedings affecting the child, either directly, or through a representative or an appropriate body, in a manner consistent with the procedural rules of national law.

Article 18

1. States Parties shall use their best efforts to ensure recognition of the principle that both parents have common responsibilities for the upbringing and development of the child. Parents or, as the case may be, legal guardians, have the primary responsibility for the upbringing and development of the child. The best interests of the child will be their basic concern.

2. For the purpose of guaranteeing and promoting the rights set forth in the present Convention, States Parties shall render appropriate assistance to parents and legal guardians in the performance of their child-rearing responsibilities and shall ensure the development of institutions, facilities and services for the care of children.

3. States Parties shall take all appropriate measures to ensure that children of working parents have the right to benefit from child-care services and facilities for which they are eligible.

Article 22

1. States Parties shall take appropriate measures to ensure that a child who is seeking refugee status or who is considered a refugee in accordance with appli-

cable international or domestic law and procedures shall, whether unaccompanied or accompanied by his or her parents or by any other person, receive appropriate protection and humanitarian assistance in the enjoyment of applicable rights set forth in the present convention and in other international human rights or humanitarian instruments to which the said States are Parties.

2.   For this purpose, States Parties shall provide, as they consider appropriate, co-operation in any efforts by the United Nations and other competent inter-governmental organisations or non-governmental organisations co-operating with the United Nations to protect and assist such a child and to trace the parents or other members of the family of any refugee child in order to obtain information necessary for reunification with his or her family. In cases where no parents or other members of the family can be found, the child shall be accorded the same protection as any other child permanently or temporarily deprived of his or her family environment for any reason, as set forth in the present Convention.

Article 40

1.   States Parties recognise the right of every child alleged as, accused of, or recognised as having infringed the penal law to be treated in a manner consistent with the promotion of the child's sense of dignity and worth, which reinforces the child's respect for the human rights and fundamental freedoms of others and which takes into account the child's age and the desirability of promoting the child's reintegration and the child's assuming a constructive role in society.

2.   To this end, and having regard to the relevant provisions of international instruments, States Parties shall, in particular, ensure that:

(a)   No child shall be alleged as, be accused of, or recognised as having infringed the penal law by reason of acts or omissions that were not prohibited by national or international law at the time they were committed;

(b)   Every child alleged as or accused of having infringed the penal law has at least the following guarantees:

(i)   To be presumed innocent until proven guilty according to law;

(ii)   To be informed promptly and directly of the charges against him or her, and, if appropriate, through his or her parents or legal guardians, and to have legal or other appropriate assistance in the preparation and presentation of his or her defence;

(iii)   To have the matter determined without delay by a competent, independent and impartial authority or judicial body in a fair hearing according to law, in the presence of legal or other appropriate assistance and, unless it is considered not to be in the best interest of the child, in particular, taking into account his or her age or situation, his or her parents or legal guardians;

(iv)   Not to be compelled to give testimony or to confess guilt; to examine or have examined adverse witnesses and to obtain the participation and examination of witnesses on his or her behalf under conditions of equality;

(v)   If considered to have infringed the penal law, to have this decision and any measures imposed in consequence thereof reviewed by a higher competent, independent and impartial authority or judicial body according to law;

(vi)   To have the free assistance of an interpreter if the child cannot understand or speak the language used;

(vii)   To have his or her privacy fully respected at all stages of the proceedings.

3.   States Parties shall seek to promote the establishment of laws, procedures, authorities and institutions specifically applicable to children alleged as, accused of, or recognised as having infringed the penal law, and, in particular:

(a)   The establishment of a minimum age below which children shall be presumed not to have the capacity to infringe the penal law;

(b) Whenever appropriate and desirable, measures for dealing with such children without resorting to judicial proceedings, providing that human rights and legal safeguards are fully respected.

4. A variety of dispositions, such as care, guidance and supervision orders; counselling; probation; foster care; education and vocational training programmes and other alternatives to institutional care shall be available to ensure that children are dealt with in a manner appropriate to their well-being and proportionate both to their circumstances and the offence.

INDEX

INDEX OF STATUTES